ACB-2251

W9-CCW-658

MAKING FACTS COME ALIVE

LIBRARY

MAKING FACTS COME ALIVE: CHOOSING QUALITY NONFICTION LITERATURE K-8

Edited by
Rosemary A. Bamford
Janice V. Kristo

Christopher-Gordon Publishers, Inc.
Norwood, Massachusetts

Credits

Every effort has been made to contact copyright holders for permission to reproduce borrowed material where necessary. We apologize for any oversights and would be happy to rectify them in future printings.

Excerpts from Russell Freedman's Fact or Fiction in *Using Nonfiction Trade Books in the Elementary Classroom: From Ants to Zeppelins*, edited by Evelyn Freedman and Diane Person, copyright © 1992 by the National Council of Teachers of English. Reprinted by permission.

Excerpt from Brent Ashabranner, "Did You Really Write that for Children," *The Horn Book Magazine*, Nov./Dec. 1988, reprinted by permission of The Horn Book, Inc., 11 Beacon Street, Ste. 1000, Boston, MA 02108.

Excerpt from Kathryn Lasky, "Reflections on Nonfiction," *The Horn Book Magazine*, 1985, reprinted by permission of The Horn Book, Inc., 11 Beacon Street, Ste. 1000, Boston, MA 02108.

Excerpt from Milton Meltzer, "Where do all the Prizes Go? The Case for Nonfiction," *The Horn Book Magazine,* 1976, reprinted by permission of The Horn Book, Inc., 11 Beacon Street, Ste. 1000, Boston, MA 02108.

Figure from *In Search of the Grand Canyon: Down the Colorado with John Wesley Powell* by Mary Ann Fraser, copyright © 1995 by Mary Ann Fraser. Reprinted by permission of Henry Holt & Co., Inc.

Illustrations from *The Life and Times of the Honeybee*, copyright © 1995 by Charles Mucucci. Reprinted by permission of Houghton Mifflin Company/Ticknor & Fields Books for Young Readers. All rights reserved.

Figure from *Fire in the Forest* by Lawrence Pringle, paintings by Bob Marstall. Reprinted by permission of Atheneum Books for Young Readers, an imprint of Simon & Schuster Children's Publishing Division. Illustrations copyright © 1995 by Bob Marstall.

Spring Tide Diagram from *Oceans* by Seymour Simon, Copyright © 1990 by Seymour Simon, used by permission of Morrow Junior Books, a division of William Morrow & Company.

The Amazing Potato diagram is used by permission of the Potato Association of America.

San Andreas Fault Broken Fence photograph courtesy of the National Geophysical Data Center/AOAA.

Dust jacket of *A Twilight Struggle: The Life of John Fitzgerald Kennedy*, by Barbara Harrison and Daniel Terris. Jacket photography by Douglas Jones, courtesy of the *Look* magazine collection of the John Fitzgerald Kennedy Library. By permission of Lothrop, Lee, & Shepard Books, a division of William Morrow & Co., Inc.

Underwater Journey, by Brian and Jillian Cutting, 1988. Illustrated by Jeff Fonilek. Bothell, WA: The Wright Group.

Excerpt from *Puffins Climb, Penguins Rhyme*, by Bruce McMillan, copyright © 1995, used by permission of Harcourt Brace & Company.

Excerpts from *I See Animals Hiding* by Jim Arnosky, copyright © 1995 by Jim Arnosky. Reprinted by permission of Scholastic, Inc.

Excerpt from *Animal Homes* by Peter Sloan and Sheryl Sloan, copyright © 1995. Used by permission of Sundance Publishing.

Excerpt from *Little Car* by Joy Cowly, illustrated by Martin Baley, copyright © 1987. Used by permission of The Wright Group.

Excerpt from *Beavers*, text copyright © 1996 by Helen H. Moore. Used by permission of Mondo Publishing, One Plaza Road, Greenvale, NY 11548.

Excerpt from *Some Machines are Enormous*, text copyright © 1988 by Bettina Bird and Joan Short. Used by permission of Mondo Publishing, One Plaza Road, Greenvale, NY 11548.

Excerpt from *What Comes First?*, text copyright © 1995 by Mondo Publishing, One Plaza Road, Greenvale, NY 11548.

Excerpt from *My New Kitten*, by Joanna Cole, photography by Margaret Miller, text copyright © 1995. Used by permission of Morrow Junior Books, a division of William Morrow & Company, Inc.

Excerpt from *Mother Jones* by Betsy Harvey Kraft, text copyright © 1995 by Betsy Harvey Kraft. Reprinted by permission of Clarion Books/Houghton Mifflin Company. All rights reserved.

Excerpt from *Kids at Work* by Russell Freedman, text copyright © 1994 by Russell Freedman. Reprinted by permission of Clarion Books/Houghton Mifflin Company. All rights reserved.

Excerpt from *Selected Poems* by Langston Hughes, copyright © 1926. Reprinted by permission of Alfred A Knopf, Inc.

Excerpt from *Cactus Hotel* by Brenda Z. Guiberson, copyright © 1991 by Brenda Guiberson. Reprinted by permission of Henry Holt & Co., Inc.

Christopher-Gordon Publishers, Inc.
1502 Providence Highway, Suite 12
Norwood, MA 02062
Tel: 617-762-5577

Copyright © 1998 by Christopher-Gordon Publishers, Inc.

All rights reserved. Except for review purposes, no part of this material protected by this copyright notice may be reproduced or utilized in any form or by any means, electronic or mechanical, including photocopying, recording, or any information and retrieval system, without the express written permission of the publisher or copyright holder.

Printed in the United States of America

10 9 8 7 6 5 4 3 2 1   02 01 00 99 98 97

ISBN: 0-926842-67-6

DEDICATION

Rosemary A. Bamford would like to dedicate this book to her dear and loving husband, Mark, who has been endlessly patient and almost as dedicated to seeing this project come to completion as the two coeditors!

Janice V. Kristo would like to dedicate this book to her students of children's literature at the University of Maine. Their thoughtful comments and questions about books always have a way of leading us into new understandings about nonfiction literature.

TABLE OF CONTENTS

PREFACE

Nonfiction literature for children is plentiful. We see these titles everywhere—from bookstores to libraries, to the reading corners of classrooms. We are, indeed, in an age flourishing with nonfiction for children. As these titles edge out textbooks in classrooms and thematic or inquiry studies take a prominent place, educators face a veritable "banquet" of nonfiction titles. How, then, do we go about making critical choices about what is the best for students in kindergarten through grade eight? Why is it important to consider what is the best quality in nonfiction? Isn't it good enough that a classroom collection of children's nonfiction on a particular topic is extensive? We'd respond that educators need not become the mediators (Saul, 1993) of inferior nonfiction for children. There are too many well-written and beautifully designed nonfiction books available to include out-of-date and poorly written titles in our classroom collections. We need to provide children with the highest quality to expect optimum learning.

This volume brings together sixteen educators who write about selecting and sharing the best in nonfiction with elementary and middle school students. It is divided into four parts, each focusing on an important aspect of the world of nonfiction. In Part I readers will find information on what kinds of books are considered nonfiction literature and how to select the best titles. Part II focuses on finding out what nonfiction titles are available in specific content areas and ways to make decisions about which to choose. In Part III readers will look inside primary, intermediate, and middle school classrooms where nonfiction is a critical component of the reading, writing, and inquiry of students. In Part IV, the finale of the book, we include response guides to eleven notable nonfiction titles. Readers will also find an annotated bibliography of National Council of Teachers of English Orbis Pictus award-winning books.

As editors, we envisioned this book to be more than simply a collection of readings. Instead, we wanted the book to have a seamless quality— one in which readers would make connections between and among chapters. There is a progression of ideas in the book building from trends in nonfiction, criteria for selection, and nonfiction in specific curricular areas to use in the classroom. Readers can certainly pick and choose individual chapters to read, but we recommend a cover to cover reading to gain a depth of understanding about the abundance of nonfiction available for children and why and how to make good selection decisions. We have attempted to limit repetition in the text. However, readers will notice some nonfiction titles are repeated in several chapters. This is due to the fact that the book is notable for a variety of reasons and, so, is described for different reasons. Within many chapters readers will notice specific references to other chapters as a way to help readers make connections between chapters and sidebars containing additional information.

Part I–Choosing Quality Nonfiction Literature, begins with a chapter by Susan Hepler in which she explores new directions in nonfiction books for children, as well as challenges in using these books. The authors of chapters two through five take a critical look at the criteria for choosing exemplary nonfiction titles for children. Four chapters are devoted specifically to the topic of evaluation criteria because this is such a crucial issue in the selection of the highest quality nonfiction. In Chapter 2, Bamford and Kristo specifically examine aspects of accuracy and organizational structures. Amy McClure, in Chapter 3, discusses some of the features of writing style evident in outstanding nonfiction titles. Richard Kerper explores visual aspects and those of design and layout that make for premier nonfiction in Chapter 4. To complete this section of the book, Paula Moore, in Chapter 5, discusses the challenges emergent readers face in reading nonfiction and teaching strategies that facilitate independence by these novice readers.

Part II–Quality Nonfiction Literature: Gateway to Imagination, Investigation, and Inquiry, focuses on nonfiction selections for a variety of curricular areas. In Chapter 6, Myra Zarnowski writes about how well-written nonfiction in the social studies area impacts learning. Anthony Fredericks, in Chapter 7, examines the importance of using nonfiction in science programs and how to determine the best titles. In Chapter 8, Sandra Wilde investigates what nonfiction is available to study mathematics and how a variety of children's literature offers embedded mathematical concepts and ways to work with these in the classroom. Barbara Kiefer, in Chapter 9, completes this section by exploring a host of books that focus on an appreciation of the arts.

Part III–Quality Nonfiction Literature: What Happens When Students and Books Come Together?, begins with Chapter 10, Using Read-Aloud to

Explore the Layers of Nonfiction by Sylvia Vardell. In this chapter Vardell makes a case for reading nonfiction aloud and ways to use this time to help children understand how good nonfiction "works." In Chapter 11, Yvonne Siu-Runyan explains the components of a successful writing program in which children write about topics to teach others what they know. Linda Levstik, in Chapter 12, discusses how children are inspired to seek answers to their inquiries through using a variety of nonfiction materials. Carol Avery, Donna Maxim, and Jeffrey Wilhelm have written chapters about their lives in schools where nonfiction is at the centerpiece of learning how to learn. In Chapter 13, Carol Avery focuses on the ways in which nonfiction shared aloud stimulates thoughtful discussions and questions about the world. Donna Maxim, in Chapter 14, presents ways in which nonfiction is a vital component of how her intermediate students think, talk, and write about science. Finally, Jeffrey Wilhelm, makes an elegant argument for the power of nonfiction, combined with drama, to "smash the frozen seas" within the minds and work of middle level students.

Part IV of this book includes a selection of eleven response guides for notable nonfiction books. This selection of guides represents well-written nonfiction titles across science, social studies, mathematics, and the arts. Each guide is comprised of distinguished features found in each book, such as the inclusion of a glossary, index, or other access features. Also included for each guide are response suggestions designed to help students apply the content or format of the book to their own inquiries and a list of connecting books.

Part IV also includes an annotated bibliography of Orbis Pictus Book Award-Winners, Honor Books, and Notable Books. These outstanding nonfiction books are chosen each year by the Orbis Pictus Committee of the National Council of Teachers of English.

At the end of the book is a bibliography of all children's books cited throughout the text.

R. A. B.

J. V. K

ACKNOWLEDGMENTS

We would like to thank our administrative assistant, Susan Russell, for her patience, her endurance in harsh conditions—namely a cold office on weekends during the Maine winter, and her tireless efforts in working with us from start to finish on the manuscript.

We also wish to thank the staff at the Bangor Public Library and Diane, Krista, Sarah, and Josh at the University of Maine Bookstore for their infinite patience in dealing with our seemingly endless phone calls.

We are grateful to the eleven nonfiction authors who we interviewed for our response guides. What began as 20 minute conversations over the phone usually lasted an hour!

Thanks to our colleagues at the University of Maine—Phyllis Brazee, Paula Moore, Brenda Power, and Jeff Wilhelm for their good humor and advice. And, thanks, too, to Dean Robert Cobb, Associate Deans Walter Harris and Anne Pooler, and Kay Hyatt for their support, patience, and encouragement of our project.

We also want to acknowledge Gail Garthwait—librarian extraordinaire, colleague, and friend for her meticulous editorial work on our manuscript.

Lastly, we wish to thank Sue Canavan for giving us an opportunity to write about a subject we love.

Part I

Choosing Quality Nonfiction Literature: Evaluation and Selection

By our very nature, humans are a questioning and curious lot. We are interested in learning what makes things tick; we want to search for the reasons things happen—we, simply, want to make sense of our world. We know that this fascination with life begins early. Children in kindergarten love to pour over books about animals, trucks, dinosaurs, whales, and all kinds of interesting things. They have questions about the world around them, and they want to begin finding the answers. As children grow, their questions continue and their curiosity about the world expands. Teachers and librarians need to help fuel this fire of knowledge and inquiry by sharing the best in nonfiction literature with students.

This section of the book will focus on what is available in nonfiction and evaluative criteria for selecting the best books for children in kindergarten through grade eight. Our intent in this first part is to lay a solid foundation for the importance of choosing high quality nonfiction and ways to make that determination. In Chapter 1, Susan Hepler examines trends in nonfiction, the kinds of nonfiction available for elementary and middle school students, and classroom issues in using nonfiction. Next, in Chapter 2, Rosemary Bamford and Janice Kristo discuss the importance of choosing the best nonfiction for children. They begin the conversation about important criteria in examining nonfiction, focusing mainly on accuracy and organizational structures in nonfiction. In Chapter 3, Amy McClure continues the discussion of selection criteria by exploring issues of style in well-written nonfiction. Richard Kerper, next, examines the access features and visual aspects of nonfiction in Chapter 4. Paula Moore concludes this first section of the book with a discussion about the challenges emergent readers face in nonfiction titles as well as strategies for helping teachers scaffold learning experiences for novice readers in Chapter 5.

CHAPTER 1
NONFICTION BOOKS FOR CHILDREN: NEW DIRECTIONS, NEW CHALLENGES

by Susan Hepler

This is a halcyon age for children's literature, especially in the areas of nonfiction or informational trade books. Children everywhere are fascinated by the world and how it works. Rising to the challenge, children's book publishers have provided parents, teachers, librarians, and children with a tremendous and increasing number of book choices to satisfy a readers' need to know.

How powerfully a nonfiction book can complement and augment children's world experiences! A toddler who studies the colorful pages of the beginning informational picture book *Big Machines* (Barton, 1995) or the preschooler who considers the eyecatching photos of footwear modeled by children in *Whose Shoe?* (Miller, 1991) will look at their environments differently after hearing these books read aloud. Older children marvel at the eating habits of medieval people when they read James Giblin's *From Hand To Mouth* (1987). There are books for everyone and on every subject or topic that might interest a reader, preschool to middle school and beyond. As one adult put it, "You want to learn something about any subject? Read a good children's nonfiction book!"

In 1992, because of the dramatic increase in nonfiction titles, Lillian N. Gerhardt, editor of *School Library Journal*, ceased publishing an annual "Nonfiction Forecast." Publishers had been invited to submit three nonfiction titles, but this format increasingly left out many important and excellent titles. Gerhardt estimated that about half of the 4,000 children's books published in that year were nonfiction titles. Presently, the picture is holding steady. In 1996, of over 7,000 children's books catalogued by the Library of Congress, about 3,500 were classified as nonfiction.

Why are there so many nonfiction books available now? Partly, it is a

AMERICAN LIBRARY ASSOCIATION NOTABLE CHILDREN'S BOOKS

The Notable Children's Book Committee for the Association for Library Service to Children, a division of the American Library Association, selects yearly notable fiction and nonfiction books. The complete list appears yearly in the March 15 issue of *Booklist*, a journal of the association.

INTERNATIONAL READING ASSOCIATION CHILDREN'S CHOICES

The Children's Choices Committee of the International Reading Association-Children's Book Council Joint Committee selects a group of books to be presented to children for their consideration and vote. The final list consists of those books receiving the highest votes. The complete list appears yearly in the November issue of *The Reading Teacher*, a journal of the association. The International Reading Association also publishes "Teacher Choices" and "Young Adult Choices" lists.

response to the market. Parents are buying more books, and schools and public libraries purchase titles to match the demands of literature-based instruction. Any quick look at the paperback book clubs will reveal that many students are choosing informational books for their recreational reading—books about the Titantic, collections of gruesome facts, biographies of their favorite sports heroes, etc. Although the quality may vary greatly, the interest in information is as high in children as it is in the general adult population. *Publisher's Weekly* data regularly shows nonfiction is the most popular genre (how-to, self-help, celebrity bios, etc.). In addition, since information has expanded exponentially, creators of children's books have responded with updated content, so libraries must weed and renew their nonfiction collection continually. For years nonfiction titles were viewed as the fusty and lackluster cousins of fiction. Now, these books look and read better than ever with snappy graphics, clear and marvelous photographs or artwork, and eloquent texts (Freeman & Person, 1992).

Informational Books Deserves More Attention

With due respect to fiction, it is time that nonfiction gets a little more center-stage attention. Years ago, noted nonfiction author Milton Meltzer (1976) lamented how few nonfiction titles had won the Newbery Medal. He counted five: Hendrik Van Loon's *The Story of Mankind* (the first winner in 1922) and four others, all biographies. Twenty years later the picture hasn't changed. The larger awards, if we do not include poetry and folktales, account for exactly two. Russell Freedman's *Lincoln: A Photobiography* won the Newbery Medal in 1988. Alice and Martin Provensen's picture book biography, *The Glorious Flight:*

Across the Channel with Louis Blériot, won the Caldecott Medal in 1984. If we include Newbery Honor books in the 20-year count, we could only add seven books by Aranka Siegel, Jean Fritz, Kathryn Lasky, Rhoda Blumberg, Patricia Lauber, Russell Freedman, Jim Murphy and (again not including poetry, alphabet books, or folktales) one Caldecott Honor book, *Bill Peet: An Autobiography* (1989).

Awards do exist for nonfiction books, however. In 1991, the National Council of Teachers of English established the Orbis Pictus Award and chooses a winner and notable books for the previous year. Since 1977, the *Washington Post*/Children's Book Guild Nonfiction Award has been given to an author for his or her total body of work. But it is rare that nonfiction gets the proper award attention even though informational titles account for more than 50% of the books published each year. Various other associations publish notables lists for their particular fields, such as social studies, science, and language arts. These annotated lists usually first appear in the association's journal and are later reprinted and purchasable.

While teachers have always been sporadically informed of informational literature that enlivens curriculum, the education presses are making increasing and valiant efforts to bring topic-related titles together. The magazine *Book Links* is an important source for annotated lists and lively dialog about children's books and their creators.

Critics, librarians, and educators have paid increasing attention to nonfiction over the years. Margery Fisher led the way with *Matters of Fact* (1972). Jo Carr's provocative collection of essays titled *Beyond Fact* (1982) furthered the dialog. Educators such as Margaret Meek in *Information and Book Learning* (1996) and Christine Duthie in *True Stories* (1996) help teachers consider what

(continued from page 4)

NOTABLE CHILDREN'S TRADE BOOKS IN THE FIELD OF SOCIAL STUDIES
Notable books are selected by the National Council for the Social Studies-Children's Book Council Joint Committee. The annotated list appears yearly in the April/May issue of *Social Education*, the association's journal of the National Council for the Social Studies.

ORBIS PICTUS AWARD FOR OUTSTANDING NONFICTION FOR CHILDREN
Presented annually by the National Council of Teachers of English for the outstanding nonfiction book for the previous year. Honor books and notable nonfiction literature are also recognized. Annotated list of awards are published in the October issue of *Language Arts*.

OUTSTANDING SCIENCE TRADE BOOKS FOR CHILDREN
National Science Teachers Association, in cooperation with the Children's Book Council, each year selects a list of notable books that appears in the March issue of the association's journal, *Science and Children*.

readers do when they read nonfiction and how this can be helped or hindered by curriculum. Periodicals such as *Appraisal: Science Books for Young People* (issued quarterly) is a helpful resource for evaluating and selecting books. *The Kobrin Newsletter* has reviewed nonfiction exclusively since 1980. *Eyeopeners I* (Kobrin, 1988) and *Eyeopeners II* (Kobrin, 1995) evaluates and categorizes informational books around topics children commonly ask questions about. Every major textbook of children's literature now includes its own sections on informational books and biographies.

What Are Nonfiction Books?

Books that present knowledge factually are referred to as both *nonfiction* and *informational books*. In this book, we will use the terms interchangeably.

Whatever we call the genre, it includes books about all of the sciences—natural, social, and physical; biography; history; sports; handicrafts; languages; geography; music; drama; and more. Surprisingly to some, informational books also include folktales and traditional literature because they bear information about the culture from which they come. In the Dewey Decimal system favored by school and public libraries, books are categorized by number so that a folktale with a documentable ethnic source may be found in the area of 398s. But those without provenance are often found in the picture book category, or the Easys (Es). Teachers note, however, that a version of "John Henry" may be found in both sections of the library; poetry is also classified numerically in the Nonfiction section (800s). But some poetic picture book texts are found in the Easy section; some informational books, such as the two picture book biographies *The Glorious Flight* (Provensens, 1983) or *Flight* (Burleigh, 1991) are poetically written and the illustrations boldly conceived. These official categories can seem somewhat arbitrary.

The Library of Congress has a section of cataloguers whose entire job is to decide where a book should be placed in their system, a complicated combination of "Ps" for fiction and other letters for nonfiction and poetry. While the highly narrative *The Magic School Bus Inside a Hurricane* (Cole, 1995) is placed in the nonfiction category (O-L) because it carries an impressive load of weather information, a book like *The Great Kapok Tree* (Cherry, 1990) will be found in the animal fiction category (PZ-10) even though it conveys information about what kinds of animals use the giant tree. The former is now called an *informational picture storybook*.

Increasingly, children's books defy easy classification as fiction or nonfiction. However, this slithery issue can pose problems for librarians, teachers, curriculum teachers, and for young readers.

How Do We Talk About Them? Classifying Nonfiction Books

It may make little difference to a child whether adults classify a book as fiction or nonfiction, poetry or folktale, if this is a book a child wants to read. And it's helpful to remember that as we parse this rich genre. That said, one helpful way to look at nonfiction books is to categorize them by the ways in which they are presented or organized.

Concept Books

Concept books explore the characteristics of a class of objects or of an abstract idea. Concept books for very young children typically discuss size, color, shape, or spatial relationships in a class of objects. For instance, Tana Hoban's excellent photo concept books examine shape in *Spirals, Curls, Fanshapes, and Lines* (1992). Kathy Darling's *Amazon ABC* (1996) features clear color photographs illustrating many of the animals found in this rainforest. In an afterword, Darling provides more description about each animal. Seymour Simon's narrative *Autumn Across America* (1993) notes the changes region by region that occur as the angle of sunlight lessens in the hemisphere. Hana Machotka's concept books, such as *Breathtaking Noses* (1992), show animal features in close-up photos while the text explains how each variety of nose functions specifically for that species. *I Spy a Freight Train: Transportation in Art* (Micklethwait, 1996) spans the globe to select artwork that pictures both antique and present day trains. Books such as these ask children to generalize and see patterns in a class. Sometimes this may be a developmentally difficult task, but one worth pursuing if only to challenge a child to focus attention on the wider world.

Currently, there seems to be many books that take a cross-cultural look at common features and subtle differences of a global topic. In fine photographs and minimal text, Ann Morris and Ken Heyman contrast food in *Bread, Bread, Bread* (1989) as well as social customs in *Weddings* (1996). Mary D. Lankford's two books, *Jacks Around the World* (1996) and *Hopscotch Around the World* (1992), show that these two favorite games vary slightly but still remain discernable no matter where you play them. Ted Lewin's *Market!* (1996) depicts in highly detailed watercolors and short descriptive paragraphs the open-air markets from the Andes to Morocco, from New York City to Nepal. These concept books for older children may pose challenges to classroom teachers whose geographical themes or units are more often regionally specific than whole-world in orientation, but they do point out to children that the distinctions in games, bread, or social customs are what make the world interesting.

Photographic Essays

Not all books that use photographs can be called photographic essays. The true photographic essay particularizes and personalizes information, making it emotionally involving for the reader, or documents and validates the truth of the text with photographs. George Ancona's *The Piñata Maker/El Piñatero* (1994) shows readers how Don Ricardo makes elaborate and beautiful pinatas as decorations for birthdays, festivals, and other special occasions. In *Koko's Kitten* (Patterson, 1985), Ronald Cohn's photos validate and confirm the story of the lowland gorilla who communicated grief for its dead pet cat and joy when a new pet arrived. *Rosie, A Visiting Dog's Story* (Calmenson, 1994) presents an endearing dog and its compassionate owner who bring happiness to shut-ins, the elderly, and others. Many photo essays, such as *Pueblo Storyteller* (Hoyt-Goldsmith, 1991) or *Chi Hoon, A Korean Girl* (McMahon, 1993), show contemporary life in a particular culture or land as seen through the eyes of one family or person.

Identification Books

Identification books in their simplest form present a phrase or two with labels and diagrams to show how something may be identified. Many of the transportation books published by Dorling Kindersley fall into this category as they point out in detailed photographs and drawings how vehicles are distinguished from each other. Nancy Winslow Parker's *Frogs, Toads, Lizards and Salamanders* (1990) discusses and identifies sixteen reptiles and amphibians in scientific terms complete with scale indicators and introduces the topic to older children by means of humorous rhymes.

Life Cycle Books

In life-cycle books the life of an animal is presented in part or in whole. For very young children, the "See How They Grow" series published originally by Dorling Kindersley, such as *See How They Grow: Rabbit* (Watts, 1991), shows the development of baby animals from birth to sixth months in clear winsome photographs, a changing and informative border, and controlled vocabulary for beginning readers. Patricia Lauber's lively text and Holly Keller's charming pictures for *An Octopus is Amazing* (1990) compel and reward a child's interest in this fascinating species. Jean Craighead George's newly reissued *Vulpes the Red Fox* (1948, 1996) shows in descriptive prose the predators and the disastrous elements a red fox faces throughout the year.

Experiment and Activity Books, Craft, and How-To Books

Books that explain how to do something exist on many topics from bubble blowing and hair bow tying, to paper airplane making, cooking, and bracelet braiding. Sometimes this sort of book is packaged with an object (a bubble wand, satin ribbons, origami paper, measuring spoons, or gimp or embroidery floss) to attract buyers and assure them that they can get started on this project right now! Joan Irvine's *Build It With Boxes* (1993) invites children to create origami boxes, or build clubhouses and sportscars out of cardboard. Directions are clearly laid out and illustrated to help children follow the steps. Bernie Zubrowski's series of experiment books leads the field with his clearly illustrated and interesting activities in such books as *Blinkers and Buzzers: Experiments with Electricity and Magnetism* (1991).

Documents, Journals, and Diaries

In recent years, documents and journals have provided the basis for either the content of a nonfiction book or the organizational principles for the presentation of a topic. For instance, James Haskins frequently uses archival photographs, actual letters, and accounts of the times in his books such as *The Day Fort Sumpter Was Fired Upon* (1995). Russell Freedman's excellent biographies and historical books, such as *Children of the Wild West* (1983), include the same type of primary source materials. While photographs lend an immediacy to the period and people depicted, images of paintings or sculptures, quotes, and eyewitness accounts also document a period as in *Cowboys, Indians, and Gunfighters* (Marrin, 1993) and *Cowboy: An Album* (Granfield, 1994).

Mary Lyons chose excerpts from the diaries of seven extraordinary 19th-century women writers that revealed the way these women discovered themselves in *Keeping Secrets* (1995). By using other primary sources, Lyons also deduced a life from what the diary writers left out, making these biographical sketches exceptional. Joan Blos uses the form of an impossible diary, "kept" by *Nellie Bly's Monkey* (1996), to interest readers in a factual account of this famous journalist's trip around the world.

Survey Books

The survey book serves as an introduction to a topic and includes representative subtopics, but it may not necessarily cover all information. The first Newbery Award was given to a survey book, Van Loon's *The Story of Mankind* (1921, 1985). For the nineties, Joy Hakim offers the "History of US" series, a multiple-format varied set of books written in a lively engaging style. In *Liberty for All?* (1994), she traces life in the United States from 1800 to the eve of the Civil War. Gail Gibbons has written and illustrated many different types of informational books. Her *Beacons of Light: Lighthouses* (1990) shows young readers not only how these beacons work but something of their history, famous landmark lighthouses, and interesting facts. For older children, *The Book of North American Owls* (Sattler, 1995) surveys general owl information but also identifies some 20 owl species, making it a hybrid of two categories—survey and identification. Milton Meltzer roams throughout 500 years of world history to explain the incredible rise of *The Amazing Potato* (1992) to its staple food status.

Informational Picture Storybooks

Informational picture storybooks look and read like picture story-books because information is carried within the narrative by invented characters or situations but is undergirded by facts. Examples include *Christmas in the Big House, Christmas in the Quarters* (McKissack & McKissack, 1994) and *My Visit to the Aquarium* (Aliki, 1993). Another kind of informational picture storybook where facts are more prominent is the extremely popular *The Magic School Bus* series by Joanna Cole and Bruce Degen. In each title, Ms. Frizzle and her mostly willing and indefatigable class take the Magic School Bus under the ocean, into a hurricane, to the waterworks, back in the time of dinosaurs, or most recently, through a bee-hive. Sidebars in the form of notebook paper reports, informative labels, diagrams, dialogue balloons, and text work together to impart information and carry the story but make the texts somewhat challenging to read aloud. Humor, both in Cole's text and in Degen's apt cartooning, encourages readers to browse each page for various purposes and return for repeat readings because no reader can "get" it all in one sitting.

Problems with informational picture storybooks arise when it is not clear to the reader what is fact and what is fiction. Gloria Skurzynski (1992) calls those books that fold facts into a fictionalized account *blended books*. She holds herself to a high standard of accuracy and fact checking and points to David Macaulay, Joanne Ryder, and Paul Fleischman as other children's book writers of blended books who do the same. Skurzynski says:

> I'm willing to sugarcoat hardcore information with every sweetener in the storyteller's bag of tricks, providing the coating doesn't obscure the fact. My job is twofold: to attract young readers to the book, and to make sure the information in it is absolutely correct. (p. 46)

To separate fact from fiction, the McKissacks include a foreword stating that while the conversation, dialogue, and setting are authentic, events are condensed and relocated to help the story flow. In an afterword, Degen and Cole always help children separate the fantastic from the factual. If books carry information in a story, teachers need to help readers separate fiction from nonfiction by highlighting text notes, afterwords, and acknowledgments, so that children learn to make these evaluative distinctions.

It is easy to see that there is no lack of fine nonfiction books available. In fact, all of the authors and illustrators mentioned in this book are creators of notable informational books for children. Many have won awards for their work. All are well known in the field. And each one has done his or her part to elevate, define, and extend the craft and artistry of creating nonfiction books for children.

Changing Times: Trends and Issues in Publishing

We have already seen that there are greater numbers of books about more diverse topics by an increasingly varied group of writers and illustrators than ever in the history of children's book publishing. We have also noted the snail-like but steadily increasing pace with which the awards and citations have been bestowed. There are several other important trends that indicate new directions for informational books but that also raise questions for teachers to consider. Barbara Elleman (1995), former editor of *Book Links* magazine, cites the vast increase in series books, that are often uneven in quality and lacking in passion and substance. She applauds the impeccable research in books by authors such as Jean Fritz, Albert Marrin, Jim Giblin, and Milton Meltzer and the creative approaches taken by authors such as Russell Freedman, Gail Gibbons, and Jim Murphy to sustain children's interest in a topic. Elleman also praises the increasing range of titles especially in the areas of multiculturalism and greater accuracy in the use of historical fact to inform historical fiction. There are other trends, as well.

Fast Response to Timely Topics

If it is true that the market drives publishing, publishers are quick to respond to issues of the day. Jane Martin, Chief of the Library of Congress cataloging department, states: "If we see it on the front pages of the *Washington Post*, you can be sure we will get a book on it." Books about the 1996 Olympic winners and the American Presidential campaign appeared quickly on publisher's lists. Books that are published in response to an event may be ephemeral in appeal or they may, like Patricia Lauber's *Volcano: The Eruption and Healing of Mt. St. Helens* (1986), remain an important teaching resource in the field of earth sciences.

The Visual Revolution

In the 1990s, illustrations have become increasingly sophisticated, visually packed with information, and amazingly varied in format and content. This is in part due to the immense influence of the British publisher Dorling Kindersley (Lodge, 1996a) whose first *Eyewitness* book (*Bird* by David Burnie) was published in 1988. In this *Eyewitness* title, readers enjoy a well-laid out text with interestingly displayed information drawn from a variety of sources to help readers discover various facts about birds. While similar content could be found in other books, no publisher had packaged it so seductively.

Scholastic's *Voyages of Discovery* series has pushed further the look of nonfiction. One such book, *Boats and Ships* (1995), features fold-out pages, inserts, acetate overlays, three-dimensional parts, and a smorgasbord of visual formats. New techniques in close-up photography have helped authors such as Vicki Cobb produce extraordinary vivid full-color microscopic views of bacteria and household germs (*e.g., Natural Wonders*, 1990). Science photography techniques have also given Seymour Simon an incredible array of pictures for his books on outer space, weather, and geologic upheavals.

Both foregrounds and backgrounds of illustrations depict children or adults with greater diversity than in previous decades. For instance, books such as Bruce McMillan's *Eating Fractions* (1991) show an African American and a Caucasian child dividing food into parts and Aliki's *My Visit to the Aquarium* (1993) shows racial diversity, people in wheelchairs, and all ages making the trip.

With the rise of snappy graphics and interactive illustrations have come interesting new formats and variations on the old ones. Candlewick's "Newspaper" books, such as *The Roman News* (Langley and DeSouza, 1996), describe events in catchy headlines and tabloid newspaper layouts so middle schoolers can read about Caesar's stabbing, the opening of the Colosseum, or banquet etiquette tips as if they were current events (Lodge, 1996b).

Other series create immediacy in unconventional ways, such as using photographs of an historical period staged to look as it did then. For example, Russ Kendall's photographs for Kate Waters' *Samuel Eaton's Day* (1993) and *On the Mayflower* (1996) cleanly depict a Pilgrim child's possible existence. Chapter 4 will examine in detail the visual aspects of nonfiction books.

Information Is Where You Find It

After a midcentury period of undocumented information books, nonfiction texts are increasingly packed with references to sources. Forewords, afterwords, and acknowledgments distinguish fiction from nonfiction and give readers added information. Annotated glossaries, pronouncing gazettes, and a detailed index are also more frequently a part of today's nonfiction. Many authors add final pages of related but extraneous material and it is not unusual for one to generously cite in source notes other informational children's books on the topic. Some nonfiction books seem to overflow with information as if, in this budget-conscious era, authors want to be sure readers are getting their money's worth. These aspects will be discussed in greater detail in Chapter 2 and Chapter 3.

New Attention to Old Topics

Certain subject areas in the school curriculum have been regularly updated in children's informational titles. Books about animals and plants, occupations, certain historical eras, and folktales from Western Europe have always been available. But other curricular areas are now being illuminated by nonfiction. Folktale selections from Central and South America, Asia, and Africa have been massively refurbished (Elleman, 1995). Among the best versions, great care has been given to cultural authenticity, the listing of sources, and the use of culturally specific illustrations (Hearne, 1993a, 1993b). Mathematics has suddenly received more attention from publishers (Maughan, 1996) who are creating series and single books about numbers and concepts (see Chapter 8). Art books, too, have come into their own with numerous connections to the art curriculum as well as to biography and history (Elleman, 1995; Boulanger, 1996). There are art books about historical periods, particular artists (*e.g.*, Krull, 1995), certain features across artists (*e.g.*, Micklethwait, 1996; Roalf, 1993), and books that teach readers to observe closely (see Chapter 9).

An interesting aside to the increase in informational art books has been the marked increase of books by and about artists (and writers) of children's literature (Helper, 1997). Starting with *Bill Peet: An Autobiography* (1989), the children's book field has become increasing self-reflective. In Richard C. Owen's glistening "Meet the Author" series (*e.g.*, Asch, 1997; Fritz, 1992; McKissack, 1997; Pringle, 1997), authors and artists have been able to show how they draw on childhood experiences, research, art techniques, and an abiding love of literature to create their work for children. For example, Pat Cummings (1992, 1995) interviewed some two dozen artists of children's books, and recently Heinemann initiated the *Creative Sparks* series with *On the Bus with Joanna Cole* (Cole, 1996), which explains how she and Bruce Degen created *The Magic School Bus* books.

New Audiences

Nonfiction titles on nearly any topic are now aimed at the preschool reader. Concept books and identification books have traditionally been a part of early childhood but newer selections use clear photographs and minimal text, often suitable for new readers.

Biographies, both in series and in individual titles, now exist for nearly all ages. Stanley and Vennema's distinguished picture-book biographies (*e.g.*, *Leonardo de Vinci*, 1996) are of interest to middle school readers. However, the picture-book format and text layout may suggest that this book is for younger children. It would be unfortunate if older readers missed Stanley's scholarly and appealing presentations. Biographies series for very young children run the risk of oversimplifying a person's contributions or the times in which he or she lived. These series often omit unpleasant facts and controversies surrounding a person's actions or life, and may lead children to mistrust books on the same subject when they read a more complex biography years later.

Changing Times: Classroom Issues in the Teaching of Nonfiction

Some of these trends raise certain issues for publishing. How much glitz and fancy format, for instance, can readers handle before the format overwhelms the book's content? Do texts have a certain responsibility to behave like texts? That is, should information unwind in an orderly fashion (and the related question—do readers understand best in a linear way)? Another concern is whether there needs to be a book on every subject for every age reader? For instance, do we need an "I Can Read" book about the holocaust, World War II, or AIDS? A related issue is the dire tone found in some natural science and ecological nonfiction. A book that arouses a child's regret and guilt rather than a sense of wonder may leave the child without optimism and hope.

There are also challenges posed for the teacher in these changing times. There appears to be a bias toward using fiction to teach reading. While teachers display informational books that relate to classroom inquiry, most shy away from reading nonfiction aloud or including it in book discussion groups (see Chapters 10 and 12). Many schools do not have multiple copies of nonfiction for use in small groups. Why is this? Don't children need just as much help in unpacking a dense text, understanding the author's purposes, evaluating points of view, or deciphering visual information as they do in understanding fiction's vagaries? If teachers use fiction exclusively to teach emergent readers, what is the consequence to their later reading of informational texts, and what losses does their writing incur?

A related question is genre preference by gender. While many older studies of children's reading preferences suggest this, is it currently true that boys prefer nonfiction more strongly than girls? There is some evidence (Pappas, 1991) that kindergartners of both genders like both genres equally. Is genre preference inherent in the child or is it instilled by the culture and emphasized in the school? If children have an affinity for informational books and the curriculum emphasizes fiction, then what are the consequences to readers of both sexes?

We don't really know much about how a reader reads informational texts. Is reading nonfiction substantially different from reading fiction? Louise Rosenblatt (1991) speaks to the need for children to adopt a predominant stance as they read; but that in one reading, stances may flicker between efferent and aesthetic. And in successive readings, stances may differ widely from previous encounters. Meek (1996) has proposed the term *radial reading* to describe how one moves back and forth in informational text to manage unfamiliar content. Do nonfiction texts, some often the visual equivalent of marbles scattered on the floor, demand a different kind of reader? What does this kind of reading look like? How can we help children toward richer readings of informational text? Does helping children refine or define their purposes for reading help or hinder their understandings?

Teachers often feel obligated to help children separate fact from fancy. It takes a lot of experience with books before children are familiar with conventions of the genre, and so many books stretch the boundaries of what nonfiction is and how it works that the problem of definition and evaluation is a complicated one. Rather, teachers need to decide what are age-appropriate ways to help children read for facts, appreciate distinctions, make inferences, understand the visuals, and begin to grasp the author's purposes. We also need to take a long hard look at the books we ask children to read to determine if they are truly relevant or merely peripheral to the subject under study (Zarnowski, 1995).

Our curriculum should begin to explore what it means to be visually literate. We ask children to make inferences constantly, but we are less likely to ask them how visuals work. What are scale diagrams? Sidebars? Close-ups? What things does this circle or bar graph tell us? How does an overlay work and why is it used here? What can be learned from this timeline? What can be inferred from this archival photograph? These are all questions that beg to be asked as we work with nonfiction and will be explored further in Chapter 4.

Teachers also need to know how to make the link between informational books and children's writing. While children are increasingly report-laden as they move through elementary school, few teachers invite children to use writing and illustrative techniques present in nonfiction. There is no reason for instance why a child could not use questions and answers to organize text, or use acetate overlays, sidebars, and circled closeups to complement it. These techniques lighten text, allow for the inclusion of additional information, draw on higher level thinking, and ask children to consider what creative approaches they can use to interest a wider audience. But children need to be invited (Moline, 1996; Hepler, 1994; Saul et al., 1993). (See Chapter 11.)

Conclusions

We need more professional books, such as this one, which help us think more deeply about the world of nonfiction. We are awash in information but so are today's children. For the 21st century, as they have in all centuries, children will need to know, to evaluate, to discern, to infer, and especially, to marvel and to wonder at the world so that they can act more intelligently. If our curriculum and our practices are ready to lead them in that direction, excellent children's books stand ready to assist, as well.

References

Book Links: A bimonthly publication from American Library Association, 434 W. Downer, Aurora, IL 60506

Boulanger, S. (1996). Language, imagination, vision: Art books for children. *The Horn Book Magazine, 72*, 295-304.

Carr, J. (1982). *Beyond fact: Nonfiction for children and young people.* Chicago: American Library Association.

Duthie, C. (1996). *True stories: Nonfiction literacy in the primary classroom.* York, ME: Stenhouse Publishers.

Elleman, B. (1995). Toward the 21st century—Where are children's books going? *The New Advocate, 8*, 151-165.

Fisher, M. (1972). *Matters of fact: Aspects of non-fiction for children.* New York: Crowell.

Freeman, E., & Person, D. G. (Eds.). (1992). *Using nonfiction trade books in the elementary classroom: From ants to zeppelins.* Urbana, IL: National Council of Teachers of English.

Gerhardt, L. N. (1992). Publishers nonfiction forecast: Fall 1992. *School Library Journal, 38* (5), 39-46.

Hearne, B. (1993a). Cite the source: Reducing cultural chaos in picture books, part one, *School Library Journal, 39* (7), 22-27.

Hearne, B. (1993b). Respect the source: Reducing cultural chaos in picture books, part two. *School Library Journal, 39* (8), 33-37.

Hepler, S. (1994). Supporting children's informational writing with books. *Teachers Networking: The Whole Language Newsletter, 13* (2), 1, 3-5.

Hepler, S. (1997). The writing life: Autobiographical reflections. *Book Links, 6* (4), 44-47.

Kobrin, B. (1988). *Eyeopeners: How to choose and use children's books about real people, places, and things.* New York: Viking.

Kobrin, B. (1995). *Eyeopeners II: Children's books to answer children's questions about the world around them.* New York: Scholastic.

Lodge, S. (1996a). Giving kids' references a fresh look. *Publishers Weekly, 243* (18), 42-43.

Lodge, S. (1996b). Not just the facts. *Publishers Weekly, 243* (33), 24-25.

Maughan, S. (1996). The numbers game. *Publishers Weekly, 243* (18), 30-31.

Meek, M. (1996). *Information and book learning.* Gloucester, Great Britain: Thimble Press.

Meltzer, M. (1976). Where do all the prizes go? The case for nonfiction. *The Horn Book Magazine, 52*, 17-23.

Moline, S. (1996). *I see what you mean: Children at work with visual information.* York, ME: Stenhouse.

Pappas, C. (1991). Fostering full access to literacy by including information books. *Language Arts, 68*, 449-462.

Rosenblatt, L. (1991). Literature—S.O.S.!. *Language Arts, 68*, 444-448.

Saul, W., Reardon, J., Schmidt, A., Pearce, C., Blackwood, D., and Bird, M. D. (1993). *Science workshop: A whole language approach.* Portsmouth, NH: Heinemann.

Skurzynski, G. (1992). Up for discussion: Blended books. *School Library Journal, 38* (10), 46-47.

Zarnowski, M. (1995). Learning history with informational storybooks: A social studies educator's perspective. *The New Advocate, 8,* 183-196.

CHAPTER 2
CHOOSING QUALITY NONFICTION LITERATURE: EXAMINING ASPECTS OF ACCURACY AND ORGANIZATION

by Rosemary A. Bamford and Janice V. Kristo

Barbara, a fourth-grade teacher, is about to embark upon a very different learning experience with her students. The class will begin a unit on the solar system incorporating lots of nonfiction literature. This is a change as Barbara usually relied on the science textbook as the primary source for reading and learning about science. She has several reasons for changing from a textbook emphasis to the use of nonfiction children's books. Barbara found herself explaining what was in the text more than students were actually reading from it. She often had children read in round-robin fashion to get through the material because there was a range of reading and comprehension abilities in the class. Students also had limited exposure to reading from a variety of science-oriented materials. And, lastly, Barbara wanted to incorporate nonfiction into the curriculum because she believed that exposure to these books would improve her students' abilities to read nonfiction as well as to write their own expository pieces.

With all this in mind, Barbara searched for as many nonfiction titles about the solar system as possible. She found some at bookstores, yard sales, and acquired others from the school and public libraries. Barbara's first priority was to have a huge selection of literature available for her students, to literally flood the classroom with books. She believed that a *book-flood* model where as many books as possible are collected would give every student an opportunity to experience reading and responding to nonfiction.

Why We Need to Select Quality Nonfiction

We begin this chapter by describing a common classroom scenario in which the teacher has good intentions about the needs of her students.

Barbara wants to share her enthusiasm for books with students and give them the opportunity to read nonfiction material. However, a very significant ingredient is missing—consideration of quality. The *book-flood* model brings many books into the classroom, but determining which are the best is ultimately of greater importance.

A number of decisions are involved in selecting high-quality nonfiction. One layer of decision making involves examining issues such as accuracy, organizational structure, style, access features, and format of books. The other layers deal with the role of nonfiction in the curriculum and how the books fit the needs of students. We believe that choosing the best nonfiction for the classroom needs to be a multilayered approach—one of examining the merits of the book as well as how the book will work with children and the curriculum.

In examining issues of quality, Saul (1993) discusses two varied perspectives. She suggests that librarians tend to take an unmediated approach to book selection viewing the merits and quality of books; whereas, teachers take a more mediated view in book selection. Teachers often view even mediocre books as having value in terms of what can be done instructionally with the books. Saul offers examples of teachers suggesting that students write to the author about inaccuracies or drawing their own illustrations if those in the book are poorly done. Saul states, "Teachers need to become more cognizant of the fact that they are, in fact, making a choice when they select a book. Books should be actively and consciously chosen for the classroom. As teachers realize that they have neither the time nor the inclination to undertake significant bibliographic work, they might become more skilled in asking librarians for help" (p.175). She goes on further to suggest that, "In sum, my hope is that both librarians and teachers come to base their *judgments* of children's trade books not on assumptions *about* readers but rather on experience *with* readers" (p.177).

It is easy to understand why Barbara was excited about making available a variety of books on a topic and did not place much emphasis on the selection process. When we go beyond gathering books to carefully weighing their inclusion in our classrooms, a number of valuable changes occur. Close examination of each book causes us to think about the best ways to integrate the information of the book with the curriculum. We may be more apt to note the differences in structures and presentations as well as the subtle differences between books and where there may be contradictions or errors. This kind of examination provides an opportunity to plan critical thinking and reading events. It also invites thinking about the special structures and features of each book. These kinds of judgments can lead to considering how each book might meet the needs of particular students as well as how it will be presented in the classroom. For example, students can hypothesize about the decisions made by the author and illustrator in terms of writing style, choice of words, graphics, and layout in considering the book as a model for their own writing and presentation of material.

Further, choosing high-quality nonfiction provides teachers with the opportunity to engage students in appreciating and examining a wide range of ways in which authors view the world—through mathematics, science, the arts, and social studies. Many teachers view literature as a way to help children design their own questions and inquiry, rather than simply reading to acquire facts. Short and Armstrong (1993) discuss their view of textbooks as "distillations of already known knowledge written to inform, they do not include enough evidence to recreate the author's inquiry process" (p.185). They go on to state:

> Well-written nonfiction, in contrast, is more modest and focused, with a more intimate and personal perspective. Instead of simply informing, the perspective is that of authors sharing their inquiry with other interested people, one enthusiast to another. Enough data is provided so readers can form their own opinions. (p.185)

Providing high-quality fiction for sharing aloud and literature discussion groups has been advocated for many years. We have known that children of all ages, though, have gravitated toward nonfiction eager to find out such things as the newest information about dinosaurs, to search for photographs of sharks, to read the truth behind their favorite sports hero, or to learn how to draw cartoons. As nonfiction becomes more prevalent in classrooms, teachers, at all grade levels, need to explore its use as the focus of literature circle discussions, for sharing aloud, as examples for writing minilessons, as the heart of the inquiry process, and in a myriad of other ways. Opportunities that bring nonfiction and children together may also lead students to recognize that nonfiction may not only be read for information but also for enjoyment.

Examining Ways to Determine
High-Quality Nonfiction Literature

In the evaluation process there are four major aspects that need to be considered: accuracy, organizational structure, writing style, and visual aspects. The focus of this chapter will be on accuracy and organizational structure. We refer readers to the next two chapters in this book: Chapter 3 "Choosing Quality Nonfiction Literature: Examining of Aspects of Writing Style," and Chapter 4 "Choosing Quality Nonfiction Literature: Features for Accessing and Visualizing Information." In addition, Chapter 5 focuses on these aspects as they apply to selecting titles for emerging readers.

How Do We Find Out What the Author Knows?
Examining Aspects of Accuracy

As you read an informational book, have you thought about the writer behind the words? It is important to guide students in becoming critical and thoughtful readers by encouraging them to consider the author's credentials, research process, involvement of other experts, etc. The internalization of such considerations will help them refine their selection process. For example:

- When was the book written?
- What are the author's credentials?
- Who is acknowledged?
- Does the reader find out any information about the author's research process?
- Are author/illustrator notes included?
- To what extent is the writing biased?
- To what extent is the information accurate?
- Are additional readings suggested?

Teachers and librarians are responsible for many content areas in the elementary and middle school, so it is virtually impossible to be an expert in all topics. Instead, we must rely on others to help determine issues of accuracy. Bruce McMillan (1993) says this about his own writing: "When I work on a nonfiction book for children, I've found that there is no such thing as overdoing the research. After I've completed my first draft, I have the text checked by scientists familiar with the subject" (p. 99). McMillan goes on to state: "The ultimate responsibility for accuracy in books for young readers lies with the books' authors, but publishers and reviewers also have a crucial role in assuring that the books which reach young readers are accurate" (p. 103).

The copyright date is critical in assessing accuracy. So many areas in our life are being challenged, debated, criticized, or totally changed. Being aware of the copyright date is particularly important in the *book-flood* model. If dated books are part of the collection, teachers and students need to assess current thinking on a topic and then determine how our knowledge has changed over the years and why. Also discuss with students how a book may be error free at the time of publication, but that recent changes in a field now makes the book inaccurate. Books, particularly on science topics, become rapidly out of date. Students also need to be aware that even recently published books, in any field, may have inaccuracies.

Not all authors write strictly within their area(s) of expertise.

Depending upon the writer's expertise, knowledge about a topic will understandably vary. While there may still be errors or misinformation in a book, an individual who writes about a primary area of expertise is usually a good indicator that the contents are accurate. When information about the author's credentials is provided, we are better able to assess the accuracy of the book.

Information about the author's area of expertise may be found in a variety of places in a book. Very often a short biography is provided only on the book cover or jacket. For example in *Vanilla, Chocolate & Strawberry* (1994) author Bonnie Busenberg's expertise on this topic is only described on the book jacket. However, in many recent nonfiction books, publishers are also duplicating the book jacket information on the last page of the book.

Authors who are experts in a topic, as well as those who are not, may use a variety of research or data-gathering techniques. This is the writer-researcher at work, digging and unearthing special treasures to include in a book of nonfiction. For example, an author might use quotes from interviews and primary sources such as historical journal or diary entries, personal accounts, old photographs, or museum reproductions. Documents of the time period such as newspapers and advertisements may also be used. Including materials such as these captures the depths of the human experience and takes the reader beyond mere facts. The acknowledgments often identify those who gave interviews or assisted with the gathering of primary source materials. In addition to the book jacket, information on the author's research process may also be found on the verso of the title page, in an introduction, author's notes, and bibliographies. Including this information for readers provides evidence of the author's scholarship

EXAMINING AUTHOR'S CREDENTIALS

Invite students to find examples of nonfiction books and share the information they find about the author's credentials. If the information is found only on a book cover or jacket, it can be copied and inserted inside the book. As students engage in inquiry studies, ask them to consider what they want to report about themselves as researchers.

Buried in Ice: The Mystery of a Lost Arctic Expedition by Owen Beattie and John Geiger

101 Questions & Answers about Backyard Wildlife by Anne Squire

Science to the Rescue by Sandra Markle

Unconditional Surrender: U. S. Grant and the Civil War by Albert Marrin

and attention to matters of accuracy. Examples of books that offer information on the research process include:

- *Once Upon a Horse* (Jurmain, 1989)
- *Shadow Ball* (Ward & Burns with O'Connor, 1994)
- *Harriet: The Life and World of Harriet Beecher Stowe* (Johnston, 1994)
- *The Clover and the Bee* (Dowden, 1990)

Research for the nonfiction writer, and often for the photo-essayist, involves more than researching historical documents or interviewing subjects about the topic. In order to acquire first-hand experience, it is not unusual for an author to travel or participate in special expeditions. Again, the book jacket information, acknowledgments, and the author's notes speak to this type of personalized research. Examples of books that involve on-site research include:

- *Now Is Your Time!* (Myers, 1991)
- *Summer Ice* (McMillan, 1995)
- *Panama Canal* (St. George, 1989)
- *Totem Pole* (Hoyt-Goldsmith, 1990)
- *Amazon Basin* (Reynolds, 1993)

While examining for accuracy, it is also wise to look for indicators of author bias. Interests, passions, personal experiences and values may narrow an author's presentation of information and conflicting or varied perspectives may not be included. However, at the same time, personal interests and experiences can also translate into writing that is full of passion and excitement for one's topic—the kind of writing that captures the interest of readers. We offer a caveat, though. Those making selections for children need to be cautious about books that misrepresent information. For example, significant facts may not be included, generalizations may be inadequately supported, or there may be evidence of cultural stereotyping or bias. Readers may want to examine the annotated Orbis Pictus list in Part IV of this book for a large selection of authors whose passion for their topics does not detract from their scholarship.

As readers, we are often alerted to the potential of biased writing when there are clearly defined opposing issues. Some organizations such as Sierra Club, Audubon Society, and others specializing in books about environmental and natural phenomena, state their philosophical mission on the verso of the title page or within the book. Examples include: Cone's *Squishy, Misty, Damp & Muddy* (1996), Darling and Darling's *How to*

Babysit an Orangutan (1996), Snedd en's *What Is a Reptile?* (1995), and Hirschi's *Save Our Prairies and Grasslands* (1994). It is also important to look for books that offer other points of view. However, we are not recommending using books with balanced views in the classroom. In fact, we encourage just the opposite. Students need to recognize a variety of perspectives in writing and to be aware that several or more positions may exist on any issue. An example of two books giving different views are Bash's *Ancient Ones* (1994) and Guiberson's *Spotted Owl* (1994).

Accuracy may also be affected by sources of information available about events or people of the past, or these historical materials may be written from a limited perspective. For example, much of what is known about Cleopatra was written by her enemies. We commend authors such as Diane Stanley (*Leonardo da Vinci*, 1996) and Kathryn Lasky (*The Librarian Who Measured the Earth*, 1994) who share with readers the problems faced by writers and researchers when presenting historical events or famous people in a fair way despite the biased historical information. More importantly, as authors share the decisions they make, readers are provided with an opportunity to learn that everything is not known and may never be known about a topic or person. Further, students are offered a model of how writer/researchers openly address these issues so as not to mislead readers. Therefore, as we assess the quality of nonfiction, it is important to recognize the efforts made to give young readers the best of what is known about a person or topic.

Errors of accuracy may also occur when an author is too narrow in covering a topic. For example, what to leave out due to limited space can be a difficult decision. Misunderstandings may occur in an attempt to capture the sensational or exotic aspects of a topic or

CHALLENGES FACED BY AUTHORS AND ILLUSTRATORS

Sharing nonfiction aloud is an excellent way to invite conversation about the challenges authors and illustrators faced in working on a book. (See Chapter 10 for more detail about reading nonfiction aloud.) Some good titles for exploring these issues include:

An Alphabet of Dinosaurs by Peter Dodson, Paintings by Wayne D. Barlowe, and Drawings by Michael Meaker

The Librarian who Measured the Earth by Kathryn Lasky and Illustrated by Kevin Hawkes

Now Is your Time! The African-American Struggle for Freedom by Walter Dean Myers

The Tainos: The People who Welcomed Columbus by Francine Jacobs

HELPING STUDENTS IDENTIFY AND DEAL WITH INCONSISTENCIES

Share a selection of nonfiction titles on one science topic or on a famous person or event in history. Ask students to identify any inconsistencies in information. Next steps could include locating additional books and other sources of information. A local university, college, or extension service would be good sources for locating experts in a particular area.

in making too many assumptions about the knowledge level of readers. For example, naturalist and author, Brian Cassie (1996) expressed concern about incorrect perceptions about the rainforest in some nonfiction. In these books no distinctions are made among the various rainforests around the world. The reader is left with the misconception that rainforests around the world are all similar. By trying to simplify the concept of rainforests to a common denominator, the reader is given misinformation. Only by carefully reading a collection of books on a topic and comparing them to other kinds of sources (such as experts in the field) can students begin to detect sensational information to the exclusion of more mundane but accurate information.

How Does The Book Help The Reader? Examining Aspects of Content and Organizational Structures

What drives an author to write about one topic over another, to carve out an area of content and to write about that content for children? Again, personal passions, interests, and a strong sense of what appeals to children are essential for nonfiction literature that not only provides information, but that also helps readers contrast facts or come to new understandings. Books that come from the author's enthusiasm for a topic grip readers and increase their knowledge of the world while stimulating new interests. Carr (1984) states that "[t]he author must care deeply about the subject; or the reader won't care at all" (p. 5).

Factors Influencing the Selection of Content

Enthusiasm for one's subject is not enough. Authors of nonfiction books often immerse themselves in their topic by reading widely, interviewing experts, and even visiting sites associated with the topic. Their knowledge of the topic allows them to better narrow the scope of content and to select an organizational structure for a specific audience.

Determining the target age group for a book is not always easy to assess. Even books including an age indicator, can be interesting and challenging to a wider audience than that which is designated. An appeal of a topic, a lively writing style, and the sophisticated treatment of the content may make a title a good choice for a wide audience. Additional factors such as how the book will be used with students or, perhaps, to what extent a book is appropriate for at-risk learners also needs to be considered. See Chapter 5 for a discussion of aspects of nonfiction that make it challenging for young students to read.

The scope of the topic is narrowed by selecting content along a continuum from a limited presentation to one that is more global, and also by depth of presentation desired, *i.e.*, level of sophistication and complexity of concepts or information. In addition, the type and length of the book (*e.g.*, photographic essay, identification book, survey book, etc.) will influence the scope and depth of content chosen. For example, Arnold's photographic essay *Killer Whale* (1994) is limited to information only about killer whales and in particular, Takara, a killer whale at Sea World. The book describes this species in more depth than would an identification handbook on whales of the North Atlantic. For the K-8 audience, authors also consider the sophistication of prior knowledge and interests of the children as well as the curricular topics. In 1992, for instance, the subject of Columbus and exploration became an important curricular topic, and as a result many books were pub-

DETERMINING AGE APPROPRIATENESS OF NONFICTION

One aspect in determining age appropriateness of nonfiction is connected with teaching and learning considerations. Think about whether to share the book aloud, have it available for student research, or use it for independent reading.

COMPARING SCOPE OF CONTENT

Consider these books on raptors by comparing the scope of content and depth of presentation. Is the presentation more global or limited? Does the title help to determine the depth of treatment? Which books are more challenging to read and what makes them so? To what extent are more complex concepts explored? What is the purpose and stance of each author? Which books would interest your students and why? Collect several on a topic of interest to your students. Design a similar activity in which they would compare the scope of content and depth of presentation on raptors.

The Book of North American Owls by Helen Roney Sattler

The Eagle and the River by Charles Craighead

Eagles by Aubrey Lang

lished about his exploration and its impact on indigenous populations. Biographers also make decisions about how much of a person's life they will explore: a *cradle-to-grave* approach or a description of a short, significant event. However, writers who decide to focus on a subject in its entirety need to be careful to not compress too much, provide too shallow, or poorly developed explanations, or leave out important details that would make complex ideas clear. Conversely, writers who focus on one aspect of a topic should establish an overall context so the reader is clear where the book's information fits in the overall scheme of the topic. Lastly, it is important to note that if an author has a particular belief or intends to highlight certain facts or share a personal perspective, some content may be purposively omitted.

In examining a selection of nonfiction on a particular topic, it is important for teachers to consider the complexity of treatment and the range of coverage in the collection. Careful examination and comparison will help to determine if the information is adequately treated. However, in most cases, by bringing nonfiction books into the classroom, we can more adequately explore a topic than the typical single textbook. In addition, as students initiate independent research, it is important to help them assess the coverage and treatment of topics in the nonfiction collection.

Organizational Structures Develop Naturally from Content

Expository texts, like narrative ones, are characterized by a range of structures and text patterns. These structures and patterns are usually found in combination rather than in a pure form (Raphael & Hiebert, 1996). A variety of schemas have emerged from the research on classification of expository text. Meyer (1975) found five structural patterns (cause-effect, comparison-contrast, problem-solution, description, and collection). Hayes (1989), in examining social studies textbooks, identified three common patterns: chronological, cause-effect, and enumeration. Other schemas have been developed by Armbruster and Anderson (1985) and Calfee and Curley (1984). But as Carter and Abrahamson (1990) so astutely point out, authors of nonfiction books "don't haphazardly choose one [structure] out of the air and force their information into it " (p. 106). Organizational structures and/or patterns need to flow naturally from the content and the purpose of the author. Bacon (1984) states that, "For children particularly, a factual book must communicate a sense of motion, and not random motion either, but motion with direction, a pattern, and a rational basis that can be explained and understood" (p. 197). It is important to point out that although nonfiction is often written using a combination of several organizational structures, an author may select a particular organizational structure or pattern for framing the overall book. Authors may also utilize other structures or patterns at the embedded or nested level of the sentence, paragraph, or passage. Additional internal patterns or structures such as cause-effect, compare-contrast, and chronological sequences, when used as embedded internal text patterns, often clarify relationships between facts and events. The organizational structure an author uses is important in supporting both a student's understanding of the information and serves as a model for their writing (Salesi, 1992). Therefore, it is essential that we look closely at organizational structures in order to assist students with comprehending text and learning from these more expert writers of informational books. Guiding questions to consider in evaluating organization are:

(continued from page 28)

Eagles: Lions of the Sky by Emery Bernhard and Durge Bernhard

Eagles of America by Dorothy Hinshaw Patent

Raptor Rescue! An Eagle Flies Free by Sylvia Johnson

Think Like an Eagle: At Work with a Wildlife Photography by Kathryn Lasky

- What type of organization has the author used to frame the information?
- Does the organization naturally flow from the content? Is it logical?
- Does the organization aid conceptual understandings?
- Do the nested structures (internal) clarify relationships between facts?
- Do the subheadings make the text easier to read and comprehend?
- Does the book have access features such as table of contents, index, bibliography, glossary, appendices, etc. and visual aids that make the book easy to use and read?

First, we will discuss the importance of attending to the organizational structure. Next, we will examine some of the more prevalent structures: enumeration, sequenced (alphabetic and counting), chronological, compare-contrast, cause-effect, and narrative common to nonfiction books for preschool through eighth grade. We will discuss the primary framing structures as well as structures embedded or nested in the text. An examination of organization should also include reference aids or access features (*e.g.*, table of contents, indices, sidebars, listed information), as well as notes to the reader and appendices (*e.g.*, forewords, afterwords, and epilogues). In evaluating the quality of organization of the nonfiction, the contribution these features make to the overall presentation needs to be considered. These organizational features and format aspects, such as illustrations and other visuals elements (*e.g.*, graphs, charts, and captions), will be discussed primarily in Chapter 4 on "Choosing Quality Nonfiction Literature: Features for Assessing and Visualizing Information."

Keeping in mind that the reader is often new to the topic, it is important that an author skillfully select an organizational structure and internal patterns that support exploration of new ideas or principles. In addition, the structural framework often signals the reader how to process the information, and thus supports recall (Raphael & Hiebert, 1996). For example, when we read a narrative informational picture book such as *Not So Very Long Ago* (Fix, 1994) we read it like a story noting the embedded factual information. But in *An Indian Winter* (Freedman, 1992), which is organized chronologically, it is easier to remember the temporal order of events and how those events relate to each other. In a structure using enumeration, such as *Eagles of America* (Patent, 1995), which begins with a general presentation or overview of the topic and follows with discussion of subtopics, readers will consider the collection of facts and their relationships to each other. In addition, when organization complements the content being presented the information is more accessible. The book is not only easier to read in terms of comprehending and recalling the information, but again, it becomes an excellent model for student writing. (See Chapter 11 "Writing Nonfiction—Helping Students Teach Each Other What They Know.")

Enumeration Structures

Enumeration is one of the more common structures and is often used when there is a topic that includes many subtopics. This structure may move from the simple to the more complex or provide an introduction followed by chapters devoted to specific topics. Even though *Police Patrol* (Winkleman, 1996) is not divided into chapters, each full-page spread addresses a different division of law enforcement. In longer works, such as *Poisons in Our Path: Plants that Harm and Heal* (Dowden, 1994), a brief general chapter is followed by four chapters on related subtopics. The table of contents and thoughtful selection of headings and subheadings help to guide the reader through the information.

Sequenced Structures: Alphabet and Counting Books

A sequence structure such as alphabetic or counting structure may be selected where there is a wealth of terms associated with a topic. In *Illuminations* (Hunt, 1989), a traditional alphabet book, each medieval term is alphabetically presented independently with little or no attention given to the general organizational structures of sequential order, chronological order, or hierarchical order, or cause-effect. A variation on the alphabet book is Lankford's *Hopscotch Around the World* (1992), which is organized alphabetically by countries. No alphabet letters are used and there is not a country and hopscotch game for

---

EXAMPLES OF
ENUMERATION
ORGANIZATION

AIDS: What Does it Mean to You? by Margaret O. Hyde and Elizabeth H. Forsyth

Bizarre Bugs by Doug Wechsler

Blue Potatoes, Orange Tomatoes by Rosalind Creasy

Lobsters: Gangsters of the Sea by Mary M. Cerullo

Making Sense: Animal Perception and Communication by Bruce Brooks

Venus: Magellan Explores our Twin Planet by Franklyn M. Branley

EXAMPLES OF
ALPHABETIC OR
COUNTING STRUCTURES

A Is for Africa by
Ifeoma Onyefulu

Aardvarks Disembark!
by Ann Jonas

*An Alphabet of
Dinosaurs* by Peter
Dodson

*The Butterfly Alphabet
Book* by Brian Cassie
and Jerry Pallotta

A Caribou Alphabet by
Mary Beth Owens

*One Hundred in a
Family* by Pam Munoz
Ryan

*Turtle Island ABC: A
Gathering of Native
American Symbols* by
Gerald Hausman

*V for Vanishing: An
Alphabet of
Endangered Animals* by
Patricia Mullins

Zin! Zin! A Violin by
Lloyd Moss

each letter of the alphabet.

Lankford's structure is similar to ones found in counting books, where the numbers are used to provide a framework for presentation, in combination with another structure such as chronological or enumerative. *Gathering: A Northwoods Counting Book* (Bowen, 1995) and *Emeka's Gift: An African Counting Book* (Onyefulu, 1995) are good examples of books where the counting structure is not intended to help clarify the nature of the relationship between the facts, but the numbers serve as a framework upon which facts about a topic are developed. While most alphabet books are ideal for browsing, this is not necessarily true for the counting organization where information may have relational connections from page to page.

Chronological Structures

Chronological order is a natural organizational structure when the author wants to explore changes or events over time. This structure is similar to a narration because the story of the event or topic is unfolded chronologically. A sense of drama and tension can be created when telling the story of a person's life or historical event. *The Abracadabra Kid: A Writer's Life* (Fleischman, 1996), *The Amazing Impossible Erie Canal* (Harness, 1995), *The Great Midwest Flood* (Vogel, 1995), and *In Flanders Fields: the Story of the Poem by John McCrae* (Granfield, 1996) all use a chronological approach, but each book focuses on a different duration of time—from days to years. For example, by presenting the events of the Midwest flood chronologically, Vogel unravels the cause and effect of each event helping readers experience the domino effect that results when rainfall is so great that it is measured in feet instead of inches. Often authors frame their writing chronologically, but combine it with other expository structures. In

Fly: A Brief History of Flight Illustrated Moser, 1993), the author chronologically presents the history of aviation. At the bottom of each page, he presents a history within a history by citing other occurrences at or about the same time. In this way readers are able to place the historical information about aviation into a more meaningful context. While chronological structures are often used for diaries, biographies, and descriptions of historical events, this structure may also be used as an embedded structure in which subtopics are described chronologically such as in *Vanilla, Chocolate & Strawberry* (Busenberg, 1994). Following a lengthy introduction to these three flavors, each one is discussed in its own chapter using a historical presentation.

Compare-Contrast Structures

Comparing and contrasting information allows an author to examine the characteristics or qualities of the topic. In *The News about Dinosaurs* (1989) Lauber uses a point-counterpoint pattern to contrast dated and current information about dinosaurs. The title *Wild Turkey, Tame Turkey* (Patent, 1989) alerts the reader that this book will involve similarities and differences between the wild turkey and the domestic turkey. By focusing first on the wild turkey, Patent explores the history of the turkey in chronological order. The final section is devoted to today's domestic turkey and the turkey industry.

Written as a informational picture storybook, each chapter of the award-winning book, *Christmas in the Big House, Christmas in the Quarters* (McKissack & McKissack, 1994), compares and contrasts the events surrounding the preparation and celebration of Christmas. Because this structural pattern helps readers clarify and contrast information whole by whole (life as a plantation owner or slave) and/or feature by feature (what a plan-

CHRONOLOGICAL STRUCTURES

The duration of time in chronological structures can vary significantly. Examine the following books to see how authors can use chronological structure to build tension and a sense of drama while also clarifying how events are connected.

Flight by Robert Burleigh

Fly: A Brief History of Flight Illustrated by Barry Moser

The Great Fire by Jim Murphy

Hurricanes: Earth's Mightiest Storms by Patricia Lauber

Stranded at Plimoth Plantation 1626 by Gary Bowen

The Wright Brothers: How They Invented the Airplane by Russell Freedman

Zlata's Diary: A Child's Life in Sarajevo by Zlata Filipovic

tation owner or slave eats), it is also commonly used as an internal organizational structure within other structures. For example, in Simon's photographic essay *Whales* (1989) which is organized enumeratively, he introduces his topic by comparing whales to fish (whole to whole) to address a common misconception that whales are fish. Throughout the remainder of the book, he compares various types of whales as he explores their characteristics, feature by feature (size of head). His metaphors, such as comparing the size of the tongue of a blue whale to an adult elephant, further contrast the information and connect with readers' prior knowledge.

Cause-Effect Structures

A cause-effect organizational structure demonstrates the causal connections between events, concepts, or facts, and the consequences. Cause-effect text structures are more often used as internal text patterns within other organizational structures. In *Batman: Exploring the World of Bats* (1991), which is organized chronologically, Pringle used cause-effect patterns within the text to demonstrate how bats are impacted by the actions of humans and, in turn, how humans are impacted by bats. In *Science to the Rescue* (1994), however, Markle uses cause and effect as the primary framework to show how science has solved problems. A problem is presented and discussed followed by the scientific solution.

Narrative Structures and Informational Storybooks

Although we ordinarily think of narrative as fiction, narrative structures are commonly found in informational books. Leal (1993) describes informational storybooks to describe texts which have the structural narrative elements of setting, theme, plot, and resolution blended with the expository structures for the purpose of conveying information. Raphael and Hiebert (1996) state that narrative "is a primary form of language, thinking, and stories" (Raphael & Hiebert, 1996, p. 124). They further suggest that authors often select this style of writing to humanize subjects, engender empathy, and convey that events are subject to multiple viewpoints or interpretations. The degree of fictionalized writing varies in the informational storybooks and other expository structures. For example, in *If You Should Hear a Honey Guide*, April Pulley Sayre (1995) describes the honey guide bird who seeks out bees' nests for the wax of the honeycombs. The narrative style is so engaging that readers may not distinguish the factual material from the fiction until they read the afterword where the author describes this unusual African bird. In *Summer of Fire: Yellowstone 1988*, Patricia Lauber (1991) dramatically builds the events of the fire, by tracing the course of the disastrous fire to its climax. The book ends with a discussion of the impact of the fire on the wildlife and park. Jim

Brandenburg (1993) in his book, *To the Top of the World: Adventures with Arctic Wolves,* uses personal narrative to describe his three-year experience of photographing and studying the Arctic wolves, which he presents as one summer. From extended interviews of families, Diane Hoyt-Goldsmith in her many books on ethnic families and their cultures writes in the first-person voice of the child being interviewed (*e.g., Pueblo Storyeller,* 1991). And finally, narratives fashioned as diaries such as Amelia Stewart Knight's *The Way West: Journal of a Pioneer Woman* (1993) and Susan Roth's *Marco Polo: His Notebook* (1990) adapt primary sources to create memoirs of a journey.

Zarnowski (1995) believes informational storybooks, while engaging, are potentially confusing to students. For the uninformed reader or in situations where books are not mediated by a more expert reader, it may be difficult to separate fact from fiction—the fictionalized scenes and created dialog from actual events and dialog, irrelevant information from the important facts. Narratives can hold the readers' interest, but the narrative structure should lead to clarifying information and supporting comprehension. If a narrative, story-like or poetic quality is used as a way to present information we need to ask additional questions such as:

- Is it clear to the reader that the purpose of the book is to convey information?
- Has the author made the facts clear?
- Has the author avoided anthromorphism?
- Has the information been distorted as a result of using a narrative style?

The narrative structure is also used in biographies allowing authors to merge interesting anecdotes with factual information.

SEPARATING FACT FROM FICTION IN NARRATIVE STRUCTURES

When students read narrative nonfiction, teachers need to help them understand how to separate the embedded facts from the fictional story. For example, in the following books there is a blending of factual with fiction.

Appalachia: The Voices of Sleeping Birds by Cynthia Rylant

Everglades by Jean Craighead George

Everybody Cooks Rice by Norah Dooley

From Pictures to Words: A Book About Making a Book by Janet Stevens

My Visit to the Aquarium by Aliki

The Magic School Bus in the Time of the Dinosaurs by Joanna Cole

Sky Tree: Seeing Science Through Art by Thomas Locker

Stranded at Plimoth Plantation 1626 by Gary Bowen

Theodoric's Rainbow by Stephen Kramer

The Truth about Cats by Alan Snow

The Way West: Journal of a Pioneer Woman by Amelia Stewart Knight

Today's biographies reflect a growing respect for young readers. The inclusion of bibliographies and detailed notes such as forewords, afterwords, and epilogues help clarify what research was done on the topic and where authors may have departed from documentation. Documentation on research findings often alerts readers to the information that was not available to the author. Current biographers skillfully weave quotes and information from primary sources such as letters, newspaper accounts, diaries, and interviews so as to suggest dialog without fictionalizing the biography. Authors such as Jean Fritz, Diane Stanley and Peter Vennema, Laurence Pringle, Russell Freedman, Jerry Stanley, and Jim Murphy have set new standards and scholarship for biographers.

Conclusions

The hallmark of a high-quality nonfiction book is that all aspects work as a harmonious whole. Compiler Jo Carr (1982) says this about nonfiction writers, "Teacher. Scholar. Promoter. Artist. Reporter. Catalyst. Philosopher. A fine nonfiction writer is really all these but is teacher and artist, most of all" (p. 4). Carr goes on to say:

> There are at least two characteristics common to fine nonfiction writers that can be measured by their effect on the reader: first, like the best teachers, they make us think deeply. And second, like the best teachers, they make us feel deeply. (p.4)

Selecting the best nonfiction is one step in helping all students become lifelong readers of nonfiction. The conversation continues in the next two chapters on style and visuals aspects of nonfiction. The books that we bring into the classroom need to be the best examples of nonfiction writing that we can find. We need to think about what we want students to learn about the world and how the best nonfiction literature supports this learning. The authors of these books also become teachers in the classroom—teaching readers what well-written nonfiction literature looks like and sounds like. These books invite our students to think in more creative, critical, and sophisticated ways and can open the door to students becoming authors of their own nonfiction pieces. Quality nonfiction leads to quality learning.

References

Armbruster, B. B., & Anderson, T. H. (1985). Producing "considerate" expository text: Or, easy reading is damned hard writing. *Journal of Curriculum Studies, 17,* 247-274.

Bacon, B. (1984). The art of nonfiction. In P. P. Barton & J. Q. Burley (Eds.), *Jump over the moon* (pp. 195-204). New York: Holt, Rinehart & Winston.

Calfee, R., & Curley, R. (1984). Structure of prose in content areas. In J. Flood (Ed.), *Understanding reading comprehension.* (pp. 161-180). Newark, DE: International Reading Association.

Carr, J. (1982). *Beyond fact: Nonfiction for children and young people.* Chicago, IL: American Library Association.

Carr, J. (1984). Writing the literature of fact. In P. P. Barron & J. Q. Burley (Eds.), *Jump over the moon.* (pp. 204-213). New York: Holt, Rinehart and Winston.

Carter, B., & Abrahamson. R. F. (1990). *Nonfiction literature for young adults from delight to wisdom.* Phoenix, AZ: Oryz Press.

Cassie, B. (1996, March). Rainforest books: What to expect! Paper presented at the National Council of Teachers of English Conference, Boston, MA.

Hayes, D. (1989). Expository text structure and student learning. *Reading Horizons, 30,* 52-61.

Leal, D. (1993). Storybook, information books and informational storybooks: An explication of an ambiguous grey genre. *The New Advocate, 6,* 61-70.

McMillan, B. (1993). Accuracy in books for young readers: From first to last check. *The New Advocate, 6,* 97-104.

Meyer, B. J. F. (1975). *The organization of prose and its effect on memory.* Amsterdam: North Holland.

Raphael, T. E., & Hiebert, E. H. (1996). *Creating an integrated approach to literacy instruction.* Orlando, FL: Harcourt Brace.

Robbins, K. (1996, March). Remarks to workshop participants. Paper presented at the National Council of Teachers of English Conference, Boston, MA.

Salesi, R. (1992). Reading and writing connection: Supporting content-area literacy through nonfiction trade books. In E. B. Freeman & D. G. Person (Eds.), *Using nonfiction trade books in the elementary classroom from ants to zeppelins* (pp. 86-94). Urbana, IL: National Council of Teachers of English.

Saul, E. W. (1993). Mediated vs. unmediated texts: Books in the library and the classroom. *The New Advocate, 6,* 171-181.

Short, K. G., & Armstrong, J. (1993). Moving toward inquiry: Integrating literature into the science curriculum. *The New Advocate, 6,* 183-199.

Zarnowski, M. (1995). Learning history with informational books: A social studies educator's perspective. *The New Advocate, 8,* 183-196.

CHAPTER 3
CHOOSING QUALITY NONFICTION LITERATURE: EXAMINING ASPECTS OF WRITING STYLE

by Amy A. McClure

Does [nonfiction] have to be nothing but a pastiche of facts? Is there a function for the imagination? Is there room for exercise of judgement? for the portrayal of character? for the illumination of human behavior? for the play of craftsmanship? Of course there is.

Milton Meltzer (1982, p. 33)

You can tell it's a good book when children listen spellbound as it's read aloud, when they ask questions, argue about the ideas, then rush to read it on their own. And, later, when they incorporate its language and structures into their own work responses, it's evident that the book's effect goes deep. Does this only happen with fiction? No! Well-written nonfiction which goes beyond facts to present an eloquent, informed, and well-crafted discussion of those facts can generate these same involved, enthusiastic responses.

What is the great appeal of such a book? Why do children turn to some informational books with a fervor and frequency equal to their interest in fictional stories while responding to a textbook on the same subject with boredom and frustration (Spink, 1996)? Consider Jim Murphy's *The Great Fire* (1995). Are children fascinated by this book because

RUSSELL FREEDMAN ON NONFICTION

Certainly the basic purpose of nonfiction is to inform, to instruct, hopefully to enlighten. But that's not enough. An effective nonfiction book must animate its subject, infuse it with life. It must create a vivid and believable world that the reader will enter willingly and leave only with reluctance. A good nonfiction book should be a pleasure to read. It should be just as compelling as a good story (Freeman & Person, 1992, p. 3).

they want information about the Chicago fire of 1871? Maybe. But they could learn about this event much more efficiently in a social studies textbook. They must be responding to something exceptional in Murphy's writing: the way he describes events so vividly that you feel as if you were there, his skillful weaving of individual experiences with the general historical events, or maybe his careful analysis of fact versus rumors surrounding this cataclysmic event.

This chapter will explore what makes a book of nonfiction so compelling that it "lights a fire" (Carr, 1987, p. 173) in children's minds, kindling their enthusiasm and engagement. The focus will be on writing style; that elusive quality that draws readers into a book and makes it memorable for them. We will explore how organizational structure, language use, tone, and focus work together to go beyond fact to create the "literature of fact" (Carr, 1982, p. 3) or as Jean Fritz (1988, p. 759) calls it "facts ignited by passion."

Clarity as an Element of Structure and Organization

As stated in Chapter 2, clear, cohesive organizational structure is critical for a nonfiction book because it provides the context necessary for understanding the content. Familiar patterns like enumeration, cause-effect, compare-contrast, chronological order, and narrative signal how the writer wants the reader to process the information. Skilled readers actually look for these patterns and intuitively structure their reading in response to them. Writers frequently struggle with finding just the right organizational framework as each collection of facts requires something different.

Clarity

A clear, lucid, cohesive text is one of the most important elements of structure. Without clarity a nonfiction book will fail in its purpose to inform readers. To be clear, the writing must be carefully organized, using logically ordered ideas, understandable language and examples, such as metaphors, that account for the background knowledge of readers.

In order to write with clarity, authors must know their subjects. Brent Ashabranner (1988) confirmed the importance of this in the following statement:

> A writer who wants to make a complex topic clear must understand it so well that he knows what he can leave out without distorting, oversimplifying or reducing the subject to insipid pap. (p. 751)

However, knowing one's subject isn't enough. We all know experts who can't communicate their ideas to a nontechnical audience. Authors must also respect the age group as they consider how they will structure the whole text as well as specific explanations. They must consider how much information to include, careful not to drown readers in too much detail. Endless recitation of fact after fact can numb readers who will have difficulty sorting out what is important.

Authors must also be careful to logically order their ideas within the structure of the overall book. Chapters help readers structure their thinking. The breaks should be natural segments, resulting from an overall logical pattern rather than an arbitrarily determined page count. Yet authors need to also structure chapters so they stand reasonably well as separate units since many readers skim nonfiction books, often choosing to carefully read only an isolated chapter. It's a challenge to create continuous text and autonomous chapters.

Clarity improves when explanations and examples use meaningful analogies or figurative language. A skillful writer combines these techniques in different ways to create a well-crafted text, which informs while also making the ideas more understandable and memorable to the reader. Freeman (1994) discovered that writers of selected Orbis Pictus books were much more likely to use familiar comparisons as well as extended or clustered analogies, both of which are more memorable to readers. This strategy undoubtedly led to clarity and thus added to the quality of their writing.

How do these structures facilitate comprehension? A reader must be able to connect what he/she already knows with what's presented in the book. Metaphors function as "structure maps" that link the *target* knowledge domain (the new concept) with the *base domain* (what we already know) so that we gain understanding. But the metaphors must be developmentally appropriate and use comparisons that are within the child's current experience to be effective. For young children,

BRENT ASHABRANNER ON AUTHORS WRITING NONFICTION

An author... "must then find a clear and straight forward organization for his materials; this structure may take him almost as long to locate as the actual writing takes" (Ashabranner, 1988, p. 751).

it seems if the comparisons are attributional (related on the basis of physical attributes or surface features like size, color, shape, speed, sound, taste, texture) rather than relational (based on common relational structures or functions) they are more memorable. However, the ability to interpret relational metaphors and analogies gradually increases with age (Freeman, 1994).

Seymour Simon uses simile effectively in *Sharks* (1995) to vividly describe the shark's ability to smell: "Sharks are like 'swimming noses'" (unpaged). Cynthia Rylant embeds metaphors within the poetic rhythm of the words in *Appalachia: The Voices of Sleeping Birds* (1991). Although the comparisons are original, she uses familiar objects to create a vivid picture of her subject:

> Night in these houses is thick, the mountains wear heavy shawls
> of fog and giant moths flap at the porch lights while cars cut through
> the dark hollows like burrowing moles. (p. 13)

The images resonate quietly in the mind and create a memorable picture for the reader.

Writing Style

Structuring a text is only the beginning of the process of crafting a high-quality nonfiction book. Imagination, vivid rhythmic language, and interesting descriptions are just as important in writing a book of biography or science as they are in fiction. Many nonfiction writers produce acceptable work that follows the basic principles of good writing. They carefully report how to draw cartoons, what a country's major products are, or the body parts of an ant. But their books aren't memorable or inspiring. What they lack is that elusive aspect of the writing process that we call style. Style is the author's ability to creatively combine words, form, and content with a creative vision that guides these elements.

Style is not a mechanical technique that follows a set pattern. Rather, it is idiosyncratic; the style an author uses must fit that particular person writing on a specific topic. Just as composers blend tone and rhythm to create a symphony or the media, so the author fuses elements of thought and language into a compelling text. Thus, although separate elements will be discussed here, it is important to note that it is the integration of these elements into a cohesive whole that truly exemplifies style. The following are some techniques that help nonfiction authors express their personal vision of a topic.

Emotional Involvement

One of the most critical aspects of style is that of the writer's emotional involvement or passion for the subject. It is the author's willingness to invest his/her intellectual knowledge with conviction and enthusiasm that makes all the difference. Margery Fisher terms this the "warming of facts with the fire of the writer's imagination" (Carr, 1982, p. 131). The author must then be able to communicate that passion so that the reader shares that wonder and delight.

Kathryn Lasky (1985), for example, describes how she is always "searching for the story among the truths, the facts, the lies and the realities":

> I have a fascination with the inexact and unexplainable. I try to do as little explaining as possible but I try to present my subject in such a way so it will not lose what I have found to be or suspect to be its sacred dimension. I seem to seek a nonfactual kind of truth that focuses on certain aesthetic or psychological realities. Facts are quite cheap but real stories are rare and expensive. (p. 532)

Patricia Lauber (1992) hated science as a child because she found science books dry and boring. By chance she became the editor of a science magazine and discovered a new passion. In her books she hopes to show that it is possible to read science for pleasure; that a good science book "touches the mind, the heart, the imagination" (p. 13). Do nonfiction writers have an obligation to be completely objective? In their eagerness to convey enthusiasm and involve the reader won't their writing degenerate into propaganda? These are valid concerns. Authors must be careful to provide balance or at least acknowledge that their view is but one perspective on the topic.

Many award-winning science writers also feel their books should have a point of view. Patricia Lauber further believes a science writer has an obligation to be fair and accurate and to present opposing perspectives. But she strongly asserts that a writer is also entitled to have a point of view and "care about how it all comes out" (p. 13).

Brent Ashabranner (1990) agrees, saying,

> Before I write a book, I know a great deal about my subject. I care about it and I have developed a point of view about it. I think it would be wrong for me not to let my reader know what that point of view is.... I must support my view with facts and documentation and if there are other valid points of view. I must let my reader know. (p. 102)

So the task of the nonfiction writer becomes one of warming facts with the fire of imagination while still maintaining a balanced perspective. Bias and a personal perspective are acceptable but should be acknowledged. And children should be left with enough information to continue asking questions about the subject and the impetus to search for answers to those questions.

Language

The way a writer uses words and phrases has a subtle yet significant effect on the reader. Even when dealing with facts, graceful language is an important component of the writing. However, language—the sentence structure, vocabulary, literary devices—must be appropriate for the age level. If it is too complex and sophisticated, the reader will not be able to comprehend the information. On the other hand, a simplified, stilted style that sounds like a basal will insult children. Even the young readers can appreciate finely crafted language if the words and concepts are within their experience. Carefully chosen, poetic-like language can illuminate a subject, making it resonate in the ear and the mind.

Mary Barrett Brown uses vivid imagery and descriptive language to introduce *Wings Along the Waterway* (1992), her book about wetland birds:

> The sound of wings breaks the stillness of dawn. One by one and then in flocks, birds fly from their nighttime roosts to the water and its surroundings. Suddenly the landscape is dotted with water birds. All shapes and sizes fill the marshy coves, rushing, almost in silence, to feed. Some earth-colored birds are hard to see as they stalk in the dark shadows of the shoreline. Others, starkly white, stand out sharply. Still others are so vivid they appear to glow in the morning sun. (p. 5)

Note the rhythm of her prose—first a long "all shapes and sizes fill the marshy coves," then a short one "rushing," then another longer phrase, then resolution of the sentence with "to feed." There is alliteration here too in the first line with the repetition of "s:" "The sound of wings breaks the stillness." Vivid verbs like "stalk," "rushing," and "glow" add to the vivid picture she has created.

Rita Golden Gelman uses poetic-like lan-

MILTON MELTZER ON STYLE

In the writer who cares there is a pressure of feeling that emerges in the rhythm of the sentences, the choice of details, the color of the language ...style in this sense is not a trick of rhetoric ...it is a quality of vision (Meltzer, 1976, p. 21).

guage, particularly rhythmic phrasing, to draw the reader into *Dawn to Dusk in the Galápagos* (1991). She begins with a sentence that flows, reflecting the flowing continuous rhythm of a rolling ocean. Two short sentences slow the rhythm a bit, then a sentence follows that explodes into the narrative with vivid verbs and a more staccato rhythm:

At first, there was ocean, miles and miles of ocean. No land. Just wind and waves.

Then the hot center of the earth burst through the ocean bottom and red molten lava shot through the water (unpaged).

Helen Roney Sattler also uses well-crafted language to describe an owl hunting in *The Book of North American Owls* (1995):

> Shortly after sunset, a barn owl awakens and leaves its perch. Silently it patrols the pasture, skimming over the ground just a few feet above the vegetation, looking and listening for small animals. Spotting a meadow mouse, it hovers momentarily, then, with its talons spread, it plunges and lands on the animal, pinning it to the ground. (p. 3)

Precise, vivid verbs like "skimming" and "plunging" (what a wonderful contrast between the two), rhythmic sentences and alliteration (shortly after sunset) combined with a compelling incident make an attention-grabbing description.

Rhythm, in particular, can be carefully crafted to help convey the feel of a topic. Jean Fritz uses a rollicking, rhythmical style to begin her biography *Bully For You, Teddy Roosevelt* (1991)! This style works perfectly to convey a sense of this colorful, larger-than-life American legend:

> What did Theodore Roosevelt want to do? Everything. And all at once if possible. Plunging headlong into life, he refused to waste a single minute. Among other things, he studied birds, shot lions, roped steer, fought a war, wrote books, and discovered the source of a mystery river in South America....(p. 9)

It seems the sound of sentences and phrases can have just as much power to influence readers as the meaning. Vivid description, which uses imagery, rhythmic phrasing, and fascinating detail can be a powerful device for capturing a reader's attention and interest.

Leads and Conclusions

The way one begins a story can draw readers in or cause children to abandon a book. Writers of nonfiction need to engage their readers right away, particularly if the book is on a technical subject that may prove to be less compelling reading as the book progresses. Additionally, because readers often start at different points throughout a nonfiction book, a writer of this genre has the added challenge of making the beginning of each chapter or section interesting.

Aliki (1996), a notable author of nonfiction, describes the writing of the introduction as critically important for her:

> Establishing my first paragraph is essential. It introduces the subject, provides the flavor and sets the mood....It is the anchor to which the second and subsequent paragraphs will link....I write in longhand, over and over, changing words and phrasing, until the Great Breakthrough comes when words begin to flow, towed out on a thread of thought. (p. 211)

Some begin by posing a question. This immediately engages readers and focuses their attention on the content to follow. Milton Meltzer uses this strategy quite effectively in his book *Cheap Raw Material* (1994), that describes the use of child labor through history to the present day. For example, Chapter 11 begins in the following way:

> Working, everyone agrees, can be a valuable part of growing up. But how often is that the case? Is every job an apprenticeship for adulthood? (p. 120)

Sometimes a provocative statement will be made. Diane Swanson does this effectively in the Orbis Pictus award-winning book, *Safari Beneath the Sea: The Wonder World of the North Pacific Coast* (1994):

> Imagine fish that tie themselves in knots, plants that flash lights in the dark, sea stars that turn their stomachs inside out and mammals that hammer their food. Life in the sea is bizarre, beautiful, funny and fabulous....(p. 1)

Some writers use narrative episodes or case studies that are placed at the beginning of a chapter or the entire first chapter. Russell Freedman uses this strategy to start *The Wright Brothers: How They Invented the Airplane* (1991). The book begins:

> No one had ever seen what Amos Root saw on that September afternoon in 1904. Standing in a cow pasture near Dayton, Ohio, he looked up and watched a flying machine circle in the sky above him. He could see the bold pilot lying facedown on the lower wing, staring straight ahead as he steered the craft to a landing in the grass. (p. 1)

Amos Root returns home to write an eyewitness account saying, "These two brothers have probably not even a faint glimpse of what their discovery is going to bring to the children of men." He was hooked and so are readers of this book.

In *Wildlife Rescue: The Work of Dr. Kathleen Ramsay* (1994), Jennifer Owings Dewey opens with a dramatic incident in which a family out on a walk in the New Mexico mountains are attacked by a beaver. After killing the beaver in self-defense, they are surprised:

> ...A moment later, she gasped, "Look! There's a baby coming...." The man and the woman and both children watched in amazement as a minute, wet beaver baby nose began to slide out of the dead mother's back end. (p. 11)

Two babies are rescued and taken to Ramsay's Wildlife Center to be cared for. The narrator then describes the many other rescues performed by the center.

Some nonfiction writers use poetry to set a context for their chapters. Harrison and Terris use excerpts from Robert Frost's "Birches" to frame each chapter in *A Twilight Struggle: The Life of John Fitzgerald Kennedy* (1992), their biography of John F. Kennedy. Amazingly, there is a segment from the poem that provides an apt commentary on each major event in the president's life. Other authors use quotes from subjects to accentuate the personal accounts, such as in *Hiding to Survive* (Rosenberg, 1994), or they use folktales and stories that frame the information that follows as in *Once Upon a Horse* (Jurmain, 1989).

Some writers artfully design chapter titles to pique interest. Milton Meltzer does this effectively in *Cheap Raw Material* (1994). Titles like "I Looked Up and My Leg Wasn't There," "Fast Food—High Abuse," and "Bargains Black and White" are compelling: the reader is repelled but intrigued, which is probably Meltzer's intent. Penny Colman combines a title with a quote in *Rosie the Riveter* (1995). For example, Chapter 8 is entitled "Pioneers in the American Workplace: 'I had the chance to prove that I could do something.'" Chapter 6 draws the reader in with the title, "The War Wears On—'I'll do anything for my country.'"

Writers also often work hard on the con-

RUSSELL FREEDMAN ON BIOGRAPHY

Russell Freedman is particularly diligent about trying to present his subjects as multi-faceted characters. Their strengths and weaknesses, successes and failures, are carefully woven into the story line. He believes his responsibility as a writer is "not just to be accurate as I muster my facts but to pursue that elusive quality called 'truth'" (Freedman, 1992, p. 3).

clusions of individual chapters to provide a transition into the next one, thus compelling the reader to continue. Sometimes they do this by leaving questions in the mind of the reader or posing a problem as a chapter closes. The issue or question can only be answered by reading on. Penny Colman uses this technique in *Rosie the Riveter: Women Working on the Home Front in World War II* (1995). Chapter 1 concludes in the following way:

> Now that America was involved in the fighting, almost everything in the United States began to change—some things immediately, other things gradually. Some things changed forever, other things changed just for the duration of the war. But almost everything changed. (p. 7)

The next chapter begins:

> One change that Dot soon noticed was that many everyday items were in short supply.... (p. 8)

Authors also often take great pains to craft a conclusion to their book which will leave the readers with a feeling of satisfaction or cause them to want to know more. Rita Golden Gelman does this effectively as she concludes *Dawn to Dusk in the Galápagos* (1991):

> The sky darkens.
> The stars appear.
> And the sliver moon is a little bit bigger.
> And still, and forever, the ocean explodes into foam against the cliffs.
> Wave after wave after wave.

The softly, rhythmic description reflects the end of the day and gives the reader a satisfying feeling that life will continue.

Vocabulary

The language used to explain complex or technical vocabulary is another important aspect of writing nonfiction. The proper words for things should be used in even the simplest books. Children need nonfiction to learn about the world. To be able to do this, they must be given the correct words for the ideas and concepts they encounter. Aliki (1996) spoke for many authors on the question of using the "real" words in the following statement:

> When I titled one of my books *Communication*, I was told I'd have to find an easier word. But there was no clearer one, and I decided that if children can pronounce (and spell!) Tyrannosaurus, they can cope with *Communication*. (p. 211)

There is an art to introducing specialized and technical vocabulary so that it is understandable and memorable. These words must be introduced, carefully defined, and then used in context so that the reader remembers them, yet the sentences read smoothly. Sometimes these words are italicized to set them apart and alert the reader to pay special attention. But good writers do more. Often they continue to use the word, when appropriate, in subsequent text, providing examples, juxtaposing it with a synonym, or telling a related story so that the reader's understanding deepens. For example, in *Learning From the Dalai Lama: Secrets of the Wheel of Time* (1995), Karen Pandell and Barry Bryant use synonyms to clarify the meaning of difficult words. When readers first encounter the term *lamas* it is italicized and immediately followed by a synonym: "or religious masters" (p. 16). The word is then used repeatedly in subsequent text which allows readers to become accustomed to the term and to see how it relates to other aspects of the Buddhist religion. Diane Hoyt-Goldsmith uses a similar technique in *Pueblo Storyteller* (1991). Additionally, she adds a pronunciation guide after each word:

> People still live in adobe (*a-doh-bee*) houses. Just as our ancestors did, the Cochiti people make adobe bricks by mixing the clay found near our village with straw from the fields and water from the river. When bricks dry, they are very strong and we use them to build our homes. (p. 2)

Hoyt-Goldsmith has clearly explained adobe using natural language and an expanded definition. A photograph of adobe bricks further clarifies this concept.

Some authors don't set the words apart at all, depending on the narrative flow and context to help readers understand new words. Examples or descriptions are used that provide a context for introducing the word. In *Shadows of Night: The Hidden World of the Little Brown Bat* (1993), Bash skillfully introduces the word *echolocation*, by broadening her readers' background before they encounter the word itself:

> Much more important [than eyes] is the bat's ability to "see with its ears." As it flies, the bat makes a continuous clicking sound too high-pitched for humans to hear. By listening for the echoes from the clicks, the bat can instantly determine the size, speed, and direction of objects in the dark. This process is called echolocation. (unpaged)

Tone

How an author conveys information can be just as important as *what* is conveyed. Carter and Abrahamson (1990) suggest five possible subcategories of tone: condescending, conversational, humorous, neutral, and partisan. Only the condescending voice is inappropriate for children's nonfiction because it is patronizing, didactic, and authoritative. It is not effective in engaging readers or drawing them into the book.

In contrast, writers who use a conversational tone write as if they're settling down to an enjoyable chat among friends. Sometimes they address questions which are then discussed or sometimes the style is more narrative, as if the readers are drawn around a storyteller. Morgan Monceaux (1994) effectively uses a narrative conversational tone to recount his recollections of the people who created the sounds of American jazz in *Jazz: My Music, My People*. His first-person biographical sketches, which include anecdotes and interesting personal tidbits, make for entertaining as well as informative reading.

Some writers use humor to make their books more palatable or interesting. Joanna Cole and Bruce Degen's *The Magic School Bus* books are renown for incorporating humorous incidents that occur to the class as they adventure through the waterworks or solar system. Tomie dePaola also uses humor effectively in stories like *The Popcorn Book* (1978) and *The Quicksand Book* (1977). Sometimes a lighthearted humorous tone goes too far and trivializes the information, undermining the purpose of the book. As long as credibility is maintained, humor can be an effective stylistic tool.

Writers who use a neutral voice present material dispassionately and objectively. In contrast, a partisan tone takes a stand on the issue being discussed. In his introduction to *Now Is Your Time: The African-American Struggle for Freedom* (1991), Walter Dean Myers is clearly partisan to his thesis that African-Americans have a heritage they can be proud of:

> If we believe that we are fully deserving of the rights to life, liberty and the pursuit of happiness, then we will fight to retain those rights. But if we believe we are not capable,

---

AUTHORS WHO USE CONVERSATIONAL TONE EFFECTIVELY

Kathleen Krull uses a similar tone in *Lives of the Writers: Comedies, Tragedies (and What the Neighbors Thought)* (1994) as she relates the "inside scoop on twenty literary luminaries." In *Take A Look: An Introduction to the Experience of Art*, Rosemary Davidson (1994) uses questions and informal, conversational language to draw in readers and encourage them to interact with the content:

Stare at This Ink Blot for a While.

What Do You See?

A Man?

A Bird?

Something Else? (p.6)

that the stars that others reach are not for us to grasp, then we will never achieve our goals....Those who have accepted themselves as failures will only find ways of failing well. In the last analysis, it is what we believe about ourselves that is our history. (p. ix-x)

Helping Children Appreciate the Art of Writing Nonfiction

Teachers and librarians can help children appreciate the style and structure of well-written nonfiction trade books while reading aloud. Nonfiction informs children and expands their awareness of how language effectively communicates complex ideas. Teachers can first discuss the story's content and then say, "Listen again to how the author described this" or "How is the author trying to make you feel about bats? What words has the author used to persuade you to feel this way?" These are typical questions that help children begin noticing style.

Teachers can also help children notice the structure of books. Fourth-grade teacher Sherry Fewin, for example, showed her students strategies for responding to structure by using questions and prompts like "Let's discuss what we think are the big ideas. This chapter has topic headings. Let's talk about that" (Farest, Miller, & Fewin, 1995, p. 285). Then creating a chart that lists the main ideas, followed by children's comments on the information they think goes under each heading, is effective in making structure clear.

Children are also quite capable of appreciating the language of books read aloud to them. Backer, *et al.* (1996) shares the following student's reaction to Jamake Highwater's *Songs for the Seasons* (1995): "The illustrator really listened to what the author had to say. You can hear the story through the pictures and you can see the pictures through the words" (p. 154). Students can also be encouraged to create charts of interesting words and phrases that various authors use to write about a topic.

Once a book has been read, children can be encouraged to retell it emphasizing the memorable words and language that stuck in their minds. Brown and Cambourne (1987) found that children demonstrated increased incidental, unconscious learning of text structure, vocabulary, and linguistic features when asked to retell a story. Although children use their own language in this activity, they will also invariably use the structure and language of the original story. Brown and Cambourne do suggest that teachers thoroughly immerse children in the text first, displaying vocabulary, creating charts or maps, sharing predictions, and similar activities—before requesting the retelling of expository text.

Children can also create a readers' theatre from a nonfiction book. The process of taking the text and turning it into a script really helps them pay close attention to language structure and style (Young & Vardell, 1993).

COMPARING THE USE OF PRIMARY SOURCES

Students could compare Murphy's *The Long Road to Gettysburg* (1992), a nonfictional account of the battle that skillfully uses primary sources to create dialogue, and Hunt's *Across Five Aprils* (1964), a fictional account of the Civil War that incorporates letters into the narrative. Introducing Murphy's *The Boys' War* (1990), a book that recounts the experiences of one young soldier from each side, can add another perspective. Teachers can ask students to consider what they learned about the war from each book. How were letters and other first-hand documents woven into the narrative? What did the author do to draw you in and compel you to read more?

As children become familiar with various books on a topic they can begin focusing on how writing styles differ across genres, authors, and even the books of one author. For example, a group could examine fictional and nonfictional books on the same topic. Compare how Jean Craighead George describes living among wolves in *Julie of the Wolves* (1972) with Jim Brandenburg's account of *Scruffy* (1996); Lawrence's *Wolves* (1990) and Simon's *Wolves* (1993) can make clear how writers use language differently in fiction and nonfiction. Introducing poems on the topic like Sarrett's "Wolf Cry" (1968) or Durston's "The Wolf" (1968) can add yet another dimension.

Children can also compare how different nonfiction authors write about the same topic. Sometimes the focus differs; often the style does. For example, Seymour Simon uses a very straightforward, neutral expository voice in *Volcano!* His focus is on providing the reader with a general understanding of these geological occurrences. In contrast, Patricia Lauber uses a narrative, chronological style to recount the story of one volcanic eruption in *Volcano: The Eruption and Healing of Mt. St. Helens* (1986). Her voice is more personal and conversational. Each book has a unique voice and perspective. Children can be asked to consider how these differences in style, focus, and structure influence their response to the book as well as the kind of information they obtain from it. They can then be asked to probe deeper and analyze what it is about the author's writing that influences their responses.

Similarly, children can compare one author's style across several books. Are there similarities? Or do authors change their style as the topic changes? Aliki, for example, uses a distinctive style throughout her books in which she integrates "asides" or additional information with her main text through captions, speech bubbles, and other unusual devices. Jerry Stanley uses the structure of individual voices against the backdrop of a larger historical context for his chronicles of American history. Russell Freedman usually begins his biographies with a compelling incident from the subject's life and then returns to chronologically document major events. He always incorporates quotes from the person, his/her contemporaries, excerpts from letters, and other primary sources. In contrast, Freedman's *An Indian Winter* (1992) uses narrative integrated with chronological structure to describe one winter in the life of the Mandan Indians. Students can learn much about the art of writing nonfiction by exploring these similarities and differences. Small groups could each study a different author and then compare them.

Children who write their own versions of simple, predictable nonfiction books or create reports, journal entries, or other written responses can learn much about text structure and writing style of nonfiction. Although they use their own language, which is often more narrative than expository, they also frequently use a book's organizational scheme, vocabulary, and language patterns in their responses. They naturally link what they've heard with what they produce in their own pieces. Teachers can encourage this process by allowing it to happen and considering this "borrowing" from nonfiction texts as an important part of learning. They can also help children become aware of their use of structures from stories by jointly creating evaluation rubrics for children's work.

Students can also be encouraged to consider how the author's writing style makes it easier or more difficult to learn about the topic. Do they understand how a system of locks operate after reading Gail Gibbons' *The Great St. Lawrence Seaway* (1992)? Do they have a sense of how the brown bat navigates through the dark forest after reading Betsy Maestro's *Bats: Night Fliers* (1994)? A good way for children to think about these questions is to consider: "What kind of teacher would this author make?" Good teachers must instruct but also help their students enjoy learning. The same holds true for good nonfiction writers.

Conclusions

Good nonfiction writers go beyond the basic conventions of language, letting the beauty and artistry of words illuminate their vision of a topic. They know how to select a structure that appropriately grounds their work. They can create just the right phrasing and image so that a topic comes alive. They can develop ideas so that understanding comes easily. In the process they help children learn about the world while engaging their hearts as well as their minds.

References

Aliki. (1996). The language of my books. In A. McClure and J. Kristo (Eds.), *Books that invite talk, wonder and play* (pp. 209-212). Urbana, Illinois: National Council of Teachers of English.

Ashabranner, B. (1988). Did you really write that for children? *The Hornbook Magazine, 59*, 749-754.

Ashabranner, B. (1990). A conversation with Brent Ashabranner. In B. Carter and R. Abrahamson (Eds.), *Nonfiction for young adults: From delight to wisdom* (pp. 96-105). Phoenix, AZ: Oryx Press.

Backer, J., Chiou, R., Colon, C., Davis, J., Harwayne, S., Hindley, J., Hudes, L., Mayer, P., Michaels, C., Pak, S., Siegman, L., Taberski, S., & Tallat-Kelpsa, K.. (1996). Weaving literature into the school community. *The New Advocate, 9,* (2), 153-168.

Brown, H., & Cambourne, B. (1987). *Read and retell.* Portsmouth, NH: Heinemann.

Carr, J. (1982). *Beyond fact: Nonfiction for children and young people.* Chicago, IL: American Library Association.

Carr, J. (1987). Filling vases, lighting fires. *The Hornbook Magazine, 59,* 710-713.

Carter, B., & Abrahamson, R. (Eds.). (1990). *Nonfiction for young adults: From delight to wisdom.* Phoenix, AZ: Oryx Press.

Farest, C., Miller, C., & Fewin, S. (1995). Lewis and Clark: An incredible journey into the world of information books. *The New Advocate, 8,* 277-288.

Freedman, R. (1992). Fact or fiction. In E. Freeman and D. Person (Eds.), *Using nonfiction trade books in the elementary classroom: From ants to zeppelins* (pp. 2-10). Urbana, IL: National Council of Teachers of English.

Freeman, E. B., & Person, D. G. (Eds.). (1992). *Using nonfiction trade books in the elementary classroom: From ants to zeppelins.* Urbana, IL: National Council of Teachers of English.

Freeman, M. (1994). Trope densities, analogy clusters, and metaphor types: metaphors, similies, and analogues in elementary science textbooks and trade books. Unpublished doctoral dissertation. Orono, ME: University of Maine.

Fritz, J. (1988). Biography: Readability plus responsibility. *The Hornbook Magazine, 64,* 759-60.

Lasky, K. (1985). Reflections on nonfiction. *The Hornbook Magazine, 61,* 527-532.

Lauber, P. (1992). The evolution of a science writer. In E. Freeman and D. Person (Eds.), *Using nonfiction trade books in the elementary classroom: From ants to zeppelins* (pp. 11-16). Urbana, IL: National Council of Teachers of English.

Meltzer, M. (1976). Where do all the prizes go? The case for nonfiction. *The Hornbook Magazine, 52,* 17-23.

Spink, K. (1996). The aesthetics of informational reading. *The New Advocate, 9* 135-149.

Young, T., & Vardell, S. M. (1993). Weaving readers theater and nonfiction into the curriculum. *The Reading Teacher, 46* (5), 396-409.

CHAPTER 4
CHOOSING QUALITY NONFICTION LITERATURE: FEATURES FOR ACCESSING AND VISUALIZING INFORMATION

by Richard M. Kerper

Nonfiction is more than information conveyed through words. It is a carefully crafted genre. It is a *literature of fact* that combines both verbal and visual texts. Authors and illustrators "arrange factual materials into artful, literary" (Roundy, 1989) presentations. They take as much care with the illustrations, photographs, diagrams, maps and tables as they do with the paragraphed text. Their creations speak to the reader-viewer about more than facts. They excite the senses and the imagination; they stimulate the formation of images, questions, and hypotheses. They invite a child to participate in the world of the book.

Literary nonfiction, states Aidan Chambers, "deserves and demands the respect and treatment—the skill and care—of art (Meltzer, 1976, p. 19). It is no less creative than Avi's novels, Greenfield's poetry, Yolen's tales, Van Allsburg's picture books or Gilbert Stuart's portraits, Lewis Hine's photographs, or John McPhee's prose. The crafting evident in these talents' creations is strikingly similar to the "making, shaping, forming, [and] selecting" (Meltzer, 1994, p. 25) achieved by creators of nonfiction. In this chapter I will focus on the design of nonfiction and will highlight visual and specific linguistic aspects such as captions. The creative decisions of artists and writers often challenge young readers. These challenges will be discussed and instructional suggestions provided.

Affordances of Nonfiction

An author and illustrator in consultation with their publisher make decisions about a book's design. They select a format as well as a size and shape for a book that is appropriate to the concepts presented and their artistic vision for the work. They also make decisions about the inclusion of access features such as a table of contents, an index, and a glossary and the inclusion of visual features such as photographs, diagrams, and maps. In the process of building these special features (some of which are the more traditional reference aids) and characteristics into their literature, an author and an illustrator create opportunities to engage in specific acts of reading and viewing. The perceptual psychologist J. J. Gibson (1979) refers to such opportunities as *affordances*. For example, just as an index affords the location of a special piece of information, a map affords the visualization of locational relationships, and a hand-sized book affords perusal by a toddler in contrast to a full-sized book.

The opportunities provided by a book do not exist independent of the audience. Affordance is a relational concept involving characteristics of the reader-viewer and characteristics of the book. For instance, a standard-print book affords a sighted child an opportunity to engage with the material that a blind child is not afforded. In addition to physical characteristics, a person's purpose in interacting with a book is another critical aspect of affordance (Heft, 1989).

Children investigate nonfiction selectively. They explore these books with particular intentions in mind. Sometimes they select books in the genre to explore their world. This general interest leads to a reading process that is linear with embedded recursion (Kerper, 1995). For example, young readers may begin at the front of a book perusing the illustrations and reading the print as needed. They skip over what does not make sense and progress toward the final page. However, as the visual experience expands their knowledge, the memory of anomalous material causes children to flip back and forth through the pages as they construct new meanings. At other times, children want to investigate an aspect of a topic in greater detail. This leads to close reading of the material. And yet, in other situations young readers and viewers hope to find a specific fact that is important to their lives. This purpose leads to scanning the words and the images in order to locate the detail that is needed. Various characteristics of a book's design influence the degree to which a purpose can be realized or, in other words, contribute to the creation of an affordance. The sum of book characteristics, reader characteristics, and the reader's purpose equal the affordance. For instructional strategies, see Chapters 10 and 11.

Creators of nonfiction can control only one aspect of this affordance equation—the book characteristics. As they write and illustrate, it is important for them to anticipate the audiences' purposes and physical characteristics. They need to consider:

- book size
- access features relative to the age and development of the intended audience

- possible reasons that children will choose the book
- the ways in which children are likely to use the book

All of these factors are important in the creation of an engaging, informative, and useful volume.

Decisions about Format

In designing a work of literary nonfiction, authors must select an overriding format that is appropriate for the content and the purpose of the book. Brent Ashabranner (1988) acknowledges that "structure may take him almost as long to locate as the actual writing takes" (p. 751). Jean Fritz (1988), the first recipient of the Orbis Pictus Award, writes that while "the art of fiction is making up facts; the art of nonfiction is using facts to make up a form" (p. 759). Whether a picture book, photographic essay, field guide, how-to, or chapter book format is selected, the final decision must result in a design that helps a child to understand and to feel.

In *Flight*, one of the recent Orbis Pictus winners, Robert Burleigh and Mike Wimmer (1991) selected the picture book format so young readers and viewers could experience the transatlantic flight of the Spirit of St. Louis. Burleigh's third-person narrative text uses excerpts from Lindbergh's writing to capture the events, his thoughts, and his emotions. The words are printed on Wimmer's full-page and double-page paintings that extend the drama of the event, amplify the emotions, and cast an American hero as a boyish young man. The print, superimposed on the illustrations, unifies the paragraphed and pictorial texts. The humanizing quality of the interior illustrations connect the accomplishment of Lindbergh's dream to the dreams that most children have. The brow briefcase cover invites a child to delve into the contents of Lindbergh's papers. The selection of the picture book format allows the drama to unfold in words and pictures and affords a child an opportunity to fly with Lindbergh.

Seymour Simon (1991) made a different decision in writing *Earthquakes*. He chose a photographic essay format. Simon's paragraphed text appears next to color photographs. In this format the images show specific cases of the effects of an earthquake. For young readers and viewers who have no firsthand experience with this natural phenomenon, the photos document the catastrophic destruction and the unusual changes. In a journalistic fashion they convince a child of the truth of the paragraphed text (see Plate 4.1).

Beyond these format choices, decisions must be made about book size and shape, cover, endpapers, type size, margins, and placement of print and illustrations. Sylvia Johnson and Ron Winch's (1995) *Raptor Rescue!:*

Plate 4.1

This fence was broken and offset eight feet by the movement of the San Andreas Fault during the 1906 earthquake.

An Eagle Flies Free uses an oversized format to emphasize the grandeur and power of the bald eagle. In *A Twilight Struggle: The Life of John Fitzgerald Kennedy*, Barbara Harrison and Daniel Terris (1992) employ rich burgundy endpapers, a conventional chapter structure, crisp unadorned typography, wide margins, and sharp black and white photographs to create a formal look and to convey the stateliness and tradition of a United States President. The dust jacket illustration uses shadow and pose to capture the contemplation of serious matters and to convey Kennedy's inner struggle (see Plate 4.2).

The hybrid format of *The Magic School Bus Lost in the Solar System*, written by Joanna Cole and illustrated by Bruce Degen (1990), uses the traditional picture book format but borrows comic strip, storyboard, and classroom report structures. The continuous narrative text provides general information about the solar system while the speech balloons and the notebook pages provide more specialized information. In addition to these for-

Plate 4.2

mat decisions, the inclusion of access features in some nonfiction potentially may help children depending on their reading and viewing purposes.

Access Features

Creators of nonfiction lay down multiple avenues into their work.
Through a table of contents, an index, a glossary, a sidebar, a bibliography,
or an author-illustrator's note, nonfiction artisans provide children with

many ways of gaining access to their ideas and images. These features provide young readers and viewers with opportunities to use the literature for their selective purposes.

Table of Contents and Chapter Titles

In *Franklin Delano Roosevelt*, Russell Freedman (1990) begins his biography with a table of contents. Concise and pointed chapter titles such as "Growing Up Rich," "To the White House," "FDR and the Great Depression," and "War Clouds" make it possible for a child to investigate the period of Roosevelt's life that is of specific interest at a given moment. Not all tables of contents make it easy to locate the material within. Some encourage readers to formulate questions that guide the viewing and the reading of the book. Chapter titles from Jim Murphy's (1995) award-winning book, *The Great Fire*: "'Everything Went Wrong!;'" "'The Dogs of Hell Were Upon the Housetops;'" "'A Surging Ocean of Flame;'" and "'Chicago Is in Flames'" encourage purpose-setting questions but do not afford easy access to information about a particular aspect of the Chicago fire. Their figurative and dramatic nature is not descriptive of the content. Instead, the chapter titles engage a child in the same way that titles in fiction do. They draw a young reader into a dramatic event and foster sustained engagement from the beginning of the book to the end.

As children encounter the diverse use of chapter titles in nonfiction literature, they may need support from the teacher. Conversations that encourage students to articulate the textual framework derived from the titles will enable them to understand the different opportunities that nonfiction books may offer. While the table of contents in *Franklin Delano Roosevelt* (1990) lends itself to focused research, the one in *The Great Fire* (1995) is better suited to recreational reading. Students seeking specific information could use the extensive index. Grasping these distinctions will help children to experience the wonders of nonfiction and to gain information on selected topics in ways that are appropriate for each piece of literature.

While chapter titles in a table of contents afford opportunities for varied reading experiences, indices in nonfiction books enable children to locate specific information. In *Unconditional Surrender: U. S. Grant and the Civil War*, Albert Marrin (1994) includes a detailed index that guides children to many facts and concepts contained in the paragraphed text. In many other books the index provides access to the visual text as well as the verbal text. Access to both print and visual material is critical for children who are reading about phenomena they have never experienced. The ability to associate images with print is important in their assimilation of new concepts.

During the past 15 years creators of nonfiction have included increasingly more and a greater variety of access features in their books. While they have sometimes included a table of contents, an index, and a glossary, today more authors, illustrators, and publishers incorporate glossaries, sidebars, bibliographies, and authors' notes in their books. This change appears to represent a reconsideration of the audience. Young readers and their teachers seem to be taken more seriously. Their desire and need for detailed, supplemental information and indicators of meticulous research and accuracy have been addressed.

Glossaries

Glossaries appear with increasing frequency. They present specialized vocabulary that may not be clear in context. They serve as a reference tool for students who may read selectively and need clarification of terminology that is used. Patricia Lauber uses a glossary in *Seeing Earth from Space* (1990) to define key terms, but in *The News About Dinosaurs* (1989) she also capitalizes on the chance to guide children in the pronunciation of dinosaur names by including a pronunciation guide. In *Making Sense: Animal Perception and Communication*, Bruce Brooks (1993) goes beyond a simple definition of terms. He provides expanded information about key concepts in the book. In this way, he appends additional information without disrupting the flow of the main text.

Sidebars

Sidebars are another access feature that facilitate the inclusion and retrieval of information. Set off in the margin beside the main text, they provide interesting sidelights to the main focus. Diane Swanson (1994) stimulates interest in the main text of *Safari Beneath the Sea: The Wonder World of the North Pacific Coast* by including intriguing factual material in marginal blocks. The barely opened scallop shell included at the top of each sidebar draws

Some indices highlight illustrations in special typeface.

The Amazing Potato by Milton Meltzer—italic type

The Great American Gold Rush by Rhoda Blumberg—boldface type

Seeing Earth from Space by Patricia Lauber—underlined type

Glossaries vary in the type of information included.

Beneath Blue Waters: Meetings with Remarkable Deep-Sea Creatures by Deborah Kovacs and Kate Madin

Frogs, Toads, Lizards, and Salamanders by Nancy Winslow Parker and Joan Richards Wright

We Remember the Holocaust by David A. Adler

Whaling Days by Carol Carrick

a child's attention and visually suggests that ideas may be slipping out. This visual metaphor becomes a powerful tool for engaging young readers and suggests a visual technique that children can use in their own writing to focus their readers' attention. In *A Tree is Growing,* Arthur Dorros and S. D. Schindler include print and illustrations in sidebars that add detail to the body of the book and provide a different model for children's work.

Inserted Information

Information inserts between chapters and blocks of bulleted ideas serve a similar purpose. They contribute information that would interrupt the flow of the main text and provide new dimensions on the topic. *Hurricanes: Earth's Mightiest Storms* by Patricia Lauber (1996) incorporates information on weather instruments, hurricane naming, and infamous hurricanes between chapters. The light blue pages, in contrast to the white pages of the main text, draw a viewer's attention to this supplementary information. In *Safari Beneath the Sea,* Swanson (1994) includes interesting facts under headings such as "Ocean Oddities," "Sea Critter Quirks," and "Fabulous Fish Feats." The bullets and bold print immediately draw a child's eyes to this material. This presentational technique provides a fine model for students' report writing. It provides them with a means for incorporating interesting ideas that are not the main focus of their reports but certainly would motivate their readers.

Bibliographies

Another important access feature that has become more common in nonfiction for children is a bibliography. This reference tool supports students' efforts to conduct further investigation. It provides them with an oppor-

Bibliographies include primary and secondary sources.

Picture books:

Illuminations by Jonathan Hunt

Leonardo da Vinci by Diane Stanley

Chapter books:

Children of the Dust Bowl: The True Story of the School at Weedpatch Camp by Jerry Stanley

Full Steam Ahead: The Race to Build a Transcontinental Railroad by Rhoda Blumberg

tunity to delve more deeply into a topic. The list of primary and secondary sources used enables the reader to evaluate the source material. An author's note, like the one included by Mary D. Lankford (1992) at the beginning of her bibliography in *Hopscotch Around the World*, helps to document the research process carried out by the author. In this case, the note records the difficulty encountered in tracking down information and the fortuitous location of some sources. As students further investigate the topic, the bibliography provides additional material to explore as well as research issues to consider. Similarly, a list of photo credits document the sources of illustrations included in the books. Like the bibliographies, these source lists can encourage further investigation.

Author's Notes

Finally, some nonfiction books contain an author's note in an independent section, thus providing access to related information and to the production aspects of the book. At the end of *Summer Ice: Life Along the Antarctic Peninsula*, Bruce McMillan (1995), who identifies himself as a photo-illustrator (McMillan, 1991), provides some background on Antarctica, offers credit for one photograph he did not shoot, and documents the equipment he used to produce his illustrations in the same way that other artists indicate the media used in their illustrations. Similarly, Russell Freedman (1996) offers information about the origin of the pictographs included in *The Life and Death of Crazy Horse*. These types of information are vital in a critical appraisal of paragraphed and visual text. Like the other access features discussed, the inclusion of this material represents a trend toward increased respect for nonfiction as a literary form and for its readers both as customers and writers.

Photo credits document visual sources.

Full Steam Ahead: The Race to Build a Transcontinental Railroad by Rhoda Blumberg

Kids At Work: Lewis Hine and the Crusade Against Child Labor by Russell Freedman

The Oregon Trail by Leonard Everett Fisher

Displaying Text Visually

The creators of nonfiction literature convey information through iconographic displays such as photographs, diagrams, maps, graphs, and charts. Each refers to a real-world object or phenomenon; however, the degree of connection varies. While some displays are clearly representational, others are highly stylized abstractions. Photographs, for example, are highly representational. They show many of the object's features as they appear in their environment. For example, a whale looks like a whale. In contrast, charts are extremely limited in their representation of the phenomena they report. They are more abstract and their features do not resemble the object or phenomenon to which they refer (see Figure 4.1).

Figure 4.1 Continuum of representationality for visual displays of information.

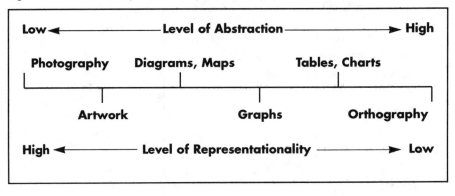

Nonfiction picture books for young children frequently contain visual displays such as photographs and pictures that fall at the high representationality end of the continuum. Their closer connection to the real world make them appropriate for the cognitive development of the intended audience. Nonfiction books for older readers have a greater tendency to be scattered along the entire continuum. This range of visual displays reflects the cognitive ability of the intended audience to deal with relatively concrete and abstract material. However, for many elementary school students abstract presentations are difficult to understand. Students need the support of a teacher who can help them make the connection to more concrete or more representational displays of information. For example, connecting a bird's eye view of an area to a map view is the type of scaffolding that a teacher can provide. Supportive measures of this kind can assist students in expanding their literacy.

Creators of nonfiction select the visual text that is best suited to convey the concepts to be introduced. Moline (1995) states that "...visual texts support (or explain) the paragraphed texts, which in turn offer generalisations that give the visual texts their context" (p. 15). The various types of visual displays found in nonfiction challenge children's understandings in different ways.

Photography

Viewers, young and old alike, often assume that photographs capture the world. In fact, our language reflects that thinking. Looking at a photograph of a lily, we say that the image is a lily. We forget that it is an artistic rendering of a lily just as much as a Monet painting is a rendering. Steven, a first grader in a school that I frequently visited, often perused nonfiction picture books. He strongly objected to illustrations in these books that used an artistic medium other than photography. As he stated, "These books are not true." For Steven a lack of representational detail in illustrations was an indicator that a book was not factually accurate. From a young age the seductive nature of photography lures us into a false sense of being in the real world. The representational detail of a photograph tricks us into equating it with objective reality when it is truly the artist's perspective, a constructed reality.

As the creators of nonfiction develop their books, photographs become a primary tool for illuminating their texts. These illustrations need to be more than filler, and they also need to go beyond the mere identification of objects, people, and places. Therefore, creators must consider the overall design, content, and themes of their books. The relationship between illustrations and paragraphed text is an important consideration in this design process.

In *Surtsey: The Newest Place on Earth* (1992), Kathryn Lasky and her husband, photographer Christopher Knight, create a symbiotic relationship between the paragraphed text and the illustrations. The photograph of the leading edge of a lava flow shows blazing,

Information on using photography in the classroom is available. On the World Wide Web access:

Kodak Photography—education solutions
http://www.kodak.com

Polaroid Education Program
http://www.polaroid.com

red-orange offshoots from the main flow. Figurative references to the flow such as "looked more like giant lobster claws pinching the island in a red-hot grip" (p. 29) complement the photograph while the illustration extends the crustacean simile from the text. Similarly, Lasky's description, "from a plane it looked like Surtsey wore a necklace of diamonds" (p. 31), comes alive with the accompanying photographs. In another context, each of Knight's illustrations as well as Lasky's words might lose their impact. It is the unity created by image and word that is of critical importance in the design of an outstanding nonfiction book (Goldsmith, 1986).

Part of this unity includes the captions. They can be equally important as the photograph they accompany. Writers and book designers can include brief descriptive phrases, detailed explanations, or no captions at all. In *Antarctica: The Last Unspoiled Continent*, Laurence Pringle (1992) uses all three approaches. The endpaper and the first three photographs of the land, sea, and penguins bear no captions and as a result invite the viewer to consider the nature of life and the environment. Further into the book, Pringle shows whales surfacing that need only the words "Killer Whales." But, at another point he includes a photograph of a reddish rock with an image on it. This image requires an explanation that fossils indicate that Antarctica's climate was once much warmer. The degree of inference required to construct meaning from an image is an important factor for the author to consider in writing a caption.

In working with photographs in books, children need to experiment with photography. Just as teachers provide students with opportunities to explore the effect of different stylistic decisions as they write and as they draw, they also need to provide opportunities to compose photographs and to link them to their own writing. Children need to see the effect of their choices on the rendering of an object. Cameras that produce photographs instantly provide this feedback immediately. Today, many photo developing labs and photography corporations sponsor programs to assist teachers in introducing photography to their students. Some help teachers to obtain cameras for classroom use and provide curricula to guide them in developing children's visual literacy.

Diagrams

A common visual display found in nonfiction books is the diagram, which links the illustration and words. From the most rudimentary diagrams such as drawings with labels and scales to the more complex cutaways, cross-sections, webs, and flow diagrams, these graphic displays simplify, generalize, and symbolize a subject rather than present it representationally like photographs (Moline, 1995).

A labeled diagram is one of the simplest diagrammatic displays. Using outlining and shading, these diagrams simplify an object by eliminating surface features such as color, which in turn highlights the labeled structural features. In *The Amazing Potato, Milton Meltzer* (1992) identifies the parts of the potato plant and the seed potato (see Plate 4.3) with greater detail and clarity than words alone can achieve. The diagram shows relationships and complexity more easily than a pure linguistic form could.

Another relatively simple, visual display is the scale diagram. The juxtaposition of objects, an object's positioning near a scale, and the verbal presentation of scale enable students to judge the size of an object. Laurence Pringle (1995) juxtaposes a lodgepole pine with a deer in *Fire in the Forest: A Cycle of Growth and Renewal*. This composition feature affords a comparative consideration of size (see Plate 4.4). Charles Micucci (1995) places a scale beside the icon of the queen bee in *The Life and Times of the Honeybee* providing for the measurement of the bee's size (see Plate 4.5). And in *Ancient Ones: The World of the Old-Growth Douglas Fir*, Barbara Bash (1994) labels inset images of insects and microscopic life with the degree of enlargement (*e.g.*, enlarged five times). This information challenges students to cognitively adjust to the size of the life form presented in order to create a size-appropriate mental image.

Cross-sections are frequently found in nonfiction making it possible for children to analyze what is beneath the surface of an object. In the book, *In Search of the Grand Canyon: Down the Colorado with John Wesley Powell*, Mary Ann Fraser (1995) clarifies the geologic layers of the Grand Canyon by showing a cross-section of the canyon walls. The key included in the diagram identifies the rock type and the environment in which it was formed (see Plate 4.6). But, not all cross-sections include keys. Many less complex diagrams include labels within the cross-section.

The characteristics of captions vary among books.

Across America on an Emigrant Train by Jim Murphy

To the Top of the World: Adventures with Arctic Wolves by Jim Brandenburg

Unraveling Fibers by Patricia A. Keeler and Francis X. McCall, Jr.

This technique presents fewer challenges to students' understanding because the parts of the diagram bear their names. However, the use of a key requires child readers to relate a defined symbol system to the diagram. This added dimension increases the complexity of the visual interpretation process. Teachers can support children's efforts to understand this type of visual display by having them (1) cut open a piece of fruit, (2) draw the parts seen, (3) shade each part with a different color, and (4) prepare a key labeling each color with the part of the fruit it represents. Based on a concrete experience like this one, teachers then can discuss with students the use of keys in cross-sections encountered in books.

Finally, flow diagrams, often using

Plate 4.4

LODGEPOLE PINE
75-80 ft.

Plate 4.3

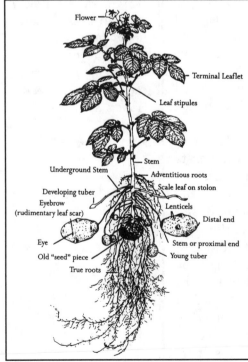

Plate 4.5

A healthy queen may live for up to four years and lay over one million eggs during that time.

arrows or lines, are useful in showing cause and effect and in explaining processes. These diagrams encourage the synthesis of information. In *Oceans*, Seymour Simon (1990) shows that the alignment of the sun, the moon, and the earth cause the highest tides (see Plate 4.7). Visually this diagram provides an explanation for the spring tides that occur twice a month.

Time lines can be a special type of flow diagram. Some present the flow of time by using arrows but do not attempt to measure time in equal units. For example, in *Take a Look: An Introduction to the Experience of Art*, Rosemary Davidson (1994) shows in words and pictures the highlights

Plate 4.6

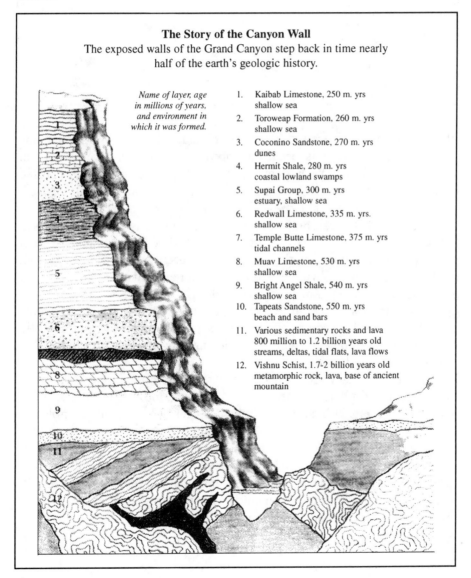

The Story of the Canyon Wall
The exposed walls of the Grand Canyon step back in time nearly
half of the earth's geologic history.

Name of layer, age in millions of years, and environment in which it was formed.

1. Kaibab Limestone, 250 m. yrs
   shallow sea
2. Toroweap Formation, 260 m. yrs
   shallow sea
3. Coconino Sandstone, 270 m. yrs
   dunes
4. Hermit Shale, 280 m. yrs
   coastal lowland swamps
5. Supai Group, 300 m. yrs
   estuary, shallow sea
6. Redwall Limestone, 335 m. yrs.
   shallow sea
7. Temple Butte Limestone, 375 m. yrs
   tidal channels
8. Muav Limestone, 530 m. yrs
   shallow sea
9. Bright Angel Shale, 540 m. yrs
   shallow sea
10. Tapeats Sandstone, 550 m. yrs
    beach and sand bars
11. Various sedimentary rocks and lava
    800 million to 1.2 billion years old
    streams, deltas, tidal flats, lava flows
12. Vishnu Schist, 1.7-2 billion years old
    metamorphic rock, lava, base of ancient
    mountain

Plate 4.7

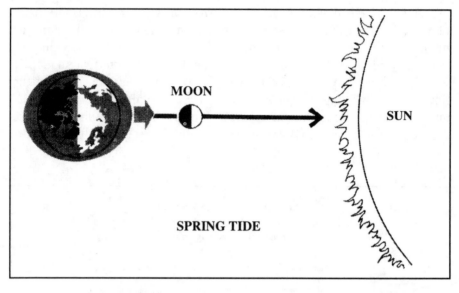

MOON

SUN

SPRING TIDE

of the history of art from 100,000 BC to today. Periods in which many notable artistic triumphs occurred appear much longer than others in which very little of note happened, even though the number of elapsed years is identical. Such visual distortions of the equal intervals of time must be pointed out to children. The reason for them must be clarified.

An activity that can help students understand this presentation technique is to have them construct a flow time line of the highlights of their lives. First, students record the key events in each year of their lives. It is likely that more events will be recorded for more recent years than for very early years. As students make sketches along a time line to present these key events, they will begin to recognize that the unequal number of events among years result in some covering more space on the time line than others, and they will develop a fuller understanding of flow time lines that they encounter in books.

Images, unlike words, present the relationships among their parts simultaneously rather than sequentially (Langer, 1957). The human mind apprehends them holistically making it easier to deal with complexity (Hunter, Crismore, & Pearson, 1987). Diagrams, therefore, are an important communicative tool for children to understand and to use. Teacher-guided group experiences in constructing various types of diagrams will scaffold children's attempts to understand them and to use them in their own writing. It is the quality of the conversation surrounding diagram development that is critical in children's learning.

Maps

Maps frequently appear in nonfiction books aimed at children who have begun to develop a sense of place in the world. This graphic feature provides authors with a way of spatially contextualizing the information presented. Maps are used to set the stage, document change, and record movement. The stage is set for *Jacks Around the World* (Lankford, 1996) by

Plate 4.8

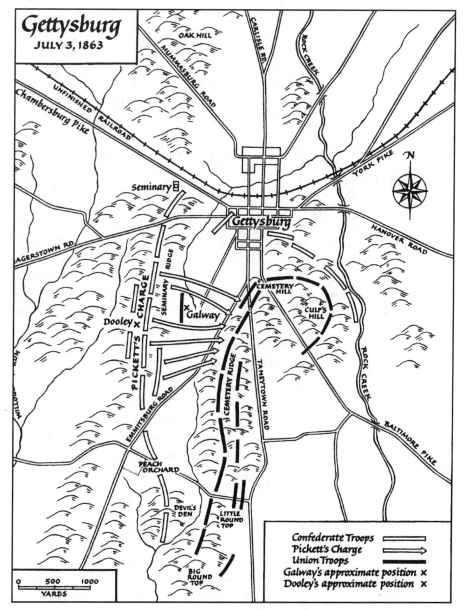

CRITICAL

Tables present information in different ways.

Frogs, Toads, Lizards, and Salamanders by Nancy Winslow Parker and Joan Richards Wright—verbal row and column (p. 46)

The Life and Times of the Honeybee by Charles Micucci—pictorial row and column (p. 9)

The Magic School Bus Lost in the Solar System by Joanna Cole—numerical row and column (unpaged)

CRITICAL

the inclusion of a world map immediately after the title page. The countries colored yellow and bearing a number defined in the key represent the nations whose versions of jacks are presented. Jim Murphy (1995) sets the stage for *The Great Fire* of Chicago by including a street map in the first chapter of the book. However, the repeated inclusion of this map with different parts shaded enables him to show changes in the area engulfed in flames. These maps document the fire's spread and emphasize its uncontrollable nature. Similarly, in *The Long Road to Gettysburg*, Murphy (1992) records troop locations and movements by using symbols such as Xs and arrows that are defined in the key (see Plate 4.8). These books, like many other works of nonfiction, depend on maps to clarify the spatial connections among the information presented. Since maps are abstract presentational forms and most use keys to define the symbols used, intervention strategies like those mentioned in the discussion of cross-section diagrams and the introduction to the section, "Displaying Text Visually," might be valuable as teachers work with children. Focusing on the way in which maps place information into spatial contexts provides students with an alternative means of displaying ideas in their writing.

Tables

Tables most commonly present information in rows and columns that are separated by lines or white spaces. Each of the blocks created is known as a *cell*. Children construct meaning by associating the information in each cell with column and row headings of which they are a part (see Plate 4.9). This need to connect two dimensions of the table provides a challenge for novice readers. The use of two straight edges or vertical and horizontal finger-tracing of the table can help students understand the information in a table. Teachers can model this process as they read nonfiction aloud or conduct shared reading in their classrooms.

Plate 4.9

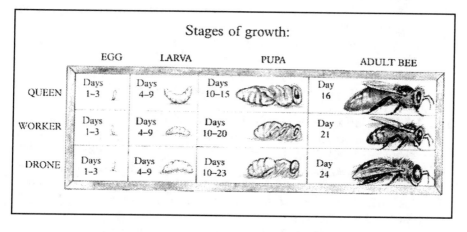

Conclusions

As authors, illustrators, and publishers with increasing frequency use the visual dimensions of a book to engage children and to inform them, the need to derive meaning from photographs, diagrams, maps, and tables as well as how to use tables of contents, glossaries, sidebars, information inserts, bibliographies, and author's notes becomes more apparent. In the classroom the talk that focuses on visual displays and access features largely determines students' success in handling these important elements of nonfiction. Classroom and library talk that is both conversational and instructional (Goldenberg, 1992) enables educators to scaffold children's learning experiences with the visual dimensions of nonfiction and to guide their development. Instructional conversations are not a panacea, but they do enable children to realize an affordance of a book. They guide them in the important process of visualizing nonfiction.

References

Ashabranner, B. (1988). Did you really write that for children? *The Horn Book Magazine, 64* (6), 749-754.

Fritz, J. (1988). Biography: Readability plus responsibility. *The Horn Book Magazine, 64* (6), 759-760.

Gibson, J. J. (1979). *The ecological approach to visual perception.* Boston: Houghton Mifflin.

Goldenberg, C. (1992). Instructional conversations: Promoting comprehension through discussion. *The Reading Teacher, 46* (3), 316-326.

Goldsmith, E. (1986). Learning from illustrations: Factors in the design of illustrated educational books for middle school children. *Word and Image, 2* (2), 111-121.

Heft, H. (1989). Affordances and the body: An intentional analysis of Gibson's ecological approach to visual perception. *Journal of the Theory of Social Behaviour, 19* (1), 1-30.

Hunter, B., Crismore, A., & Pearson, P. D. (1987). Visual displays in basal readers and social studies textbooks. In H. A. Houghton & D. M. Willows (Eds.), *The psychology of illustration: Instructional issues* (pp. 116-135). New York: Springer-Verlag.

Kerper, R. M. (1995). Three children viewing and reading: Transactions with illustrations and print in informational books. (Doctoral dissertation, The Ohio State University, 1994). *Dissertation Abstracts International, 56* (01-A) [On-line]. (University Microfilms No. AADAA-I9517029).

Langer, S. K. (1957). *Philosophy in a new key.* Cambridge, MA: Harvard University Press.

McMillan, B. (1991). Photographer or photo-illustrator: What's the difference? *School Library Journal, 37* (2), 38-39.

Meltzer, M. (1976). Where do all the prizes go? *The Horn Book Magazine, 52* (1), 17-23.

Meltzer, M. (1994). Where have all the prizes gone? In E. W. Saul (Ed.), *Nonfiction for the classroom: Milton Meltzer on writing, history, and social responsibility* (pp. 24-29). Newark, DE: The International Reading Association.

Moline, S. (1995). *I see what you mean: Children at work with visual information.* York, ME: Stenhouse.

Roundy, J. (1989). Crafting fact: Formal devices in the prose of John McPhee. In C. Anderson (Ed.), *Literary nonfiction: Theory, criticism, pedagogy* (pp. 70-92). Carbondale, IL: Southern Illinois University Press.

CHAPTER 5
CHOOSING QUALITY NONFICTION LITERATURE: ASPECTS OF SELECTION FOR EMERGENT READERS

by Paula Moore

One of Zach's favorite little books is *Underwater Journey* (Cutting & Cutting, 1988). He chooses to read it over and over again, both to me and to his family. I selected the *Underwater Journey* for Zach, an engaging seven-year-old, because, as he declares, "I love science!" In addition, the book is about at his instructional level, and it presents some new learning opportunities while providing adequate support for him to use strategies he has learned.

The major difference between *Underwater Journey* and other instructional books I have used with Zach is the language structure. Zach is used to books with repetitive language patterns, like *Little Car* (Cowly, 1987), another book at his instructional level. In that book the heavy Lump family gets into a car that is way too small for them, and it can't go. While there are many lines of text on each page, the repetitive language structure makes the book easy for an emerging reader:

> "Silly little car," said Mr. Lump.
> "Silly little car," said Mrs. Lump.
> "Silly little car," said Linda Lump.
> "It won't go!" (p. 8)

In *Underwater Journey*, a book with only 61 words, each page has only one line of text, and the language structure varies from page to page. In addition, there are many unfamiliar words and concepts for Zach: explore, coral reef, squid, dolphins. In order to make the book's concepts accessible for Zach, I spent a longer time than I usually do discussing the pictures on each page and introducing key concepts, such as the idea of exploration. With the thorough introduction under his belt, Zach confidently read the Underwater Journey for the first time with very little difficulty.

Sharing Nonfiction in a Balanced Early Literacy Program

Usually reading emerges between kindergarten and second grade. A few children may learn how to read before entering kindergarten, and some may take many more years beyond second grade to learn how to read. But regardless of age and prior experiences, emerging readers, like Zach, need to learn a range of strategies before becoming independent readers, including strategies for reading nonfiction text.

Nonfiction is different from fiction in several ways. For example, while there are a range of genres within fiction, texts tend to have a similar organizational structure (*e.g.*, initiating event, internal response) with consistent literary features (*e.g.*, setting, plot, characters). Conversely, the organizational structures of nonfiction text vary, based on the author's purposes and the content addressed (Raphael & Hiebert, 1996). However, nonfiction text often has some identifiable structures that are used to organize and convey information (*e.g.*, headings, subheadings, table of contents, glossary, index). Knowing about these organizational structures and access features appears to help students with comprehension and writing of nonfiction text. See Chapter 2 for information on organizational structures and Chapter 4 for descriptions of access features.

Also, reading for information requires different comprehension processes than reading to follow a story plot. For example, a useful strategy for reading fiction is that of predicting or anticipating a logical sequence of events. In contrast, readers of nonfiction need a strategy for identifying the author's organizational schema in order to acquire and remember information. One of the reasons that many young readers have difficulty reading science and social studies texts in upper elementary grades may be that they have not had adequate opportunities at the lower elementary level to develop strategies for reading nonfiction texts.

In an early primary classroom that has a well-balanced literacy program (Depree & Iversen, 1994; Fountas & Pinnell, 1996; McGee & Richgels, 1996; Mooney, 1990; Morrison, 1994a; Morrison, 1994b; Tompkins, 1997) the teacher is engaging children in reading and writing nonfiction in a variety of ways. They include read-alouds, shared reading, and guided reading. Reading aloud is a powerful instructional strategy. This helps to familiarize children with the sound of nonfiction language structures and the role of access features, just as fiction read-alouds help children learn to use story language as a cue source and knowledge of story organization to anticipate events. See Chapter 10 for more detailed information on nonfiction read-alouds.

Shared reading is another excellent way to scaffold emergent readers as they learn about the new and different demands of nonfiction text. The teacher introduces and reads an enlarged version of a text (*e.g.*, Big Book) or the teacher and the students all have copies of the book that the teacher reads while the students follow along in their copies. Students join in the reading in unison on favorite parts or particular refrains. An additional shared reading technique is for the teacher to make overhead copies of particular pages in nonfiction books; children "share" the reading while looking at the screen. This provides an opportunity for the teacher to point out some of the conventions of nonfiction text and to teach strategies for reading for information.

Research findings are quite clear that children learn how to read by reading (e.g., Adams, 1990; Clay, 1991; Holdaway, 1980; Smith, 1988; Stanovich, 1986). Therefore, it is important to have a variety of nonfiction available in the classroom that emerging readers can read. In addition, in order to learn how to extend their use of strategies in more complex and mature ways, emerging readers need opportunities to read nonfiction books that are steadily increasing in difficulty. Guided reading instruction provides an opportunity for the teacher to support emerging readers as they attempt to read a slightly more challenging text on their own.

First, the teacher chooses a book that is close to a child's, or group of children's, instructional level. The teacher discusses the topic of the book, helping children access their prior knowledge and build new prior knowledge, before the children read the text silently to themselves (or in whispers for the most novice readers). Then, the teacher attends closely while the children attempt to read on their own in order to help them learn problem solving strategies for deciphering the text. It is critical for children to be able to read as independently as possible during guided reading instruction because only they can teach themselves what they need to learn. Just like in any skilled human activity (e.g., piano playing, skating, driving) it helps to have a "coach" who can point out some ways to extend skills, but it is in the doing of the activity that we construct our understanding and skill. A carefully planned guided reading program that includes nonfiction texts at each gradient of difficulty provides children with the opportunity to act on new challenges in nonfiction text with the support of the teacher. In that way, their competence increases.

In the following sections of this chapter, I will discuss issues around using nonfiction in the guided reading portion of a balanced literacy program. Specifically, I will address gradients of difficulty in instructional books for emerging readers by selecting instructional nonfiction books for emerging readers, and finally, the role of the teacher in helping emerging readers learn how to read nonfiction.

Gradients of Difficulty in Books for Emerging Readers

Identifying gradients of difficulty in books for emerging readers is not the same as applying readability formulas. Readability formulas do not account for a reader's prior knowledge or interest about the subject matter.

In particular, when reading nonfiction texts, prior knowledge or interest about the topic is the factor most likely to determine how "readable" the text is. Furthermore, readability formulas are based on the questionable concept of grade level. Instead, gradients of difficulty in books for emerging readers are based on what research suggests emerging readers must learn and what makes it easy for them to learn it (Clay, 1991; Ferreiro & Teberosky, 1982; Henderson, 1986; Hiebert, 1986; Holdaway, 1986; Sulzby & Teale, 1991).

There are a variety of ways to label a range of text gradients and systems for organizing them. For example, some publishers label gradients with letters or numbers. Some teachers use colors to designate easier from harder texts. Frequently, systems for displaying the level of the text are not interchangeable. Teachers who level their own books by trying out the gradients on their students are often the most reliable determiners of gradients. The most important concept about leveling for teachers to understand is what the gradients of difficulty offer novice readers in terms of opportunities to extend reading strategies on books that are increasing in complexity in several ways: conceptually (semantic), structurally (syntactic), and graphophonically. In the next section are suggestions for selecting instructional books for emergent readers that further clarify how to distinguish easier from more difficult nonfiction texts.

Selecting Nonfiction Books for Emergent Reading Instruction

In general, all the criteria presented in Chapter 2 through Chapter 4 also apply to choosing good nonfiction for young children. High-quality nonfiction books that are too difficult for young children can always be read aloud to or shared with children. However, books that teachers use to help children learn how to read nonfiction text require additional criteria. Aspects to consider in choosing nonfiction text to use for instruction include considering what aspects of the reading task young children can already control and what new challenges and supports a nonfiction text will provide. Some specific considerations include the following.

Directionality, Print, and Voice-to-Print Match

All novices learning how to read English print, whether the novice is an English-speaking child of four or a 40-year-old Vietnamese immigrant, must first understand directionality principles of English print. For example, they must grasp that print goes left to right and top to bottom, with a return sweep on multiple lines of text. They also have to learn the direction in which books are read. In addition, very young children must also learn how pictures relate to print.

Novice readers also need to learn that spoken words match print in a specific and one-to-one relationship. There-fore, print size and spacing between words should be generous for emergent readers and can decrease as the novice's experience with print increases. This may seem too simple to mention, and yet, undergirding this simple concept is a complex factor about how oral language relates to written language.

Oral language is a continuous stream of sound. There are no breaks, except when the speaker decides to take a breath or pause. Mature readers in print-dominated cultures think they hear separate words because that's what they are used to reading. However, writ-ten words, and the spaces between them, are an invention of humans. Other societies throughout history developed other conven-tions for recording thoughts, speech, and action in order to communicate them over time and space (see Smith, 1988 for thorough discussion of this).

Research indicates that many young chil-dren begin to get confused at the earliest stages in learning to read because they fail to grasp this important convention about how print represents spoken language (Adams, 1990; Clay, 1991; Holdaway, 1980). Therefore, for guided reading interactions, young chil-dren need texts that emphasize spaces between words and which have words in large print. These kinds of books make it easier for them to learn how words and spaces are relat-ed. Large print also makes it easier for chil-dren with less developed fine motor coordina-tion to point to or touch the words as they learn the complex task of integrating motor movement (pointing and touching) with look-ing at words and speaking. That is actually three complex actions which must be com-bined. Adults in literate societies have forgot-ten what it is like to learn how to coordinate the reading act. To make the complexity explicit on an adult level, the first steps in

Books to Foster Voice-to-Print Match and Directionality Concepts

I Love Bugs by Mary Lake

Is this a Monster? by Scarlett Lovell and Diane Snowball

Melting by Faye Bolton

Tarantulas are Spiders by Norman Platnick

EASY BOOKS FOR MORE
EXPERIENCED NOVICES

Breathing by Honey
Anderson

Caterpillars by Robyn
Green

Floating and Sinking by
Honey Anderson

How to Make Salsa by
Jaime Lucero

learning how to read are like the first steps in learning how to play tennis; you must learn how to look at a tennis ball coming toward you, while you bring up the racket and try to make it connect with the ball.

Children who cannot yet match speech with print or demonstrate consistent directionality need nonfiction texts that are characterized as *concept books*. Concept books focus on a single idea or have a simple narrative line close to a young child's experiences (*e.g.,* going shopping, pets, family members). The book language, while not exactly duplicating oral language, includes naturally occurring syntactic structures found in everyday speech (*e.g.,* I put on my _____; I see a _____; This is my _____). An example of books at this level is *Animal Homes* (Sloan & Sloan, 1995). Only one animal in its home is on each page, and the illustrations make the animal and its home explicit. The sentence structure is the same on every page: "A _____ lives in a _____."

Conversely, a book like *I Like Me!* (Carlson, 1988) looks like it would be easy for the most novice readers to learn the earliest concepts about how reading works; it has large print, simple illustrations, and uses common words. However, the text is positioned on a different place on each page and may even begin at the midpoint of a line. This makes it difficult to learn directionality concepts. The most inexperienced readers might be tempted to read a right page before a left page, because there is print on both pages.

Language Structure

More experienced emergent readers who control directionality and voice-to-print matching still need nonfiction texts with predictable language structures, but they can cope with more complex language patterns than concept books provide. A typical child entering first grade copes best with language structures found in concept books. By the middle of first grade, a text like *Some Machines are Enormous* (Bird & Short, 1996) may be easy reading for a child. The book has more complex words, but the text is still straight forward: "A combine harvester is one of the biggest machines used on farms" (p. 7). At the end of first grade or beginning of second grade, most children can cope with complex structures such as this sentence found in *I See Animals Hiding* (Arnosky, 1995): "Because of this protective coloration, called camouflage, wild animals can hide by simply staying still and blending in" (unpaged).

Vocabulary

The number of words or lines of text per page, alone, are not an indication of the difficulty of a nonfiction text. The teacher must assess the balance of common and specialized vocabulary that the text includes. Most emergent readers can cope with unusual and specialized vocabulary if concepts are discussed before reading. A comparison of two books for emergent readers that vary greatly in level of vocabulary sophistication are *Fall* (Kinney, 1995) and *The Reasons for Seasons* (Gibbons, 1995). In *Fall* the vocabulary is simple and typical of events occurring in the northeast. However, in *Reasons for the Seasons*, Gail Gibbons writes using complex vocabulary to describe more abstract ideas, such as how seasons are created by the rotation of the Earth around the sun. What initially appears to be fairly simple vocabulary, on closer examination it is clear that Gibbons' book is more appropriate for advanced readers.

My New Kitten (Cole, 1995) is an example of a longer book for emergent readers having a good balance of common and specialized vocabulary with illustrations that make the text explicit. For example, instead of writing

BOOKS FOR THE END OF FIRST GRADE

Be a Friend to Trees by Patricia Lauber

The Dancing Dragon by Marcia Vaughn

Dinosaurs by Michael Collins

Thinking About Ants by Barbara Brenner

about the birth of the kittens using medical terms, Cole uses common language to describe the event: "Soon Cleo had her kittens. She pushed each one out of her body" (unpaged).

Book Length, Number of Words, New Challenges

Research suggests that successful emergent readers have had more opportunity to read because they read more books and longer books (Hatfield, 1994). Therefore, if children are to learn to read through reading, the gradient level needs to steadily increase. One of the many competencies that emerging readers acquire by reading is how to learn words. Imagine how difficult it would be to read any text if a reader had to stop and puzzle each time over words like "a," "the," "is," and "to," which make up nearly half of any English print. Novice readers must learn how to quickly and automatically recognize a large number of words so that they can attend to making sense out of the story or informational text. The only way to quickly learn both words and the process for learning words is by reading. Books that are longer provide more opportunities for emerging readers to do both. As many of the easiest nonfiction texts are very short, a steady diet of them in an instructional reading program would not provide adequate learning opportunities for emerging readers. Therefore, emerging readers need opportunities to practice what they already know and move to new challenges, just as bike riders, skaters, and baseball players need practice in order to perfect and extend their competencies.

Greenspun's *Daddies* (1991) meets many of the criteria for good nonfiction children's literature. However, most pages have only two or three words and very large pictures. While the book is excellent for discussion purposes, the book is not really suitable for an instructional text because it does not have enough opportunities for actual reading. In contrast, *Meet the Octopus* (James, 1996) has a short paragraph on each page. The common and specialized words are well balanced. With a careful introduction, many emergent readers would be able to read most of the text independently by the middle of their first grade year.

Illustrations

Pictures need to be highly supportive in nonfiction texts for emergent readers, and print must be separated from the pictures for the most novice readers. It seems too simple to even need to include this point, but it is surprising how many nonfiction texts for young readers do not have illustrations that make the text explicit. A delightful nonfiction book, which looks like it would be easy for young readers, is *Puffins Climb, Penguins Rhyme* (McMillan, 1995). Quite a few of the illustrations show penguins and puffins standing in different poses. The pictures do not make it explicit that the "Puffins peer," "Puffins hear," "Penguins glare," or "Penguins share" (all unpaged). A reader has to be able to read the words first, in order to appreciate the relationship of the bird's pose to the text, or to enjoy the rhyme.

In contrast, in the book *What Comes First?* (Swanson-Natsues, 1995), the illustrations, along with the repetitive language structure, allow the young reader to predict exactly what the word in the text will be. For example, each page has two pictures, the second of which is an effect of the first: "First comes the rain. Then comes the rainbow" (p. 6) or "First comes the spider. Then comes the web" (p. 7). Once the child knows the structure, the illustration makes explicit the only word that changes.

Page Layout and Format

Page layout and format must be consistent in nonfiction text so that novice readers are not confused about where to read. In books with complex layout and format, teachers must not make assumptions that emergent readers know where to look for information. The reasons that page layout and format are important are the same as for print size. Young readers need to learn the basic convention about how speech maps onto written language. We make it hard for children to learn this, and in some cases we create their learning difficulties when we present them with books that have busy or inconsistent formats.

Books such as *I Eat Leaves* (Vandine, 1995) have a nonfiction format that makes it easier for novice readers. The simple, repetitive text is located in the same place on each page. Even though the names for the different kinds of leaves that animals eat are printed in the illustrations, it won't be confusing for young children once the teacher explains that the pictures are labeled with the type of leaf eaten by each creature. A book with a slightly higher gradient of difficulty is *Chickens* (Snowball, 1995). While the language structure changes on each page, the format is still consistent; pictures are at the top of the page, and text is at the bottom. Several pages have a pop-up format in which the child reads a question about when the chicken's eggs are ready to hatch. Then, the child must lift up a picture of the egg to see "inside" it and read a simple yes or no answer. The formats of these two books make it easy for a novice reader to learn how to read and to learn new information at the same time.

Access Features

Generally, nonfiction with sophisticated and conventional use of access features such as headings, glossaries, and sidebars are beyond the scope of emerging readers' instructional and independent reading levels. Extraneous graphic information distracts a young reader from learning where and how to look at print. However, once young readers know how to read nonfiction text at the concept book level, they are ready to learn how some common access features work, such as the table of contents and title page. In addition, a simple glossary in the back of the book, such as the "Goat Farm Words" in the back of the book *700 Kids on Grandpa's Farm* (Morris, 1994), makes it easy for young readers to learn how special vocabulary is often part of many nonfiction texts. This simple glossary makes it easy to teach young children the strategy of using the glossary to help themselves understand more difficult words that they may encounter in nonfiction text.

Another book, *Beavers* (Moore, 1996), is an example of a nonfiction text that many first graders could read near the end of the year. It has long sections of text and variable sentence structure and vocabulary. It provides young readers with an opportunity to learn how to use several simple access features such as graphic organizers: a table of contents, a glossary, and an index. In addition, the text is organized using enumeration with simple headings, such as "Why Do Beavers Gnaw?", which makes it easy for the young child to learn how to read for information. The heading, "Why Do Beavers Gnaw?" also serves as an advanced organizer.

In summary, to select nonfiction books for guided reading instruction, a teacher must consider how all the characteristics of the text fit. In general, a good nonfiction text for instruction at the emergent reading level is consistent across all of the following dimensions:

- A good early nonfiction book makes it easy for young children to point and read

- Vocabulary and sentence structure are simple

BOOKS FOR SECOND GRADE

Elephant Families by Arthur Dorros

Exploring Tree Habitats by Patti Seifert

Slugs and Snails by Robyn Green

What Makes a Bird a Bird by May Garelic

- Illustrations make explicit the information in the text
- Print size and spaces between words are generous
- Page layout is consistent and it is easy to distinguish print from illustrations
- There are few graphic distractions

Conversely, a "good" nonfiction instructional text at a harder emergent level will have the following:

- More technical vocabulary and complex sentence structure
- Illustrations that support the text, but not "tell" all the information
- Print size is smaller
- Format and layout may be less consistent
- Other access features might be present
- There may be more print overall so that there are more opportunities for the child to learn by reading

However, text gradients are guidelines at best. They must be used in a flexible way. A gradient is only useful in relation to a particular reader or group of readers. A teacher must carefully observe what the young readers already know how to do, and then choose instructional texts that provide them with the opportunity to extend those competencies in a new way. In the next section I address the critical role of the teacher in helping emerging readers learn how to read nonfiction.

The Teacher's Role

Giacobbe (Fountas & Pinnell, 1996) cautions that providing appropriate books is only the beginning. The critical element is the skillful teaching that helps young readers learn the effective strategies they need to become independent. How a teacher decides to use a particular nonfiction text with a particular group of emerging readers is what determines the richness of the learning opportunities for children. Many high-quality nonfiction texts for young children are suitable for classroom use in some way. Books that a teacher judges too difficult for novice readers because of page layout, print size, or language structure can always be read aloud to children or shared with children. In fact, a well-balanced literacy program provides opportunities for young readers and writers to interact with nonfiction literature in many ways.

The role of the teacher in selecting and introducing books for guided reading instruction is critical. It is important to choose texts carefully so that they offer children an opportunity to extend their competencies without overwhelming them. Books that are too difficult for young children (*e.g.*, books that young children cannot read 90% of themselves) impede learning. However, a difficult book that is carefully introduced to a young reader can make it accessible.

In general, books for emerging readers, even at the most difficult level, need to stay close to children's everyday experiences. This ensures that the most important cue source in reading, prior knowledge, is accessible for the reader. This is one reason why most instructional books at the emergent level are fiction. They deal with typical events and plots in the life of children—losing a pet, finding friends, playing games, making choices. Some nonfiction texts are out of the range of everyday experience for some children. For example, a book about sea creatures may be difficult to read if a child has not heard about coral reefs, octopus, or sea cucumbers. Teachers may need to provide a very thorough introduction of the concepts included in a nonfiction book before the children read it, especially if the topic is far from their everyday experiences.

Another area in which teachers need to bring careful decision making and expertise is in supporting and instructing children during guided reading. When children encounter difficulties in reading a text, teachers will need to scaffold them by supporting their use of cues from meaning, language, and graphophonic sources as appropriate. In addition, they may need to supply more concept knowledge in order for children to use the full range of meaning cues. Also, it is especially important for nonfiction readers to be able to search for cues from a variety of sources, because they may not bring adequate prior knowledge to the task. Telling children the words they cannot read for themselves or, conversely, not giving enough help in figuring out words, prevents children from developing independent reading strategies. This is an example of the way in which I supported and taught Zach as he read *Underwater Journey* (Cutting & Cutting, 1988) for the first time.

Zach: I can't remember that word! (After reading "execute" for "explore," Zach noticed his miscue, but did not know how to fix it.)

Teacher: You don't have to remember that word. Think about what would make sense—think about what these people are doing on their underwater journey. They've got this special underwater boat that lets them look at all the interesting creatures way down in the ocean. See what they are doing?

Zach: They're looking all around at all the stuff.

Teacher: Yes! What's a good word for "looking around at all the stuff?"

Zach: (No response)

Teacher: What else could you try? What do you know about how the word looks that could help you? You know that it starts like "execute." Can you say more of the word? (I knew that Zach had the concept, but I wanted him to search for more cues so that he would learn how to use information from more than one source when he got stuck.)

Zach: (Puzzled look on Zach's face.)

Teacher: Try saying just this bit. (To make the strategy explicit, I covered up most of the word and left just "expl-" showing.)

Zach: Ex-pl—explore!

Teacher: Does explore make sense here? Are they exploring on their under water journey?

Zach: (Nods.)

Teacher: OK! Keep on reading, and when you get stuck, think about what makes sense and how the letters in the word can help you.

Guided reading instruction is a delicate balance requiring expert decision making. I knew that Zach had to learn how to search for information from a variety of sources, including the graphophonic information, in order to successfully read nonfiction independently. Sometimes young readers have the concept but not the exact word to describe the concept. Even when I provided more prompting around the concept it didn't help, and Zach did not know how to use other sources of information to help himself. I could have told him the word. It would have made the reading easier for the moment, but then I would have missed an excellent opportunity to help Zach learn how to problem solve in a more flexible way.

Zach did not actively search for further information when he encountered an unknown word, even in fiction reading. Thus, this is the "next step" he needs to acquire in his learning-how-to-read journey. Remembering is not a good strategy as text becomes more complex. I knew that Zach had the word explore in his spoken language vocabulary because I had used it in my introduction. If he could "hear" just a few more of the letters in the printed word, it would trigger a link with the spoken word. I wanted him to know how to search for sources of information in a flexible way for both nonfiction and fiction text. Then, he will be an independent reader and can continue to teach himself more about reading each time he reads.

Conclusions

The guidance given in this chapter about how to identify gradients of text difficulty, how to select instructional texts, and the role of the teacher is not meant to be a recipe. Teaching is a complex process; it just can't be simplified. The guidance in this chapter is meant to provide teachers with greater understanding about the many factors that must be considered when selecting and using nonfiction texts with emerging readers.

Identifying gradients of text difficulty helps teachers select instructional nonfiction texts that will allow children to learn how to read by reading. Consideration should be given to a range of text characteristics in making the determination whether or not a particular book should be used for reading instruction. Text characteristics to consider include: language structure, sophistication of vocabulary, amount of learning opportunities in the text, how explicitly the illustrations match the text, print size and spacing between words, page layout and format, and access features.

However, there is much more to selecting books for instruction than identifying a gradient of difficulty. For example, a more difficult gradient can be made easier by the way in which the teacher matches a particular book with a particular reader, keeping the reader's interest and prior knowledge in mind. Another way in which a difficult book can be made easier is by giving students a thorough introduction before they read, thereby building their prior knowledge. In addition, a teacher can make a more difficult text easier by being right there to prompt for strategy use while the student reads the book for the first time.

Finally, the message I want most to convey is that emergent readers need frequent access to quality nonfiction text. But, providing children with lots of books is not going to make them better nonfiction readers and writers. The secret is in how teachers use the books to foster changes in children's knowledge, understanding, and strategies for reading informational texts. All the understanding teachers have about the characteristics which make it easy or hard for a child to read a particular text is useless if they don't know how to match their particular students with the appropriate book or instructional technique. Reading aloud nonfiction is always an appropriate teaching strategy to help all learners develop an "ear" for the type of text that they must learn how to read. Shared reading works well when readers are just learning about the conventions of nonfiction text and need extra scaffolding as they try out new reading strategies. However, if children are to learn how to read nonfiction by reading, then choosing appropriately leveled texts for them to read during guided reading is imperative. As always, it is what the teacher knows about making teaching decisions, not the books or the program, that makes the difference.

References

Adams, M. (1990). *Beginning to read: Thinking and learning about print.* Cambridge, MA: MIT Press.

Clay, M. (1991). *Becoming literate: The construction of inner control.* Portsmouth, NH: Heinemann.

Depree, H., & Iversen, S. (1994). *Early literacy in the classroom: A new standard for young readers.* Bothell, WA: The Wright Group.

Ferreiro, E., & Teberosky, A. (1982). *Literacy before schooling.* Portsmouth, NH: Heinemann.

Fountas, I. C., & Pinnell, G. S. (1996). *Guided reading: Good first teaching for all children.* Portsmouth, NH: Heinemann.

Giacobbe, M. E. (1996). Foreword. In I. C. Fountas & G. S. Pinnell, *Guided reading: Good first teaching for all children* (pp. ix-x). Portsmouth, NH: Heinemann.

Hatfield, P. (1994). *Performance characteristics of discontinued versus not dis continued children in the Reading Recovery program.* Unpublished dissertation. University of Maine, Orono, Maine.

Henderson, E. (1986). Understanding children's knowledge of written language. In D. Yaden & S. Templeton (Eds.), *Metalinguistic awareness and beginning literacy: Conceptualizing what it means to read and write* (pp. 65-78). Portsmouth, NH: Heinemann.

Hiebert, E. (1986). Issues related to home influences on young children's print-related development. In D. Yaden & S. Templeton (Eds.), *Metalinguistic awareness and beginning literacy: Conceptualizing what it means to read and write* (pp. 145-158). Portsmouth, NH: Heinemann.

Holdaway, D. (1980). *Independence in reading.* Portsmouth, NH: Heinemann.

McGee, L. M., & Richgels, D. J. (1996). *Literacy's beginnings: Supporting young readers and writers* (2nd ed.). Needham Heights, MA: Allyn & Bacon.

Mooney, M. (1990). *Reading to, with, and by.* Katonah, NY: Richard Owen.

Morrison, I. (1994a). *Getting it together: Linking reading theory to practice.* Bothell, WA: The Wright Group.

Morrison, I. (1994b). *Keeping it together: Linking reading theory to practice.* Bothell, WA: The Wright Group.

Raphael, T. E., & Hiebert, E. H. (1996). *Creating an integrated approach to literacy instruction.* Fortworth, TX: Harcourt Brace College Publishers.

Smith, F. (1988). *Understanding reading* (4th ed.). New York: Holt, Rinehart and Winston.

Stanovich, K. (1986). Matthew effects in reading: Some consequences of individual differences in the acquisition of literacy. *Reading Research Quarterly, 21,* 360-407.

Sulzby, E., & Teale, W. (1991). Emergent literacy. In R. Barr, M. Kamil, P. Mosenthal, & P. D. Pearson (Eds.), *Handbook of reading research, volume II* (pp. 727-758). New York: Longman.

Tompkins, G. E. (1997). *Literacy for the 21st century: A balanced approach.* Upper Saddle River, NJ: Prentice-Hall.

Part II

Quality Nonfiction Literature: Gateway to Imagination, Investigation, and Inquiry

Who started the Great Chicago Fire? What was the Dust Bowl? How do bees make honey? Who invented a way to measure how big the earth is? How do I take care of my pet tarantula? I want to learn about the best ballerinas in the world. Inquiring minds have lots of questions, a desire to search for answers, to come up with more questions, and the need to know.

How do we go about selecting books that invite young minds into the debates of the past, that explore answers to today's dilemmas, and that expose students to the challenges of tomorrow? In Chapter 6, Myra Zarnowski examines six important features of nonfiction that help readers learn and appreciate the social studies. Anthony Fredericks emphasizes the importance of incorporating high-quality nonfiction to study science in the classroom in Chapter 7. Sandra Wilde discusses issues of accuracy and treatment of mathematics in nonfiction books, explains how social studies and science nonfiction can be used to explore mathematical topics, and suggests ways to use these books appropriately in the classroom in Chapter 8. Lastly, in Chapter 9, Barbara Kiefer argues that the experiences children have with the arts are instrumental in building aesthetic understandings and that excellent nonfiction in the arts contributes to this knowledge.

CHAPTER 6
IT'S MORE THAN DATES AND PLACES: HOW NONFICTION CONTRIBUTES TO UNDERSTANDING SOCIAL STUDIES

by Myra Zarnowski

Controversy, debate, and outright disagreement are no strangers to the field of social studies. What really happened? How do you know? What is significant and, therefore, worth knowing? What isn't? Social studies is a lively arena dealing with questions like these about how we see ourselves—our past, present, and future—and how we see others. It even helps us appreciate how others see us.

When teaching social studies, the books we select for young readers need to introduce them to this liveliness and debate so that they can learn about the social world in all of its fascinating complexity. Of course, the features shared by all good nonfiction (accuracy, organizational structure, writing style, and visual aspects) apply to social studies books as well, but there is more to consider. In this chapter I will focus on six important features of nonfiction that help readers learn and appreciate the social studies. I will pay particular attention to how books can promote historical understanding, since history is so often the foundation of elementary and middle school programs. Above all, I will emphasize books that show the ongoing dialog within the field of social studies, instead of books that emphasize "the archival tradition" (Greene, 1994) of amassing facts to remember.

How Nonfiction Helps Readers Envision the Social World

Until recently, discussions of literary envisionments—how readers build and refine their understandings—have largely concentrated on how

The author wishes to thank Lila Alexander, sixth-grade teacher at P.S. 201 in Flushing, New York, for collaborating on the study of students' responses to learning about plague.

fiction is read and understood. But observers of literature-based social studies programs are amassing a complementary body of research. This research shows how readers build rich envisionments of the real world through their reading of nonfiction (Levstik, 1993; Spink, 1996; Zarnowski, 1996). Although these studies show the impact of good literature, they also draw our attention to the importance of selecting appropriate books. Nonfiction used to teach social studies needs to be enlightening, interesting, and inspiring.

Writers of successful nonfiction rise to this challenge. To help young readers build envisionments of the social world, they employ a number of writing techniques that promote interest and understanding (see Figure 5.1). An awareness of these techniques can help teachers select the best materials for social studies instruction. What follows is a more detailed discussion of how outstanding writers help readers envision the world and some examples of the excellent nonfiction that results.

Figure 6.1 How Quality Nonfiction Writing Helps Readers Envision the Social World

How Quality Nonfiction Helps Readers Envision the Social World

- Offers a coherent explanation
- Integrates primary source material
- Establishes an author presence
- Presents the possibility of reinterpretation and multiple interpretations
- Presents vivid descriptions and visual materials
- Offers a sense of hope for the future

Offers a Coherent Explanation

As McClure points out in Chapter 3, skillful writers meet the young reader's need for overall clarity, or coherence. They provide their readers with sufficient background information, clear distinctions between main ideas and supporting details, and information about who is doing what to whom. In this way they provide a framework that readers can use as they continue to learn about the social world. This writing contrasts sharply with social studies textbooks which have been found to perplex readers more than to edify (Beck & McKeown, 1994; McKeown & Beck, 1994). Textbooks have been termed *inconsiderate* because they don't support the reader's efforts to build understanding. They don't take time to show the connections between the reader's world and the world described in the textbook.

In contrast, a look at several recent non-fiction trade books illustrates how readers can benefit when authors are *considerate*. In *Pony Express!* (1996), author Steven Kroll provides readers with enough background information so that they can envision the Pony Express as a sensible response to people's real need for communication, not some exotic stunt. He does this by dividing the book into three parts: "Before," part one, explains how the discovery of gold in California triggered an onrush of people from the East who craved mail from back home; "The First Ride," part two, describes the physical difficulties Pony Express riders encountered; and "After," part three, explains why the service was no longer needed once the transcontinental telegraph was completed. An "Author's Note" connects this historic story with our continuing search for improved communication through E-mail and fax. This book places past events in a meaningful context.

Ogbo by Ifeoma Onyefulu (1996) develops the important idea of civic responsibility by describing how everyone in a Nigerian village belongs to an age group, or *ogbo*. Each ogbo contributes to the life of the village by providing services. Readers learn about the various responsibilities of children, parents, and elders. This book makes clear that activities of various ogbo such as sweeping, building houses, and offering wisdom are all examples of the larger idea of community responsibility.

James Cross Giblin's book, *Be Seated: A Book About Chairs* (1993), illustrates one major idea: ordinary household items—in this case, chairs—reveal a great deal about the people who use them. Readers learn about chairs in ancient Egypt, ancient Greece, medieval Europe, and elsewhere. But they learn about more than chairs. They learn how even simple belongings help define us and

Other books that offer coherent explanations about the social world:

Coming to America: The Story of Immigration by Betsy Maestro

One World, Many Religions by Mary Pope Osborne

With Needle and Thread by Raymond Bial

those who came before us.

Nonfiction literature that is appropriate for social studies learning offers coherent explanations by developing big ideas in sufficient detail. When authors provide their readers with sufficient information, and when they clearly distinguish between main ideas and supporting details, they are being *considerate* of their readers' needs.

Integrates Primary Source Material

Another way nonfiction writers support a reader's understanding of the social world is by including documents such as letters, diaries, and newspaper accounts. These documents enliven social studies books by introducing the voices of the people involved and letting them speak for themselves.

But even more importantly, by using documents, writers can introduce readers to the historian's practice of *sourcing* (Wineburg, 1991a, 1991b). Sourcing involves paying attention to the source of information and considering the social situation in which a document was written. Sourcing means thinking about the writer's motivations and bias. It is "wide awake" reading that requires readers to critically examine what they read.

Even picture books designed for use in the primary grades can begin to introduce readers to primary sources. In *Dear Benjamin Banneker* (1994), author Andrea Davis Pinkney includes excerpts from the 1791 correspondence between Benjamin Banneker and the then Secretary of State, Thomas Jefferson. In an exchange of letters, Banneker, a free black, criticizes Jefferson for failing to extend to blacks the freedom he proclaimed for all men in the Declaration of Independence. Banneker's passionate accusations of "fraud," "violence," and "oppression" are stirring in a way that merely summarizing this correspondence could never be. Similarly, *Starry Messenger* (Sís, 1996), a picture book biography of Galileo, provides excerpts from Galileo's writing that forcefully illustrate his unshakable belief in the scientific method.

In *The Children of Topaz* (1996), a book for older readers, authors Michael Tunnell and George Chilcoat deal with the impact of forced imprisonment on Japanese-Americans during World War II. As the authors narrow their focus on the impact of the internment on children, they provide excerpts from a diary kept by a teacher and her third-grade class inside the internment camp in Topaz, Utah. Twenty pages from this diary are reproduced and commented on by the authors. Background information about conditions inside Topaz is provided in order to help the reader understand the diary. But the authors go beyond simply supplying background information to speculate about why the diary is totally uncritical of the events and conditions within the camp. They state that "Perhaps Miss Yamauchi [the teacher] was trying to protect the children and herself by not writing anything she thought might anger the camp officials" (p. 29). This speculation is a fine example of how historians question their sources and consider people's motives.

When writers introduce primary source material, they bring the process of "doing history" closer to children, showing them that history involves examining primary sources and hypothesizing about their meaning. As picture book authors have demonstrated, we can begin quite early to acquaint children with this process.

Establishes an Author Presence

A more immediate and personal way of promoting historical understanding is when authors speak directly to their readers. In *The Great Fire* (Murphy, 1995), author Jim Murphy illustrates the two ways this can be done. First, authors can guide readers by giving them an overview of what will follow. They tell how their work is organized and what they hope to accomplish. In the introduction of *The Great Fire*, Murphy writes, "You will meet a number of survivors in this book, most of them just once or twice and only briefly" (p. 11). Second, authors can tell us their thoughts and opinions about the topic they are writing about. In the final chapter of *The Great Fire*, Murphy tells us that when the editor in chief of the *Chicago Tribune* described the neighborhood in which the fire started as an area of crime, debauchery, and disease, "such a description of the O'Leary neighborhood was grossly unfair" (p.134). This kind of communication between author and reader is called *metadiscourse* because it is about understanding and interpreting the information given (Crismore, 1984).

Both types of *author presence* are important. The first type—when authors tell us how their information is organized—allows readers to anticipate what will follow and,

When discussing primary source material, consider asking some of the following questions:

- Who wrote this document? When? Why?

- What was the writer trying to accomplish?

- Am I convinced that the person is telling the truth? Why?

When discussing books like *Bard of Avon* and *Cleopatra,* pay particular attention to the authors' preface and notes. Ask questions such as the following that highlight the work historians do:

• What are the authors telling you about how historians work?

• How do historians fill in the gaps in their information?

therefore, promotes comprehension. But the second type—when authors tell us their attitudes and opinions—is even more important. Here authors show themselves as judges, critics, interrogators and ultimately as pattern-seekers and case builders. These are precisely the roles students need to assume in their reading and writing to learn social studies.

There are a number of examples of author presence in nonfiction literature for young readers, especially in biographies that present a dramatically new interpretation of a person's life. *Bard of Avon* (1992) by Diane Stanley and Peter Vennema begins with an Authors' Note that explains the nature of historical writing. The authors tell us that a historian's work is much like that of a detective and that throughout the book they are attempting to show this. As a result, the authors spend a great deal of time pointing out the gaps in the story—what we don't know about Shakespeare. We don't know his date of birth, the first play he saw and when he saw it, what work he did after attending grammar school, when and why he first went to London, and when he wrote his sonnets.

Stanley and Vennema alert readers to the role of the historian in finding meaning in whatever evidence is left behind—evidence that will always, by its nature, be incomplete. This is an important insight into the nature of biography and history, and it goes a long way toward explaining why it is still possible to write about Shakespeare even today. Not only is there the possibility that new information will surface—which, in fact, did happen recently when a "new" poem was attributed to Shakespeare—but there is also the possibility that we will interpret even "old" information in new ways.

Another example of author presence, this time for older readers, can be found In *Mother Jones* (1995) by Betsy Kraft. In this book, the author deals with historical understanding by cautioning readers against accepting any account at its face value. Kraft writes about the need to consider the reliability of historical sources, focusing here on the autobiography of Mother Jones:

> With any historic figure, it is often hard to separate fact from fiction. Much of the labor movement in America took place on unruly picket lines or tent camps of Appalachia and the West where scholarship and careful record-keeping were nonexistent. Feelings on both sides of the labor issue ran high and both sides exaggerated their own virtues and the other's evils. Mother Jones was no exception. Her autobiography is full of vain references to her own importance, and her own portrayal of her role in the labor movement does not always coincide with other accounts. Occasionally she deliberately misrepresented the facts to gain support for what she thought was right. (p. 3)

Author presence does a great deal to promote a case building or constructivist view of history. According to this view, interpretations of the past are not scientifically fixed, but they are offered for discussion, debate, and possible revision. By sharing their thoughts about how cases are made, authors of nonfiction let children walk through the process with them. They show children that interpreting history is an ongoing task, one that they can participate in. Here is a viable alternative to history presented as a closed case full of irrelevant facts about dead people.

Presents the Possibility of Reinterpretation and Multiple Interpretation

Not only can authors present their own ideas, but they can present a range of contrasting views. Providing multiple perspectives is "fundamental to good history teaching" (Tunnell & Ammon, 1996, p. 212), and contrasts with the more "selective tradition," which has been generally identified in children's historical fiction (Taxel, 1983; Trousdale, 1990). One researcher (Taxel, 1983), for example, found that historical fiction dealing with the American Revolution offered young readers only a narrow range of possible interpretations of this event, leaving out other, more controversial, interpretations.

In contrast, a number of books for young readers provide a wide range of historical perspectives on selected issues. Jim Murphy, for example, addresses the subject of historical reinterpretation of the Civil War in *The Boys' War* (1990). In Chapter 1, Murphy notes that the causes of the Civil War are so complex that historians still argue about them. In the Afterword, he writes that the role of boys in the Civil War had been largely "forgotten" in books written by adults right after the war. He states, "Not until fairly recently did historians take a serious look at who had partici-

Compare two or more biographies of the same person in order to compare each author's interpretation. For example, read *Galileo* by Leonard Everett Fisher and *Starry Messenger* by Peter Sís, two picture book biographies of Galileo. How are the books similar? How are they different? What does your analysis reveal about the role of the author in writing a biography?

pated in the war and realize how many boys managed to enlist" (pp. 99-100). This process of reseeing or reevaluating the past leaves open the possibility that readers, too, can enter the discussion, forming their own interpretations.

Milton Meltzer's *Voices from the Civil War* (1989) presents a variety of voices, largely those of ordinary people, directly involved in the events of the Civil War. In the Foreword to the book, Meltzer tells us that these voices are not disinterested observers; instead "their words carry the passions and the prejudices of their time" (xi).

Each of the 29 chapters in Meltzer's book uses the same format: A topic is introduced (e.g., the Fugitive Slave Law, John Brown's Raid, and the Kansas-Nebraska Act) and individuals holding widely differing perspectives on that topic speak for themselves. Meltzer makes use of diaries, speeches, letters, public testimony, songs—all sorts of written material that he refers to as "bits and pieces of human life—and death—that taken together may catch the spirit of the time" (xii).

For example, in discussing the spread of slavery into the territories acquired as a result of the war with Mexico in 1846-47, Meltzer introduces three widely different perspectives. He quotes from (1) an antislavery congressman from Massachusetts who claims that in the North there is "a strong religious conviction that slavery is a curse" (p. 9); (2) a pro-slavery congressman from Georgia who declares in response to the possibility of legislation abolishing slavery in the territories and in Washington, D.C., "I am for disunion" (p. 9); and (3) the Great Compromiser, Henry Clay, who cautions both sides "to pause at the edge of the precipice" (p. 11) before leaping into certain calamity.

When authors allow voices from the past to speak for themselves, they indicate that readers can join in the conversation and reach their own conclusions. Young readers need to know that there is much more to be said about the past.

Presents Vivid Descriptions and Visual Materials

Understanding the factors that influenced daily life in the past is difficult, even for adults (Wineburg & Fournier, 1994). We tend to judge the past using the standards of the present. As a result, we have difficulty understanding why people once believed it was acceptable to own slaves, deny women the right to vote, or claim land already settled by others. Children often conceive of the past as a straight march toward a more perfect present; along the way things improved because people "figured it out" by "getting smarter" (Barton, 1996).

Nonfiction can promote a more accurate understanding of the past by providing vivid descriptions and visual material that enhances these descriptions. A book like *The Underground Railroad* (1995) by Raymond Bial helps readers understand the conditions under which slaves risked their lives in pursuit of freedom. Bial not only invites the reader to imagine what it was like back then, but he supports the reader's imaginings with staged evocative photographs. Many escapes on the Underground Railroad preceded the invention of photography, but Bial shows us recent photographs that help us picture the drama, tension, and even the terror involved. His photos show a view of a slave cabin at night, the starting point of the journey; the Ohio River, which many slaves crossed in order to enter free states; and the places where slaves hid as they traveled the Underground Railroad, places such as behind a fake wall, in a wagon with a false bottom, and in an underground tunnel. These visual materials, combined with the stories of runaways, both successful and unsuccessful, help the reader step inside this historical context.

Kids at Work (1994) by Russell Freedman also extends the reader's understanding of the past, this time the early 1900s. *Kids at Work* is both a biography of the social reformer, Lewis Hine, and a story of his crusade against child labor. To help readers understand the conditions in which many children in this country labored, Freedman has included numerous photographs taken by Lewis Hine—photographs showing children working in canneries, factories, coal mines, laundries, mills, and on the streets. A particularly striking photograph at the beginning of the book shows a 5-year-old who works in a cannery peeling shells from shrimp.

Freedman helps readers understand the overall need for reform by providing many specific details about the deplorable working conditions children endured. How bad was it? According to Freedman:

> Thousands of young boys descended into dark and dangerous coal mines every day, or worked aboveground in the stifling dust of the coal breakers, picking slate from coal with torn and bleeding fingers. Small

girls tended noisy machines in the spinning rooms of cotton mills, where the humid, lint-filled air made breathing difficult. They were kept awake by having cold water thrown in their faces. Three-year-olds could be found in the cotton fields, twelve-year-olds on factory night shifts. Across the country, children who should have been in school or at play had to work for a living. (p. 2)

With this description, Freedman brings the problems of child labor to life.

Nonfiction that combines vivid writing like this with illustrations, particularly photographs of people and places, helps readers understand the past. To strengthen this understanding, readers should also consider how some things change over time while others remain the same. The process of change is uneven. The authors of both *The Underground Railroad* and *Kids at Work* anticipate this need. Freedman ends his book by noting that while conditions have improved, child labor continues, while Bial also ends his book by noting that the struggle for equality still continues. By doing this, these authors help readers connect the past with the present.

Offers a Sense of Hope for the Future

Social studies highlights the importance of *social efficacy*, the ability to effect change. One of the major strands in the *Curriculum Standards for Social Studies* (NCSS, 1994) is civic ideals and practices. The *Standards* suggest that among the questions learners need to confront is "How can I make a positive difference?" (p. 30).

Nonfiction provides us with many examples of people who have made a difference in the lives of others. One of the most inspiring examples is found in Jerry Stanley's *Children of the Dust Bowl* (1992), which tells how one man, Leo Hart, helped a group of migrant children while others turned their backs. The

To become more aware of the vivid descriptions of the past found in nonfiction literature, have children collect samples of vivid writing. Works by Russell Freedman are especially good sources. Other books by Freedman include *Children of the Wild West, Cowboys of the Wild West, Lincoln: A Photobiography,* and *The Wright Brothers.*

book describes the terrible suffering of the Okies, Oklahoma families and others, who left their farms during the Dust Bowl of the 1930s and traveled to California in search of jobs and a better life. What they found was just the opposite: hunger, disease, and prejudice. Children, in particular, suffered terribly. They were shunned in school, even by their teachers who believed that the Okie children were just too dumb to learn.

Leo Hart, school superintendent in Kern County, changed the lives of the Okie children in Weedpatch Camp, a federal work camp near Bakersfield, California. Through his persistence, determination, and love, he built a school for these children—a school that taught them the skills they needed along with self-respect. Leo Hart wanted to have these children take their "rightful place" (p. 41) in society, and they did. The success of the Weedpatch School is an uplifting story about what can be done to counter intolerance.

Readers of *When Plague Strikes* (Giblin, 1995), a book for older readers, learn what they can do to combat our current plague, the AIDS virus. Author James Cross Giblin claims that by studying how people responded to plague in the past, we can learn how to act today. Accordingly, Giblin traces the parallels between three plagues—the Black Death, smallpox, and AIDS. He concludes that in the past people's responses ranged from compassion to outright hostility, and that we are likely to respond the same way unless we pursue a rigorous program of medical research while at the same time showing compassion for people infected with the disease.

Books like *Children of the Dust Bowl* and *When Plague Strikes* present children with some of the harsh realities of life. But along with these realities, they present evidence that people can effect positive change. In this way, nonfiction provides an important message about citizenship.

Selecting Nonfiction to Teach Social Studies

When selecting nonfiction to teach social studies, the six features discussed above can serve as a guide. While not every book will have every feature, books should have at least some of them. Figure 6.2 contains questions to ask when evaluating books for social studies programs.

These same six features can also be used as models for writing instruction. A class can collect examples of how authors present main ideas, introduce primary source material, reveal their attitudes toward information, and so forth, and make data charts illustrating how this is done. A data chart can serve as a guide when teachers write collaboratively with their students or when students write independently.

The next section will briefly describe how a sixth-grade teacher and I used nonfiction—in this case *When Plague Strikes*—to scaffold, or support, her students' understanding of the past using data charts. This book

Figure 6.2 Selecting Nonfiction to Teach Social Studies

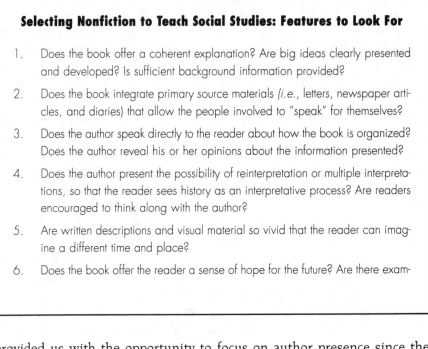

Selecting Nonfiction to Teach Social Studies: Features to Look For

1. Does the book offer a coherent explanation? Are big ideas clearly presented and developed? Is sufficient background information provided?

2. Does the book integrate primary source materials (i.e., letters, newspaper articles, and diaries) that allow the people involved to "speak" for themselves?

3. Does the author speak directly to the reader about how the book is organized? Does the author reveal his or her opinions about the information presented?

4. Does the author present the possibility of reinterpretation or multiple interpretations, so that the reader sees history as an interpretative process? Are readers encouraged to think along with the author?

5. Are written descriptions and visual material so vivid that the reader can imagine a different time and place?

6. Does the book offer the reader a sense of hope for the future? Are there exam-

provided us with the opportunity to focus on author presence since the author makes a strong case for seeing parallels among the three different plagues he discusses—the Black Death, smallpox, and AIDS.

Using Nonfiction to Teach Social Studies: Examining Parallels in History

Last year, sixth-grade teacher Lila Alexander and I used *When Plague Strikes* (Giblin, 1995) to help her students develop their historical thinking. We planned that, as a class, we would closely examine examples of the kind of thinking we wanted to promote. We thought that a number of ideas in *When Plague Strikes* deserved attention. In the Prologue to this book, Giblin claims that the plagues he will be discussing—the Black Death, smallpox, and AIDS are similar in three ways: people's immediate reactions, the disastrous impact on population, and the lasting consequences that resulted. In the main sections of the book, Giblin documents this claim, and then, in the Afterword, he draws implications from this information.

Lila and I felt that Giblin's clearly stated historical interpretation, followed by his well-written account of the three cases of plague, would allow children the opportunity to think along with him about a critical social issue. We planned to first identify Giblin's thesis with the children, and then focus their attention on reading to discover how this thesis was (or was not) substantiated. We would be looking at how Giblin engaged in pattern-seeking and case building as ways to understand the past. Second, Giblin's book would provide enough information so that children could compare the three plagues and begin to think about the parallels that can be found in history. In this case, we decided to take a closer look at the similarities and differences between the Black Death and AIDS. And finally, we hoped to generate enough interest in the topic so that students would be motivated to find out more about AIDS through independent research, thereby extending our discussion of the topic.

As the book was read aloud and discussed, Lila and the students collected information about each plague. Using a large data chart, Lila recorded the information as the students suggested it. The format of the data chart focused students' attention on documenting the parallels among the three plagues. A separate chart was made for each plague. Figure 6.3 shows a portion of the chart for the Black Death.

Figure 6.3 Data Chart for the Black Plague

The Black Plague: Data Chart

People's Immediate Reaction	Impact on the Population	Lasting Consequences
confusion, fear, frustration	Approximately 36 million people in Western Europe died.	Workers got more money because so many had died of the plague that workers were hard to find.
built walls around victims' houses		
looked for "scapegoat," someone to blame	Thousands of Jews were killed. Many of the rest went to Poland.	Nobles got poorer. They couldn't sell their crops because there weren't people to buy them. Nobles lost power.
blamed: (1) Jews, (2) outcasts (3) themselves		
Some people became flagellants, whipped themselves so God would take the plague away.		Churches lost power. People didn't believe because the church couldn't do anything about the plague. Some priests ran away so people lost faith in them.
felt hopeless and helpless		Changes in people's beliefs about science: 1. People could study the human body. 2. People didn't believe in Galen's ideas about "humors" any more. 3. People used the scientific method.

As the three charts were completed, students' attention was focused on considering the similarities between the Black Death and AIDS. Among the statements they made were the following:

- With both diseases, people were used as scapegoats: AIDS (Haitians), Black Death (people who were different).
- Both are infections, but AIDS is much harder to catch.
- Both can be fatal. AIDS is always fatal. Black Death is usually fatal.
- Both diseases started from an animal. AIDS from monkeys. Black Death from rats.
- At first no one wanted to deal with the problem.

Students generally concluded that there were, indeed, parallels between the two plagues. To extend the conversation we gathered books about AIDS, and encouraged the students to read, respond in journals, and discuss the additional information they found.

Finally, we asked students to put their ideas into writing, so that their classmates and others could read them. We asked them to focus on two main challenges: (1) comparing the Black Death and AIDS and (2) sharing thoughts about AIDS, especially those resulting from independent reading.

Excerpts from one student's writing indicates the quality of thought involved. She began a comparison this way:

> AIDS is caused by a virus, Plague is caused by a bacterium which lives in rat-fleas. With AIDS, the virus is spread by the exchange of body fluids, especially by coming into contact with another person's blood. Plague is not spread in that way, Plague is airborne. You could inhale Plague just from being in casual contact with another person....

This competent, well constructed comparison only hints at what students can do. When given time, sufficient information, and support from their teachers, students—like historians—can find patterns within data, find parallels among different events, and build cases that highlight their own interpretations.

When Plague Strikes taught children a great deal about plague. But it did much more. First, it taught them that when authors write about the social world they do more than retell the story; they interpret it. James Cross Giblin's original interpretation provided a clear example of that. Second, through the process of responding to this book, students learned that they, too, can interpret. These are powerful understandings derived from nonfiction.

Conclusions

Other books, like the ones mentioned in this chapter, introduce students to social studies as a vibrant, living, relevant subject—one that requires active thinking. Nonfiction not only provides students with important content to think about; it also provides them with a model for setting forth their own ideas. In the short term, reading and responding to powerful ideas about the social world promotes the learning of content, skills and values related to citizenship. In the long term, it provides a bridge toward active citizenship. Social studies educators know how important it is to move in this direction.

References

Barton, K. C. (1996). Narrative simplifications in elementary students' historical thinking. In J. Brophy (Ed.), *Advances in research on teaching: Vol. 6. History teaching and learning* (pp. 51-83). Greenwich, CT: JAI Press.

Beck, I. L., & McKeown, M. G. (1994). Outcomes of history instruction: Paste-up accounts. In M. Carretero & J. F. Voss (Eds.), *Cognitive and instructional processes in history and the social sciences* (pp. 237-256). Hillsdale, NJ: Lawrence Erlbaum Associates.

Crismore, A. (1984). The rhetoric of textbooks: Metadiscourse. *Journal of Curriculum Studies, 16,* 279-296.

Greene, S. (1994). The problems of learning to think like a historian: Writing history in the culture of the classroom. *Educational Psychologist, 29,* 89-96.

Levstik, L. S. (1993). Building a sense of history in a first-grade classroom. In J. Brophy (Ed.), *Advances in research on teaching: Vol. 3. Case studies of teaching and learning in social studies* (pp. 1-31). Greenwich, CT: JAI Press.

McKeown, M. G., & Beck, I. L. (1994). Making sense of accounts of history: Why young students don't and how they might. In G. Leinhardt, I. L. Beck, & C. Stainton (Eds.), *Teaching and learning in history* (pp. 1-26). Hillsdale, NJ: Lawrence Erlbaum Associates.

National Council for the Social Studies. (1994). *Expectations of excellence: Curriculum standards for social studies.* Washington, DC: National Council for the Social Studies.

Spink, J. K. (1996). The aesthetics of informational reading. *The New Advocate, 9,* 135-149.

Taxel, J. (1983). The American Revolution in children's fiction. *Research in the Teaching of English, 17,* 61-83.

Trousdale, A. M. (1990). A submission theology for black Americans: Religion and social action in prize-winning children's books about the black experience in America. *Research in the Teaching of English, 24,* 117-140.

Tunnell, M. O., & Ammon, R. (1996). The story of ourselves: Fostering multiple historical perspectives. *Social Education, 60,* 212-215.

Wineburg, S. S. (1991a). Historical problem solving: A study of the processes used in the evaluation of documentary and pictorial evidence. *Journal of Educational Psychology, 83,* 73-87.

Wineburg, S. S. (1991b). On the reading of historical texts: Notes on the breach between school and academy. *American Educational Research Journal, 28,* 495-519.

Wineburg, S. S., & Fournier, J. (1994). Contextualized thinking in history. In M. Carretero & J. F. Voss (Eds.), *Cognitive and instructional processes in history and the social sciences* (pp. 285-308). Hillsdale, NJ: Lawrence Erlbaum Associates.

Zarnowski, M. (1996). Constructing historical interpretations in elementary school: A look at process and product. In J. Brophy (Ed.), *Advances in research on teaching: Vol. 6. History teaching and learning* (pp. 183-205). Greenwich, CT: JAI Press.

CHAPTER 7
EVALUATING AND USING NONFICTION LITERATURE IN THE SCIENCE CURRICULUM

by Anthony D. Fredericks

Science is an exploration of, and an investigation into, the unknown. Science is learning more about what we don't know...filling in gaps in our knowledge base, changing old ideas, modifying concepts, and discovering that we don't necessarily have all the answers just because we know a bunch of facts. In some ways, science is a testament to our own innate ignorance—an ignorance borne of a desire to know more about ourselves and our world, not one signifying a complete lack of knowledge.

For children, science can and should become a dynamic and interactive discipline. It should allow children to examine new ideas, play around with concepts and precepts, and discover that there is no such thing as a body of finite knowledge. What does this mean for teachers? It means that children must be given a multitude of opportunities to probe, poke, and peek into the mysteries of the universe—whether that universe is their own backyard or a galaxy far away.

Those opportunities exist in the wealth of science literature available for children. Opening up doors of understanding and comprehension and building bridges to increased awareness and appreciation of science as an everyday aspect of youngsters' lives are viable goals for any teacher. Those goals can be promoted through the judicious use of high-quality children's books.

A Classroom View

The piercing cries of macaws, the incessant chatter of distant monkeys, and the buzzing of colorful insects filled the air with a cacophony of sounds. The gurgling of a nearby stream and the occasional crash of an enormous Kapok tree mixed with animal sounds to create a clamor that ebbed and flowed across the landscape.

Visitors entering Lowell Brigg's fourth-grade classroom often feel as though they have been transported to some dark and distant Amazonian forest. Lowell's room is less of a classroom and more of an ecological wonderland awash in a diversity of sights and a medley of sounds. He and his students have worked hard to transform their room into a rainforest ecosystem that is so close to the original that one might expect a family of tapirs to creep out of the shadows or a giant python to coil itself around the leg of a desk.

In order to actively involve his students in a host of positive learning experiences, Lowell set out to create a unit on "Rain Forests"—one based on the introduction and reading of selected nonfiction books. By offering his students active opportunities to become involved in nonfiction literature, Lowell was able to emphasize authentic learning within a specific area of the science curriculum. So too, was he able to focus on a *process approach* to science instruction—one that provided students with meaningful hands-on experiences.

Let's look in on Lowell's class as his students explore some of the mysteries and marvels of rainforest life:

1. Based on the book *Exploring the Rainforest* (Fredericks, 1996) a small group of youngsters was constructing a handmade terrarium.

2. Three pupils were constructing a series of papier mâché—bromeliads based on what they had learned in *A Walk in the Rain Forest* (Pratt, 1992).

3. Two students were replaying a rainforest audiotape and matching animal sounds with creatures in *Rainforest Animals* (Chinery, 1992).

4. Another group was tracking the movements of the class frog and comparing its behaviors with those detailed in *A Chorus of Frogs* (Hunt, 1995).

5. Three students were putting together a bibliography of rainforest literature that could be shared with their "pen pals" in another fourth-grade class.

6. Two students were assembling a list of questions to pose to a visiting biology professor.

7. A small group began looking through several books *Frogs and Toads* (Parker, 1994); *Extremely Weird Frogs* (Lovett, 1992); and *Amazing Frogs and Toads* (Clarke, 1990) to construct an information guide about the life of the Poison Dart Frog.

Lowell's students were not involved in haphazard activities, but rather in well-planned *process learning*. The rainforest unit combined an assortment of non-fiction literature and authentic learning activities into a sequential series of lessons designed to assist students in appreciating the rainforests of the world through an active processing of data. Lowell had introduced the unit with a collection of nonfiction books about the rainforest—including those dealing with the climate, explorations, rates of destruction, medicines obtained from rainforest plants, and some of the most unusual animals found anywhere in the world. The literature selections became the vehicle for a host of holistic activities. Some activities had been planned by teachers; however, a large majority were suggested by students as an outgrowth of the books read and shared in class.

ADDITIONAL "RAINFOREST" ACTIVITIES

a. the drafting of a letter to political leaders sharing students' concerns about rainforest destruction;

b. the writing of an editorial for the local newspaper;

c. a "learning vine" containing "leaves" on which are recorded new words and terms learned throughout the unit;

d. posters of selected creatures that live in each of the four major layers of the rainforest;

e. a scrapbook of amazing facts and figures;

f. a series of terrariums and aquariums containing representative rainforest flora and fauna;

g. an ongoing newspaper of the life and times of various rainforest inhabitants; and

h. charts, graphs, and tables chronicling the rate of destruction taking place in the world's rain-forest (daily, weekly, yearly).

Literature and Science

Lowell is one of a growing legion of teachers who have discovered the enormous value and impact nonfiction has on the entire science curriculum. In many ways, children's literature (both fiction and nonfiction) allows Lowell to "energize" his science program and demonstrate the logical connections that exist between classroom learning and the natural world outside the classroom. In essence, Lowell's classroom is one in which nonfiction literature provides both a foundation and a launching pad for his students' self-initiated discoveries. Nonfiction literature provides breadth and depth to the entire science curriculum—offering innumerable opportunities for students to become immersed in the dynamics of specific science topics.

The advantages of nonfiction literature in the science curriculum are many. Meinbach, Rothlein, & Fredericks (1995) point to the following six significant "markers" for any classroom teacher:

- Nonfiction literature provides youngsters with an ever-expanding array of information in a welcome and familiar format. Youngsters begin to realize that science is not relegated to the pages of a textbook, but can be found on the shelves of the local bookstore or public library.

- Teachers are free to help students look at a scientific principle, discovery, or enigma from a variety of perspectives, rather than a single viewpoint frequently demonstrated in a text book or curriculum guide.

- Nonfiction literature provides kids with appropriate models for their own writing experiences. Students learn how scientific information is gathered, assembled, and presented in coherent, comprehensible, responsible, and interesting ways.

- A well-written trade book offers readers a variety of information from several angles or several points of view. Youngsters learn that scientific knowledge is never static.

- Current nonfiction literature provides children with new information and knowledge unobtainable in any other format. Topics in which new discoveries are being made at a rapid rate (i.e., space exploration, medical research, tectonic plate theory) can be shared through recent publications.

- With nonfiction literature, children have sustained time and opportunity to investigate topics thoroughly and to engage in reflective inquiry.

The points above have been given additional emphasis with the release of the National Science Education Standards—particularly the first section of that document addressing the new Science Teaching Standards (National Research Council, 1996). These standards provide teachers and administrators with pertinent guidelines and an operational outline for developing improved science curricula. Note how the following teaching standards can be effectively promoted and implemented through the judicious use of nonfiction literature:

- Select science content and adapt and design curricula to meet the interests, knowledge, understanding, abilities, and experiences of students [Teaching Standard A].

- Orchestrate discourse among students about scientific ideas [Teaching Standard B].

- Use multiple methods and systematically gather data about student understanding and ability [Teaching Standard C].

- Structure the time available so that students are able to engage in extended investigations [Teaching Standard D].

- Enable students to have a significant voice in decisions about the content and context of their work...[Teaching Standard E].

Each of the aforementioned standards can be effectively supported and logically promulgated via an increased emphasis on nonfiction literature. In reviewing the classroom activities of Lowell Briggs' students, it is apparent that the *systematic and sustained* inclusion of nonfiction literature in his science curriculum not only promotes scientific literacy and viable teaching principles, but it underscores the basic tenets of the National Science Education Standards.

I'm certainly not suggesting that we "throw" trade books into our science curricula simply for the sake of "reviving" it. What I am suggesting is the judicious and reasoned utilization of nonfiction literature in concert with a process ("hands-on") approach to science education. While many children's nonfiction science books are available in our local bookstores and libraries, not all are satisfactory in terms of information or presentation. Lutz (1996) laments the fact that the vast majority of them are not written by scientists or in consultation with scientists. She goes on to state that any science book must "pass" three tests:

- It must have an authentic connection to science and scientists;

- There must be a story involved (as opposed to a simple reporting of facts);

- The book must suggest, in some way, why scientists have a particular fondness for their work.

Lutz's concern is that a reporting of facts is no more a science book than a mixture of flour, milk, and sugar is a cake. She concludes her essay with the following statement: "Facts are cheap, but enthusiasm is rare" (p. 173). Just as teachers must have an enthusiasm about teaching science in order for science instruction to be effective and lasting; so, too, must science literature evidence a high measure of excitement above and beyond the facts shared or the data presented.

Bruce McMillan (1993) makes a poignant argument for accuracy in science books. He provides a plethora of convincing data that points to an ever-increasing use of misinformation in nonfiction books. His criteria for quality science writing include the need for science book authors to have appropriate science credentials, the elimination of value statements or personal viewpoints as factual information, and the importance of the most up-to-date information available. He states that many authors rely on the work of others without going to the trouble of double- and triple-checking their data with current research or with reliable and respected experts. According to McMillan, too many books are rife with factual errors or errors in presentation. The old maxim—"Old wine in new bottles"— seems to be a common condition for a large proportion of science books currently on the market.

While there are excellent examples of science trade books available for classroom use, their distribution among all the sciences is not equal. For example, the market is dominated by books on the biological sciences, while books on the physical sciences are few and far between. Not surprisingly, teachers tend to incorporate more trade books into their studies of the life sciences and, conversely, tend to over-rely on the textbook for information related to the physical sciences. Obviously, this fosters an imbalance in the minds of youngsters who tend to believe that plants and animals are more worthy of study (they must be, because there's so many books about plants and animals) than are simple machines, atomic power, and water power (for which there is an obvious dearth of resources). The fact that an overwhelming majority of students report "animals" as their favorite science topic may be due, in some measure, to the trade books available in that area as opposed to quality literature available in the other disciplines of science.

Of no less importance is the fact that science changes! Knowledge is never static—it's always in a state of flux. What we know in the 20th century about space exploration, for example, may be erroneous, misinterpreted, or unnecessary in the 21st century. By the same token, the information presented to students in science books may be "right on the mark" today, but 20% incorrect four years from now. As stated in the introduction to this chapter, it is important for children to realize that science knowledge needs to be weighed, evaluated, and reassessed periodically. Just because it's in a book doesn't necessarily mean it's true! Although both adults and kids have a tendency to believe whatever we read in print, it's particularly important for teachers to help their students develop a "critical eye" about what they read. The copyright date, the experiences and background of the author, substantiated facts, and clear organization are all important factors in the "appropriateness" of any single book (Fredericks, Blake-Kline, & Kristo, 1997).

Particularly important is the relevancy of science information to the lives of the readers of science trade books. Fredericks, Meinbach, & Rothlein (1993) place considerable emphasis on the fact that science literature that relies on the simple presentation of dates, names,

EXAMPLES OF NONFICTION ON THE PHYSICAL SCIENCES

Adventures with Rocks and Minerals: Geology Experiments for Young People by Lloyd H. Barrow

Air: The Elements by Ken Robbins

Atom Bomb by Tom Seddon

My Balloon by Kay Davies and Wendy Oldfield

One Giant Leap by Mary Ann Fraser

Pioneering Ocean Depths by Sandra Markle

Shadow Play: Making Pictures with Light and Lenses by Bernie Zubrowski

Venus: Magellan Explores Our Twin Planet by Franklyn M. Branley

Water, the Source of Life: Glaciers, Springs, Oceans, Tide Pools, Lakes, Swamps, Rivers, and Oases (Scholastic Voyages of Discovery Series)

Weather: A National Geographic Action Book by Tom Kierein

places, facts and figures is boring! They further state that "placing this information in a context that has meaning for students helps them appreciate significant data as it relates to their lives" (p. 30). In short, readers must be able to understand the application of science concepts to their everyday lives. Knowing that one million acres of rainforest trees are chopped down or burned every single week may have little relevance to most children. The relevancy of that information comes from the fact that more than 1,000,000 new cases of cancer are diagnosed in this country each year and the rainforests of the world are the most important source for new medicines, particularly drugs used in the fight against cancer (Fredericks, 1996). Reducing the rate of rainforest destruction has direct implications for probable cancer treatments. That's something many children can "sink their teeth into."

Given these concerns, it's important to keep in mind that the dynamics of nonfiction literature hold enormous possibilities for both teachers and students throughout the entire science program. Science books open up the curriculum, facilitate the integration of subject matter, and stimulate creative and divergent thinking in a host of arenas. In short, nonfiction literature in the science program helps teachers emphasize and promote the natural curiosity and inquisitiveness of children.

A Process Evaluation of Nonfiction Literature

The investigation of science is dynamic! That is, children's daily contacts with the scientific world involve a constant interaction between the known and unknown. New ideas are discovered and others are modified, strengthened, or rejected. What helps children develop a scientific outlook is the processes to which they are exposed to science in school. In other words, science should not be merely a study of finite answers, but rather an application of processes that aid in discovering and learning about the world in which we live. These universal processes apply to a wide variety of learning opportunities for students—opportunities that help them think for themselves and apply more of what they learn to their own lives.

A *process approach* to science stimulates divergent thinking and provides a means for children to investigate their world based on what they know as well as on what they wish to discover. The following seven processes should be embedded in the science nonfiction you share with students. This is not to say that *all seven processes* will be in every book; rather that there should be several processes utilized or promulgated within a single piece of nonfiction. What is important is the need to offer children multiple opportunities to use nonfiction literature as a springboard to new and varied learning opportunities throughout the world of science. With each process, I have identified several books that would support that learning opportunity.

Observing

Observation involves all the primary senses: seeing, hearing, smelling, tasting, and touching. It is how we react to our environment and is the source of knowledge that humans employ most. Nonfiction literature should offer students opportunities to actively utilize their observational skills, gain a sense of importance of this process, and become more alert to the panorama of science that surrounds them every day. Scientific skills are enhanced when children use observation in combination with other processes, such as predicting and experimenting.

- *Jack-in-the-Pulpit* by Jerome Wexler
- *Nature All Year Long* by Claire Walker Leslie
- *Squishy, Misty, Damp & Muddy: The In-Between World of the Wetlands* by Molly Cone
- *Castle: Stephen Biesty's Cross-Sections* by Richard Platt and Illustrated by Stephen Biesty
- *Unseen Rainbows, Silent Songs: The World Beyond Human Senses* by Susan Goodman

Classifying

Classifying is the process of assigning basic elements to specific groups. All the items within a particular group share a basic relationship. As new ideas are encountered, they are added to previously formulated groups on the basis of similar elements. Quality nonfiction literature encourages children to strengthen their background knowledge and expand their mental categories and the items within those categories. Classifying enhances scientific comprehension because it provides children with the opportunity to relate prior knowledge to new concepts.

- *Darwin: Nature Reinterpreted* by Piero Ventura
- *Spiders Near and Far* by Jennifer Owings Dewey
- *Surprising Swimmers* by Anthony D. Fredericks
- *A Wasp Is Not a Bee* by Marilyn Singer

Measuring

Scientists are constantly measuring. Measuring provides the scientist with the hard data necessary to confirm hypotheses and make predictions. Measuring includes gathering data on size, weight, quantity, and number. It is also a valid means of making comparisons using very definite terms; rather than using indefinite language such as large, small, huge, heavy, light, etc. Good nonfiction literature assists youngsters in understanding the need for scientific accuracy as well as ways in which that data can be shared with others. This also provides young authors with appropriate writing models.

- *Backyard Birds of Winter* by Carol Lerner
- *One Giant Leap* by Mary Ann Fraser
- *One Small Square: Cactus Desert* by Donald Silver
- *Coral Reefs: Earth's Undersea Treasures* by Laurence Pringle

Inferring

Children often need to make conjectures and suppositions on the basis of a minimum of data. Inferring is of two types: *deductive* (going from the general to the specific) and *inductive* (going from the specific to the general). Making inferences requires children to have a sufficient background of personal experiences as well as opportunities and encouragement to draw tentative conclusions or explanations. Purposeful nonfiction literature provides readers with just enough data to develop inferential abilities. They can draw conclusions in much the same way as scientists.

- *Fire in the Forest: A Cycle of Growth and Renewal* by Laurence Pringle
- *Making Sense: Animal Perception and Communication* by Bruce Brooks
- *The Iceman* by Don Lessem
- *A Drop of Water: A Book of Science and Wonder* by Walter Wick

Communicating

Communication is the means by which information is shared and disseminated. It involves not only interacting with others but organizing data so that it can be effectively passed on to others. Communicating can take many forms, including gestures, electronic, verbal and written responses, reading, listening, showing, and questioning. Good nonfiction literature stimulates students to share and disseminate information with each other. Readers' interests are piqued through literature, and their desire to pass information on to others is aroused.

- *Look!* by April Wilson
- *Ten Little-Known Facts about Hippopotamuses: And More Little-Known Facts and a Few Fibs about Other Animals* by Douglas Little

- *Wild in the City* by Jan Thornhill
- *101 Questions & Answers about Backyard Wildlife* by Anne Squire

Predicting

Predicting is the process of extrapolating potential information based on a minimum amount of data or on information already known. The scientist then tries to confirm or refute the prediction based on the gathering of new data. Predictions provide scientists with a road map by which they can conduct their experiments. They provide goals—albeit tentative ones—but at least something to aim for. The data-gathering process provides scientists with the evidence they need to verify their original predictions. Nonfiction literature, too, gives young readers scientific opportunities to formulate predictions during the reading process as well as information to follow through on those predictions. In short, literature should stimulate the posing of questions and the opportunities to search for answers.

- *Sky Tree* by Thomas Locker
- *Zero Gravity* by Gloria Skurzynski
- *Why Mammals Have Fur* by Dorothy Hinshaw Patent
- *Extinction Is Forever* by Donald Silver
- *Mistakes That Worked: 40 Familiar Inventions and How They Came to Be* by Charlotte Foltz Jones

Experimenting

By definition, a true scientist is one who is constantly experimenting. Through experimenting, ideas and hypotheses are tested. Experimentation involves the identification and control of variables in order to arrive at a cause-effect conclusion. Experimenting also involves manipulating data and assessing the results. Children need to understand that they conduct experiments every day, from watching ice cream melt to deciding on what clothes to wear outside. Scientific experimentation, however, involves a more formalized process, albeit one that also touches our everyday activities. Not all nonfiction literature will have (or should have) detailed formal experiments. Nevertheless, students' curiosity should be sufficiently provoked to pursue their own self-initiated experiments and discoveries.

- *Cricketology* by Michael Ross
- *Science to the Rescue* by Sandra Markle
- *Making Waves: Finding Out about Rhythmic Motion* by Bernie Zubrowski

- *Adventures with Rocks and Minerals: Book II Geology Experiments for Young People* by Lloyd Barrow
- *Backyard Safaris: 52 Year-Round Science Adventures* by Phyllis S. Busch

Let's take a look at one science book—an outstanding piece of nonfiction literature—and how it embodies the basic processes of science:

America's Deserts: Guide to Plants and Animals by Marianne Wallace

Summary: This book provides readers with an exciting examination of North America's four major desert areas. Crisp and clear illustrations complimented by a fascinating and detailed text offer young scientists a close look at this wondrous ecosystem. This is a fun and lively field guide that is sure to spark interest in one of the world's most misunderstood environments.

OBSERVING: Detailed illustrations encourage readers to examine the desert environment and many inhabitants.

CLASSIFYING: The four major deserts of the United States and the flora and fauna that are indigenous to each of those areas are profiled.

MEASURING: The size, length, and shape of plants and animals is provided in both standard and metric measurements.

INFERRING: The illustrations provide youngsters with opportunities to determine the interrelationships that exist between members of a specific biome.

COMMUNICATING: Fascinating facts and interesting information encourage readers to share and discuss that data with others.

PREDICTING: Textual information encourages readers to formulate predictions, which are then confirmed through illustrations that follow those discussions.

EXPERIMENTING: No formal experiments are provided in this book. Experiments with desert flora and fauna detailed in this book can be conducted (*i.e.*, in a desert terrarium) with projects from other books.

Conclusions

Science is one of the most dynamic subjects youngsters will encounter in their lifetimes; thus, it stands to reason that it must be joyous, exciting, and purposeful to them while they are in school as well as when they leave the confines of your classroom. Helping children achieve a measure of success and comprehension throughout all the sciences is a challenge for teachers. That challenge can be met when students are provided with a rich and varied foundation of high-quality nonfiction literature. Through that literature, students will understand that science is never static—it is a constant and ongoing process of investigation, discovery, and intellectual growth.

References

Fredericks, A. D., Meinbach, A. M., & Rothlein, L. (1993). *Thematic units: An integrated approach to teaching science and social studies.* New York: HarperCollins.

Fredericks, A. D. (1996). *Exploring the rainforest: Science activities for kids.* Golden, CO: Fulcrum Publishing.

Fredericks, A. D., Blake-Kline, B., & Kristo, J. V. (1997). *Teaching the integrated language arts: Process and practice.* New York: Addison-Wesley.

Lutz, D. (1996). Science is what scientists do, or Wetenschap is wat wetenschappers doen. *The Horn Book Magazine, 72,* (2), pp. 166-173.

McMillan, B. (1993). Accuracy in books for young readers: From first to last check. *The New Advocate, 6,* (2), pp. 97-104.

Meinbach, A., Rothlein, L., & Fredericks, A. D. (1995). *The complete guide to thematic units: Creating the integrated curriculum.* Norwood, MA: Christopher-Gordon.

National Research Council. (1996). *National science education standards.* Washington, DC: National Academy Press.

LIBRARY

Chapter 8
Mathematical Learning and Exploration in Nonfiction Literature

by Sandra Wilde

Children's literature is increasingly being seen as an avenue for deepening mathematical understanding. Current approaches to curriculum and instruction emphasize mathematics in the context of human experience and other curricular areas as well as its affective and aesthetic dimensions (National Council of Teachers of Mathematics, 1989). The use of children's literature supports all of these goals. Despite the large numbers of children's books, particularly picture books, that can be used to explore mathematical topics (Thiessen & Matthias, 1992; Whitin & Wilde, 1992, 1995), there are surprisingly few nonfiction mathematics books for children that are of good quality. For instance, none of the Orbis Pictus books has mathematics as its subject. In this chapter I will discuss a sample of mathematics nonfiction books, explain how social studies and science-oriented books can be used to explore mathematical topics, examine issues of accuracy and the treatment of mathematics in nonfiction, and suggest how these books can be used appropriately in the classroom.

When David Whitin and I recently compiled a list of what we felt were the 20 best new children's books with mathematical content (Whitin & Wilde, 1995), five were fiction, eleven were nonfiction, and four were new prototypes of counting books. One of the fictional books was Rod Clement's *Counting on Frank* (1991), the humorous picture storybook of a young boy who sees mathematics everywhere he looks. Of the eleven nonfiction books, only five dealt specifically with mathematical topics (*e.g.*, numbers, fractions, circles, money, and time). The other six focused on topics that involved some mathematical content, such as the construction of the transcontinental railroad and examining microscopic creatures. This selection of "best books" is generally representative of the state of affairs when looking for mathematical content in children's books. Looking under headings such as "Mathematics—Juvenile literature" in a library's database or in the mathematics section of a children's bookstore (if there is one) produces little beyond books of math puzzles and activities and often dreary workbooks. Illustrators continue to find the counting book genre a provocative way to show off their talents, but readers looking for more advanced mathematical content may have to search hard for it.

The line between fiction and nonfiction children's books is, perhaps, a more nebulous one for mathematics than for other content areas. In books that are technically fiction, a story is often a bare pretext for the mathematical content rather than being a fully developed narrative. Many of these books are of high-quality since they use a story as a way to contextualize and enliven mathematical content. Two recent examples are Sciezka and Smith's *Math Curse* (1995) and *One Hundred Hungry Ants* (Pinczes, 1993). However, for the purposes of this chapter I will first focus on books that are clearly nonfiction. Some of these books deal with "pure" mathematical topics relating to numbers and computation. A second group of books deals with applied topics such as geometry (particularly optical illusions), games and puzzles, and measurement of qualities like value (as measured by money), size, and time. The third group consists of nonfiction books on other topics that include mathematical content. I have chosen selected books that are especially good for integrating mathematical explorations into other curriculum areas, as well as some Orbis Pictus books that demonstrate how good nonfiction books on many topics often include mathematical content. Each group of books suggests slightly different criteria for evaluation and classroom use.

Numbers, Computation, and Other "Pure" Mathematics Topics in Nonfiction

Since mathematics is sometimes viewed as a relatively dry topic, it is probably not surprising that there are few nonfiction books devoted to it. Authors usually choose to embed theoretical mathematical information in a story, particularly when writing for young children.

A few new books from Dorling Kindersley attempt to deal with early mathematical topics in a nonfiction format. The most comprehensive of these is *My First Number Book* (Heinst, 1992), which uses two-page pictorial spreads to develop concepts of classification, one-to-one correspondence, and ordering that eventually lead to simple and more advanced concepts of number as well as basic computation. Its strength is its use of vivid photographs and well-phrased questions to develop concepts systematically. However, the text lacks an author's voice and does not use language to develop concepts beyond captions and questions. Related books from the same publisher include *My First Book of Time* (Llewellyn, 1992) and *My First Cookbook* (Wilkes, 1989).

Some books on fractions, while technically nonfiction, illustrate how books on abstract mathematical topics almost always end up verging on narrative. Bruce McMillan's photographic concept book *Eating Fractions* (1991) uses pictures of children eating a meal to illustrate various fractions. Food, such as pizza, is first shown as a whole and then divided into fractional parts accompanied by fraction terminology and graphic representations. A recipe for each dish appears at the end of the book providing opportunities for the additional mathematical activity of measurement. However, it is only the absence of a written story that keeps this book in the nonfiction camp; the photographs clearly carry a narrative storyline.

Loreen Leedy, author of *The Monster Money Book* (1992) and *2 X 2= Boo!: A Set of Spooky Multiplication Stories* (1995), also wrote *Fraction Action* (1994) in which she presents a series of short lessons on fraction concepts such as fractional parts of areas and sets. These are framed as a series of cartoon stories that are slightly more developed than story problems. Although appreciably more didactic than the narrative fraction book, *The Doorbell Rang* (Hutchins, 1986), it manages to cover a number of concepts in a lively way. It again illustrates, however, the difficulty of avoiding narrative entirely in mathematical nonfiction, particularly for topics such as basic fraction concepts that do not work easily into expository text.

Precise visual representation is a major criterion in selecting nonfiction dealing with abstract mathematical topics. The accuracy, appropriateness, and quality of the illustrations are also crucial to the success of these

MORE BOOKS USING FRACTIONS

Half and Half by Joanne Nelson

The Little Mouse, the Red Ripe Strawberry, and the Big Hungry Bear by Don Wood and Audrey Wood.

The Teacher from the Black Lagoon by Mike Thaler

MORE BOOKS ABOUT BIG NUMBERS

The Biggest Birthday Cake in the World by Elizabeth Spurr

The King's Chessboard by David Birch

Land of Dark, Land of Light: The Arctic National Wildlife Refuge by Karen Pandell

A Million Fish...More or Less by Patricia McKissack

One Grain of Rice: A Mathematical Folktale by Demi

One Million by Hendrik Hertzberg

Pumpkins by Mary L. Ray

books in a way that may not be as decisive for books on other topics. A mathematics book misses the point entirely if an illustration of a set of 100 objects actually contained 99 or 101, or if an area were divided into parts labeled "1/3," but that were of unequal sizes.

Two contemporary authors for children focus on presenting more challenging mathematical content. David Schwartz's books about large numbers, *How Much is a Million?* (1985) and *If You Made a Million* (1989), use real-life or fanciful examples such as the length of time it takes to count to a million (or billion or trillion) and the size of a goldfish bowl for a million (billion, trillion) fish in order to make these numbers comprehensible to young readers. Steven Kellogg's illustrations are a crucial component of the concept development, as readers see goldfish bowls the size of a whale, a stadium, and a city harbor.

Mitsumasa Anno, who illustrates his own books, explores topics such as factorial numbers, mathematical logic, permutations, and combinations. *Anno's Mysterious Multiplying Jar* (Anno & Anno, 1983), on factorial numbers, is the most successful of these for young readers. A magical jar contains a sea with an island that has two countries. Each of the two countries contains three mountains, each mountain is home to four walled kingdoms and so on, until we come across nine boxes, each one holding ten jars that look just like the one we started with. The pictures and accompanying number sentences help to make this an intriguing book. The mathematical content appears explicitly in the second half of the book, and it defines the concept of factorial numbers by showing that the visual sequence represents "10 factorial," which can also be expressed as 10! or $10 \times 9 \times 8 \times 7 \times 6 \times 5 \times 4 \times 3 \times 2 \times 1$. Despite their picture book format, *Socrates and the Three Little Pigs* by Mori (1986) about permutations and combinations and *Anno's Hat Tricks* (Nozaki, 1985) on mathematical logic are too hard for elementary school children. However, I'd recommend them as introductions to these topics for older students or even adults.

The best set of nonfiction books on pure mathematical topics was the "Young Math Books" published by Crowell in the 1970s. Although out of print, it is available in libraries. Edited by Max Beberman, director of the Committee on School Mathematics Projects at the University of Illinois, and Dorothy Bloomfield of Bank Street College of Education, this extensive series of short books written for the middle elementary grades introduces topics such as binary numbers, odd and even numbers, statistics, and topology to young readers. A typical example, *Yes-No, Stop-Go: Some Patterns in Mathematical Logic* (Gersting and Kuczkowsky, 1977) uses a railroad switching device and a castle with two arrangements of drawbridges to develop the concept of truth tables. Although illustrations are simple and use only two colors unlike today's more sophisticated ones, the quality of writing, concept development, and clarity of illustration are uniformly high. Many of the books explore "New Math" topics and focus on the intrinsic interest and beauty of mathematical concepts rather than applications. This series deserves to be reprinted.

All of these books, which directly explore mathematical topics, work well as starting points for discussion. For example, teachers working with young children could discuss *My First Number Book* (Heinst, 1992) a page at a time. *Eating Fractions* (McMillan, 1991) may be shared with young children just beginning to study the idea of one-to-one correspondence or beginning fraction concepts, respectively. These nonfiction books can also be used with the fictional children's books that

OTHER BOOKS BY MITSUMASA ANNO

Anno's Counting House

Anno's Faces

Anno's Math Games

Anno's Math Games II

Anno's Math Games III

Anno's Medieval World

deal with the same topics. The advantage of the nonfiction books is that they "teach" the topics more explicitly, but they may not have the appeal of fiction.

Although subjects like factorial numbers and concepts of million, billion, and trillion aren't part of the standard elementary school mathematics curriculum, *Anno's Mysterious Multiplying Jar* (Anno & Anno, 1983) and the two Schwartz books are useful for introducing these ideas as enrichment and to excite children about the possibilities of large numbers. The richness of these books is that they can be used profitably with both younger children, where the focus would be mainly on enjoying and marveling at the story, and with older students, who could try some of the computations suggested or develop their own.

Applied Mathematics in Nonfiction

When we turn to books that deal with applied mathematical topics, the possibilities for authors and illustrators expand and so do the quantity and variety of books. Many make mathematics aesthetically appealing or show the role it takes in a variety of human activities. Many of these books, because of the nature of their topics, are structured as collections of short pieces rather than as cohesive wholes with a strong author's voice. This is perhaps why they are so rarely chosen as award winners. Typical of such books is *The Kids' World Almanac of Amazing Facts about Numbers, Math and Money* (Facklam and Thomas, 1992), a fascinating collection of mathematical trivia such as the number of ways a deck of cards can be arranged and the longest attack of hiccups ever—65 years! Although not of high literary quality, such books are worth having in the classroom. A book that seems similarly fragmented, but is actually more ambitious and sophisticated, is *Circles* (Ross, 1992), which uses a variety of articles and activities to explore the nature of roundness. For example, the reader learns that ancient towns were often round because a circular shape can be defended by the smallest possible surrounding wall. Students are invited to slice up the skin of a grapefruit as a way of understanding the difficulty of creating a rectangular map of a spherical surface. Even for readers for whom the information in this book isn't new, it is exciting to see dozens of concepts come together as aspects of the same big idea.

William Edmonds' *Big Book of Time* (1994) achieves similar effects with two-page spreads on units of time ranging from seconds to eras. I was especially fascinated by the discussions of "now" defined as the "no time" that lies between the present and the future, and of moments, the times of change from one state to another like the moment that lightning strikes a tree.

A third book made up of a collection of ideas is *A Gallery of Games* (Marchon-Arnaud, 1994), which is part of a series called "The Young

Artisan" and has a particularly strong aesthetic dimension. Histories of games are accompanied by instructions for making several games in multiple formats. For example, readers learn how to make a checkerboard out of window screen with small magnets for checkers, or in the sand with stones for squares and shells for checkers. Books that collect a number of mathematical ideas seem to work best when they have a strong unifying force of some kind: a central idea, a progression from one thought to the next, or an artistic vision.

Children's books are a rich resource for the applied areas of mathematics that get little attention in the curriculum. Geometry and measurement can involve more than textbook exercises if they are treated as ways of representing and understanding the world around us. Optical illusion books both delight and provoke us to think about how our perceptions work. The topic of optical illusions illustrates the range of choices that authors and illustrators often have in dealing with mathematical content. They can choose to focus on either the aesthetic pleasure of visual patterns, like impossible staircases or identical circles that look different, or on understanding how such illusions work and learning how to create them. Seymour Simon's *The Optical Illusion Book* (1976) represents a comprehensive explanation of the various types of optical illusions, including many relating to the size and shape of circles. The impossible staircases are part of a chapter discussion of optical illusions in art. In *Picture Puzzler*, Kathleen Westray (1994) offers a much briefer collection of optical illusions portrayed in folk art style. Although there are brief discussions of each picture, the emphasis is primarily on the vivid full-color illustrations. There is generally only a single example of each type of illusion. Both of these excellent books are valuable for classroom use—*Picture Puzzler* to

OTHER BOOKS ABOUT TIME

A Book of Days: Then and Now by Starr Ockenga

Keeping Time by Franklyn M. Branley

My First Book of Time by Claire Llewellyn

What Do I Do at 8 o'clock? by Carla Dijs

BOOKS ABOUT PUZZLES AND GAMES

Ancient Puzzles: Classic Brainteasers and Other Timeless Mathematical Games of the Last 10 Centuries by Dominic Olivastro

Math Fun with Money Puzzlers by Rose Wyler and Mary Elting

Math-a-Magic: Number Tricks for Magicians by Laurence B. White, Jr. and Ray Broekel

Mathemagic by Raymond Blum

Puzzlooney! Really Ridiculous Math Puzzles by Russell Ginns

OTHER BOOKS ABOUT
VISUAL ILLUSIONS

*Magic Eye: A New Way
of Looking at the World*
by N. E. Thing
Enterprises

*Magic Eye II: Now You
See it...* by N. E. Thing
Enterprises

*Magic Eye III: Now You
See it...* by N. E. Thing
Enterprises

*Mirror: Finding Out
about the Properties of
Light* by Bernie
Zubrowski

Mirror Magic by
Seymour Simon

generate interest in optical illusions and *The Optical Illusion Book* for a more detailed exploration.

Three books on measurement exemplify some of the qualities that make for a good nonfiction book on applied mathematics. These books are different in many ways, but all are well written and illustrated. These present the mathematical content in precise and interesting ways. *Is a Blue Whale the Biggest Thing There Is?* (Wells, 1993), the briefest of these books, uses a picture book format to explore concepts and examples of large size. The author has also written a related book, *What's Smaller than a Pygmy Shrew?* (1995). The blue whale book begins with information about the size of the whale, which is the biggest animal that exists. It is shown juxtaposed to an elephant and other large mammals to compare its size to more familiar animals. The whale is, however, just the starting point for examining the concept of largeness. Ingenious illustrations show 20 imaginary jars filled with 100 whales each looking quite small on top of Mount Everest, 100 earths in a string bag looking tiny next to the sun, and other comparisons, ending with a representation of the entire universe as "the biggest thing there is." This book is an excellent example of how to present an aspect of mathematics that is difficult to grasp intuitively and to make it visible and exciting.

Kathryn Lasky's picture book, *The Librarian Who Measured the Earth* (1994), is a mathematical biography of Eratosthenes. In the third century B.C., he devised a means of measuring the circumference of the earth. We now know that he was off by only two hundred miles. The appealing biographical material on Eratosthenes is accompanied by a mathematical exploration that clarifies his feat in words and pictures. It shows how knowing the distance between two points on the earth and the difference in the angle at which the sun hit them enables one to calculate the planet's circumference. An especially interesting fact for readers is the difficulty of calculating the distance between points long before the days of cars with odometers. After discovering that travel rates for camels were too erratic to provide an accurate measure, Eratosthenes borrowed the king's surveyors, who were trained to walk with consistent-length steps.

A longer book on measurement, notable for its comprehensiveness, is *Keeping Time* (Branley, 1993). The former head of the Hayden Planetarium answers questions about time and timekeeping. These topics discussed range from the pre-clock era of sun and seasons to a remarkably clear explanation of why the theory of relativity predicts that passengers in high-speed spaceships will age more slowly than those they leave behind on earth. Many of Jill Weber's excellent illustrations carry valuable information, ranging from how to make clocks to how the International Date Line works. Time is an especially rich subject for mathematical explanation because it involves the interaction of human needs and capacities with the unchanging realities of the physical world. For instance, defining noon as the time the sun is directly overhead created a dilemma in designing timetables for trains traveling between distant locations. So, time zones were established.

Finding the Mathematics in Other Nonfiction Books

Other nonfiction books lend themselves to mathematical study. Mathematical content is often embedded within books on other topics. For example, Joanna Cole's *Large as Life* animal books (1985a, 1985b; also available in a single-volume version, 1990) use a large format to portray animals' actual sizes. These are especially intriguing to children since animals are usually shown in scaled-down format. Although primarily an avenue for learning about the animals, these books suggest classroom activities such as making life-sized models of animals. A similar book, *The Life-size Animal Counting Book* (van Noorden, 1994), may appeal to children who are too old for counting books. It begins with one life-sized gorilla's head and paws and progresses to greater numbers of smaller animals, up to 100 creepy crawlers.

Magnification (Norden & Ruschak, 1993) uses electron microscope photographs to help readers see animals and objects too small to be seen with the naked eye. These representations are larger than life-sized, and much of the fun of this pop-up and lift-the-flap book lies in trying to guess what odd creatures and structures we are seeing. For example, what looks like the bark of a palm tree is actually a human hair magnified 1,500 times. The mathematical value lies in the precision of information. We are told exactly how many times each item is magnified. This data enables us to compare the relative size of hair and eyelashes, or to imagine similar enlargements of things we can see.

Mathematics is often evident in history. *Anno's Medieval World* (Anno, 1980) tells how human beliefs about the nature of the world changed from medieval to Renaissance times, and in particular from a Ptolemaic to a Copernican viewpoint. Anno uses ingenious visual devices depicting people at the beginning of the book on a perfectly flat expanse of land that gradually takes on the curvature of the spherical earth, eventually turning into a globe. Although the story is about the history of science, both the illustrations and information in the afterword about the orbits of the solar system help readers to understand that perceptions may be misleading about underlying geometrical reality. This information places geometry in the context of human thought and comprehension.

An excellent example of embedded mathematics is *Ten Mile Day and the Building of the Transcontinental Railroad* (Fraser, 1993). It examines a small piece of American history, the day when the builders of the Transcontinental Railroad met the challenge of laying an unprecedented 10 miles of track in one day. Included are the number of workers, the rate at which track was laid, and the total number of rails, spikes, nuts, and bolts used. Although this book is about social history, it is also about the history of technology, and technology usually involves mathematics. Readers who look for numbers will find them throughout, including the endpapers that show not only a map of the Transcontinental Railroad and of the track from the 10-mile day, but they will also find an elevation map of the railroad's route. This mathematical content enables readers to deepen their understanding of both this event and of technological feats in general. Encourage students to scale models and research similar ventures like the building of the interstate highway system.

Books on history, science, and technology often contain mathematical content and provide excellent opportunities to appreciate mathematics in its human context. Such books are more likely to be read in connection with the science and social studies curriculum than in conjunction with the study of the embedded mathematical concepts, but this doesn't mean the mathematical content should be ignored. Three excellent avenues for exploiting the mathematical content of general nonfiction books are integrating mathematical ideas into content area units of study, using nonfiction books to enrich mathematics units, and developing thematic units that have a strong mathematical component and go beyond traditional curriculum topics.

Seymour Simon's *Oceans* (1990), one of his many picture book explorations on earth science, uses a variety of photographs, maps, and diagrams to demonstrate the role oceans play in the life of the planet. After sharing the book, do a number hunt with students through its pages. The teacher might ask how many numbers can be found that help us learn about oceans, and do we understand them? The first two numbers alone are fascinating. Seventy percent of the earth's surface is covered by oceans, which can be verified by looking at a globe. The ocean floor has mountains twice as tall as Mt. Everest. Students might be helped to understand this concept by comparing the height of Everest to the height of the tallest building they know. Since many of the numbers in *Oceans* relate to measurement, it can be included as part of a measurement unit in mathematics. For example, Simon writes about how in some places tides rise and fall only a few inches a day, while in parts of the Bay of Fundy there may be a 50-foot difference. Students could measure these distances in the school hallway and also discuss measurements for tides if they live near a coast. Using a variety of nonfiction books, a thematic unit on "Highs and Lows" could be an opportunity to explore extremes of height, tides, and other phenomena.

For older students, use *Panama Canal: Gateway to the World* (St. George, 1989) to investigate mathematical topics in a variety of ways. Understanding the mathematics of building the canal helps children to understand the grandeur of this project in terms of both cost and engineering. Students can identify the most interesting numbers in the book. A class exploring multiplication might find it useful to convert some of the dollar amounts in this book to today's values. For example, in 1903, Panama was paid $10,000,000 for the rights to build a canal, and the canal's chief engineer was paid $25,000 a year (which interestingly was the second-highest government salary). Both this book and *Ten Mile Day and the Building of the Transcontinental Railroad* fit well into a thematic unit on great technological feats. Learning about massive projects like the canal is an opportunity to explore not only many aspects of mathematics but scientific and social history as well.

Conclusions

Good mathematical nonfiction books for children are not typically found from quickly looking at the mathematics shelf in the library or bookstore. However, plenty of material is available if we expand our search to include books on broad mathematical topics or other topics in which mathematics is embedded by the nature of the subject matter. As with other children's books on specialized topics, book reviews by subject matter specialists (e.g., in professional journals such as *Teaching Children Mathematics*) can help classroom teachers and librarians assess high-quality books. In addition to the usual criteria for good nonfiction, it is crucial that mathematical content be made interesting and accessible, since there is more potential for dryness and boredom than with many other topics. Two avenues seem the most profitable ways of accomplishing this: getting in touch with the natural wonder and excitement of mathematics and finding the mathematics in curricular topics that are of great interest to children.

References

National Council of Teachers of Mathematics (NCTM). (1989). *Curriculum and evaluation standards for school mathematics.* Reston, VA: National Council of Teachers of Mathematics.

Teaching children mathematics. A publication of the National Council of Teachers of Mathematics, 1906 Association Drive, Reston, VA 22091.

Thiessen, D., & Matthias, M. (Eds.). (1992). *The wonderful world of mathematics.* Reston, VA: National Council of Teachers of Mathematics.

Whitin, D. J., & Wilde, S. (1992). *Read any good math lately? Children's books for mathematical learning.* Portsmouth, NH: Heinemann.

Whitin, D. J., & Wilde, S. (1995). *It's the story that counts: More children's books for mathematical learning K-6.* Portsmouth, NH: Heinemann.

CHAPTER 9
CREATING POSSIBILITIES, DEEPENING APPRECIATION: NONFICTION LITERATURE TO STUDY THE ARTS

by Barbara Kiefer

A friend and I recently visited the Guggenheim Museum in New York City to view works by 20th-century painter Ellsworth Kelly. We looked at the massive canvases—a brilliantly pure square of vermilion, joined panels of black and white rectangles, a curving fan of ultramarine blue. My friend turned to me with a slightly perplexed look and asked, "Now, why is this art?"

It wasn't a stupid question, nor a simplistic one. It leads us into the realm of aesthetics and asks us to grapple with issues that have confounded scholars and philosophers for centuries. Elliott Eisner (Brandt, 1988) has said that aesthetics asks the question "What is art and what do I know about it?"(p. 6). These questions must remain central to our thinking as we evaluate nonfiction books about the arts for children and plan curricula that will lead children to explore their own answers in significant ways.

The arts are generally defined as the graphic arts (drawing, painting, sculpture, ceramics, and architecture), music, dance, theater, and literature. Significant works in the arts represent what Suzanne Langer (1957) called life symbols, "the logic of consciousness itself" (p. 26). Our responses to them are highly complex and difficult to summarize. As Purves and Beach (1972), said of literary response,

> Response consists of cognition, perception, and some emotional or attitudinal reaction; it involves predispositions; it changes during the course of reading; it persists and is modified after the work has been read; it may result in moification of concepts, attitudes or feelings. (p. 178)

Substitute the words "the experience" for the word "reading" and the definition holds equally well for other art forms.

Each individual's experience with a work of art may be affected by social and cultural considerations. For example, a musical work may be more meaningful when experienced or performed in the company of others. Chinese Opera may seem less pleasing to an audience that is used to different cultural definitions of musical form. Our knowledge of history, elements, and techniques of an art form can influence our encounter with it. Familiarity with historical styles or an artist's personal story may also affect our perception of a work. Finally, because, as human beings, we change and grow over time, there is a potential for our aesthetic experience with a work of art to change, to grow, to deepen with subsequent encounters.

Langer and others have argued that the arts are basic human symbols for representing meaning and, as such, may predate discursive language. In children, we may find the evolution of the arts as mediums of expression recreated with each new generation. Infant cries may be early expressions of musical forms with pitch, rhythm, stress, and juncture meant to convey the very essence of their life force and their need to survive. Babies' movements and gestures are exploratory as well as informative, and once they can grasp a crayon (or a tube of lipstick), no adult has to urge children to explore visual possibilities on a piece of paper or a wall. They build happily with blocks or sticks. They construct sculpture out of found objects. They return to a favorite story again and again. Dramatic play is a basic way of knowing for the preschooler. It is clear that young children are as passionately and wholly engaged by the arts (perhaps more so) as they are by exploring the natural world.

Can the products young children create be called works of art? Are children capable of experiencing aesthetic responses? These questions will have to be left to other forums. However, in this chapter I will argue that children's experiences with the arts form the basis for building artistic creation and aesthetic understanding, just as the language competencies they bring to school settings are the foundations on which they develop literacy. The classroom context for such learning must be one that provides continuing opportunities for engaging with the arts, for learning about techniques relating to various art forms, and for deepening understanding of critical and historical perspectives on the arts. Discipline-Based Art Education, a program developed by Elliott Eisner and The Getty Foundation, is one such approach to arts education that seeks to involve children in art production, art criticism, art history, and aesthetics (Brandt, 1988). Howard Gardner and his colleagues at Harvard Project Zero have developed alternative programs with similar aims (Burton, Lederman, & London, 1988; Gardner, 1988). Elementary and Middle School classroom teachers who develop curricular studies around literature-based themes can also plan to use the arts to explore topics and identify learning (Pappas, Kiefer, and Levstik, 1995). In these and other well-developed arts programs good nonfiction books about the arts can play a vital role.

Kinds of Nonfiction About the Arts

Nonfiction books about the arts take many forms. Books may simply introduce children to an art, focus on developing appreciation of an art, provide a historical or cultural perspective on the arts, or connect styles of an art through themes. Many titles are profiles or biographies of creators or performers, while other books explain techniques and/or basic elements that comprise a particular art form. A survey of the *Subject Guide To Books In Print* show that the majority of publications for children seem to focus on the visual arts, perhaps because the medium of the book makes it possible to reproduce pictures of paintings, sculpture, architecture, and drawings.

There are fewer works on the other arts, however. We may find some nonfiction books about the literary arts such as biographies and profiles of authors or books about bookmaking, but most often we take it for granted that the literary work itself serves to teach children about the aesthetics of literature. However, authors of informational books on music, dance, and the theater, because of the nature of these art forms, may find it more difficult to engage children directly with the art experience. These authors may show photographs of symphony orchestras playing, reproduce musical notation of a song, or provide examples of dancers in various poses. They may create rhythm and movement in the design of each page and layout of the book. However, they cannot replicate the sensory aspects of a live musical, dramatic, or dance performance within the two-dimensional pages of a book. Thus, nonfiction books about music, dance, and theater seem to fall most often in the categories of history, biography, or profile. Many books on music such as Wynton Marsalis's *Marsalis On Music* (1995) now include compact discs, and the advent of CD-ROM makes it more likely that in the future the printed word will combine with computer graphics and animation to engage children more directly with the experience of a performance.

Of course, even books on the visual arts have their limitations. Books cannot show the size of a painting, sculpture, or building, nor can they present children with the three-dimensional qualities of constructed art forms or the textures of materials such as stone or metal or oil paint. With these limitations in mind, we can proceed to survey some of the many wonderful information books on the arts for children. In the remainder of the chapter, I will discuss the types of nonfiction books that teachers might include as part of the curriculum and at the same time highlight key qualities to look for in nonfiction books about the arts. Finally, I will briefly suggest some ways to organize classroom studies in the arts.

Beginning Books

The best books for young readers may simply engage children with the art forms and elements rather than try to teach them about principles, techniques, or history. In particular, early exposure to visual images in books can make a profound impression on babies and toddlers, educating their eyes to differing styles, cultural norms, and historical methods of depicting (Butler, 1980). We know the interaction that takes place between parent and baby over the pages of a good book is the single most important factor in language and literacy learning. It may be an important introduction to the world of fine arts as well. Early experiences with a variety of images could stay with children for years, mediating, perhaps, the preference for realism that seems to overtake children in the late middle grades.

Lucy Micklethwait has created several series of visual art books for young children that will attract their attention and engage them with the world of painting. Her "I Spy" series is perfect for engendering interaction between baby and adult. Her first book, *I Spy: An Alphabet in Art* (1992) has been followed by *I Spy a Lion: Animals in Art* (1993), *I Spy: Two Eyes: Numbers in Art* (1994), and *I Spy a Freight Train: Transportation in Art* (1996). The books are all attractively designed with inviting covers, bright endpapers, and glossy paper that allows for faithful reproduction of the paintings included. In each double-page spread the phrase, "I spy with my little eye..." invites children to hunt for an object in the reproduction of a painting placed opposite. The alphabet book, for example, asks the child to find something beginning with the letter E in an Indian miniature dating from the late 16th century. Most of the objects to be found are fairly common in the young child's world, and if the child is too young to make the connection between letters and beginning sounds, the adult reader can supply the object to look for. The *I Spy a Freight Train* includes a rowboat in Vasily Kandinsky's "The Birds," a wagon in Van Gogh's "The Langlois Drawbridge," and a car in Mel Ramos's "Batmobile." A key in the back of the book provides parents with the answers (just in case their eyes aren't as sharp as their child's) and also provides brief information about each painting. Young children's delight in this type of visual game serves as a way of drawing their attention to details in paintings.

Micklethwait's *A Child's Book of Art: Great Pictures, First Words* (1993), and *A Child's Book of Play in Art* (1996) are formatted on a much larger scale. A trim size of 11 X 14 inches allows the placement of more reproductions on each page without sacrificing clarity of detail. This approach allows the author to make explicit comparisons of artistic styles that were introduced in the "I Spy" books. In both books, each double-page spread provides several reproductions of paintings that follow categories, statements, or questions such as "At Home," or "Where Will We Live?" Several reproductions are provided to illustrate each statement or question. Unlike the previous titles, these books provide guidance to parents and teachers in a two-page introduction and a note section that includes the painting's original media, its dimensions, its title and date, and the dates of the artist's birth and death. Although aimed at younger audiences, Micklethwait's books can be used with any age group. All these titles will inspire, delight, and invite readers of all ages to take time to relish, explore, and talk about visual art.

Inviting Exploration of the Arts

Some nonfiction books seek to involve children with the arts directly, providing information about the elements of an art form, suggesting activities and projects that children can do on their own, or introducing the steps in training for performance. *Color Sampler* (Westray, 1993) is an excellent introduction to the element of color. Westray uses combinations of simple geometric shapes to introduce primary, secondary, and intermediate colors, tints, and shades to build understanding of how color schemes affect perception and feelings. The shapes are taken from American quilt patterns and provide both a sample book of quilt designs and a lively introduction to color theory.

Going to My Ballet Class (Kuklin, 1989) shows young children what they can expect if they wish to undertake formal instruction in an art form. For children wondering about taking lessons, the first-person narration by little Jami is both appealing and reassuring. The brief text and large clear photographs of a class of young boys and girls provide clear explana-

BOOKS THAT INVITE
EXPLORATION

An Introduction to Watercolor by Ray Smith

Join the Band by Marjorie Pillar

Perspective by Alison Cole

Twins on Toes: A Ballet Debut by Joan Anderson

tions of the different positions and movements that dancers learn, inviting students to try these on their own. A note for parents at the end of the book explains the teacher's philosophy of movement exploration and suggests ways for them to choose the right ballet class for their child.

The best hands-on books should invite children to explore materials and investigate their world rather than direct them in what to do. Often hands-on books dictate ideas rather than invite imaginative creation. In other cases, some hands-on books look beautifully simple but demand more skill than young children may possess. For example, instructions for making musical instruments require more knowledge of acoustics and harmonic scales than children may have acquired. An instrument that looks nice but sounds terrible may be disappointing and defeat that purpose of helping children to appreciate art.

Art Appreciation Books

Many excellent nonfiction books on the arts serve to introduce basic understandings about an art form, a historical period, or a cultural style. Two of the best of these have been written by Phillip Isaacson. *Round Buildings, Square Buildings and Buildings That Wiggle Like a Fish* (1988) is an introduction to architecture for middle graders and up. *A Short Walk around the Pyramids and Through the World of Art* (1993) provides an overview of visual art theory and lays a firm foundation for further exploration of art history and styles. Both books could serve as models of good expository writing, clarity of message, and beautiful book design. The size of the books, 10 X 9 1/2 inches, their layout, and the high quality of paper and reproductions are as pleasing as the way in which Isaacson's ideas are presented, which underscore the very concepts he is discussing. The photographs and reproductions of the art works are placed with the accompanying text and so they need no captions, which would have cluttered up the harmonious page design. For those who want more information, an explanation for each reproduction is given in more detail in the book's back matter.

Isaacson begins *A Short Walk around the Pyramids and Through the World of Art* with a large picture of the Step Pyramid of King Zoser in Egypt, inviting the reader into the book to admire this ancient form. He then takes us to great pyramids at Giza and writes of these forms with a sense of awe.

> They seem too large to have been made by human beings, too perfect to have been formed by nature, and, when the sun is overhead, not solid enough to be attached to the sand (plate 3). In the minutes before sunrise, they are the color of faded roses (plate 4), and when the last rays of the desert sun touch them they turn to amber (plate 5). But whatever the light, their broad proportions, the beauty of the limestone, and the care with which it is fitted into place create three unforgettable works of art. (pp. 5-7)

The accompanying photos, showing the essence of these simple shapes against a desert sky, capture Isaacson's sense of wonder.

By beginning with photographs of familiar shapes, Isaacson leads readers into understandings about visual representation, helps us to see our world with an artist's eye, and shows how we can all be captivated by some aspect of visual experience. He then goes on to explain, clearly and simply, why these structures are works of art. Subsequent chapters on "Sculpture," "Color," "Images," "Photographs," "Useful Things," and "Towns and Cities" are built upon the concepts he introduces in the first chapter, concepts that underlie the creation of all works of visual art. By linking the discussion of disparate visual art objects back to the pyramids he makes strong connections between art and the visual world. He also helps us to see the logical progression of artistic styles from the forms of the pyramids to the massive canvases of the abstract expressionists, from centuries-old buildings to massive city skyscrapers.

Jan Greenberg and Sandra Jordan build nicely on Isaacson's general introduction to visual art in *The Painter's Eye* (1991), *The Sculptor's Eye* (1993), and *The American Eye* (1995), three books about 20th-century art. These books also help us to understand that the artist doesn't try to reproduce the world but to transform it, conveying what painter Ellsworth Kelly refers to as the "rapture of seeing" (Cotter, 1996, p 43). Like Isaacson's books, *The Painter's Eye: Learning to Look at Contemporary Art*, the first book of the three, sets forth basic concepts about modern art and then builds upon them in subsequent chapters. The chapter titles such as "New Art and Frankenstein's Monster" have great child appeal but also outline the premise of the book. In chapters such as "The Language of Art," "What does It all Mean Anyway?", and

OTHER BOOKS ABOUT VISITS WITH AUTHORS

Henry Moore: From Bones and Stones to Sketches and Sculptures by Jane Mylum Gardner

Introducing Picasso by Julie Heslewood

A Weekend with Rousseau by Giles Plazy

A Weekend with Degas by Rosabianca Skira-Venturi

A Weekend with Leonardo by Rosabianca Skira-Venturi

A Weekend with Rembrandt by Pascal Bonafoux

A Weekend with Renoir by Rosabianca Skira-Venturi

A Weekend with Van Gogh by Rosabianca Skira-Venturi

A Young Painter: The Life and Paintings of Wang Yani—China's Extraordinary Young Artist by Z. Zhensun and A. Low

"Putting It All Together," Greenberg and Jordan support generalizations about modern art with details and help us understand the highly complex world of 20th-century visual art. *The Sculptor's Eye* and *The American Eye* provide a closer look at 20th-century sculpture and American art of this century. In all three books the high quality of the reproductions of original art, photographs of artists at work, quotes from artists, and the detailed back matter to help deepen our appreciation and may help to answer the common question, "Now, why is this art?"

Readers introduced to the concepts and understandings in these fine nonfiction books will certainly want to explore other books about the arts and to look for the connections underlying these different ways of knowing. These and other titles can help extend our understandings and deepen appreciation by creating the possibility that each new experience with an art form is richer and more satisfying than the one before.

Profiles and Biographies

Another way to deepen understandings of an art form may be to connect children directly with its creators and performers. Well-written and instructive biographies or profiles are available for many ages and cover most of the arts. Often these books seek to link the child reader to the artist through an imaginary child character who knows the artist. *Linnea in Monet's Garden* (1985) by Christina Björk was one of the first to do this and its success (witness a Linnea doll, gardening book, and almanac) has been followed by several similar series.

Beethoven Lives Upstairs (1993) by Barbara Nichol is an account of the last years of Beethoven's life told through fictionalized letters between a 10-year-old neighbor boy and his uncle. Like Linnea, young Christoph, a music student, is a fully realized character with his own story that will connect to young readers. Our sympathies are totally engaged as we first meet Christoph who is agonizing over his father's death and complaining to his uncle about Ludwig Von Beethoven, the crazy man who lives upstairs. Then as the boy comes to know and respect this troubled genius the reader does also. The climax of the book comes as Christoph writes about his attendance at the first performance of the Ninth Symphony. His awe and passion are evident in his words:

> I cannot describe the music, Uncle. I can only tell you what the music made me feel.
>
> Uncle, how difficult Mr. Beethoven's life must be. To feel so much inside, even so much joy, must be almost more than he can bear. (unpaged)

Although the book is fictionalized biography it serves as a good introduction to Beethoven's life and times. Christoph's profound excitement in the middle of the night as he struggles to write the letter may be the book's true strength for it may give children information about the rich possibilities inherent in an aesthetic experience. The simple picture book format and the glowing illustrations by Scott Cameron are in keeping with the emotional qualities of the story, and they reinforce Suzanne Langer's (1957) argument that in a work of art "feeling is conceived, formulated and presented" (p. 113).

African-American painter Morgan Monceaux uses words and paintings to personalize his passion for jazz in *Jazz: My Music, My People* (1994). The book, a collection of 41 vignettes about jazz musicians and singers, begins with Buddy Bolden and W. C. Handy who worked in the late 1800s and early 1900s and ends with modern-day legends Lena Horn and Johnetta. This is a book about what made these men and women jazz musicians rather than a book about what jazz is. Monceaux portrays each artist as a unique individual often weaving his own personal life experiences into their stories. He also creates "jazzy" visual portraits of each musician using mixed media collage and words (much as artist and author Faith Ringgold includes written narrative into her story quilts). Along with the expressionistic portraits, Monceaux also includes abstract paintings that are full of vivid color, contrasting values, and high energy. Taken together, the art, words, and the overall design of the book convey the lively essence of this unique musical form. Monceaux provides an important glimpse of African-American culture and helps us to understand the essential characteristics of their music, a broad overview that locates jazz in the stream of history.

Kathleen Krull has written an engaging series of lively books that introduce children to the human quirks and qualities of famous artists (1995), musicians (1993), and writers. All of the books feature brief profiles, each accompanied by a delightful caricature by illustrator Kathryn Hewitt. In *Lives of the Writers: Comedies, Tragedies (And What the Neighbors Thought)* (1993), we learn that Jack London loved to put on boxing gloves and go a few rounds with his wife Charmian, to fly kites, and to ride bicycles. We also find out that Zora Neale Hurston *always* wore hats, loved to travel, and once borrowed a coin from a beggar's cup for a subway fare. Although these aren't necessarily the facts found in the usual nonfiction books, they help to highlight the personality of each artist. The books also prove to children that famous creators are not always perfect and sometimes are perfectly awful.

Pat Cummings has provided similar insights into the lives of illustrators of children's books in two volumes of *Talking with Artists* (1992). Illustrators such as Victoria Chess, Denise Fleming, Brian Pinkney, Chris Van Allsburg, and Vera B. Williams respond to Cummings' questions and reflect upon their current work as well as their childhood memories. Each profile is accompanied by examples of the illustrator's childhood art as well as his or her current work.

These personalized profiles are natural introductions to more traditional biographies of art makers. Women's contributions to the visual arts are recognized in several accessible books for middle school children. *Inspirations: Stories About Women Artists* (1989) and *Visions: Stories About Women Artists* (1993), both by Leslie Sills, and *Focus: Five Women Photographers* (1994) by Sylvia Wolf are fine introductions to the stories of women who excelled in the arts. Robyn Montana Turner has written short biographies of such artists as *Rosa Bonheur* (1991), *Mary Cassatt* (1992), *Frida Kahlo* (1993), *Dorothea Lange* (1994), and *Georgia O'Keefe* (1991). Illustrated with photographs and many reproductions of each artist's work, these books offer important insights into each artist's approach to her work as well as details about her life. Mary E. Lyons has developed a fine series of books about African-American artists including painters Bill Traylor and Horace Pippin, quilt maker Harriet Jacobs, and woodworker and carpenter Tom Day. Through words and pictures, Lyons gives readers glimpses of social history, fascinating details about the lives of these artists, and information about the links each of them had to their African heritage.

For older children there are many profiles or biographies that address an artist's life and times, style, and method of work. Books such as Lou Ann Walker's *Roy Lichtenstein: The Artist at Work* (1994) or Wendy Thompson's *Claude Debussy* (1993), one of the "Composer's World" series, provide more detailed accounts of an artist's life and times. Middle school and high school students with a serious interest in the arts, will find books such as Beverly Gherman's *Agnes DeMille, Dancing off the Earth* (1990) engaging and inspiring. The best of these books help readers to understand the "how-to" of art making as well as the "why" of a particular art form.

Whatever the format of the presentation, or whether the author's purpose is to simply highlight an artist's work or to cover the person in depth, the best of these biographies should help children understand that no matter what the form, a work of art is an expression of the artist's idea, as Langer (1953) states:

> ...something that takes shape as he articulates an envisagement of realities which discursive language cannot properly express. What he makes is primarily a symbol to capture and hold his own imagination of organized feeling, the rhythms of life, the forms of emotion. (p. 392)

Themes in Art

One of the aims of nonfiction books on the arts should be to help children understand that an artist, musician, dancer, or poet is trying to convey profound human experiences and understandings in ways that cannot be expressed by words and sentences alone. Nonfiction books that focus on a theme rather than on an art, artist, or historical period, may help children grasp this concept more readily. Several series about visual art are based around themes common to childhood. The Millbrook Art Library includes *Nature in Art* (1991), *People in Art* (1991), *Places in Art* (1991), all by Anthea Peppin, and *Stories in Art* (1991) by Helen Williams—all titles that make connections among artists across cultures and centuries. For example, *Places in Art* shows how the artist is affected by special places including his or her studio, and how artists have represented place and created space on two-dimensional canvases. All the books include color reproductions, diagrams, and pictures of materials that invite children to try expressing the theme in their own work. Short biographies of some of the artists and an index are included in the back matter. These

OTHER PROFILES OR BIOGRAPHIES

Giotto and Medieval Painting by Lucia Corrain

E. B. White: Some Writer by Beverly Gherman

Painting Dreams: Minnie Evans, Visionary Artist by Mary E. Lyons

Mary Cassatt by Susan E. Meyer

What Makes a Bruegel a Bruegel? by Richard Mühlberger

Leonardo DaVinci by Diane Stanley

Wolfgang Amadeus Mozart by Wendy Thompson

The Ingenious Mr. Peale by Janet Wilson

books all connect children to styles of art and artists' many unique ways of seeing.

Other books cut across art forms, creating strong links between poetry, music, literature, and visual art. *Singing America: Poems that Define a Nation* (1995) by Neil Philip combines poetry, song lyrics, and hymns with elegant scratchboard illustrations by Michael McCurdy to give children an artistic tour of American history. Alan Axelrod brings together a collection of prose, songs, and paintings in *Songs of the Wild West* (1991), and he provides a view of a unique time and place in America's past. In books such as *Children of Promise: African American Literature and Art for Young People* (1992) and *Here is My Kingdom: Hispanic-American Literature and Art for Young People* (1994), author Charles Sullivan has developed especially powerful connections across the arts for older readers. In addition to celebrating the artistic contributions of many cultures and subcultures, Sullivan's books and others like them encourage children and young adults to make their own connections to art and among the arts.

The Arts in the Classroom

Although this chapter has addressed nonfiction books on the arts, good fiction and poetry can also extend children's understanding and appreciation of the arts. Music educator Michael Nord (1996) prefers to use books such as Chris Raschka's *Charlie Parker Played Be-Bop* (1992) to introduce children to the world of music and music making. Dance educator and choreographer Barbara Basho argues that books should inspire children to create their own problem solving through dance, inviting them to move from a quiet time to a creating time. To engage young children with movement and dance Basho (In Press) suggests a story making and dance curriculum using books such as Nikki Giovanni's *The Genie in the Jar* (1996) or Carole Lexa Schaefer's *The Squiggle* (1996).

Whatever the age of the student, whatever the topics or concepts under study in a classroom, arts educators generally agree that children should have as many opportunities to respond to their learning through art, music, drama, and dance as they do through talking and writing. The many types of nonfiction books about the fine arts discussed here certainly have a contribution to make to classroom studies, especially when combined with firsthand experiences in the arts and art makers and the many excellent works of fiction about the arts.

Teachers who have no formal training in the arts do not need to be afraid to make books and materials available in the classroom and to explore the arts with their students. Teachers can demonstrate their own exploration of the arts just as they share their struggles and experiences with reading and writing. Often school or district arts specialists or local arts associations are more than pleased to team up with classroom teachers to plan a curriculum that will extend and deepen children's aesthetic response and enhance their learning.

Teachers may want to plan a special unit that concentrates on a single art form such as "Music," "Poetry," or the "The Art of the Picture Book". But broader themes are worth exploring for their potential to center the arts in the everyday life of the classroom rather than only highlight an art form once a year. Themes such as "Spaces and Places," "Time," "Sounds All Around," and "Explorations"(see Pappas, Kiefer, and Levstik, 1995) could take children beyond the question of "Why is this art?" to ask "What do I see? How does it make me feel? What does it mean? How am I changed?"

Conclusions

Children's literature can help readers reflect on and generate similar questions about the arts. Good nonfiction books also can aid teachers in planning curricula that will lead children to explore their own answers to these questions in significant ways.

The best of these books will engage readers with the arts and deepen understandings of critical and historical perspectives. The books should involve children in the "how-to" of art making as well as the "why" of a particular art form, and help them to make personal connections across time and across art forms. Whatever the format of the presentation or the author's purpose, books should give children information about the rich possibilities inherent in an aesthetic experience.

In nonfiction books about the arts, the book's design is as important as the quality of the author's writing. The format of the book should express the emotional qualities of an art experience as much as the written text conveys the facts about an art form. As previ-

BOOKS TO HELP IN THEMATIC PLANNING

Cities: Through the Eyes of Artists by Wendy Richardson and Jack Richardson

Colors by Phillip Yenawine

Dancers by Peggy Roalf

Families by Peggy Roalf

Imaginary Gardens: American Poetry and Art for Young People by Charles Sullivan

Lines by Phillip Yenawine

People by Phillip Yenawine

Places by Phillip Yenawine

Shapes by Phillip Yenawine

Stories by Phillip Yenawin

ously discussed in Chapter 4, books should be attractively designed with inviting covers, endpapers, and high-quality paper that allows for clarity of reproduction and detail. Indexes, glossaries, and author's notes are important, and diagrams and other graphic organizers should help readers to understand art elements, processes, and qualities of a specific art experience.

Maxine Greene (1995) argues that we should provide children with situations "where there are always the possibilities of new clearings, new openings...if we want to awaken them to their lived situations and enable them to make sense of and to name their worlds"(p. 150). By giving children opportunities to know their world through many art forms and by providing them with books of all types, we may truly cement the arts as life foundations.

References

Basho, B. (In Press). Spotlight on dance. *Dance Education.*

Brandt, R. (1988). On discipline-based art education: A conversation with Elliott Eisner. *Educational Leadership, 45,* 6-9.

Burton, J., Lederman, A., & London, P. (Eds.). (1988). *Beyond DBAE: The case for multiple visions of arts education.* North Dartmouth, MA: University Council on the Arts.

Butler, D. (1980). *Cushla and her books.* Boston, MA: The Horn Book Co.

Cotter, H. (1996, October 13). A giant of the new surveys his rich past. *The New York Times,* Section H, p. 43.

Gardner, H. (1988). Towards more effective arts education. *Journal of Aesthetic Education, 22,* 157-167.

Greene, M. (1995). *Releasing the imagination: Essays on education, the arts, and social change.* San Francisco, CA: Jossey-Bass.

Langer, S. K. (1953). *Feeling and form.* New York: Charles Scribner & Sons.

Langer, S. K. (1957). *Problems of art: The philosophical lectures.* New York: Scribner's.

Nord, M. (1996). Personal communication.

Pappas, C., Kiefer, B., & Levstik, L. (1995). *An integrated language perspective in the elementary school* (2nd ed.). White Plains, NY: Longman.

Purves, A. & Beach, R. (1972). *Literature and the reader: Research in response to literature, reading interests, and the teaching of literature.* Urbana, IL: National Council of Teachers of English.

Also see:

For information on Discipline-Based Arts Education, ArtsEdNet URL: http//www.artsednet.getty.edu

For dance literature prepared for the child contact—chldnslit@aol.com

Part III

Quality Nonfiction Literature: What Happens When Students and Books Come Together?

What are some effective ways for bringing nonfiction literature and children together? Are there particularly good starting places for integrating nonfiction literature at different grade levels? What challenges do nonfiction literature present to young readers? These and other questions about nonfiction use will be explored in Part III. In Chapter 10, Sylvia Vardell presents a persuasive argument for using read-aloud as an effective way to investigate all the many rich layers of high-quality nonfiction. Yvonne Siu-Runyan discusses how children need opportunities to explore and write about topics they are passionate about. She also discusses how nonfiction can be a model for students' own expository writing in Chapter 11. In Chapter 12, Linda Levstik explores learning as a process of inquiry and the place of nonfiction in investigating the issues that really matter to students.

The last three chapters highlight the use of nonfiction in a variety of classroom settings. Carol Avery, in Chapter 13, discusses the successful use of nonfiction literature in her primary classroom. In Chapter 14, Donna Maxim describes what happens when science, children, and lots of good nonfiction come together in the intermediate classroom. Starting with students' experiences, interests, and inquiries, Jeffrey Wilhelm, in the closing chapter, writes about the potential of good nonfiction to "smash the frozen seas within" so the "magic called LEARNING can happen."

CHAPTER 10
USING READ-ALOUD TO EXPLORE THE LAYERS OF NONFICTION

by Sylvia M. Vardell

Think for a moment about the board books and toy books we share with babies and very young children. When a little one curls up on your lap with a book in hand, what kind of book is it? Quite often this little cardboard book is full of pictures of objects with labels or scenes of everyday life to identify and discuss. Less often do these "first" books provide long story narratives to read aloud and simply listen to. Much of the literature we first share with children before they come to school is indeed nonfiction. These simple board books show photographs or information about the everyday life of the child—dog, toy, bed, cup, etc. Sometimes these objects are organized along topical lines, such as items of clothing, means of transportation, kinds of animals, etc. In each instance, the intent is to provide young "readers" with information about the world around them. Beginning with familiar images, early books provide an opportunity for children to see literature as a vehicle for understanding their surroundings, for finding answers to their questions.

There is even a growing body of nonfiction picture books designed particularly for the very young child. One example from Japan is the popular *Everyone Poops* by Taro Gomi (1993). In a very matter-of-fact way, this bodily function is presented in a way any child can comprehend. Because the topic is so important to the 2- to 3-year-old, this nonfiction book is bound to stimulate discussion. For a look at different kinds of jobs and the tools required for them, consider *Who Uses This?* by Margaret Miller (1990). With giant letters, bold color photographs, and a question-answer approach, she introduces a juggler, carpenter, football player, baker, gardener, conductor, dog walker, barber, and artist. Nonfiction for young children includes many more outstanding titles, including many alphabet and counting books, as well as clear and focused concept books (Vardell, 1994). See Chapters 5 and 13 for discussion of nonfiction books for emerging and young readers.

Nonfiction appropriate for young readers can be found in a variety of formats including alphabet books, counting books, and concept books.

Count Your Way Through Mexico by Jim Haskins

The Icky Bug Counting Book by Jerry Pallotta

Of Colors and Things by Tana Hoban

The experience of reading such simple informational books is an excellent example of the dynamics for a read-aloud for sharing nonfiction literature. Adult and child pore over the illustrations together. Sometimes, the adult reads the labels or text, sometimes they simply identify the pictures or relate to the images together. "Dog." "Yes, that's a puppy like our little dog." "Do you see the puppy on the page? Can you point to the puppy's tail?" Sometimes the pair works methodically through the pages in sequence, but it is also possible to skip around as the child's interest dictates, noting objects and details that catch the eye. Reading such a book aloud is rarely a passive activity. Child and adult typically interact as they identify pictures, point out labels, and make connections between the images and the child's experiences in an overlapping dialog of reading and talking. This form of scaffolding or support seems to come naturally to many parents. As discussed in Chapter 5, it is a strategy that teachers can also employ as they allow children to openly explore and question their way through a new nonfiction trade book.

In reality, reading aloud nonfiction at any age level can be as spontaneous and interactive as these first book experiences. There is no reason why such an approach cannot be just as pleasurable and meaningful in the classroom or library as it is at the bedtime reading for preschoolers. For example, a teacher or librarian might "preview" a nonfiction book with the class, showing the incredible photographs that illustrate Carole G. Vogel's book *Shock Waves Through Los Angeles: The Northridge Earthquake* (1996) while inviting student commentary. "Wow, that apartment building looks like it's breaking in half." "Why would you guess that happened?" "Where is this?" "Where might you guess this is—based on what details?"

Unfortunately, adults often fall into the trap of believing that older children who are independent readers should be more systematic and thorough in their reading. They should proceed from beginning to end, reading every word. They should not look only at the pictures, and they should most certainly not read the ending first. A book like *Earthquakes*, however, may best be enjoyed by browsing through the pictures first to develop a visual understanding of the phenomenon before tackling the vocabulary and explanations describing it within the text.

The most basic and fundamental approach to sharing literature of all kinds with children has long been the practice of reading aloud. As was noted in the landmark study, *Becoming a Nation of Readers* (Anderson, Hiebert, Scott, & Wilkinson, 1985), "The single most important activity for building the knowledge required for eventual success in reading is reading aloud to children" (p. 23). Reading aloud nonfiction, however, rarely seems to occur. There seems to be a widespread, but unspoken understanding that fiction is for read-aloud time, and nonfiction is for research time. Perhaps this is due to the kinds of nonfiction that were published in the past or to the general adult assumption that children prefer stories. Yet, this view has now been refuted by several sources, including the work of Pappas (1991) and Doiron (1994). Choosing appropriate nonfiction, then, is based partly on student interest in the subject as well as on literary criteria relevant to nonfiction such as accuracy, organization, and style (Vardell, 1996; Vardell, 1991). See Chapters 2-5 for a more thorough discussion of the literary criteria appropriate to the nonfiction genre.

The key then to sharing nonfiction books out loud with children is twofold: we must expand our own knowledge base of the kinds of nonfiction available for children, and we must learn a variety of ways of sharing nonfiction orally with children. In this chapter, these two goals will be examined together. Ideas for reading aloud nonfiction will be shared along with recommended titles.

The first step to successfully sharing nonfiction in read-aloud sessions is to recognize that there are many ways to share books. The traditional approach of choosing a book and reading the entire text out loud from cover to cover (in one session or across several sessions) is only one way. It is still an excellent introduction to informational literature, and many examples of books will be presented for this method. With nonfiction, however, this is probably not the most typical approach for presenting informational literature. Quite honestly, most nonfiction books do not lend themselves to a cover-to-cover read-aloud. The concept density is simply too intense for one sitting. That is, students may be overwhelmed by the amount of new information and terminology presented in one book when presented with it all at once. Keep in mind, however, that many excellent works of fiction also do not lend themselves to being read aloud, but they are much more enjoyable when pored over individually in silent reading. Therefore, this chapter will provide examples of both traditional and non-traditional ways to read aloud nonfiction. This will include: cover-to-cover read-alouds, participatory read-alouds, chapter read-alouds, caption reading, browsing, believe-it-or-not sharing, and introducing structural elements through reading aloud. Examples of several excellent titles of nonfiction to use with each technique will also be shared.

Cover-to-Cover Read-Alouds for All Ages

There are probably two practical ways to share nonfiction books in their entirety during read-aloud sessions: as a "stand alone" high-quality work of literature or in conjunction with a particular unit of study. There are many works of nonfiction which are so well written and so beautifully designed that they come alive through the read-aloud experience. The best measure of this is to simply choose a page or paragraph and try it out loud beforehand. How does it feel and sound? Do the sentences feel overly long and complicated? Would quite a bit of explanation be necessary? Such a book is not ideal for reading aloud. If however, the language captures you, or the information (and perhaps the illustrations) "grab" you, then it might be a candidate for reading aloud. This may include picture books as well as lengthier titles that may be read over several sittings. Look to the winners (and the honor books) of the Orbis Pictus award for outstanding nonfiction for children. The Newbery, Caldecott, and Coretta Scott King award winners and honor books also include some titles of nonfiction that lend themselves to being read aloud.

A perfect exemplar of effective writing for a read-aloud is *Flight* by Robert Burleigh (1991). Don't let the picture book format of this book mislead you into thinking it's only appropriate in the primary grades. This true story will captivate listeners of all ages. In fact, nonfiction is a genre ideally suited to sharing across the grade levels since the content of the books offer new information not necessarily linked to particular grade levels. For example, did you know Charles Lindbergh flew with no radio or parachute (so he could accommodate extra fuel) and brought five chicken sandwiches with him that he didn't eat (so he wouldn't get sleepy)? Even adults learn something new from nonfiction books designed for the juvenile market. Listeners of all ages respond to the fascination of facts found in the best nonfiction literature.

Another excellent example of lyrical language for oral sharing is found in *Winter* by Ron Hirschi (1990) with phrases like "winter is weasel white" and "winter is a time for robins and sparrows to search for the last summer berries" (unpaged). Nature photographs add to the beauty of the whole. Or share Zack Rogow's *Oranges* (1988) with its methodical chronology and colorful drawings showing the production of oranges from the clearing of the fields to planting, grafting, irrigating, picking, hauling, selling, etc. "A world of work is in this ripe orange that I pry apart" ends the book (unpaged). What an opportunity to bring an orange to see and smell and taste after the read-aloud.

In fact, if the topic is food or food production, there are several excellent read-alouds to consider. And often linking books with units of study heightens students' interest in the text and provides the scaffolding necessary to process and understand new concepts and information. Teachers and librarians often find this approach successful because it helps insure a high level of motivation and comprehension. Two examples that fit easily into a unit in health, nutrition, or social studies are *Make Me a Peanut Butter Sandwich and a Glass of Milk* by Ken Robbins (1992) and *Extra Cheese, Please! Mozzarella's Journey from Cow to Pizza* by Cris Peterson (1994). Robbins' book could be read in three sittings: the process of making peanut butter, the making of bread from growing wheat to transporting the packaged bread to the store, and finally the manufacture of milk. Cris Peterson's account of her own dairy farm is full of fascinating details like: "Annabelle is quite a cow. In one year, she produces 40,000 glasses of milk, enough to make cheese for 1,800 pizzas. If your family ate one pizza a day, it would take you nearly five years to eat that many pizzas" (unpaged). It should be mentioned, however, that each of these books is so lively and interesting that they can stand alone as a read-aloud text without a unit context.

Each of the sections of Margy Burns Knight's *Talking Walls* (1992) and *Talking Walls: The Stories Continue* (1996) could stand alone as a read-aloud excerpt, but in combination they make a powerful statement about the similarities and differences among the world's peoples. These nonfiction picture books introduce famous wall landmarks from around the world with fascinating details and insights into what the walls tell us about each culture. From the Great Wall of China to the Berlin Wall, brief passages and colorful illustrations lend themselves beautifully to being read aloud. Additional historical notes for each wall are also included in the back for readers who want even more information. These would add even greater depth to a second read-aloud of the book. Just as children enjoy hearing favorite selections of fiction read aloud over and over again, don't be surprised by repeated requests for favorite nonfiction titles to be shared during read-aloud time. Each read-aloud session deepens the understanding and comprehension students have of the text. With some nonfiction texts, multiple readings may be essential to absorb all the layers of information and detail available in the text and illustrations, sidebars and boxes, captions and graphic aids.

Oyler and Barry (1996) describe an approach to reading aloud nonfiction that even encourages students to make connections to previous reading. During the read-aloud experience in their classroom, students often commented on how new information presented in the book connected with something they had read in another book. Rather than sidestep this digression, the teacher welcomed and encouraged the students' initiative in retrieving and sharing this remembered book and passage with the class. In this way, "classroom talk becomes an opportunity to construct shared understandings through the connections made visible by intertextuality" (p. 328). For example, a read-aloud of Ann Morris' *Houses and Homes* (1992) includes a mention of white houses with photographs of houses that are white as well as the White House in Washington, D.C. Noticing the latter may lead students to make connections to other sources of White House photographs such as a CD-ROM encyclopedia or another nonfiction text like Leonard Everett Fisher's *The White House* (1989).

Longer nonfiction works can also be shared during read-aloud time much as a novel is read aloud one chapter at a time over several days or weeks. This is especially useful for the intermediate grades where the sustained study of a topic can be linked with a particular nonfiction title. For example, many of the works of Russell Freedman lend themselves to a chapter by chapter read-aloud: *Children of the Wild West* (1983), *Buffalo Hunt* (1988), and *The Life and Death of Crazy Horse* (1996) are just a few. Each of these books begins with a chapter that summarizes the total work. Thus the listener gets "the big picture" before all the details are shared in succeeding chapters. For example, each section of Freedman's books has a title that helps provide the main idea for the text. For example, "From the Brains to the Tail" gives the listener a pretty good idea of what to expect from this chapter in *Buffalo Hunt* (1988). His use of primary source data for both text and illustration is also an excellent example for middle grade researchers.

Other longer texts for extended sharing include the work of Susan Campbell Bartoletti or Rhoda Blumberg, Dennis Brendell Fradin, or Steven H. Jaffe. Bartoletti's *Growing Up in Coal Country* (1996) will fascinate older listeners as they hear what life was like for children in coal mining towns. *Full Steam Ahead: The Race to Build a Transcontinental Railroad* (Blumberg, 1996) reveals not only the hardships and dramas of building the railroad, but also the behind-the-scene politics. When scientific discoveries are made, often there are debates of whom gets credit. Fradin's *We Have Conquered Pain: The Discovery of Anesthesia* with a touch of old-fashioned melodrama explores the on-going debate. And speaking of debates, Steven Jaffe in *Who Were the Founding Fathers?* (1996) addresses the political arguments of the many intents of the Founding Fathers in the writing of our nation's most important documents, The Declaration of Independence and the Constitution of the United States.

Older students may even want to participate in the read-aloud experience by volunteering to read instead of the teacher. They may also make recommendations of favorite nonfiction texts they've encountered or suggest topics of interest that can guide book selection. As longer texts are shared with older readers, students may be motivated to "read more about it." They may be intrigued by the research each author reveals in his/her work through sources cited and author notes. Like younger listeners, they will benefit from having expository prose shared and modeled for them as they begin to experiment with this mode in their own writing.

Biographies are also possible candidates for read-aloud time. The picture book biographies by Diane Stanley are excellent examples for the middle grades. *Good Queen Bess: The Story of Elizabeth I of England* by Diane Stanley and Peter Vennema (1990) is illustrated with paintings and portraiture reminiscent of the Elizabethan era. The narrative of her life unfolds with as much drama as any contemporary novel. And best, the act of reading aloud helps give biographies a voice. It's almost as if the subject comes to life through reading aloud. *Starry Messenger* by Peter Sís (1996) and *Mandela* by Floyd Cooper (1996) are two other picture book biographies that make interesting read-alouds.

Autobiographies can also be very effective texts for reading aloud. More and more authors and illustrators of children's literature are penning their autobiographies for juvenile audiences. These nonfiction texts make excellent companions to the author's works themselves. Consider, for example, *Under My Nose* by Lois Ehlert (1996), author in the Richard C. Owen's "Meet the Author" series, in which she shares pictures and details of her childhood, her cat, her studio, even rough drafts of her work. Combine this read-aloud with her book, *Red Leaf, Yellow Leaf* (1991) or *Feathers for Lunch* (1990). (See Chapter 1 for other authors in the series by

Other biographies suitable for reading aloud are:

Champions: Stories of Ten Remarkable Athletes by Bill Littlefield

Hoang Anh by Diane Hoyt-Goldsmith

Things Change by Troy Aikman and Greg Brown

Wood-Song by Gary Paulsen

Richard C. Owen.) An examination of her life and her work in this combined context is sure to elicit responses from students. Pat Cummings' collected interviews, *Talking with Artists* (1992) and *Talking with Artists, Volume II* (1995) can function in the same way, matching autobiographies with works by the subjects. Those autobiographical interviews could, in fact, be read aloud by two readers, in a kind of "press conference" format similar to readers theater.

Each of these works is typical of many others available that can captivate audiences in a read-aloud session. They can be read in one sitting with mature listeners, or spread over several sessions. Some have a narrative thread and others rely on sequence or organization to maintain reader interest. Each is effective as a successful read-aloud experience in its entirety. All have one major attribute in common—they're true stories, real people, actual fact—and as such exert a powerful pull on students' attention spans. It is also important to recognize these works as quality literature in their own right to read, savor, and enjoy, not just as texts to teach, discuss, and analyze.

Participatory Read-Alouds

As students and teachers each gain experience with the nonfiction genre, more creative alternatives to traditional teacher read-alouds can be explored. Ultimately, it would be most beneficial to involve the students in presenting the information directly. What may seem surprising is how many nonfiction works lend themselves to more participatory or interactive read-aloud modes. For example, *Come Back, Salmon: How a Group of Dedicated Kids Adopted Pigeon Creek and Brought it Back to Life* by Molly Cone (1993) contains several sections built on a dialog between a teacher and students. Chapter 3 "The Fish that Went to School" and Chapter 6 "Come Back, Salmon" both lend themselves to a read-aloud in parts, with the teacher and students sharing aloud respective lines from the book. With practice, this may even lead to the adaptation of nonfiction texts for readers theater, an exciting combination for collaboration and enhanced comprehension (Young and Vardell, 1993).

Other nonfiction texts, such as Patricia McMahon's *Chi-Hoon, A Korean Girl* (1993) feature the voice of one character throughout. This individual's lines or parts could be read aloud by a student, while the teacher or librarian reads the remaining text. In this example, Chi-Hoon's diary entries are interspersed among the narrative, including this one for Wednesday:

> We went on a school picnic. We went to Kyongbuk-kung. After lunch, it rained. First the boys had their pictures taken together. Then the girls. Because of the rain, we couldn't play games. Instead, we sang and told riddles on the bus. It was fun. (p. 37)

Student participation in reading aloud texts from the child's point of view enriches the read-aloud experience for both the participant who engages in a closer reading of the text, as well as for the audience who hears at least one interpretation of it.

Some nonfiction texts, however, do not involve student perspectives, but they still lend themselves to effective participatory read-alouds. Passages that describe or provide direction can be used to lead students in related activities during the read-aloud experience. For example, students can participate as they listen to the teacher or librarian read aloud the step-by-step guidelines for figuring out the day of the week you were born from Marilyn Burns' *Math for Smarty Pants* (1982). Many other nonfiction titles detail the how-to's of experiments, games, and other activities. These hands-on activities provide a concrete connection with the read-aloud experience and keep attention spans focused on the task and the text. Whether students are reading aloud dialog or diary-like entries or responding with practical activities while listening, students who participate actively in the read-aloud session will find their direct involvement helps insure a higher level of motivation and comprehension. Nonfiction literature can help provide this experience in a unique and distinctive way.

Chapter/Excerpt Read-Alouds

When it comes to using nonfiction literature in the classroom or library, it may be most practical to consider more nontraditional methods of reading aloud than the cover-to-cover approach to sharing. Many informational books are perfect for sharing orally in "bits and pieces" because they are often organized enumeratively. In addition, once the teacher or leader has shared a section or sections and the students become familiar with the text format, they may well want to volunteer to participate in the oral reading process themselves, particularly when the topic interests them on a personal level. An often-used school library technique is to present *Booktalks* or *book teasers*. A wide variety of books (sometimes within a specific topic area) are introduced to a class, with the purpose of enticing students to select one or more for independent reading. A well-prepared librarian with short, fascinating comments about each book may be mobbed after the Booktalks as students vie to check out those that caught their interest.

The format of *Families: A Celebration of Diversity, Commitment, and Love* by Aylette Jenness (1990) is such that any of the family profiles could be read aloud and discussed. Real children and their families are pictured and detailed in first-person narratives, including the adoptive family of Tam, the blended family of Jody, Jennifer's family on a commune, and Nhor's foster family, among others. The entire book is excellent, but need not be read from cover-to-cover in order to discover the variety of families representative of our society today. Another example of an excellent work

Other excellent examples of books with chapters or excerpts that work effectively for reading aloud include:

Blood and Guts by Linda Allison

50 Simple Things Kids Can Do To Recycle by The Earth Works Group

It Happened in America: True Stories from the Fifty States by Lila Perl

Kids' Guide to Social Action by Barbara Lewis

Kids Explore the Gifts of Children with Special Needs by the Westridge Young Writers Workshop

Paul Harvey's: The Rest of the Story by Paul Harvey

Mistakes that Worked by Charlotte Foltz Jones

of nonfiction, any chapter of which makes interesting sharing, is *From Hand to Mouth: Or, How We Invented Knives, Forks, Spoons, and Chopsticks and the Table Manners to Go with Them* by James Cross Giblin (1987). Just reading aloud the chapter entitled "The rise and fall of table manners" is a fascinating story about how forks came to America, among other things.

Even some biographies work effectively in excerpts or sections read aloud. Share the chapters, "How Yani Paints" or "Yani and Her Father," from *A Young Painter: The Life and Paintings of Wang Yani—China's Extraordinary Young Artist* by Zheng Zhensun and Alice Low (1991). These two chapters, in particular, give student audiences a feeling for how the young artist works as well as how her gift affects her family. The excellent biographical work *Sojourner Truth: "Ain't I a Woman?"* by Patricia McKissack and Fredrick McKissack (1992) is a fascinating study. Reading aloud the chapter "Free Belle" or "Ain't I a Woman?" might be just enough to lure readers in the middle grades to read the rest of her story on their own. Each of these chapters functions as a story in itself about this fascinating woman and the times she lived in, first as a slave, then as a free woman. In addition, the mini-biographies in the section "More about the people Sojourner Truth knew" also stand alone as interesting read-aloud material. Many collective biographies also include pieces lively and short enough for reading aloud, such as those found in *Inspirations: Stories about Women Artists* by Leslie Sills (1989) or *Book of Black Heroes From A to Z* by Wade Hudson and Valerie Wilson Wesley (1988). These brief, biographical selections from a variety of sources could form the basis of a read-aloud series, featuring famous as well as less familiar people worth hearing about.

Browsing

Many works of nonfiction include such breadth of information that simply sampling information here and there can be an effective introduction to a topic. This kind of *browsing* approach is most effective when the topic is somewhat familiar to the students or related to a unit of study currently under investigation. Otherwise, such a random sampling could seem haphazard and obscure.

Skim through Bruce McMillan's *Going on a Whale Watch* (1992) and note the new whaling terms he introduces alongside the color photos and scenes. Invite students to browse through nonfiction books in pairs to lead each other in discovering and sharing their findings. Browsing through *Linnea's Windowsill Garden* (Björk & Anderson, 1988) will yield all kinds of details about plant and plant care, including "how-to" directions to read aloud and follow. As adult readers, we typically browse through magazines and newspapers digesting all kinds of new and unconnected information. We stop and read aloud to family or friends nearby those juicy tidbits that strike us as interesting. Why not also apply this spontaneous reading strategy to nonfiction books rich in information or illustration?

Reading aloud only a chapter or section from a nonfiction book may be an obvious alternative to the cover-to-cover approach usually taken. Another approach, however, which may be less obvious can also be effective with the nonfiction genre: reading aloud captions only. Much of the nonfiction literature published for young people today is packed with illustrations and photographs, often in full color. Often skimming through only the pictures and captions provides a "bird's eye view" of the overall content of the book. It also helps to fine-tune students' visual literacy skills, guiding them in using illustrations as informational cues in the reading process. Sometimes pictures provide information that isn't discussed in the text. Extracting new knowledge from photographs is also a valuable skill. Showing pictures and sharing captions in the read-aloud session can be a kind of "sneak preview" for the book as a whole. Students with further interest in the topic may then choose to check out the book for individual reading.

Consider, for example, the following captions for the gripping photographs in Charlotte Wilcox's book *Mummies and Their Mysteries* (1993):

> When farmers found this body in a Danish bog in 1950, they immediately called the police. The 2000-year-old body was so well preserved, the farmers thought the man had been recently murdered. The rope used to hang him was still around his neck. (p. 51)

Later in the book the reader discovers this caption:

> Few people in modern times want to be mummified, but some like

CAPTIONS AND READ-ALOUD EXAMPLES

Captions can take many different forms in nonfiction books, from simple labels to a more lengthy or expanded form. They may even contain new information that may not be found in other places in the book. Additional nonfiction titles that offer read-aloud opportunities include many of the works of Gail Gibbons, for example, *Weather Words and What They Mean* (1990); the photographic essays of Kate Waters, for example, *Sarah Morton's Day* (1989) or *Samuel Eaton's Day* (1993); and the "Eyewitness" and "Eyewitness Junior" series, such as *Ancient Egypt* by George Hart (1990), which incorporates both labels and paragraph-length descriptions of photos and illustrations.

the idea of keeping a favorite cat or dog around the house even if it's no longer alive. Chemical mummification of this cat, including the gold plating, cost its owner $5,000. (p. 59)

Dorothy Hinshaw Patent uses captions and photographs very effectively throughout her nonfiction works. For example, see the photographs that accompany these captions (from *Yellowstone Fires: Flames and Rebirth*, 1990): "Smoke from the fires often blocked out the sun" (p. 21). "Most of the fires created a mosaic of burned places, killed trees, and unburned areas. As time passes, these varied patches will result in a greater variety of habitats for the park plants and animals" (p. 34). Even without pictures, the vivid descriptions found in these captions provide excellent material for a read-aloud and discussion.

Other outstanding sources for good caption writing and exciting illustration, include: *To Space and Back* by Sally Ride with Susan Okie (1986) including full color National Aeronautics and Space Administration (NASA) photographs; *Inside Dinosaurs and Other Prehistoric Creatures* (1993) by Steve Parker with cutaway illustrations and detailed captions; *For Home and Country: A Civil War Scrapbook* (1995) by Norman Bolotin and Angela Herb with captions describing the original photographs and documents. Reading and sharing captions and illustrations during read-aloud time is an excellent way to incorporate nonfiction into the curriculum and can lead to mini-lessons on descriptive writing or identifying main ideas.

Perusing nonfiction may also be an excellent strategy for the students' first introduction to *The Magic School Bus* series. A first read-aloud might simply share the story narrative. In any of these books, listeners can follow Ms. Frizzle and her class on their magical tours. Successive read-alouds can highlight expository passages, share captions, and point out additional details. Students can join in on each layer of the read-aloud.

When nonfiction titles employ multilayered formats and access features, these more "chaotic" formats can be made to seem less formidable by the read-aloud experience that guides students in processing all the multiple sources of information. In fact, students can also participate in pointing out and reading aloud information chunks when they are particularly familiar with the text or topic. For example, Richard Platt's *Incredible Cross-Sections*, illustrated by Steven Biesty (1992), is a favorite among students. As pages are unfolded and spread out, student volunteers may point out their favorite scenes or details to the group or class. Through the interactive read-aloud, the depth and richness of these nonfiction formats can be better appreciated.

Believe It or Not, Best Lists, Almanacs, and Trivia

Though literary critics would discount these as having any literary value at all, books of trivia, almanacs of facts, and accounts of strange and bizarre occurrences make up one of the most popular forms of nonfiction with children and young adults. These "believe it or not " books also often lend themselves to being read aloud. In fact, students usually share their findings quite spontaneously while poring over the latest edition of *The Guinness Book of World Records* (McFarlan & McWhirter, 1996) or *Kids' World Almanac of Animals and Pets* (Felder, 1996). Because these passages are rarely very long, this makes an excellent "sponge" activity for those few, but inevitable unplanned moments in the day.

Russell Ash's *The Top 10 of Everything of 1996* (1996) contains an incredible variety of lists to share aloud. Each can serve as a springboard for speculation and discussion. Just consider: the 10 best-selling children's books of all time in the U.S.; the 10 highest-earning entertainers in the world; and the 10 deadliest snakes in the world. New editions are published for each calendar year. *Strange Creatures* by Seymour Simon (1981) contains anecdotes describing "a real vampire," "the snake that plays dead," and "the lizard that can walk on the ceiling," among others.

Finally, the most accessible nonfiction of all is the paperback collection of weird and bizarre "real life" information. Many of these are detailed in short story narrative fashion that is ideal for reading aloud. Read aloud tales of talking horses or the dog who swallowed a wrench collected in Stephen Mooser's *The Man who Ate a Car and Tons of Other Weird True Stories* (1991). For the sports-minded reader, stories about baseball, football, basketball, hockey, and even the Olympic games are available in Phyllis and Zander Hollander's *Amazing But True Sports Stories* (1986). These "believe it or not" stories have incredible appeal to students and usually make short and pithy read-alouds.

Introducing Access Features and Expository Text Structures Through Reading Aloud

As we build students' exposure to nonfiction through a variety of read-aloud strategies, many possibilities for extension and instruction will present themselves. It is important, however, that students first become familiar with the genre and discuss their observations and responses. When this foundation is in place, it is possible to use the read-aloud time as a kind of "think-aloud" session to introduce or highlight the technical aspects of nonfiction text. This includes the internal structure or how the author has organized the information. In addition, the read-aloud can model how nonfiction authors use access features, reference aids, placement of illustrations, and graphic aids. See Chapter 4 for a more extensive discussion of these format elements in nonfiction.

To the novice reader, all these elements can be intimidating and confusing. It's like stepping off the train in a foreign country and hearing announcements being called out, seeing billboards with advertisements, noticing shop windows and signs, seeking out directions for turning left or right, and wondering if you are in the right spot. The reader is being bombarded by multiple sources of information that all seem to be vying for attention at the same time. The teacher can use the read-aloud experience to explain what each of these text elements are, providing the labels. For example, the teacher can indicate the glossary when reading from *Mummies* (Wilcox, 1993) and explain that the glossary is a list of words and meanings that helps readers with a subject or topic. In the give and take of an interactive read-aloud session, teachers can help students clarify their understanding of all these "pieces" of text. Using high quality nonfiction trade books helps provide an interesting and meaningful context for identifying these elements. As students become more familiar with how these work in books they enjoy, they may be better equipped to experiment with using these tools in their own writing. This kind of modeling is essential if students are also expected to write their own expository texts. Building upon examples from authentic literature helps provide some of the necessary scaffolding for students' early efforts.

These reference tools can also be presented quite naturally in the read-aloud experience. Deciding which excerpt to read aloud can provide a need for referring to a table of contents. Penny Colman's comprehensive work *Rosie the Riveter, Women Working on the Home Front in World War II* (1995) offers many choices for a read-aloud. Reading aloud the table of contents can involve the students in choosing a starting chapter. Afterwards, a discussion of how the author chooses titles for each chapter and why the chapters are organized the way they are is a rich opportunity for developing the *thinking* behind the writing and organizing of expository text.

The same kind of practice can be used for demonstrating the value of an index. This time, begin at the end with an overhead transparency of the index pages. Enlist the school librarian to co-teach this type of information literacy skills. Stress the importance of brainstorming key words, understanding the concept of subtopics, and noting that the quantity of index varies from book to book. Again, students can choose intriguing topics. The read-aloud leader looks for the reference within the text. Show students how to read only the relevant material. So often, less able readers need "permission" not to read the entire page, not realizing that skimming and scanning is appropriate and necessary. Try Patricia Lauber's excellent nonfiction work, *Seeing Earth from Space* (1990). Look up "drought" on p. 48 or "oil spill" on p. 72, and find the references to read aloud. Be sure to show the incredible photographs from space showing actual droughts and oil spills.

Expository text is full of all kinds of access features that can be systematically introduced during a nonfiction read-aloud time. One at a time, in the context of a quality nonfiction title, these tools can be demonstrated as the useful and informative devices they are. *The Great Fire* (Murphy, 1995) is an excellent example of how helpful maps can be in telling a story, as described in Chapter 4. The scale and magnitude of the great fire of Chicago is vividly conveyed by the expanding gray area on the maps provided throughout the book. As the details of the fire unfold throughout the read-aloud experience, transparencies of the maps can reveal the extent of the fire in a very concrete and visual way.

The chronological timeline, on the other hand, is incredibly helpful in David Adler's work, *We Remember the Holocaust* (1989). This device provides a helpful mechanism for relating and connecting the events that unfold throughout the text. Students can make a poster-sized version of this chronology for display and refer to it throughout the read-aloud of the text itself. In addition, this book also includes maps, a glossary, and a reading list.

Guiding students to understand the internal text structure of nonfiction writing may be the most challenging layer of all. But using the read-aloud experience is an excellent method for bringing this to light. For example, *The News About Dinosaurs* by Patricia Lauber (1989) has a clearly defined structure for the presentation of information. The author presents a brief summary of previously held beliefs regarding dinosaur lore, and then breaks the text with the words, "The news is:" Then the most current, and often contradictory findings are shared. Reading aloud one segment, and discussing it, help reveal to students one possible method for organizing information. This use of point-counterpoint is one way a nonfiction author may choose to lay out a book.

Another method of organizing expository text is to rely on chronological order to guide the sequencing of information. As the teacher reads aloud chapters or excerpts from the Orbis Pictus award-winning, *Across America on an Emigrant Train* by Jim Murphy (1993), students can identify each year or period of years that serves as the backdrop for the chapter. They might even work together to create a time line to accompany the book as Robert Louis Stevenson's journey is detailed in this account of the development of the train industry. Creating a visual aid may help the students to see that the author chose to present the information in a linear sequence for a very specific purpose.

The organizational structure of *compare-contrast* can be illustrated by reading aloud *Christmas in the Big House, Christmas in the Quarters* (McKissack and McKissack, 1994). Having two oral readers (one reader for the chapters about the Big House, one for those about the Quarters) could help students clearly hear the two distinctive points of view. This could be followed by a discussion of why the authors chose the *compare-contrast* layout for their organizational structure, rather than simply sharing information chronologically or in some other fashion.

As students become more and more familiar with nonfiction as a genre and with its peculiarities of form and format, the read-aloud session can expand into demonstration and explication from both a reader's and a writer's point of view. Just as we point out how fiction writers use setting to create a mood, we can direct students to notice how and why nonfiction writers use a great variety of tools and devices to organize their ideas and to make that organization more reader-friendly.

Conclusions

Reading aloud provides an important role model for students (Trelease, 1989). Hoffman, Roser, and Battle (1993) describe an ideal "model" scenario for the classroom read-aloud based on their research of current practices which includes a well-stocked classroom library, an accessible display of books, 20 minutes or more daily for reading aloud, encouraging open-ended responses to literature, small and large group discussions, journal writing, drawing, and paired sharing, and opportunities to revisit favorite texts (p. 502). This model is an excellent framework for integrating the use of nonfiction. Informational literature can indeed evoke responses from students, expand units of instruction, and lead to connections across topics, formats, authors, and genres (Vardell & Copeland, 1992). Choosing nonfiction books also presents students with additional possibilities for their own independent reading. The adult (or student) who leads the read-aloud experience can and should exercise some flexibility and creativity in presenting nonfiction orally to students. The techniques presented here are some which can be effective, but there are bound to be many other possibilities. In fact, as new books are published, each will suggest its own way into the classroom or library. The key is to keep current on what resources are available, then do all we can to provide our students with access to these resources. Once students discover there are answers to their questions about the world and how it works, their interest in the new nonfiction published each year will be voracious. Read-aloud time is one place where we may join them in this quest for knowledge.

References

Anderson, R. C., Hiebert, E. H., Scott, J. A., & Wilkinson, I. A. (1985). *Becoming a nation of readers: The report of the Commission of Reading.* Washington, DC: The National Institute of Education.

Doiron, R. (1994). Using nonfiction in a read-aloud program: Letting the facts speak for themselves. *The Reading Teacher, 47* (8), 616-624.

Hoffman, J. V., Roser, N. L., & Battle, J. (1993). Reading aloud in classrooms: From the modal toward a "model." *The Reading Teacher, 46* (6), 496-503.

Oyler, C., & Barry, A. (1996). Intertextual connections in read-alouds of information books. *Language Arts, 73,* 324-329.

Pappas, C. C. (1991). Fostering full access to literacy for including information books. *Language Arts, 68,* 449-461.

Trelease, J. (1989). *The new read aloud handbook.* New York: Penguin.

Vardell, S. M. (1991). A new "picture of the world": The NCTE Orbis Pictus award for outstanding nonfiction for children. *Language Arts, 68,* 474-479.

Vardell, S. M. (1994). Nonfiction for young children. *Young Children, 49* (6), 40-41.

Vardell, S. M. (1996). The language of facts: Using nonfiction books to support language growth. In A. A. McClure & J. V. Kristo (Eds.), *Books that invite talk, wonder, and play* (pp. 59-77). Urbana, IL: National Council of Teachers of English.

Vardell, S. M., & Copeland, K. A. (1992). Reading aloud and responding to non fiction: Let's talk about it. In E. B. Freeman & D. G. Person (Eds.), *Using nonfiction trade books in the elementary classroom: From ants to zeppelins* (pp. 76-85). Urbana, IL: National Council of Teachers of English.

Young, T., & Vardell, S. M. (1993). Weaving readers theater and nonfiction into the curriculum. *The Reading Teacher, 46* (5), 396-409.

Chapter 11
Writing Nonfiction: Helping Students Teach Others What They Know

by Yvonne Siu-Runyan

I met David when I did a demonstration lesson on writing for fourth-graders. This particular group of fourth graders had very little experience with writing nonfiction and the teachers wanted to see how I would work this group of students. I started by reading aloud the chapter on how the wolf became a dog from *Out of the Wild: The Story of Domesticated Animals* (Ryan, 1995) because I knew it would capture the students' interests immediately. I expected that the students would be enthusiastic to share their own experiences with animals. David, one of the few students who owned neither a cat, dog, fish, or bird, offered that he had two pet chinchillas. The students were curious about them, and David willingly answered their questions.

I continued to invite discussion about their animals as rehearsal for writing. Following our discussion, the students immediately got to work, except for David. Even though the children were captivated by all that David had shared orally, it was obvious he was not going to write. I approached David and asked, "Aren't you going to write?"

He responded with, "No, I'm not going to write. I hate writing and you can't make me do it." I decided that this was the perfect time to model how an interview can generate information for writing.

"I understand how you feel. Not everyone likes to write. But, David," I continued, "could you tell me more about your chinchillas? I didn't know you could actually keep them as pets. This is new to me. Tell me more about them. How did you get them? What are all the different kinds of foods they like to eat? Can they be house trained? What do you do with them when you go on trips and cannot be at home to take care of them?" I was curious, and David answered all my questions and more.

I knew that if I wanted David to write, I needed to tap his passion and knowledge for chinchillas. So, I suggested, "You might be willing to help me learn about chinchillas by writing down what we talk about. I know I'll never remember everything we discuss unless you help me remember and record the information we talk about on paper. Can you do that?" To my relief, David agreed.

As I walked around the room checking on the other students and responding to their emerging drafts, I noticed that David was sitting quietly, but he seemed confused and frustrated. When I approached him, he said he didn't know how to begin. I discussed how he might brainstorm ideas by making a web or list. To our surprise, David immediately got busy and wrote for the next hour. That day David found his voice as a writer. What helped David to find his voice as a writer? The following points illustrate the ways in which teachers can empower students as writers of nonfiction.

How Can We Help Students Find Their Voices?

Why did David, a reluctant writer, decide to write after proclaiming to me that he hated to write and wasn't going to do it? Simply put, David felt empowered. He felt passionate about his pet chinchillas, others were interested in his knowledge, and he learned through our discussions that he could teach others what he knew by writing.

Like adult authors of nonfiction, in order for students to write with voice and fluency, they must know and love their topics. Too often teachers forget that children have deep passion about things they care about, know about, and want to learn more about. If we are concerned about helping them develop their ability to write, we must first tap into these "burning" issues and show them we are interested in what they have to say. When we talk with students, we must use language that empowers them. This means we first need to focus on the information they share and be truly interested in this content. We need to let them know that through their writing, they become the teachers who help others learn what they know. That is, as writers of nonfiction, their primary goal is to teach others (their audience) what is inside of their heads.

Considering one's audience is an important aspect of writing. When discussing audience for writing, Tyler, a second-grade boy, offered, "We didn't write all the information down like the book does. We wrote only the information we thought would be the most interesting....Interesting to our readers, you know our classmates" (Siu-Runyan, 1996, p. 6-7).

Tyler also discussed the importance of being interested in the topic when doing research. When asked, "What would you say to other kids your age who want to do research and write but they just don't know how to do it? What would you say to them?" (Siu-Runyan, 1996):

> I'd say, read the books, talk to someone about the information, then
> write it down using interesting words. Draw pictures if they help and

then share the information with your classmates. One last thing, always research something you're interested in. (p. 8)

How Can We Help Students Learn About Their Topic?

Over the years, I have found that students get in trouble when they write about a topic for which they have little information. In fact, many students think they have little to write about. Another problem may occur when students do not know their subject. The topic doesn't develop and the writing lacks fluency and details. Thus the writing is uninformed, uninteresting, and has little voice. It meanders, makes no point, and the reader is left with an empty, "So what?" feeling.

So, how can teachers make the point that in order to write well it is important to know one's topic? Too often we have been guilty of simply telling students, "You need more information. Go to the library and get some books and read them." Without guidance about the variety of print sources to explore (e.g., nonfiction literature, other genres, magazines, brochures, almanacs, maps, the World Wide Web, etc.), many students go directly to the encyclopedia, copy the information down word for word, and claim it as their own. Discuss these concerns with your school librarian and you'll probably find a powerful, on-site ally who will be more than happy to co-teach these information literacy skills.

A good place to begin the research process is listing everything you know about the subject—such a list will assist in formulating key words as well as identifying misunderstandings, a necessary part of research.

In addition to print sources, Graves (1989) and Calkins (1991) suggest that students collect data by interviewing, observing, conversing, and "mining" their learning logs. In other words, novice researchers need to be encouraged to learn about their topic from many resources. Wide data gathering also presents an opportunity for children to experience multiple points of view and contradictory perspectives. Raphael and Hiebert (1996) recommend that students develop a repertoire of strategies for organizing, categorizing, or describing their information such as using graphic organizers, charts, webs, and concept maps.

Many students are not aware that authors must often do research before they write. Two questions that work well in helping students understand the importance of knowing one's subject is to ask after reading a piece to the students: "What do you suppose the author had to know in order to write this piece?; How do you think the author went about gathering that information?" These questions help students think about what authors do when rehearsing to write a piece and can be followed by examining books that describe the author's research process. The following books listed in Figure 11.1 include information about the author's research process as discussed in Chapter 2. Descriptions of the author's research process can be located in the following places within a book—acknowledgments, index, bibliography, preface, and author's note. Because information may be found within only one section or a combination of sections, encourage students to explore the books.

Recommend that students keep an annotated record of the different sources they consult in researching their topics. They can then fashion a description of their research process and include it as part of their finished products.

Figure 11-1 Nonfiction Titles Containing Information about the Author's Research Process

Bard of Avon: The Story of William Shakespeare by Diane Stanley and Peter Vennema and Illustrated by Diane Stanley

Buddha by Susan L. Roth

Cleopatra by Diane Stanley and Peter Vennema and Illustrated by Diane Stanley

Good Queen Bess: The Story of Elizabeth I of England by Diane Stanley and Peter Vennema and Illustrated by Diane Stanley

A River Ran Wild by Lynn Cherry

Houses and Homes by Ann Morris and Photographs by Ken Heyman

The Last Princess: The Story of Princess Ka'iulani of Hawai'i by Fay Stanley and Diane Stanley

Listen for the Bus: David's Story by Patricia McMahon and Photographs by John Godt

Loving by Ann Morris and Photographs by Ken Heyman

Marco Polo: His Notebook by Susan L. Roth

On the Go by Ann Morris and Photographs by Ken Heyman

Sharks by Gail Gibbons

Spiders by Gail Gibbons

Tools by Ann Morris and Photographs by Ken Heyman

Whales by Gail Gibbons

Your Cat's Wild Cousins by Hope Ryden

What Do Student Writers Learn as They Read Nonfiction?

Immerse Students in Nonfiction

As children progress through the grades, they will be asked to write nonfiction more often. Students need to be immersed or "marinated" in the genre in which they are expected to write, before they can be successful. However, as Sylvia Vardell notes in Chapter 10, nonfiction books are not typically the first choices for reading aloud. Children need to develop an "ear" for the language of well-crafted nonfiction by hearing many different kinds read aloud. They need exposure to a variety of formats, styles, illustrations, and be given time to browse and sample high-quality titles. As we read aloud and invite students to examine and talk about a variety of ways authors write nonfiction, they become more aware of the decisions writers make about language and style, organizational patterns, layout, and format. Frank Smith (1983 comments that "...in order for students to recognize pattern, examples of good writing must be found in what other people have written, in existing texts" (p. 560). Smith goes on to say that, "Teachers must also ensure that children have access to reading materials that are relevant to the kinds of writers they are interested in becoming at a particular moment; teachers must recruit the authors who will become the unwitting collaborators" (p. 564). In fact, students often use what they have learned from reading when writing; this is called "intertextuality." As Cairney (1990) stated, "It seems that children do indeed dip into a cauldron of literary experiences as part of the writing process. Each new text written reflects in some measure the shadows of texts experienced in the past" (p. 484).

Use Organizational Structures as a Way into Writing Nonfiction

Plan a minilesson on a nonfiction title such as Jonathan London's *Voices of the Wild* (1993). This book discusses animals in the wild with two pages devoted to each wild animal. Discuss London's organizational structure in this book with children. Since information about each animal can be read separately, transitions from one animal to the next need not be made. This book is actually a collection of individual pieces about wild animals. Share other nonfiction titles organized in similar ways and compare and contrast how authors have used the organizational structure. Students may find that this kind of organization is easy for them to use in their own pieces. Other excellent nonfiction books organized in this way are:

- *Arctic Memories* by Normee Ekoomiak
- *Children Just Like Me: A Unique Celebration of Children Around the World* by Barnabas Kindersley and Anabel Kindersley and Photographed by Barnabas Kindersley
- *A Kettle of Hawks and Other Wildlife Groups* by Jim Arnosky

Organizing by Chronology

Another easy way for students to organize nonfiction writing is chronologically. Since most students already understand this organizational structural technique from many of the fictional stories they read and write, they will be successful at using chronology to order informational writing. Some outstanding books that fit the bill are:

- *Cactus Hotel* by Brenda Z. Guiberson and Illustrated by Megan Lloyd

- *Ininatig's Gift of Sugar: Traditional Sugarmaking* by Laura Waterman Wittstock and Photographed by Dale Kakkak

- *Let's Go Traveling in Mexico* by Robin Rector Krupp

- *Sea Elf* by Joanne Ryder and Illustrated by Michael Rothman

Organize by Question and Answer

Using the question and answer format to organize nonfiction writing leads students into thinking deeply about their topics. While it is not difficult to organize one's writing using the question and answer format, students will soon discover that they must know the answers to the questions they ask. Deciding on this structure can actually stimulate young writers to do even more research than originally anticipated. Also, students can easily ask their classmates about the questions they have concerning the topic being researched. Thus, using this format can help writers direct their research and reinforce the notion that one of the things good writers do is to answer their readers' questions.

- *Guess Who?* by Margaret Miller

- *What is the Sun?* by Reeve Lindbergh and Illustrated by Stephen Lambert

- *What Would You Do If You Lived at the Zoo?* by Nancy White Carlstrom and Illustrated by Lizi Boyd

- *Where Does the Trail Lead?* by Burton Albert and Illustrated by Brian Pinkney

Call Attention to the Unique Ways in Which Authors Use Language

Outstanding nonfiction writers do not use language that sounds like encyclopedias or textbooks. In fact, noteworthy nonfiction writers use language with flair, imagery, and precision just as fictional writers do. (See Chapter 3 for a thorough discussion of language and style in nonfiction.) Teachers need to share exquisite examples of well-written nonfiction and linger over the language—the subtleties and nuances of a fine-crafted piece of informational writing.

Using repetitive text

One technique students can easily incorporate into their own writing is the use of repeated phrases throughout. Author Madeleine Dunphy in *Here Is the Tropical Rain Forest* (1994), begins each new piece of information about rainforests with: "Here is..." and ends with: "Here is the tropical rain forest," the first sentence of the book. Dunphy also uses interlocking, repeated, cumulative text throughout the book giving it a sense of cohesion. An example from the first few pages follow:

> Page 1: Here is the tropical rain forest.
> Page 3: Here is the rain
>   that drizzles and pours
>   and may fall every day
>   in this lush and wet world:
>   Here is the tropical rain forest.
> Page 5: Here is the frog
>   who bathes in the rain
>   that drizzles and pours
>   and may fall every day
>   in this lush and wet world:
>   Here is the tropical rain forest. (p. 5)

In *Voices of the Wild* (1993), previously mentioned because of its organizational structure, London introduces each wild animal by simply stating: "I am _____, _____ing...." This same sentence construction works well for young authors because they will already have a structure in which to incorporate information.

Using words that show, not just tell

Excellent writers of nonfiction also understand the importance of *showing* rather than *telling* by using rich language. Writers use strong verbs and nouns to describe details and to create metaphors. For example, in *Scaley Facts* (1995) Chermayeff writes: "Alligators' mouths are very large" (unpaged). Then he *shows* what he means by the next sentence: "Some alligators grow more than forty sets of teeth in a lifetime" (unpaged). If the readers did not understand what very large means, they certainly have a better understanding after reading that line.

To help support young authors' growth in showing, and not just telling, it is important to help them notice how the use of strong verbs and nouns with specific details helps writers *show* so that readers experience the writing. For example, in *The Great Northern Diver, The Loon* (1990),

Barbara Esbensen writes: "No other bird has such a unique pattern of black and white" (unpaged). Then she follows with: "The loon's black wings and back are decorated with a dizzying display of white checks and stripes and dots. Partially circling the neck is an unusual necklace of wavy white lines" (unpaged). Invite students to discuss Esbensen's use of the words, "decorated and necklace" (unpaged), as examples of a strong verb and strong noun and how these words make a difference in the readers' ability to visualize the loon.

Other nonfiction books in which authors use language in exceptional ways are the following:

- *Everglades* by Jean Craighead George and Illustrated by Wendell Minor (strong verbs, excellent imagery)

- *How Dinosaurs Came To Be* by Patricia Lauber and Illustrated by Douglas Henderson (clear, direct writing that answers the reader's questions; outstanding images created using rhythmic language propelling the readers through the text; easily understood analogies)

- *Is This a House for Hermit Crab?* by Megan McDonald and Illustrated by S. D. Schindler (excellent use of onomatopoeia)

- *Market* by Ted Lewin (strong verbs)

Examining Layout and Format

Nonfiction text contains not only text, of course, but typically photographs, illustrations, and a variety of graphics as well. How the text and illustrative materials are situated on the page can either help or hinder readers. It is important that teachers and librarians help students understand that layout and format will affect how well readers will understand the information. By conducting a variety of mini-studies involving data collections, children can be taught how to collect or create appropriate materials for their own research project. For example, the results of a preference study on favorite animals can be presented in graph form as well as written out in text. Some books with interesting layouts and formats are:

- *Crinkleroot's Guide to Knowing Butterflies & Moths* by Jim Arnosky

- *Small and Furry Animals: A Watercolor Sketchbook of Mammals in the Wild* by Gill Tomblin

- *The Ever-Living Tree: The Life and Times of a Coast Red Wood* by Linda Vieira and Illustrated by Christopher Canyon

- *A Desert Scrapbook: Dawn to Dusk in the Sonoran Desert* by Virginia Wright-Frierson

Notable Nonfiction Writing Across the Curriculum

Students apprentice themselves to the authors they read. It is the authors that ultimately teach children how to write. Ask authors who influenced their writing, and they will typically respond that they learned to write from the authors they read. Here is a sampler of favorite authors who served as apprentices to my student writers:

Math: Mitsumasa Anno, Paul Giganti, Jim Haskins, Tana Hoban, and David Schwartz;

Science/Nature: Aliki, Jim Arnosky, Barbara Bash, Eric Carle, Lynn Cherry, Joanna Cole, Barbara Esbensen, Jean Craighead George, Gail Gibbons, Brenda Guiberson, Ruth Heller, Patricia Lauber, Bruce McMillan, Susan L. Roth, Joanne Ryder, and Seymour Simon;

People/Places/Things: Verna Aardema, Aliki, Raymond Bial, Pam Conrad, Donald Crews, Russell Freedman, Jean Fritz, James Cross Giblin, Kathryn Lasky, Ann Morris, Diane Stanley, and Peter Vennema.

Conclusions

From my own classroom research, I discovered that what I said and did had tremendous impact on student writing (Siu-Runyan, 1994). When I asked students the questions: What do I do that helps you as a writer? What do I do that does not help you as a writer? Their responses were uniformly the same. They said that (1) it helped them when I shared my writing with them and how I went about solving problems, (2) they liked the way I spoke with them about their writing, (3) I showed interest in their pieces, and (4) I offered gentle suggestions and not mandates.

The first thing we must understand as we teach writing is that it is not ours; it is the students'. In other words, we must not take control of the students' writing, but we can do the following:

- be interested in the student's message,

- provide real reasons for writing,

- offer suggestions,

- share or model our writing with them, and

- provide examples of how other nonfiction authors present their information.

To do this well, we must show ourselves to be inquisitive, interested in learning, and curious about the world. We must be enthusiastic about what nonfiction literature has to offer us and be receptive as to how authors of informational books can inform our own writing. For their writing will help us to understand the inside "scoop" about nonfiction writing—content, form, and a sense of audience, and how all these ingredients work together.

The literature on intertextuality (Cairney, 1990; Eckhoff, 1983; Stotsky, 1983) offers us new insights into writing instruction. If we want our students to develop into writers, they must hear and read excellent books from across all genres. And, it means that if we want our students to write *nonfiction*, we must read aloud and provide time for browsing and sharing well-written informational books. By "massaging and combing" text to learn what it has to offer young writers (Kristo, 1993, p. 68), both teachers and students can identify such aspects of nonfiction as an interesting use of organizational structure, powerful language, the author's note or preface, an intriguing title, the lead or conclusion, copyright date, and the format and layout of words and pictures. It also takes a safe environment, time, and a willingness to risk in order to craft a nonfiction piece of writing.

Finally, despite the importance of intertextuality and the connections between reading and writing, the one thing we must remember is this— children write with voice when they are passionate about their subjects. So, tap into those areas of student passion, by inviting them to teach others what they know through their writing of nonfiction.

References:

Cairney, T. (1990). Intertextuality: Infectious echoes from the past. *The Reading Teacher, 43*, 478-484.

Calkins, L. M. (1991). *Living between the lines*. Portsmouth, NH: Heinemann.

Eckhoff, B. (1983). How reading affects children's writing. *Language Arts, 60*, 607-616.

Graves, D. (1989). *Investigate Nonfiction*. Portsmouth, NH: Heinemann.

Kristo, J. V. (1993). Reading aloud in a primary classroom: Reading and teaching young readers. In K. E. Holland, R. A. Hungerford, S. B. Ernst (Eds.), *Journeying: Children Responding to Literature* (pp. 54-71). Portsmouth, NH: Heinemann.

Raphael, T. E., & Hiebert, E. H. (1996). *Creating an Integrated Approach to Literacy Instruction*. Fort Worth, TX: Harcourt Brace.

Siu-Runyan, Y. (1994). Holistic assessment in intermediate classes: Techniques for informing our teaching. In Bill Harp (Ed.), *Assessment & evaluation for student-centered learning, 2nd Edition* (pp. 143-177). Norwood, MA: Christopher-Gordon.

Siu-Runyan, Y. (1996). Researching: Two second graders' perspectives. *The Colorado Communicator, 19*, 4-8.

Smith, F. (1983). Reading like a writer. *Language Arts, 60*, 558-567.

Stotsky, S. (1983). Research on reading/writing relationships: A synthesis and suggested directions. *Language Arts, 60*, 627-642.

CHAPTER 12
TO FLING MY ARMS WIDE[1]:
STUDENTS LEARNING ABOUT THE
WORLD THROUGH NONFICTION

by Linda S. Levstik

> We are not afraid to entrust the American people with unpleasant
> facts, foreign ideas, alien philosophies, and competitive values. For a
> nation that is afraid to let its people judge the truth and falsehood in an
> open market is a nation that is afraid of its people.
>
> John F. Kennedy, February 26, 1962

> The textbook told exact dates, places, names....Other sources pro-
> vide more explanations of why something happened or why someone
> was famous. They give more details of actual reasoning and even feel-
> ings. For instance, I was *inside* on who wanted the states [prior to the
> American Civil War] split up, and why.
>
> Albert, Eighth-Grade Student (1995)

We sat on either side of a long library table, jackets buttoned up
against the air-conditioned chill that preserved time-worn documents.
Across the table were strewn folders full of letters whose ink had faded to
a delicate purple. The tiny antique script that had once conserved precious
paper made the letters difficult to decipher. Yet as we read, a world
emerged—one of friendships, and commitment to a cause. Using letters
and diaries, pamphlets and newspapers, we gradually pieced together the
life of a woman who spent most of her 84 years engaged in a battle against
slavery and oppression. As we worked, some questions were answered
while new ones emerged, and at the end of each day, we spent hours discussing what we had found. The experience was exhilarating. It also
reminded me of how few opportunities most people have for this kind of
learning experience.

It may be that sifting through old letters is not your idea of fun—per-

---

[1] This title is taken from the first line of Langston Hughs' poem *Dream Variation*.

haps you would rather explore tidal pools, chart the behaviors of hermit crabs, find out what is on the other side of a mountain, or learn about childrearing practices in a Kikuyu community in Kenya. Regardless of the topic that fascinates you, I hope that the experience of in-depth study is not foreign to you—that you have been pushed by challenging questions; struggled to make sense out of diverse ideas, alien philosophies, and competitive values; and felt the exhilaration of discovery and dawning understanding—because this chapter is about sharing that sense of discovery with young learners. More specifically, it is about using nonfiction in the context of integrated instruction and inquiry.

An important characteristic of authentic, integrated instruction is confidence in an open market of ideas in which teachers, children, and other interested adults examine ideas, issues, questions, and problems from many different perspectives. Students and teachers use intellectual tools drawn from their immediate environment, the school culture, and the disciplines[2], not simply to acquire knowledge and skills, but to use knowledge and skills to solve a variety of problems (Levstik & Smith, 1996; Wells & Chang-Wells, 1992). While students initiate some research activities and engage in others suggested by teachers, they also exercise choice about how to pursue their learning, have opportunities both to work alone and in groups, and participate with others in the examination of new information and ideas. Investigations also often cut across disciplinary boundaries, delving into questions that require multidisciplinary as well as multicultural perspectives (Gamberg, et al. 1988; Newmann, et al. 1995; Wells & Chang-Wells, 1992; Young, 1994). In this context, it is not enough to have ideas; we and our students must be willing to express those ideas, support them, revise them in the face of new information, or abandon them if they prove false. This requires that all members of the learning community be visible, valued, and taught (Delpit, 1994; Hollins, 1996; Levstik & Barton, 1996; Pappas, et al. 1995). It also requires that students have access to a variety of information, combined with specific instruction in the analysis and use of nonfiction such as concept books, photographic essays, documents and journals, identification books, biographies and the like (Albert, 1995; Levstik & Smith, 1996; Pappas, et al. 1995) .

There are compelling reasons for using a variety of nonfiction that have more to do with what we want our students to learn and how we want them to learn it. First, we want students to learn to consider alternate perspectives. Carefully selected nonfiction, used in conjunction with other sources, can present students with an array of points of view that no sin-

---

[2] The term "Discipline" is problematic. In this context I am using it to refer to the culturally constructed ways of categorizing knowledge that generally correspond to the academic subjects from which the content of school subjects such as science, social studies, mathematics, language arts, and the arts are drawn.

gle text, no matter how well conceived and well written, could adequately address. Second, we want students to learn to use and analyze the range of genres generally associated with a particular subject or discipline. We are not only introducing our students to particular content when we engage them in integrated study; we are also introducing them to culturally constructed ways of learning and communicating. Experience with a full range of literature and other informational sources expands students' cultural as well as intellectual repertoires. It is important to note, however, that as teachers we are not limited to the genres used by professionals in a field; rather, our task is to present children with as wide an array as possible of the ways in which cultures as a whole use information. The practice of what we sometimes call "the disciplines" is the province of us all. The intent of integrated, in-depth study is to provide students with the tools necessary to be lifelong users and creators of science and social studies, literature and the arts, writing and mathematics.

Learning the Tools of the Trade

Reading about inquiry is not the same as doing it; trying to do inquiry without knowing the most useful registers—ways to pose, investigate, and solve problems—often leads to frustration. We cannot assume that if we surround children with wonderful books or integrate the curriculum, in-depth inquiry will follow. Imagining our students as apprentices engaged in mastering these registers is a useful metaphor here. Part of an apprenticeship is developing the ability to select and use the appropriate strategies or processes for a particular task (Newmann, et al. 1995; Rogoff, 1990; Wells, 1986). Apprentices also need exposure to the array of genres available to them as they attempt to establish the significance of an idea or piece of evidence, construct a narrative, propose a theory or illuminate an issue (Newmann, et al. 1995). Too often, students are presented with books and told to "look it up" when they have questions. As one third grader explained, "I don't think they realize how hard it is for us to look things up....I'm just not very good at it!"(Levstik & Smith, 1996). Along with his classmates, he found it very frustrating to be given a huge topic and very little direction or time to conduct the research:

Joel: Like, you get India.

Sandy: That's pretty big, isn't it?....I like it when we narrow it down.

Alex: I like to do research on just one thing, so that you could see it in your mind if somebody would write it to you, and it would take me like about ten days to do it really good, and just the way....I like it.

⌐≈≋≈⌐

BOOKS THAT FOCUS ON ONE TOPIC

Be Seated: A Book About Chairs by James Giblin

Bicycle Book by Gail Gibbons

Let There Be Light: A Book About Windows by James Giblin

The Planets by Gail Gibbons

⌐≈≋≈⌐

Fortunately, nonfiction can provide models both of different genres and "narrowed-down" topics. One approach is to develop book sets—three or four books that represent both broad and more narrow aspects of the same topic. Just as close-up photographs give you details and long shots give you context, so survey texts serve different functions than narrower concept books. Thus, a book such as *Take a Look* (Davidson, 1994) or *A Short Walk Around the Pyramids and Through the World of Art* (Isaacson, 1993) provide a broader context when contrasted with more narrowly focused works such as *Master of Mahogany: Tom Day, Free Black Cabinetmaker* (Lyons, 1994), *Walking the Log: Memories of a Southern Childhood* (Nickens, 1994), or *A Young Painter: The Life and Paintings of Wang Yani—China's Extraordinary Young Artist* (Zhensun & Low, 1991). In particular, narrowly focused books often pay more attention to nontraditional content (cabinetmaking as an art form), underrepresented people (African-American folk artist Bessie Nickens), and non-Western cultures (Chinese artist Wang Yani), then do survey texts. Having both comprehensive and more focused treatments of a topic provides an opportunity to talk with students about selection, significance, and cultural silences (Hollins, 1996). The contrast in scope also illuminates different approaches to inquiry.

Some teachers introduce students to small-scale studies by having them model their work on such highly acclaimed authors as Gail Gibbons or James Giblin who often write about a single concept. After discussing these books, students pick one concept to investigate and use a limited number of sources for their study. In this context, teaching specific data retrieval techniques such as interview protocols, simple notetaking techniques, and the like is quite manageable especially if the teacher utilizes the expertise of a school librarian. Working in small groups, students pool the results of their investigations and report them in a variety of ways, often making their own concept books.

Next, students work with a related, but slightly broader problem or question. If, for instance, their initial study was on games from their parents' or grandparents' childhoods, they might broaden their investigation to look either at games that were popular a century ago, or favorite games played by students at different grade levels. Finally, they combine their findings, using a more comprehensive format. A class book entitled *Games Children Play* might take the form of a timeline, an alphabet book such as *Alphabet City* (Johnson, 1995), or a book of poetry, similar to *Animal, Vegetable, Mineral: Poems about Small Things* (Livingston, 1994). The advantage to this approach is that the initial topic is focused and manageable for the novice researcher while the culminating project requires children to think about where their individual work fits in a broader theme. The necessity for negotiation and sharing in the creation of the final product also means that students are likely to learn more than their own slice of the inquiry pie.

If students are expected to use a variety of nonfiction in their investigations, however, they need help in learning how to gather information from different genres. "It's important to follow through with this," one third-grade teacher explains. "There is a constant need to keep them focused on what they are doing—what they want to find out—whether they are going off track or not" (Levstik & Smith, 1996). In her classroom, students receive specific instruction in notetaking. Initially, taking notes from written sources or considering the perspective of these sources overwhelmed her students. Collecting data from pictures, though, turned out to be much easier for them. Unlike written texts, pictures seemed to free students to use their own words and exercise their own judgment. Initially, students were skeptical about how useful photographs would be as data sources. However, as their teacher held up a photograph and asked: "What can you tell me about this picture that's factual?" the children promptly called out about a dozen observations.

Teacher: That's what you'll be doing today, just reading pictures....Take notes on facts first. Now let's think about how we can put facts on paper. Think about that a minute and raise your hand when you've thought about how to organize your facts.

Kara: Short sentences. One line per fact.

Aya: I will write main things the caption talks about and draw circles.

Teacher: Like this? [Draws web on board, showing connecting pieces of information.]

Carl: That's a story map! It's a web!

Teacher: Butch, how do you like to do yours?

Butch: With pictures, sort of like in the book, with captions.

As students worked in groups to take notes from pictures they engaged in considerable discussion about what their observations meant. Without a text to tell them what the pictures meant, most willingly engaged in speculation, trying to confirm their hypotheses with other pictures or with reference to prior knowledge. Later, when their teacher introduced historical pictures such as those in *Daily Life in a Victorian House* (Wilson, 1994), the students had experience with making observations based on visual texts, and they were able to gather considerable information from the illustrations as well as from the written text.

Calling attention to the scope of the topic as well as the format an author selects is part of the larger issue of encouraging students to consider alternative viewpoints and to make reasoned judgments about the merits of different perspectives. Selecting nonfiction that accurately represents these alternatives is important, but providing access to such alternatives does not mean that students will use them in their studies. Like many adults, students often look for the first, most easily available answer to a question (Levstik & Smith, 1996). There may be five or six books available, each presenting an interesting, provocative perspective that could challenge students to think more carefully about a topic—if they read the books. But students are unlikely to look to multiple resources unless their study is structured to make that necessary.

In one school, the presence of an international guest sparked interest in Kenya. A fourth grader investigating the government of Kenya noted that a reference book in the class collection described Kenya as having one of the most stable governments in East Africa. Another student disagreed. He had read a more recent Kenyan newspaper, part of a culture kit on loan to the school. His source described civil unrest in some parts of the country, a possible political assassination, and a strike by doctors in Nairobi. As a result of their exchange, both students decided to ask their guest, a Kenyan studying at a nearby university, for some background on the current status of Kenya's government. His confirmation of the newspaper reports triggered a class discussion of the limitations of books in investigating current events.

Without the interest generated by the presence of the Kenyan guest, students might not have pursued this issue. In addition, without access to other sources, they might never have discovered any problems in their initial understanding of Kenyan politics, nor have thought to ask their guest about them. With such access they were able to move beyond simply reporting information to analyzing the sources of information and considering how best to use different data sources to acquire accurate information. Note, however, that each student did not have to read each source. Instead, their teacher established an environment in which certain kinds of conversation were likely to happen. First, she made sure that children working on the same problem used different sources so that each student encountered a slightly different perspective. Second, she provided opportunities for students to discuss their work with their peers. Third, she arranged an environment in which discussions were valued at least in part because they provided students with access to interesting people and activities.

Not only is it very tempting for students to resolve an inquiry by going to one source, but a particularly attractive or well-written text is likely to be accepted as "the truth" (Levstik, 1995; Levstik & Smith, 1996). Few problems worth in-depth study, however, are so easily answered. One of the hallmarks of good inquiry is that the questions children investigate are not ones that have single or simple answers or even any answers at all. Individual pieces of the puzzle may be easily answered, but the overall issue or problem requires putting the pieces together and interpreting what the finished product means. Oversimplifying issues in theme studies can mean that students persist in misconceptions or leap to make judgments without sufficient information. This does not mean that a single book cannot illuminate the complexities of an issue in powerful ways. For example, *Bull Run* (Fleischman, 1993), *Vanishing Ozone* (Pringle, 1995), and *Spotted Owl* (Guiberson, 1994) offer multiple perspectives on complex issues. However, multiple perspectives often require multiple books.

While multiple books are important, using large numbers of books does not ensure multiple perspectives. It is possible to read a variety of children's books about the American Revolution without getting any clear idea of why some colonists remained loyal to the British, or why some African-Americans threw their lot in with the British rather than put their trust in the Declaration of Independence. Similarly, while scientists regularly argue about their field, it is possible to introduce a number of science books for children that present information as if it were carved in stone, rather than the subject of debate. Good inquiry relies on teachers who know enough about the content they are teaching to search out literature that invites children into these important conversations, so that they understand that knowledge alters in the face of changing attitudes as well as new discoveries.

One approach to engaging students in conversations about how knowledge is constructed is to begin with well-written presentations of current scholarship. Books such as *The Tainos* (Jacobs, 1992) and *Discovering Christopher Columbus: How History is Invented* (Pelta, 1991) help students identify some of the myths, misperceptions, and biases inherent in much of the literature about Columbus and early contact between Native Americans and Europeans. With this background, students can critique the array of picture books available on this topic. All of these books are easily available and introduce issues that are accessible even to quite young children (*cf.* Levstik & Barton, 1996).

Another technique is to take a single concept and trace how ideas related to that concept have changed over time. A group of upper primary students explored the theme "Giants" and developed an illustrated chart of "Facts and Myths about Giant Creatures." One side of the chart included information about legendary giants such as Big Foot, the Loch Ness Monster, and the Golem; the other side provided information about actual "giant" creatures including a Vietnamese horse snake, the tallest man in the world, and a great white whale. Students read books, looked at magazine articles, visited an aquarium, and watched several videos. In follow-up discussions, they talked about "urban myths," the exaggerations common in some children's television programs, and the stories and rumors that circulated in their own class and community. For the remainder of the year, the children referred back to "giant stories" when they thought something was exaggerated.

Most of us are more likely to understand and recall information we encounter in a variety of forms, just as did the children studying giants (Gardner, 1991; 1983; 1982). For instance, some of us begin with the instruction manual when learning a new computer program, while others of us prefer to be shown how the thing works. Similarly, our students approach intellectual problems in different ways. The point is not that teachers figure out exactly which approach is preferred by each child; rather, that multiple modalities are planned for and encouraged. Students learning how to inquire in integrated study should experiment with different approaches, constantly expanding their ways of learning about the world. An excerpt from another classroom illustrates the point.

A group of students listened to their teacher read from *Shh! We're Writing the Constitution* (Fritz, 1987). They watched a video of a play from the Constitutional period in the United States, and they read other nonfictional sources as well. "What picture do you get from each of these sources?" their teacher asked. "What images come to mind?" The students immediately responded with sensory images: "hot and muggy," "a lot of white-haired, white men," "flies buzzing around, windows closed," "secretive." At this point, their teacher showed them a painting depicting the signing of the Constitution, and said:

> What we are looking at is a painting of the immediate setting of
> the writing of the Constitution. Now, when you look at this painting, I
> want you to use some of the work we have done with costume, with
> clothing, art and things of the time period. You know there wasn't any

CNN back during the writing of the Constitution. After the fact an artist did a rendering of what he thought it would look like if you had been at the Constitutional Convention. Now, you are the art critic. I want you to look at the painting and to evaluate it in terms of [she writes on the board]:

What kind of job do you think the artist did? Did he make an accurate portrait of what happened at that time? Inaccurate? Why?

Where is attention focused in the painting? What do you think the artist is trying to do here? What are the aesthetic elements of this painting? What are the political uses this painting might be put to? (Levstik & Barton, 1997, p. 148)

Working in small groups, the students began noting details that conflicted with other sources they had used. Contrary to most sources, the men in the painting seemed cool and comfortable; curtains and windows were open. They noticed that George Washington was centered in the painting. The light focused on him so "he becomes the main figure" while the men who did most of the writing were minor figures in the painting. Carter explained that seeing the painting helped him visualize what the delegates looked like: "It really assisted me knowing which figure was which." Interestingly, he also mentioned that despite having read about how many delegates had been in attendance, "I didn't realize just how many delegates participated...until I saw that picture" (Levstik & Barton, 1997, p. 148).

In Carter's case, he knew from his reading of nonfiction how many delegates were at the convention, but it had probably not struck him as either interesting or significant. Experience with another medium elevated this information to a new level of significance. This would probably not have happened if he had not been exposed to the literature as well as the painting. While the painting added a new understanding to the texts he had read, informational books helped him notice dimensions in the art that he might have otherwise missed. It is not enough, then, only to provide students with literary sources. Rather, in integrated instruction, nonfiction plays an important, but not singular role. This means that students need to learn how different sources, including nonfiction, function in the context of inquiry.

Conducting Investigations

While there is no single way to use nonfiction in integrated studies, there are several approaches that can make its use more effective. A book set including several pieces of nonfiction at different levels of difficulty can help students move beyond an attachment to a single perspective. For a study of seasons, nonfiction such as *Winter Across America* (Simon, 1994),

Rocky Mountain Seasons (Burns, 1993), and *Sky Tree: Seeing Science through Art* (Locker & Christiansen, 1995) might be paired with fiction such as *My Mama had a Dancing Heart* (Gray, 1995) and *How Does the Wind Walk?* (Carlstrom, 1993), each a more poetic approach to seasons. In some classrooms, students select one of the books for their own reading, and a selection that the teacher reads aloud serves as contrast. In early primary classes, the teacher reads each of the books aloud, encouraging students to select them for later independent reading.

One primary teacher, Ruby Yessin, often starts the school day by reading and discussing nonfiction with her first-grade class (Levstik, 1993). During these times, illustrations are discussed, facts are checked, and questions are raised about the authenticity of the information. In Ruby's class, a child may be called upon to check with the librarian for further information or to use one of the reference books in the classroom to answer questions raised in reading an informational book. Some of the nonfiction they use is difficult for Ruby's students, but they read as much as they can and allow the teacher, their partners, or other adults to help them understand the rest. It is not unusual for a visitor to be asked to read an informational book to a first grader intent on finding out about Shakers, semi-trucks, or China. Ruby explains that her extensive use of nonfiction is part of the *web of meaning* that she and the children are building.

With older students, dialog journals provide an important opportunity to discuss responses to books. In dialog journals, teachers and students carry on a written conversation about the literature students read or hear. Sometimes students respond to a specific question. During one integrated study, a journal prompt began: "What do you think are the most important differences among the photographic visions of Solomon Butcher, Mathew Brady, and Dorothea Lange?" This question relied on students having heard or read *Prairie Visions: The Life and Times of Solomon Butcher* (Conrad, 1991), *Mathew Brady: His Life and Photographs* (Sullivan, 1994), and *Dorothea Lange* (Turner, 1994). In their responses, students commented on the impact of light and shadow in the photographs, on the solemnity of so many of the people pictured by each artist, and on Lange's and Butcher's emphasis on families. In another entry, students responded to questions such as "Do you think Lange changed the lives of the people she photographed?" and "What sources helped you answer this question?" These questions required more attention to developing a historical interpretation, and they encouraged students to draw on other nonfiction sources as well.

Abby Mott, a teacher who often uses book sets, arranges two different types of reading response groups to help her students think more carefully about their reading. The first is a discussion opportunity for students who are reading the same book. Abby may start the group with a couple of questions or a problem that requires referring to the book they are reading, and she will focus on both the literary and content aspects of the book. For example, during a study of early contact between Native Americans and European colonists she asks one group to select three passages from *Thunder from the Clear Sky* (Sewall, 1995) that show how the Wampanoag Indians and Pilgrims misunderstood each other. In another group, students search for passages that capture the differences between life in the Wampanoag village and the Pilgrim settlement. A third group selects historical descriptions from Sewall's book that can be supported by evidence from one of the other informational books available to the students. Notice that the groups are not duplicating each other. Instead, each group is organized so that it will have something specific to contribute to a follow-up discussion among response groups.

The second type of response group mixes students who have read different books. The tasks for such a group might involve the following: creating a comparison chart showing patterns of Native and European contact in Massachusetts, Virginia, California, and the Caribbean; describing different farming techniques used by native peoples; or creating a map that locates important places described in the books. In one class, two groups ended up discussing misunderstandings and betrayals between the Wampanoags and Pilgrims leading to King Philip's War. When one child suggested that "someone should have stepped in," Abby asked if they could come up with a solution that might have prevented the war. The two groups recruited several other participants and staged a mock negotiation between Wampanoags and Pilgrims that resulted in a treaty agreed to by most participants. Abby followed up by sharing parts of several actual treaties, along with segments from a Public Broadcasting System (PBS) video on what happened to these treaties. She then shared excerpts from *Killing Custer* (Welch, 1994), an adult book chronicling the story of Little Bighorn from the Native American perspective.

While some of these activities were relatively short term—writing a dialog journal entry—others became extended studies such as the treaty negotiations. Students had opportunities to share what they were thinking with their teacher and small groups of their peers. Their activities sent them to other sources and gave them a framework for making sense out of what they found. The structure of the treaty negotiations encouraged them to think about how to best represent different perspectives while the literature provided them with some information on what those perspectives might be.

As students worked on these projects, questions arose that sent them back to their reading. Sometimes debates would reignite as new information came to light. By arranging opportunities to encounter and reencounter a topic, their teacher provided a context for communal construction of meaning (Atwell, 1990; Wells & Chang-Wells, 1992). Students adjusted their ideas, not just in response to the text, or to teacher comment, but on the basis of interactions with their peers. In addition, their teacher encouraged reference to other sources of information. When a dispute over the accuracy of information arose, she arbitrated first by having students check each of their sources and then sent students to the library to look for confirming or disconfirming information. Sometimes students contacted outside experts, including a local historian. Jeff Wilhelm, in Chapter 15, discusses drama as a vehicle for exploring conflicting perspectives.

As students collect information, they also need help organizing what they have found. This organization is especially important when students are investigating many different aspects of a topic. As one teacher explains, "I found some [students] will do quite odd things in organization if not shown first"(Levstik & Smith, 1996). Some teachers find the *I-Search* paper a useful tool in this regard (Macrorie, 1988). In an *I-Search* paper, students follow four simple steps to describe their inquiry: "What I Knew," "Why I'm Writing this Paper," "The Search," and "What I Learned (or didn't learn)." They keep information related to each of these categories in an *I-Search* notebook. "The Search" category is particularly important, as it records not only what books or other resources have been used, but how each source contributed to the search. In the end, students can trace their journey as researchers, identifying questions and the sources they used in answering the questions. A simple model for this research technique is *George Washington's Breakfast* (Fritz, 1969) in which a young boy, George Washington Allen, wants to find out what his namesake ate for breakfast. The book traces young George's journey through reference materials, a field trip to Mount Vernon, and, finally, the discovery of the primary source that answers his question. In the end, he finds the recipe that allows him to taste Washington's breakfast—Indian hoe cakes (Pappas, *et al.* 1995). (For further information on *I-Search* papers, see also Joyce and Tallman, 1997.)

All of this is hard intellectual work for children. As another third grad-er remarked, at the conclusion of one extended study, "Research required a lot of writing and thinking. You also had to go a lot of places just to figure out one thing. You have to make a lot of categories and lists....When you make a web you're getting more ideas about a main subject. Research is more than one thing...you're putting more knowledge into your head." Her classmate added, "You know you're learning, but it's fun to do."

In their comments, these young children indicate that they are begin-ning to move beyond information accumulation. As another of them explained, "Research is learning something. It's not just copying down information." They enjoyed having "opportunities others don't have—even some adults—sometimes you can do all this fun stuff and it really teaches you a lot and I'll come home sometimes and say, 'Mom and Dad, guess what I learned today,' and they don't even know it."

Conclusions

All students should have the opportunity to engage in integrated study and inquiry. Our instruction should encourage children to fling their arms wide and embrace a world full of complexity and challenge, rich in interesting and intriguing possibilities, where there are always new things to learn. Filling our classrooms and libraries with accurate, well-written nonfiction is an important way in which we can help students to develop the skills necessary to begin to make sense out of the world, and to have the confidence to believe that they can make a difference in it.

References

Albert, M. (1995). Impact of an arts-integrated social studies curriculum on eighth graders' thinking capacities. Unpublished doctoral dissertation, University of Kentucky, Lexington.

Atwell, N. (Ed.). (1990). *Coming to know: Writing to learn in the intermediate grades*. Portsmouth, NH: Heinemann.

Delpit, L. (1994). *Other people's children: Cultural conflict in the classroom*. New York: New Press/Norton.

Gamberg, R., Kwak, W., Hutchings, M., & Altheim, J. (1988). *Learning and loving it: Theme studies in the classroom*. Portsmouth, NH: Heinemann.

Gardner, H. (1982). *Art, mind, and brain: A cognitive approach to creativity*. New York: Basic Books.

Gardner, H. (1983). *Frames of mind: The theory of multiple intelligences*. New York: Basic Books.

Gardner, H. (1991). *The unschooled mind: How children think and how schools should teach*. New York: Basic Books.

Hollins, E. (1996). *Culture in school learning: Revealing the deep meaning*. Mahwah, NJ: Erlbaum.

Hughes, L. (1981). Dream variation. In N. J. Frederick (Ed.), *The Harper Anthology of Poetry*. New York: Harper

Joyce, M., & Tallman, J. I. (1997). *Making the writing and research connection with the I-search process*. New York: Neal-Schuman.

Kennedy, J. F. (1962). John Fitzgerald Kennedy papers. Washington, DC: National Archives and Records Administration.

Levstik, L. S. (1993). Building a sense of history in a first grade classroom. In J. Brophy (Ed.), *Advances in Research on Teaching, Vol. 4. Research in Elementary Social Studies* (pp. 1-31). Greenwich, CT: JAI Press.

Levstik, L. S. (1995). Narrative constructions: Cultural frames for history. *The Social Studies, 86*, 113-116.

Levstik, L. S., & Barton, K. C. (1996). "They still use some of their past": Historical salience in elementary children's chronological thinking.

Journal of Curriculum Studies, 28 (5), 531-576.

Levstik, L. S., & Barton, K. C. (1997). *Doing history: Inquiries with elementary and middle school children.* Mahwah, NJ: Erlbaum.

Levstik, L. S., & Smith, D. B. (1996). "I've never done this before:" Building a community of historical inquiry in a third grade classroom. In J. Brophy (Ed.), *Advances in Research on Teaching, Vol. 6.* (pp. 85-114). Greenwich, CT: JAI Press.

Macrorie, K. (1988). *The I-search paper.* Portsmouth, NH: Boynton/Cook.

Newmann, F. M., Secada, W. G., & Wehlage, G. G. (1995). *A guide to authentic instruction and assessment: Vision, standards and scoring.* Madison, WI: Wisconsin Center for Education Research.

Pappas, C. C., Kiefer, B. Z., & Levstik, L. S. (1995). *An integrated language perspective in the elementary school: Theory into action.* White Plains, NY: Longman.

Rogoff, B. (1990). *Apprenticeship in thinking: Cognitive development in social context.* New York: Oxford University Press.

Welch, J. (1994). *Killing Custer.* New York: Norton.

Wells, G. (1986). *The meaning makers: Children learning language and using language to learn.* Portsmouth, NH: Heinemann.

Wells, G., & Chang,Wells, G. L. (1992). *Constructing knowledge together: Classrooms as centers of inquiry and literacy.* Portsmouth, NH: Heinemann.

Young, K. A. (1994). *Constructing buildings, bridges, and minds: Building an integrated curriculum through social studies.* Portsmouth, NH: Heinemann.

Chapter 13
Nonfiction Books: Naturals for the Primary Level

by Carol Avery

On a blustery January morning in the mountains of Pennsylvania, I open a book in front of 35 children in a small classroom. They've been bused to school from many directions to this aging hilltop building surrounded by woods, fields, and a lake. It is time for the read-aloud that will lead into the daily writing workshop. The children are now familiar with the structure and become attentive. They love this read-aloud time and the writing that follows. "What are you going to read today?" they ask eagerly.

Today I have chosen *Cactus Hotel* (1991) by Brenda Z. Guiberson and illustrated by Megan Lloyd. "This book is about the saguaro cactus. It grows in the southwest. Once I was there and I saw saguaro cactus when I drove along the highway between Tucson and Phoenix. They look like this and they are quite large." I show the class the illustration on the book's cover as I give a brief introduction to the book. "Megan Lloyd is a Pennsylvania illustrator who lives in Carlisle, but it says here (I point to the book jacket flap) that she flew to Arizona before she did these illustrations." I read the blurb on the jacket and then reread the quotation from Lloyd, "I like to see what I am going to illustrate rather than make it up," she says. "Why do you suppose that's so?" I ask.

Helping Children Distinguish Nonfiction From Fiction

• When a nonfiction book is shared aloud invite children to talk about the differences and similarities between nonfiction and fiction.

• When nonfiction titles are shared aloud identify them as such.

• Present a variety of nonfiction and discuss how different authors write about their topics and ways in which illustrators and photographers depict topics. These discussions will help children define their definition of nonfiction.

• It is important to provide young children with many experiences with nonfiction materials in order to build their concept of the difference between fiction and nonfiction.

"Because then she'd get it right. She'd know what something really looks like."

"She wouldn't have to guess."

"It'd be fun to go there [Arizona]."

"Yes, good ideas. And I bet she did have fun going there," I respond, and we move on. Timing is important. I don't want to get bogged down exploring too much background during the first reading of this book. The focus must be on the ideas and information presented in the book: making sense of what we find in the words and pictures and enjoying the process of doing so.

"I chose this book to read today because it is nonfiction. That means it is true—it's factual information as opposed to a fiction book that tells a made-up story." I note nods of acknowledgment from many children and, from a few others, looks that tell me this is probably either a totally new concept or an emerging awareness. "But," I add, "even though this book is nonfiction, it's written like a story. That's a choice the author made as a way to present the information she had."

"What do you think the title *Cactus Hotel* means?" I ask. Brian, sitting in the front row, looks over his shoulder around the room at his classmates. Seeing no hands, he hesitantly raises his.

"The cactus is a hotel for lots of animals? Lot of animals live there?" he says.

"Oh, you think that's what the author means—that this cactus is like a hotel—a place for lots of different animals to live?" I can hear the delight in my own voice over Brian's response. He's not been one to venture predictions very often.

"Yeah." He speaks with confidence now. A glance around the class tells me that this idea had not occurred to many of them, and they are somewhat surprised and respectful that Brian came up with it.

I begin to read:

"On a hot, dry day in the desert, a bright-red fruit falls from a tall saguaro cactus. *Plop.* It splits apart on the sandy floor. Two thousand black seeds glisten in the sunlight" (unpaged).

"Do you get an image, a picture in your head, from the words?" I pause to ask before I show the illustration. I'm drawing on previous read-alouds when we discussed writing that creates images for readers and effective beginnings in books.

"Yeah."

"I see it."

"The picture helped me see the red fruit better."

"What about that word 'plop'?" I ask. "It's written in italics and that one word is a whole sentence. Why do you suppose this is?"

The children quickly articulate that the word represents the sound of the fruit falling. I add a quick explanation that the use of italics and the sentence structure help us as readers to form an image from the first three sentences. We reread this first page and realize that at the sentence "*Plop*" our mind pauses for a split second to hear that sound almost, then the text continues with the next words "It splits apart...."

I turn the page and read:

"When the air cools in the evening, an old pack rat comes out and eats the juicy fruit. Then he skitters across the sand. A seed left clinging to his whiskers falls under a paloverde tree" (unpaged).

"Ooh, I like the way the author switches from the hot day to the cool evening. And I like when she says the rat "skitters." A couple of children repeat "skitters." "I like to say that word and I like the sound of it," I say. Smiles and nods and more repetition of "skitters" dot the room and we move on.

For the rest of the reading our talk revolves around the story of the life of a saguaro cactus. On this particular reading, the slow growth and size of the cactus appeal to the imaginations of these children. We take note as a seed sprouts from the juicy red fruit. After 10 years it is "only four inches high." After 50 years it "stands ten feet tall." And Aaron comments, "Wow! That's as tall as a basketball hoop!"

"Really? I didn't know that." And I hear surprise in my voice and see several boys nod in confirmation.

"After 60 years the cactus hotel is 18 feet tall....It begins to grow an arm....After 150 years,...the giant plant has finally stopped growing. It is 50 feet tall...weighs eight tons—about as much as five automobiles" (unpaged). Wows and whews come from the class—especially the boys. They speculate just how long 50 feet really is, start to compare it with the length of a football field, then change

INVITING STUDENTS TO NOTICE ASPECTS OF NONFICTION

Authors and illustrators make decisions as they write and think through how material will be presented. Helping students notice specific qualities of good writing and format nurtures their development as readers and writers as you read aloud. Invite children to notice how language and illustrations "work" together in nonfiction. The difficulty will not be in finding examples but in choosing which ones to point out to children.

their minds, speculate on the height of the school, then decide they don't know for sure. It's just big.

"You could measure," I comment. They nod and we go on. Except for pointing out the "*Tap, tap, tap*" of a woodpecker as another example of onomatopoeia (words that imitate natural sounds) like the "*Plop*" at the beginning, we read the rest of the book without taking note of the author's strategies, style, or techniques. I drop back, let the children take the lead, and respond to what is important to them. One child states that she likes the way the illustrator drew the pictures so that you could see the inside of the holes where the animals live at the same time that you see the whole scene outside. Several children have commented on the lives of the animals that live in the cactus hotel. On a subsequent reading, they astound me at how much information they have retained about these animals—far more than I could recall and significantly more than I would have guessed had I to evaluate what they took away from the first reading. On further thought, I think, of course they remember. Children always remember details in stories they enjoy. The use of narrative to present nonfiction is a natural for young children to help them remember information.

This is the way it goes. Again, children have been my teachers. After nearly 30 years in education, these little surprises continue to bring me delight and, at the same time, evoke my profound respect for children as first-class thinkers, knowers, and learners. Part of the rewards of teaching is catching glimpses of children's thinking. I have learned that this only happens if I am willing to "drop back" and let children lead.

When I decided to read *Cactus Hotel*, my agenda was to present a well-written nonfiction book to the class, point out the difference between fiction and nonfiction, and provide an example of nonfiction writing that was not personal narrative or memoir as most of the children's writing has been. As I shared the book, I knew that we would encounter interesting aspects of the writing and illustrations. I would point out some specifics as we came upon them, making my decisions based on my sense of timing and my "read" of the class at a given moment, and I would also see what children would notice and discover on their own. We have a history together. I know what I have introduced to them and where they are in their development as readers and writers. Yetta Goodman (1985) emphasized the importance of *kidwatching*. As I watch and listen to the children, I continually discover teachable moments when I can nudge their development further. If I set my mind on all the possibilities beforehand, I have learned I tend to overlook the fundamental goal of involving the children in the book. I want them to want to return to this book again and again, to ask me to reread it, to remember it at unexpected moments later in the day and even after school.

I did not plan to have the class measure or graph the growth of the cactus. My decision to followup with such an activity would evolve out of the children's responses to the size of the cactus. This group did respond and I planted a seed for the possibility of including this kind of activity when I said, "You could measure." Whether or not we do will depend on the interest and energy of the class after the reading and during subsequent rereadings. I have learned that to plan on lots of follow-up activities and to try to get lots of curricular mileage out of a book can backfire. Children begin to approach books with an attitude of "What is she going to make us do this time?" instead of just learning, appreciating, and enjoying the book on its own merit.

So, the heart of the read-aloud time—and most of that time too—is spent enjoying and taking in the ideas presented by the author and illustrator. That is what happened with *Cactus Hotel.* Woven through this time, however, was direct teaching and specific questions designed to help children discover aspects of the book they might otherwise miss. I interjected these things briefly as one might add a touch of strong color to a painting or to a quilt. I specifically wanted the class to notice some of the strategies and techniques the author and illustrator used to help convey their ideas. In this case, I pointed out the illustrator's need for direct experience in order to illustrate, the author's use of story (narrative) to write nonfiction, the meaning conveyed in the title, the use of italics, onomatopoeia and one word sentences, a lead that creates images and uses contrasts, and the use of a strong verb, such as "skitters."

On rereading the book, other characteristics of the writing may come up. For example, Guiberson's choice of verbs throughout the text moves the writing forward in a direct, clear fashion at the same time that it enriches the images left with the reader. We know that hearing and reading well-written books helps children to develop as readers and writers. I believe that it requires more than just surrounding them with such experiences; we also need to take some time to point out, to "name" those things that writers do and invite children to try these strategies and techniques as they write. I have noticed that children frequently take up these invitations to try techniques when they are read to daily and when they have opportunity to write daily. But a little bit goes a long way; an exhaustive examination of the author's methods would be overwhelming, not be internalized, and deflate the children's enthusiasm for the book and end their talk about it. In the days that followed our reading, when the children referred to this book, they talked about the ideas the author conveyed in the content. This is what ought to happen. The readers' continued thinking and talking about the book, is, I am sure, what the author and illustrator hoped would happen when they created *Cactus Hotel.*

Nonfiction as Read-Alouds

I began reading nonfiction to classes when I was an elementary librarian in the early 1970s. My purpose then, as now, was to introduce children to the riches of nonfiction children's literature and to whet their appetites to read nonfiction as well as traditional fictional literature. Many, if not most, of the nonfiction books I read to children (no matter the grade level) do not necessarily connect with specific content areas of the curriculum. I choose books that appeal to me because they have strong, accurate content presented in a concise, creative, interesting, and fascinating manner. I quickly discovered that children love nonfiction; they crave it. Children have an insatiable desire to learn about the world they live in and the world beyond their daily experiences. Books, especially nonfiction, provide opportunity for children to explore these worlds and experience life vicariously beyond their doors.

Narrative Nonfiction

In recent years, I have noticed that many authors of quality nonfiction books use some form of narrative as they present facts, information, and ideas. I think this is one of the qualities of these books that captures the hearts and the minds of readers of all ages. Narratives—stories—have always been ways to communicate experiences and knowledge. The technique has opened nonfiction to many more young readers. We are blessed with a wonderful selection of excellent quality nonfiction to share with children today.

For the very young, Lois Ehlert's books provide children with a combination of fiction and nonfiction in the same book. *Feathers for Lunch* (1990); *Red Leaf, Yellow Leaf* (1993); and *Snowballs* (1995) all combine short narrative stories with simple scientific information. The factual information is embedded in the illustrations and labels, in appended informational pages, and in the book jacket itself. Ehlert's unusual collages provide information through the depiction of real objects. Talking about what is "true" and what is "made up" helps very young children begin to think differentially about the material in books. The books also provide models of unusual ways an author conveys information to readers. Ehlert's books have become classics that I read every year to first graders (and to the preschooler in my life).

There are other nonfiction books that I love so much that I return to them year after year as classroom read-alouds. I can count on them always being hits with children. *Think of an Eel* (1993) by Karen Wallace (one of the *Read and Wonder* series from Candlewick Press) is a fascinating book about the life of eels who are born in the Sargasso Sea south of Bermuda, swim to the rivers of Europe to live most of their lives, and return to the Sargasso to mate, lay eggs, and die. The children are particularly intrigued with the extra facts and ideas penned in handwritten note form into the margins of the pages of this book.

Oil Spill! (1994) by Melvin Berger, (one of the *Let's Read-and-Find-Out Science* books from HarperCollins) begins with the Exxon Valdez oil spill. The book explains the immensity of this spill by pointing out that the 11 million gallons are enough to fill more than 1,000 large swimming pools. The book also addresses causes of oil spills, procedures to clean oil spills, and ways to prevent them. One response to this book might be to write to a senator, although, I am not inclined to give such an assignment to the class. Rather, I point out that this is what persons do when they care very much about something; they write letters to protest, raise awareness, to suggest changes. With this kind of standing invitation in the classroom, Jeff wrote to the toy manufacturer of his action figure that lost its paint within two months of purchase. When he received a postcard reply that was obviously a form letter, he said in disgust, "I don't think I'll buy any more toys from them."

Jane Yolen's *Letting Swift River Go* (1992) is a fictionalized story based on the damming of the Swift River in Massachusetts to create the Quabbin Reservoir, which flooded several towns. Yolen researched her story thoroughly before writing, even traveling on an annual bus trip pilgrimage to the site with former residents of the flooded area. Though the book is told from the perspective of a fictional character, the information about the process of creating a reservoir is so detailed that the book qualifies as nonfiction in our classrooms. *Faction* is the word the children and I often use for books such as this. *Letting Swift River Go* evoked much discussion with children

EXAMPLES OF NONFICTION SERIES BOOKS FOR YOUNG CHILDREN

• The books in the *Read and Wonder* series provide children with models of interesting ways to write nonfiction and have a wealth of information. *I Love Guinea Pigs* (King-Smith, 1994) and *Spider Watching* (French, 1994) are favorites with children.

• The *Let's-Read-and-Find-Out Science* series introduces basic science concepts. Stage 1 books explain simple and observable concepts as in *From Tadpole to Frog* (Pfeffer, 1994). Stage 2 books include hands-on activities as in *Where Does the Garbage Go?* (Showers, 1994). Some of these books are revised and updated versions of popular old nonfiction titles while others are brand-new nonfiction books.

who live near a reservoir in Pennsylvania. "Oh, you know the place where the road goes into the water?" Shawn reminded the class when I read it aloud. The book prompted discussions about how reservoirs are created and historical discussions of communities as recalled by older family members. We even had youngsters examining the pros and cons of power plants on rivers.

The *Story of Ruby Bridges* (1995) by Robert Coles, Pulitzer Prize-winning author and Harvard research psychiatrist, shows the integration of public schools as no other book or report as ever done for me. When first grader Ruby Bridges comes to school with federal marshals guarding her passage through the schoolyard, she is the only child in the classroom. All the other families have withdrawn their children. First graders were awed when I read this book and asked to have it read again and again. It seemed to me that with each reading they grappled with the reality of and reasons for Ruby's school experience, which was so different from what they'd known.

Becoming Class Experts

Introducing children to books they might read is one of my purposes for reading to children. Reading a good book aloud usually prompts the children to read it on their own, and some of the most sought-after books in my classrooms have been nonfiction. Children do not have to be able to read the text to "read" a book. Kindergarten children and first graders read the pictures and sometimes the captions, soaking up every detail.

First-grade student Greg was our class expert on the Titanic. His parents reported he had seen a recent TV special on the Titanic when he was three and he had been fascinated ever since. He pored over every book on the topic that he could get his hands on. His interest became contagious. We all became experts on the Titanic that year. During reading workshop he often could be found with a partner scrutinizing every picture, noticing every detail, and reading the captions for clues. Eventually, Greg wrote his own book, The Death of the Titanic. He not only presented the factual details he knew about the sinking of this unsinkable ship but also shared human interest stories of the drama of the catastrophe. He carefully constructed his writing, dividing his information into chapters and alternating the chapters between mechanical explanations and human drama. "I wanted it to be interesting, not boring," he said, "That's why I did it that way."

The nonfiction read-alouds in my classroom have never been limited to short picture books. Patricia Lauber's *Volcano* (1986), which narrates the eruption of Mount St. Helens and the rebirth of life on the mountain afterwards, became one of the "tried and true" books that every first-grade class loved. I read a few pages of it every day during our read-aloud time along with other choices of fiction, poetry, etc. The topic of volcanos is fascinating to them, and my reading opened for them a treasure of information that would have been unaccessible otherwise. Children became experts on volcanos and speculated about the role of volcanos during the time of dinosaurs.

Nonfiction and the Curriculum

Of course, nonfiction books play a major part in content areas of study. When I begin such areas of study, I rely on an inquiry approach using many of the suggestions presented in Linda Levstik's Chapter 12. I may decide to launch a particular area of study by reading a nonfiction book on some aspect of that topic. Then I explore the topic with the class by brainstorming, webbing, listing, or in some way compiling the information they know that connects to this topic. We raise questions and consider ways to seek answers. The librarian becomes involved and we write notes to ask for materials, or even better yet, go to the library as a group to find resources ourselves. It is not just the answers that are important but the processes of researching, questioning, seeking, connecting, theorizing, clarifying, revising our thinking, and raising new questions. We are learning how to learn.

Because many of my students are emerging readers, I read nonfiction books aloud to my students and make them available for them to browse through on their own. My classes soon come to recognize particular authors whose work they can count on to be accurate such as Patricia Lauber, Gail Gibbons, Seymour Simon, and Aliki. As we get into topics, the children usually recognize that we need to check third or fourth sources when two books have conflicting information. We also check copyright dates. For example, when we studied dinosaurs, we soon realized that this is an area that is continually producing new discoveries that require updating information. It became important to question what we read. What information is most recent? Why would information in some books conflict with other books? Why might books have incorrect information?

We are also discriminating when it comes to determining which books are important to use for content studies. When a child found Syd Hoff's *Danny and the Dinosaur* (1958) in the classroom, he proclaimed, "Here's a book about dinosaurs. We can read it and get more information." We took time to discuss the difference between storybooks about dinosaurs, particularly fantasy, and nonfictional books about dinosaurs and why this book was not a good resource for our study of dinosaurs. All of this is part of reading instruction, and, by incorporating quality nonfiction books into our studies, I can help even first graders develop critical study and investigative skills. Repeatedly, I watched children develop an attitude of coming to investigative reading with questioning attitudes.

The children keep logs throughout our studies of particular content areas. In these logs they record the important information they find. "Important" is what is meaningful to them. For example, after reading a nonfiction book or after showing a filmstrip, I have them record their ideas before we talk. On field trips they take notepads and record what they find of interest. Drawing and labeling (strategies that we find in many nonfiction books) become part of their logs. They share and discuss their logs periodically during our investigations and sometimes I have them write a final piece about some aspect of the topic, encouraging them to incorporate all that they know about good writing from our writing workshop. Investigation and inquiry into curricular topics of study never end. We may move onto other topics in the classroom, but the children continue to read and question and learn more about the interests we have begun together. It is usual for a child to share information in May regarding a topic we studied as a group in the fall (Avery, 1993).

Conclusions

I have spent most of my educational career working with primary-age children. However, I have had enough experience with older children to know that nonfiction literature is for all ages. Sharing high-quality nonfiction aloud in the primary classroom or during library visits is a time of significant teaching. I discuss strategies for reading nonfiction, demonstrate connections to other books, invite conversation about decisions authors make in writing nonfiction, and help children make connections to their own lines. I involve children in making these connections by inviting their ideas and valuing all the responses they offer. I refrain from shaping children's ideas to conform with my own in favor of honoring the diversity of ideas that will be inherent within any group.

We speak of negotiation when we talk about decision making in the classroom. Using read-aloud as a teaching time is filled with making decisions and, thus, requires skill in negotiation. Negotiation continually occurs as we work our way through the following:

- the demands of the curriculum and the needs of children and their development,

- the tension between a teacher's responsibility to share knowledge and expertise and the child's readiness to receive and understand,

- the obvious need for direct teaching and the essential need for children to have opportunity to make discoveries through engagement in authentic tasks.

Once we read nonfiction books to children for them to "get" the specific content. I believe our reading of nonfiction involves far more than conveying content. As we incorporate the reading of nonfiction literature aloud on a regular basis in primary classrooms, we learn to negotiate the tensions inherent in teaching. Learning to do this well moves us from teachers as practitioners and implementers to teachers as crafters and even artists and, most importantly, fosters the development of literate lives for our students.

References

Avery, C. (1993). *...And with a light touch: Learning about reading, writing, and teaching with first graders.* Portsmouth, NH: Heinemann.

Goodman, Y. (1985). Kidwatching: Observing children in the classroom. In A. Jaggar & M. T. Smith-Burke (Eds.), *Observing the language learner* (pp. 9-18). Newark, DE: The International Reading Association. Urbana, IL: National Council of Teachers of English.

Chapter 14
Nonfiction Literature as the "Text" of My Intermediate Classroom: That's a Fact

by Donna Maxim

> I'm more interested in arousing enthusiasm in kids than in teaching facts. The facts may change, but the enthusiasm for exploring the world will remain with them the rest of their lives.
> —Seymour Simon (Musleah, 1996)

Seymour Simon's words best tell why I use nonfiction literature with my third- and fourth-grade classroom at the Center for Teaching and Learning in Edgecomb, Maine. However, this was not always the case.

As a third- and fourth-grade teacher for the past 23 years, I have gradually moved away from using textbooks in my classes. During my first 8 years of teaching, I had a textbook for every subject, but I rarely finished any one of them in a given year. During this time I began to collect children's literature for my classroom, usually chapter books. I was hungry to hear educators, authors, and illustrators speak; so I attended a variety of conferences and workshops. Ideas for using literature in the classroom were suggested by classroom teachers and teacher educators such as Beverly Kobrin, Don Graves, and Jim Trelease. I gathered literature from a variety of notable nonfiction authors—Seymour Simon, Jim Arnosky, Gail Gibbons, Milton Meltzer, Jean Fritz, Jean Craighead George, and Barbara Bash, among others.

When I took a position at Boothbay Region Elementary School, textbooks were provided only for reading, math, and science. We were encouraged to create our own units of study across the curriculum, as long as we worked within the curricular guidelines. A classroom library organized by subject areas filled my room. Science and history children's books were used as resources for research projects and as models for writing. Reading aloud books created a common background of knowledge for every student

TEACHER RESOURCES

Book Links
434 W. Downer
Aurora, Illinois 60506

Naturescope Magazine
National Wildlife
Federation
1412 Sixteenth Street
NW
Washington, DC 20036

The Web Magazine
Ohio State University
200 Ramseyer Hall
29 W. Woodruff
Columbus, Ohio 4321

in my class. Often only a small section of a book was shared aloud to discuss an especially interesting feature, such as intriguing chapter titles in a table of contents, a powerful lead, or an unusual organizational structure, etc. Then the book was left in an accessible place for students to use during independent reading time. Poetry was shared in all subject areas as a possible format for student writing and as a way to look at the factual side of science more aesthetically.

For the past 7 years I have taught third and fourth graders at the Center for Teaching and Learning, a demonstration school in Edgecomb, Maine. Children's literature is available throughout the school as "textbooks" for my students. A variety of genres supports every unit of study, and nonfiction is an integral part of every unit. Because our rooms are subject focused (reading/history, writing, and math/science rooms), resources are gathered in baskets for the purpose of being moved throughout the school. In addition, many other resources extend and enhance the teaching and learning that goes on in my classroom.

The faculty at the Center chooses one science and one history theme each year to be studied by all children in kindergarten through the eighth grade. We are dedicated to collecting and searching out all the possible resources available and examining them during weekly planning sessions. Some of our most helpful teacher resources are these three magazines: *The Web, Book Links,* and *Naturescope.* We also use Beverly Kobrin's *Eyeopeners* (1988) and *Eyeopeners II* (1995), and Donald Graves' *Investigating Nonfiction* (1989).

At the beginning of each unit of study, resources are recorded on a theme-planning page (including such categories as print resources for teachers and kids, vocabulary, key concepts, people, organizations, field trips, and activities, etc.), which is revised as new ideas are generated. For each theme we also develop an extensive bibliography of children's literature and teacher resources sometimes running up to 8 or 10 pages.

Snowball (1995) found that 85% of the reading done by middle school, high school, and adult readers is nonfiction. I have witnessed an increase in the use of nonfiction in my own classroom as students research and write about topics that interest them or are assigned. This percentage also demonstrates a need to provide many opportunities for my students to read more nonfiction.

There are several powerful reasons why I use nonfiction literature in the classroom:

- Excites students about new as well as familiar information
- Explores a variety of approaches to researching and presenting their research
- Arouses their curiosity and wonders about the world
- Supports my teaching and learning
- Contains more current information than usually found in textbooks

Simply having access to books, however, is not enough. I both plan and invite my students to use nonfiction literature in my classroom: sharing it in minilessons for all curricular areas; as resources for student research projects and presentations; as models for student writing; and to teach critical reading strategies and skills (*e.g.*, extracting information, making comparisons, and checking author credentials and accuracy of information). In the following section, I discuss how nonfiction can be used during reading workshop time. The remainder of the chapter will focus on the integration of nonfiction into the science program.

Nonfiction Literature as the "Text" of the Classroom

Nonfiction Literature for Reading Worshop

Students become familiar with reading a wide variety of resources and use these to search out answers to their own questions, to explore interests, and to find new information for the units that we are studying. Reading minilessons are presented to meet these needs as well as a variety of literature to demonstrate the need to double check facts while researching.

In order to help my students extract information from nonfiction materials, time is provided to discuss these books as resources when reading nonfiction texts. The focus of one reading minilesson was listing the strategies we noticed as we reread a photocopy of a text.

- We read more slowly—especially when looking for specific information.
- We paid more attention while we were reading.
- We looked at the pictures more closely and expected more pictures.
- Some books took longer to read.
- Sometimes we circled important words while reading and it slowed us down.
- We noticed the author's crafting of the piece.

To extend awareness and appreciation of writing styles and how we read nonfiction, we conducted two author studies—one of Seymour Simon and another of Ken Robbins. First, we gathered all the books by each author and used independent reading time to read the books in pairs. On separate charts, we listed what we noticed about each author's writing style. We began our comparison by reading the dedication in *The Sun* (Simon, 1986) because he tells readers that this is his one 100th book. Here are some of the things we noticed about each author's writing style.

Figure 14.1 Chart on Writing Styles of Seymour Simon and Ken Robbins

Seymour Simon's Books

1. He sure wrote about a lot of topics. He has written over one hundred books. He has edited one book of poetry.
2. Sometimes he used second-person narrative and involved the reader in his books: Earth, Big Cats, and Whales.
3. Sometimes he used a question-answer format.
4. He shared lots of information.
5. Sometimes he used comparisons to share information.
6. Sometimes he wrote from general to specific. In *Sharks* (1995) he writes first about all sharks in general, then he writes about specific kinds of sharks. He does this in *Whales* (1989) also.

Ken Robbin's Books

(See Children's Books Cited for books in the "Elements" series by Ken Robbins)

1. He put the topic on the bottom of each page.
2. On every page he told something about the topic.
3. His illustrations were different-colored photographs.
4. His photographs were all labeled where they are.
5. He used special language and words in his text: "squish" and "squash" as well as some rhyming.
6. He created clear images in his writing.

The nonfiction literature we use to conduct research in other curricular areas is also the literature used during reading workshop to help students to notice specific skills and strategies they use for research and reading independently. Reading workshop time is also used to explore possible resources and to read nonfiction literature. For additional ways to use nonfiction literature throughout the curriculum see Chapter 12. Some of our favorite nonfiction books for Social Studies and Mathematics are included in Figure 14.2.

Figure14.2 Favorite Read-Aloud Books

MIGRATION UNIT

All Times, All People: A World History of Slavery by Milton Meltzer

The Great Migration: An American Story by Jacob Lawrence

Journey to Freedom: A Story of the Underground Railroad by Courtni Wright

Nettie's Trip South by Ann Turner

A Picture Book of Harriet Tubman by David Adler

U. S. HISTORY

From Colonies to Country: A History of Us by Joy Hakim

The Great Little Madison by Jean Fritz

Why Don't You Get a Horse, Sam Adams? by Jean Fritz

MATHEMATICS

Counting Cranes by Mary Beth Owens

Counting Wildflowers by Bruce McMillan

The Doorbell Rang by Pat Hutchins

Each Orange Had 8 Slices: A Counting Book by Paul Giganti, Jr.

How Big Is a Foot? by Rolf Myller

Jelly Beans for Sale by Bruce McMillan

The King's Chessboard by David Birch

A Remainder of One by Elinor J. Pinczes

Nonfiction Literature for Science

In 1994-1995, the faculty at the Center For Teaching and Learning chose marine studies as the science theme for the year. During one part of the year we focused on the lifestyles of marine creatures. In reading workshop I began reading aloud *Newberry: The Life and Times of a Maine Clam* (Dethier, 1981), a novel that includes facts about marine creatures. Students practiced their note-taking skills by recording new information about marine creatures in their journals while I read aloud (Maxim, 1990).

Other popular titles for read-alouds included *Life in a Tide Pool* (Silverstein & Silverstein, 1990) and *Where the Waves Break: Life at the Edge of the Sea* (Malnig, 1985).

During the next science class I asked my students to read the introduction to *The Ocean Book* (Sobel, 1989) either independently or with a partner and to discuss the facts that they learned. I then read aloud *Oceans* (Simon, 1990) and asked students to again take notes in their journals about things they know, questions, and what they were learning. I wanted them to think about how different authors present their ideas, to understand that information was sometimes repeated in several sources, and to potentially use the resources for their own presentations. As my students began brainstorming ideas in their journals for research projects about marine creatures, I also shared *Whales* (Simon, 1989) aloud. We charted everything we knew about whales and wanted to learn and decided the topic would be too large for one person to research and write about.

Another minilesson began by sharing a marine creatures diagram from *The Seaside Naturalist* (Coulombe, 1984), which highlighted the major groups of marine animals. We listed all the possibilities of marine creatures we might write about, and after defining "vertebrate" and "invertebrate," we listed them in two categories.

I also shared a chapter about the three lifestyle zones—benthos, nekton, and plankton, and then we listed the marine creatures found in the Northern Atlantic Ocean by these zones. In a student-led minilesson about the zones and their characteristics, we shared our new information with the kindergartners. Working collaboratively, we created a mural entitled "The Lifestyles of Ocean Creatures" in which we used cut-out sea creatures placed in the zones of the ocean.

We explored the features of the ocean floor by looking at maps and listing all the different features we noticed on a class chart. We defined the features using: *Geography From A to Z: A Picture Glossary* (Knowlton, 1988) and *Earth Words: A Dictionary of the Environment* (Simon, 1995). Using this information, teams of students chose features to draw and write about. They created their own resource, *Ocean Features*, which we published and displayed with papier mâché models of the ocean floor. The book described the ocean features they had included as part of their models. Gretchen Hull, a parent with a degree in biology, helped the class conduct experiments on saltwater density and use microscopes to observe and study plankton. We recorded information in our journals and on class charts. (See Figure 14.3.)

Our kindergarten collaboration continued by researching and writing about marine creatures. Teams of students, composed of kindergartners and third and fourth graders, began to brainstorm questions in their journals. The third and fourth graders acted as recorders.

Figure14.3

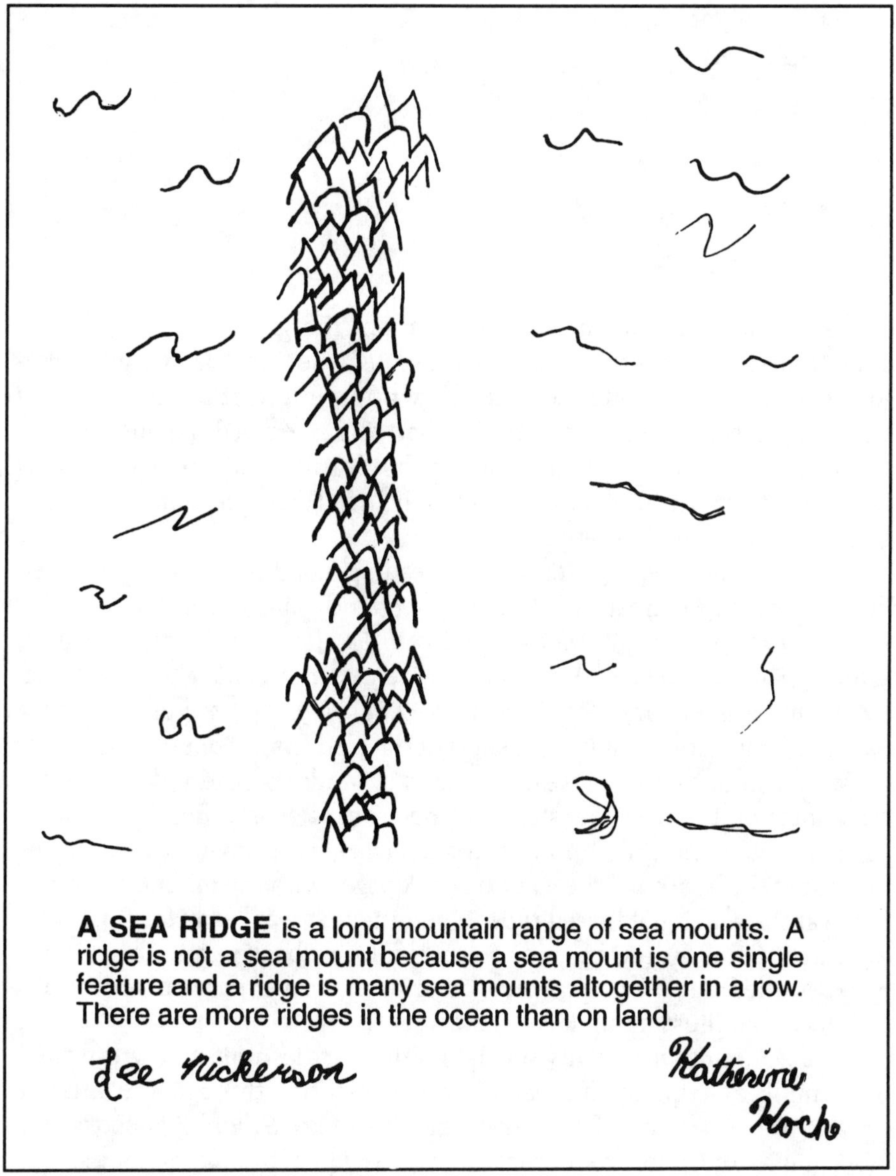

A SEA RIDGE is a long mountain range of sea mounts. A ridge is not a sea mount because a sea mount is one single feature and a ridge is many sea mounts altogether in a row. There are more ridges in the ocean than on land.

Lee Nickerson   *Katherine Koch*

The teachers used these questions to spark a discussion and create a class chart of the kinds of information we might share about marine creatures:

- What does the creature look like?

- What does it eat?

- How does it breathe?

- What eats it?
- Where does it live?
- How do they protect themselves?
- How does it move?
- How does it eat?
- How does it reproduce?
- How big does it get?

After much discussion and negotiation, the group chose a coloring book format to present their information. Because of the layout of a coloring book, children decided to limit the written information to three facts for each creature. We returned to the chart and narrowed the questions to include: what the creature ate, what ate the creature, and where it lived. As a group, we planned the page format to include three questions written as statements and an illustration.

The research began in earnest by reading aloud books that presented information on sea creatures: *Squish! A Wetland Walk* (Luenn, 1994); *Safari Beneath the Sea: The Wonder of the North Pacific Coast* (Swanson, 1995); *A Swim Through the Sea* (Pratt, 1994); *The Ocean Alphabet Book* (Pallotta, 1986); and *Discovering Acadia* (Scheid, 1988). We collected all our ocean resources and kept them in a basket that traveled from room to room while we were conducting our research. Teams of students read independently, took notes on the three questions in their journals, and then teams drafted their texts. The third and fourth graders took responsibility for typing the text at the bottom of the coloring book pages with the marine creature's name at the top in bold-faced type. When the text was ready for final copy, each student team drew pictures on their coloring book pages. The coloring book, entitled *Life at the Seashore*, began with a cover page on which each child drew an illustration. (See Figure 14.4.)

Our culminating activity for the marine studies unit was writing and performing a script for a "Magic School Bus" trip through the Atlantic Ocean. We read many of Joanna Cole's *The Magic School Bus* books (see Bibliography of Children's Books) during independent reading time in science class and recorded what we noticed about the organization of the books in our journals. Students outlined what their own "Magic School Bus" journey might look like. They decided it would begin in the benthos zone and then travel through the nekton and plankton zones. During the trip different marine creatures would swim on or alongside the bus and share information about themselves. Teams of two students planned to describe each lifestyle zone while other students negotiated what marine creatures they would become: a horseshoe crab, a swordfish, a blue whale,

Figure14.4

a manatee, zoo plankton, and phytoplankton. My entire class volunteered me as Ms. Frizzle! At the first rehearsal, suggestions for props were made, texts were shared, and comments and questions on each presentation were taken into consideration for possible revisions. One suggestion was that the shades be pulled down to represent the benthos zone, the lowest zone, and then raise the shades as we continued up through the different zones. We donned our sunglasses and microscopes for the plankton zone. After revising our script, we invited our kindergarten partners for a ride on our own "Magic School Bus" adventure!

Conclusions

When planning any unit of study at the Center for Teaching and Learning, I provide lots of opportunities for reading, talking, observing, recording, researching, and publishing. Publications and oral presentations emerge from lots of discussion, reading aloud, independent reading, field trips, questioning, recording in journal entries and on class charts, and a variety of different forms of writing. Nonfiction literature plays an important role in daily learning and teaching at the Center. Whether teachers and students are reading aloud, reading independently, working on an investigation, or just browsing for pleasure, nonfiction literature is an integral component. Nonfiction books are my students' "texts." I organize a variety of activities and collaborations for my students to use nonfiction literature during class. As nonfiction author Seymour Simon suggests, nonfiction literature has the power to excite students about learning that will remain with them forever.

References

Coulombe, D. (1984). *The seaside naturalist: A guide to nature study at the seashore.* Englewood Cliffs, NJ: Prentice-Hall.

Graves, D. (1989). *Investigate nonfiction.* Portsmouth, NH: Heinemann.

Hakim, J. (1993). *From colonies to country: A history of us.* New York: Oxford University Press.

Hakim, J. (1994). *War, terrible war.* New York: Oxford University Press.

Kobrin, B. (1988). *Eyeopeners! How to choose and use children's books about real people, places, and things.* New York: Penguin Books.

Kobrin, B. (1995). *Eyeopeners II: Children's books to answer children's questions about the world around them.* New York: Scholastic.

Maxim, D. (1990). Beginning researchers. In N. Atwell (Ed.), *Coming to know: Writing to learn in the intermediate grades.* Portsmouth, NH: Heinemann.

Musleah, R. (1996, February 18). Unveiling the panoramas of the universe for young readers. *New York Times*, Section 13, LI, 6.

Snowball, Diane. (1995, May). Building literacy skills through nonfiction. *Teaching K-8*, 62-63.

Sobel, D. (Ed.). (1989). *The ocean book: Aquarium and seaside activities and ideas for all ages.* Center for Marine Conservation. New York: John Wiley & Sons, Inc.

CHAPTER 15
BIG STUFF AT THE MIDDLE LEVEL: THE REAL WORLD, REAL READING, AND RIGHT ACTION

by Jeffrey D. Wilhelm

School is a place where you do a bunch of crap for somebody else.
                                        —Tommy, seventh grade student

A slave is anyone who does someone else's work.
                                        —Plato, Greek philosopher

"The best thing [about this inquiry project] was that we asked our own questions. And we read *real* things, you know, to...like...do *real* work...to answer our own questions and to make stuff to teach other people."
-Roper, seventh grade student, after creating a video documentary based on his Holocaust research, conducted primarily through the reading of nonfiction books

Big Stuff

FINALE! CONCLUSION! Phantasmagoric displays of FIREWORKS! Well, sorry....Since this isn't hypertext or video, I can't truly display my students' pyrotechnical virtuosity on these pages. In this book's final chapter, what I can do is to examine nonfiction use in the middle school classroom relative to big issues. In fact, let's go right after this "BIG STUFF" as my student Sean affectionately called it. After all, school should be about Big Stuff, and so should our reading. To get us started, here are some Big Questions that I think we need to ask.

*The author wishes to acknowledge the work of Brian Edmiston and Paul Friedemann in both the conception and teaching of the activities described in this chapter.

- What should middle school kids (and all others) be learning in school, and for what purposes?

- How can we teach middle level students in powerful ways that are consistent with these purposes?

- How does the classroom use of nonfiction fit into all this?

There are answers to all of these questions. Though they are not widely practiced, these answers are being enthusiastically embraced not only at the middle level, but by teachers, administrators, and theorists concerned with education at levels from prekindergarten through college (*e.g., Breaking Ranks*, NASSP, 1996).

First up: What should kids be learning to know and do? They need to learn to be learners and to be responsible citizens. This means they need to define and solve problems and become literate and civic-minded people who can participate in the personal, social, and cultural work necessary to sustain a democratic way of life.

And what are some of the kinds of exalted and significant work we do in a democracy? We become stewards for a fragile planet; we care for and understand diversity by recognizing the strength and vitality inherent in multiple perspectives and ways of being; we recognize history as the continual correction of errors and know how to participate in this kind of forward-looking problem solving; we continually argue our way into creating the highest degree of freedom and dignity for all people; we explore and express new meanings and enact new ways of "becoming" through our use of signs and symbols (*cf.* Postman, 1995). Our students, therefore, need to become wide awake and wide aware to the self and to the world, to the personal possibilities of the individual agent to care about others, and to make new kinds of things happen.

How can we teach students in powerful ways that are consistent with these purposes? As many curriculum theorists are now arguing, we can do so through problem-cored, student-centered, and inquiry-driven curricula (Beane, 1990). A prerequisite to achieving this kind of curriculum will be to free ourselves from the traditional *information-transmission* model of learning. We must make use of a *constructivist* model of learning as the building and organizing of meanings and assist students in increasing their competencies. This is so because learning requires going beyond what is currently known to create new personally relevant understandings. And this is true because students at all levels have the desire to pursue personally relevant and socially significant learnings that push them beyond their current state of being. Students want to create meanings. And they want to use these relevant learnings to do real work in the world. By allowing them to pursue questions of their own, which intersect with social and curricular concerns, and by encouraging them to act on what they learn, we can engage all of our students with significant content in such a way that we can guide them to becoming independent learners and agents in the world.

Smashing the Frozen Seas Within

How does nonfiction use fit into all this? We start with the students' experiences, interests, and questions. We guide them in choosing texts that will confront their deepest concerns in ways that will potentially change them. Such texts can engage them and serve as a personal research tool that naturally integrates curriculum, and that challenges their knowledge of the world and their reading expertise. When this occurs, the magic called LEARNING can happen.

> Writing about the greater value behind reading, Kafka had this to say: It seems to me that one should only read books which bite and sting one. If the book we are reading does not wake us up with a blow on the head, what's the point of reading? To make us happy, as you write to me? Good God, we would be just as happy without books, and books which make us happy, we can at a pinch write them for ourselves. On the other hand we have need of books which act upon us like a misfortune from which we would suffer terribly, like the death of someone we are fonder of than ourselves...a book must be the axe which smashes the frozen sea within us. That's what I think. (cited in Chambers, 1985, p. 17)

Why read stories of inventions, events, people, and places when we can use lectures or textbooks to more efficiently lay out the important facts? To borrow a phrase from my seventh graders, "Just because!" Just because learning is the act of constructing meaning, not receiving it. Just because, as Barbara Hardy (1977) points out, narrative "is a primary act of mind"—it is through stories that we contextualize our understanding and make it usable. Because, as Aidan Chambers (1985) tells us, man is the storytelling animal. Even experts in artificial intelligence recognize that computers can't think until they can recognize, receive, modify, theorize, and communicate real-life meanings in the form of stories (Schank, 1992). Theorizing about the world and how it works is essentially a storytelling act—a kind of *meta-storying*. Even scientists use stories to understand, teach, apply, theorize, and push current understandings (Bruner, 1986). What we know is almost always embedded in stories—real ones—and *meta-stories* constructed of an elaborate admixture of real-life experiential stories and those we experience as told to us by distant teachers such as nonfiction authors.

Nonfiction stories provide a context for our learning and situates it.

Nonfiction allows us to be ethnographers by observing and entering into other worlds and experiencing these places, people, and times that are often at a distance from us. Nonfiction also encourages us to imagine possibilities and ask "What if?" and to be action researchers investigating how to enact changes in the world. Students are like all other human beings (a fact that is sometimes forgotten); they read the word so that they can read the world. When they truly experience a text that speaks to them, they understand and represent the world in new ways, but they also promise to transform the world and to choose to become ethical beings in new and exciting ways.

People read for real purposes: to experience, to enjoy, to inform, to learn, and to address human concerns. We know that learning is social, human, language based and meaning centered. All of these purposes were used to advantage in the following unit.

Learning Happens!

For several years my friend Paul Friedemann and I team taught integrated units that made use of nonfiction texts. Our curriculum was integrated in the sense that it was centered on the concerns and questions students raised about major themes such as civil rights and social justice (see Chapter 12 for Levstik's discussion of learning about the world through nonfiction). Our classroom was similar to the model of a "center of inquiry" as described by Wells and Chang-Wells (1992). The aim was to "integrate learning experiences into [the students'] schemes of meaning so as to broaden and deepen their understanding of themselves and their world" (Beane, 1995). Over the course of each year, students developed a high level of ownership for their own reading and learning. They expected to negotiate with us to work in self-selected small groups as they investigated topics of their own choosing within a broad thematic unit of study. They were accustomed to doing research through their reading and a variety of other means, and they expected to design learning documents and experiences so that their findings could be shared with peers and public audiences outside of school.

Our unit, focusing on the themes of civil rights and social justice, took place close to the end of the school year. In March, to introduce the unit, our seventh graders pursued an extended *process drama*[1] lasting one week. During and after the drama work, students read and shared several nonfiction texts and one fiction book relating to the themes. Later in the unit,

---

[1] process drama is a kind of drama that uses a particular historical or story situation as its but the evolves on its own through the work of students and the structuring of a 'r-in-role. How this kind of drama works will become clearer over the next few pages.

groups were formed and members articulated research questions for the themes. Students, in consultation with Paul and me, established their own reading and research agenda. This agenda was to culminate with the design of either a hypermedia or video documentary. This electronic document was to be used to teach their peers about the issue and questions they had chosen, and it was to serve as an informational reference for the community and students at our partner schools. (These video and hypermedia documents were sent to our partner schools and featured in our library.)

As students pursued their research and document design, they read a wide variety of nonfiction texts: books, newspapers, periodicals, primary source materials, and different electronic *texts*[2] such as those available on electronic databases like SIRS (Social Issues Resource Service) or on electronic mail, listservs, and Web sites. Students also constructed their own nonfiction texts by conducting surveys and interviews with informants, and by analyzing and creating artifacts that related to their study. These various nonfiction texts all held the possibility of "smashing frozen seas" and helped students to review and reposition their perspectives and understandings, continually making these understandings more complex and sophisticated.

Because process drama involves unscripted improvisations, different versions of our Columbus process drama were created by students in five different language arts classes. The number of students in each class varied from 23 to 27. Before we did any reading, students first brainstormed what they knew about Columbus. What emerged in each class period was the traditional cultural story of

---

[2] I use "text" here as literary theorists and semioticians do, to designate *any* artifact that can be said to convey information: stories, graphs, sound bites, video, etc.

CURRICULUM THEMES: CIVIL RIGHTS AND SOCIAL JUSTICE

Topic: Columbus' meeting with the Tainos on the island of Hispaniola

Activity: Mantle of the Expert Process Drama

Nonfiction resources used throughout the drama work:

The Tainos: The People Who Welcomed Columbus by Francine Jacobs (nonfiction)

Christopher Columbus: Voyager to the Unknown by Nancy Smiler Levinson (nonfiction)

Columbus and the World Around Him by Milton Meltzer (nonfiction)

Rethinking Schools issue on "Rethinking Columbus," which included primary resources and documents

Morning Girl by Michael Dorris (fiction)

Columbus discovering the New World and bringing civilization and Christianity to the continent. Our students possessed what might be called a *monologic* (Bakhtin, 1984) or unquestioned understanding that is based on a single perspective. Through the drama we attempted to confound this monologic viewpoint by requiring the students to experience and dialog with other perspectives on Columbus. Bakhtin (1984) states "To live means to participate in dialogue: to ask questions, to heed, to respond, to agree, and so forth" (p. 293). Brian Edmiston (1994) writes that a "dialogic inter-action is a struggle to 'author' or construct meaning in relation to other understandings; the result of this struggle will inform how we think, inter-act, believe and learn" (p. 26). He continues by asserting that "in dialogue students may radically alter their sense of how they think about issues and their relationship with them." A Bakhtinian view of understanding is not about the recitation of facts, but is relational and "weblike"; "we under-stand when we appreciate how one view is placed in a web of relation-ships" (p. 26).

Our students began the process drama by articulating and acting on a particular position about Columbus. I then chose readings and dramatic activities that challenged this position of Columbus as discoverer and hero. These perspective-challenging nonfiction readings were pursued both throughout and after our drama work. They required students to dialog with understandings different than their own.

Much of what occurs in schools, unfortunately, works against dialogue and fits what Bakhtin (1984) would call a "monologue" of nonnegotiable meanings that "denies the existence outside of itself of another conscious-ness with equal rights and responsibilities" (p. 292). Nonfiction texts can serve as a tool for dialog and reaching more complex understanding by con-fronting fixed meanings, such as my students' understanding of Columbus.

These students uniformly celebrated Columbus as a hero. At the same time, many expressed very strong opinions against a treaty rights contro-versy involving local groups of Indians seeking to maintain their tradi-tional hunting and fishing rights. They expressed unquestioned main-stream opinions such as "manifest destiny" and "superior culture wins, weaker culture must assimilate." Through the nonfiction texts that framed our drama, Paul and I hoped to help students examine and rework their understandings in such a way that would lead to changes in thought and action.

We began by involving whole-classroom groups in a "mantle of the expert" drama (Heathcote and Bolton, 1995) through which students would confront these issues indirectly. Heathcote insists that in drama, instead of confronting students with their own prejudice, they need to be brought in a roundabout way to understand these issues. In a mantle of the expert drama, students are cast as "experts" who have authority to make decisions and act on these decisions to fulfill their purposes. The general idea for this particular drama on Columbus, as well as many of the particular episodes, were suggested and structured by Brian Edmiston, a renowned and gifted drama educator.

So after the students consented, I opened the drama by convening a Museum Board Meeting. In the role of curator, I asked the students, as board members, to consider renaming the Museum of American Culture as the Museum of American Cultures. After a brief debate, the board voted down the proposal. Luz, reporting from her group, said they had discussed the idea of America as a "melting pot" and felt that there was one American culture, not many cultures. Her group proposed "keeping the old name."

I problematized their decision by revealing that we had received a generous donation to design an exhibit on the topic "Columbus and his Legacy" but the donor wished us to consider changing the name of the museum. The students wanted to know who the anonymous donor was, but I could not reveal this. Luz, for one, thought the donor was "a minority person" who "wants to use the museum" presumably to present a particular political agenda. Ron said, "Our job is to present history the way it was, not do any old exhibit the way someone wants us to do it." Having established some viewpoints to which we could return, I asked the board to brainstorm some ideas for our new Columbus exhibit.

The drama continued with students considering names for the exhibit. They proposed "The Courage of Columbus" and then "The Discovery of America." They also suggested many ideas for exhibits. The next day, using some of our nonfiction texts, they dramatized short film clips of scenes from Columbus'

RESOURCES ON PROCESS DRAMA

Drama for Learning: Dorothy Heathcote's Mantle of the Expert Approach for Teaching by D. Heathcote and G. Bolton

Drama Guidelines by C. O'Neill, A. Lambert, R. Linnell, and J. Warr-Wood

Drama Worlds by C. O'Neill

Drama Structures by C. O'Neill and A. Lambert

Imagining to Learn: Drama to Support Reading, Learning, and Valuing Across the Curriculum by J. Wilhelm and B. Edmiston

odyssey: planning his journey, meeting with Queen Isabella, undertaking the voyage, and finally, planting the Spanish flag in the sand of the New World and saying "I, Columbus, have sailed the ocean and discovered this country. I claim it now for Isabella, Queen of Spain. I bring civilization and religion to all people here!" An Indian knelt at his feet and whispered, "Oh, thank you, most powerful white man!"

Time to Smash Some Frozen Seas

In my role as the historical consultant, I confronted the filmmakers. "Your job is to tell the whole story! Whose voices are you missing?" The students responded that we were missing the voices of the sailors, the sailors' families, the King, and the Indians. Using excerpts from *The Tainos* (Jacobs, 1992), *Morning Girl* (Dorris, 1992), and primary source materials such as eyewitness accounts of the atrocities committed by Columbus, the students and I continued on a different tack.

In Heathcote's terms, the students were entering into a new perspective that allowed them to "read implications" and discover hidden stories and meanings that affect the lives of human beings. Students posed as sailors and Tainos to create an interactive exhibit. When the visitor walked by, they would speak about their experience. Ron was a sailor; Luz a Taino. Luz spoke out: "We welcomed them. We were willing to share but they destroyed us. They brought greed and disease. My family is dead!" The sailors responded: "We want to go home. This is no place for us." The Tainos responded by saying, "Go home and leave us in peace. This place was given to us by the Great Spirit. It is not for you to rule or own!"

Then we all became Tainos, meeting in the tribal circle to share stories of what was happening because of Columbus' arrival, and suggesting solutions. It was decided that the Spaniards were too powerful to be resisted, and they were too "gold-crazy" to be reasoned with. Some decided to build canoes and escape, but they recognized this was only a short-term fix. "There is really nothing we can do!" one girl emoted.

After this class session, Luz responded that "The real amazing thing is that we all saw it the same way. I mean, it never even occurred to me to look at it from the Indians' point of view. And it was hard to do, I kept saying no to it and when I finally did [see from the Taino Indians' point of view] it just blew my mind." Luz admitted that she was very "upset and confused" by what she had read and experienced. "It's just so different from what I thought," she said, "It's hard to put together." Here Luz is trying to dialog and create a more complex understanding. This is hard work, and as she begins to dialog with new perspectives, she recognizes her previous resistance.

When I asked her what had helped her see other viewpoints, she said:

> Reading the descriptions [from *The Tainos*] helped. *Morning Girl* made me think of what life was like before Columbus came—how much that changed everything for the worse....Reading what the priest wrote [in the primary source materials] almost made me want to puke. How could they do that to another human being? And then I heard all the other voices [in the drama, of the sailors and Tainos] it was like it was drowning out all of the cool things I still believed yesterday about Columbus.

Bakhtin (1984) says that in artistic experience, people finalize ethics in action and "become answerable" for current understandings. This was certainly true for Luz as she answered her previous understandings of Columbus. She interrogated and examined her prior positions as she entered into dialog with new viewpoints.

As we continued the drama, students used their nonfiction reading as they wrote diary entries as Indians before, during, and after the arrival of Columbus. They adopted a boy from another tribe and discussed what "he needed to know and do to be one of us." As they did so, they entered entirely into the perspective of the Tainos and their culture as they understood it through their readings. Then we became members of Columbus' entourage before his second voyage, justifying funding and developing policies for dealing with "the savages." We reenacted Columbus' arrival. Using the drama technique of *choral montage* we created a poem made up of short powerful phrases. The phrases were composed by students taking various perspectives: a Taino chief, a Taino child, and the mountains of Hispaniola reflecting on what they had seen since the arrival of Columbus.

As the focal point of our exhibit, we ended the drama by creating a sculpture or *dramatic tableaux*—through body positioning. The result was a picture frozen in time. The caption, written by the students, read "Columbus, discovered a land for one civilization and destroyed the one that was already there."

In his reflective journal, one student wrote that "Now I understand why the Indians [in Wisconsin] are so angry about the treaty rights thing." This student had come to face the complexity surrounding his opinion, even if he did not change it. Another wrote: "It's interesting to think about things from different directions. I felt kind of like we held Columbus in our hand like a ball and turned him around to see all sides." Luz simply wrote: "Wow! That was intense!" Such is the power of nonfiction texts when used by a teacher to frame instruction and guide the creation of more dialogic understandings.

Off On Their Own

The drama was followed by reading nonfiction pieces, such as excerpts from *Coming of Age in Mississippi* (Moody, 1968), *Sojourner*

Figure 15.1 Some Featured Drama Technique

Story Drama
A series of dramatic episodes that reenact a story. Each episode corresponds to an event in the story.

Process Drama
A series of dramatic episodes that follow their own internal logic. The teacher will structure the current drama episodes based on student response in previous episodes. The initial episode may come from a story or historical incident.

Mantle of the Expert Drama
A process drama approach in which students are positioned in functional roles as knowledgeable and skillful experts. In the drama, they have something to do or create in their roles as experts. In this chapter, the students were cast as museum exhibit designers.

Tableaux Drama
Tableaux are frozen pictures or frozen moments in time. Students use their bodies to demonstrate an activity, feeling, or idea. Variants involve students providing captions, the characters in the picture coming to life to tell their feelings, the combining of several tableaux into a slide show, etc.

Role Play
Students take on the role and perspective of another person or thing. Often played out in pairs where each role has a defined purpose or problem.

Ritual
The unity created when everyone is doing the same thing, usually a ritual like "naming," "spell casting," or "voting." This builds belief in the drama world.

Truth: Ain't I a Woman? (McKissack & McKissack, 1992), and several writings of Martin Luther King, Jr. The class read the story of the fictional Logan family in *Roll of Thunder, Hear My Cry* (Taylor, 1976) who struggled to maintain their rights, dignity, and personal safety during the Depression in Mississippi.

At this point, we created a civil rights time line from the arrival of Columbus to the Rodney King trial. The students were asked to use the final 5 weeks of the school year to continue pursuing the theme of civil rights and social justice by articulating their own research questions and reading agendas about some idea suggested by the time line. Again, it is worth emphasizing that Dewey insisted throughout his writings that inquiry must begin with significant content that interests students.

Bakhtin (1986) also insisted that "Without one's own serious and sincere questions one cannot creatively understand anything other or foreign" (p. 11). The students' initial wonderings were, after reading and guidance, formalized into research questions that organized both individual and group inquiry over the remainder of the year. They were working toward a final presentation that would be a hypermedia document or video documentary. This documentary was for the purpose of teaching other members of the class and of the community.

Two groups of girls chose to research the experience of slavery. The first group asked, "What was it like to be a slave in the American South?" The second group asked, "What did people do to resist slavery?" These groups read a variety of nonfiction including *Many Thousand Gone: African Americans from Slavery to Freedom* (Hamilton, 1993) and *Now is Your Time! The African-American Struggle for Freedom* (Myers, 1991). Several girls read the McKissacks' *Christmas in the Big House, Christmas in the Quarters* (1994). All of them read *To Be A Slave* (Lester, 1968), and some read the fictional works *Letters from a Slave Girl* (Lyons, 1992) and *Nightjohn* (Paulsen, 1993) about a slave who risks everything to learn and teach reading. I have a great personal interest in jazz and lent my copy of *Jazz: My Music, My People* (Monceaux, 1994) to two students interested in music. We explored together how jazz evolved from the slaves' field hollers, the blues, and the bamboulas on Congo Square in New Orleans where the slaves were allowed to convene on Sundays.

One group of boys read Adler's *We Remember the Holocaust* (1989) and availed themselves of the Internet. I visited the Web site: http://www.ushmm.org:80/education/ed.html to retrieve an in-depth teaching manual of the Holocaust, which I shared with this group. Another group, researching the Japanese Internment in America during World War II, read the mural book *The Journey* (Hamanaka, 1990) and *I am an American* (Stanley, 1994). They also read electronic nonfiction "texts" on the Internet through the University of Kansas History Network at Telnet to: hnsource.cc.ukans.edu. The students were able to download pictures to use in their documentaries. They also sought and found an informant they could talk to over E-mail through International Email Cultural Connections (IECC). To do so they E-mailed to iec-request@stolaf.edu and subscribed to be matched with a keypal.

Getting Critical: Getting Complex

I would like to look at two more groups to consider their reading and evolving understandings. One group of girls was researching the historical role of women in this country and asked the question: "What changed things?" They read *Breaking Barriers* (Archer, 1991) and *Rosie the Riveter:*

Women Working on the Homefront in World War II (Colman, 1995). Though they initially took a feminist stance, they came to question "whether we took for granted that they [men] were prejudiced against us, when it seems more complicated than that. So maybe we were prejudiced against them. This is a neat, but disturbing thought" (from a reflective journal entry about the filming of their video documentary). One film modeled after Steve Allen's "Meeting of the Minds" involved great female reformers convening through time travel. "It made me thankful, and made me wonder where I would be today without these women that went before me," one girl wrote.

Much of these girls' research was done through interviews conducted at the local Senior Citizen Center. The girls were so moved by the "nonfiction texts" or conversations they experienced at the Center that they started to create a library of stories about various topics such as dating rituals in the twenties and thirties, Ms. Swan's School for Girls, and many other stories that illuminated the roles of women earlier in the century. Many of these oral histories were committed to audio- or videotape and were a source of much discussion and sharing. The girls came to strongly believe that prejudicial treatment of women was not only historical but continued to be the case. They were moved to social action by creating and disseminating a survey and then a petition designed to "make people more aware" of what effect harassment in the hallways had on young women. I encouraged this, and to help them, I provided several social action guides on our classroom book cart, e.g., *The Kid's Guide to Social Action: How to Solve the Problems You Choose—and Turn Creative Thinking Into Positive Action* (Lewis, 1991).

Perhaps the most obvious and dramatic change in understanding occurred for two boys researching the Vietnam War. Tony and Robby were initially most interested in the 1960s and 1970s protest music directed against the United States' involvement in Vietnam. They began with the question: "What was the most important protest music against the Vietnam War?"

These boys began by identifying solely with the antiwar perspective on Vietnam. Robby had been incredulous that anyone could have supported the war. "Who could be for a war? A war you chose to be in and that had nothing to do with you?" Tony was equally adamant. "It was a stupid war. It was just wrong."

Through their reading of some carefully chosen materials, we asked Tony and Robby to reconsider their initial points of view, to dialog with these from new positions and perspectives. They began by reading old *Rolling Stone* magazines and the lyrics of protest songs. They read excerpts from Ron Kovic's (1976) *Born on the Fourth of July*. These served only to reinforce their initial viewpoint.

Several nonfiction works were also available to them: *An Album of the Vietnam War* (Lawson, 1986) used photographs to convey an experience of the war; *Dear America: Letters Home From Vietnam* (Edelman, 1985) provided a collection of letters written by service people that gave a variety of perspectives; and *Homecoming: When the Soldiers Returned from Vietnam* (Greene, 1989) gave powerful insights into the sacrifice and purposes of our soldiers, and the atrocious treatment they received at the hands of the "antiwar" faction.

Through their reading, the students became disillusioned with their previous beliefs. Robby was one of several students who suggested using some drama work with the reading to help address their confusion. I invited Brian Edmiston to come into the school to help this group and several others with their inquiry project. Brian asked these two boys to prepare by collecting a set of artifacts: photos, letters, newspaper op-ed pieces, that could be used as resources for the drama work.

They decided to begin the drama sessions by taking on the roles of street musicians playing at a protest outside an Army Recruitment Center on draft day. In order to be arrested, they harassed the people entering and leaving the Center. Brian, in his attempt to engage the boys mentally, physically, and emotionally with multiple perspectives, next secured their agreement to imagine they were army personnel being interviewed for television about the problems caused by the protesters. Issues regarding access to the center turned to concerns about violence and the ability to do "our job...to do what we think is right" from the perspective of military personnel.

Over the course of two 40-minute drama sessions they adopted additional perspectives: political advisors to the President, American soldiers in Nam, Vietnamese villagers, and ultimately the members of a family split by the war—with one son serving his country and another who was a conscientious objector engaged in antiwar protests. Excerpts from Gioglio's *Days of Decision* (1989) and Mabie's *Vietnam There and Here* (1985) were made available. In this episode, Brian interacted with them as the son who had just returned to his family from the War in time for Thanksgiving dinner. As the son he was able to "ventriloquate" the boys by repeating some of the opinions the boys had voiced earlier—about the war being wrong—and press them to dialog with their prior positions. He wanted them to know he was hurt by their lack of support and understanding; he wanted to know why his brother was not supportive of government policy—but more importantly—supportive of him, his own brother! He shared his feelings of betrayal, and he angrily asked to know his family's position.

Through the drama session and their reading, the students played the roles of historians, informants who were experiencing the war from various imaginative stances, researchers and informants, and then again from their own personal position. Both boys reconsidered their previous monologic and dogmatic points of view through this process. The frozen seas within had been smashed by the axes of powerful interventions—nonfiction used with drama. (For fuller descriptions of this kind of drama work, see Wilhelm & Edmiston, 1997; and Edmiston & Wilhelm, in press.)

Robby explained that "We got to see that there were other ways of looking at it [the war]," and Tony had this to say: "My whole opinion changed with looking through both opponents' eyes and arguing for what I'm against." Both boys talked about the importance of reading and experiencing texts from various points of view. Tony explained that "We were so many people. We were everywhere. I was inside so many different characters. I was protesters, Vietnamese, in the army, a parent [of a soldier], a politician." He reported that he had "never really thought about what the Vietnamese people went through."

Tony made this powerful statement about the use of nonfiction in an inquiry-driven curriculum: "[My reading and the drama sessions] kind of brought doubt. My original opinion kind of went down, then up again with some doubt. I had different reasons for my opinions, like the effect on the Vietnamese people which I'd never thought about—how they got killed and their houses destroyed and stuff...so in a way, my opinion [against the war] was stronger, but it's less sure. I'm kind of more open to that there are other opinions that are strong and stuff even though you might disagree [with those other opinions]."

The boys changed their research question to "What kinds of protest were most effective" and then to "How can you change opinions to help peace?" as they critiqued violent protests and the poor treatment of American soldiers. In their video documentary, they featured encounters from opposing points of view. One scene was of two competing public service announcements asking people to protest, and then to support the war effort. The video continued with a debate between two politicians and the two sons, after Thanksgiving dinner, hashing out their differences on the family couch.

Tony explained to me that "We got to see that there were other ways of looking at it [the war] and so protests were not going to...like...automatically work." Robby wrote in his journal that, "I will put both sides in my story [video documentary], not just the antiwar side."

These boys' realizations are examples of how nonfiction, inquiry, and techniques such as drama for guiding understanding can be instrumental in constructing understandings that are "better" in Perkins' (1988) sense of being "more complex," "generative," and "open-ended." Perkins uses the metaphor of "webs" to highlight the relationships inherent in understandings that demonstrate not only more knowledge, but also finer distinctions and connections between various perspectives and themes. Inquiry based on nonfiction problematized and smashed frozen points of view. The students acknowledged the incompleteness of their understandings and made themselves open to adding other meanings to their world views.

As such, the students created their own nonfiction texts, both on video and in their minds. They wove their previous experiences and opinions with those from texts that challenged them. As they did so, they created a new and more complexly colored fabric of understanding. This weaving act is the process teachers so fondly call learning. Yeah, I would agree with Sean and call this "Big Stuff."

It's always big stuff when students meet the books they need and have the strength to dialog with them. Sean, always one with a flair for expression, calls this kind of meeting "...intense. Kind of like the American Gladiators of reading, know what I mean?" I do, and I hope you do, too—and I know that quality nonfiction holds the promise of this kind of reading and learning many times over.

References

Bakhtin, M. M. (1984). *Problems of Dosteovsky's poetics* (C. Emerson, Ed. & Trans.). Minneapolis: University of Minnesota Press.

Bakhtin, M. M. (1986). *Speech genres and other late essays* (V. McGee, Trans.). Austin: University of Texas Press.

Beane, J. (1990). *A middle school curriculum: From rhetoric to reality.* Columbus, OH: National Middle School Association.

Beane, J. (1995). *Toward a coherent curriculum.* Alexandria, VA: Assocation for Supervision and Curriculum Development.

Bruner, J. (1986). *Actual minds, possible worlds.* Cambridge, MA: Harvard University.

Chambers, A. (1985). *Booktalk: Occasional writing on literature and children.* London: The Bodley Head.

Edmiston, B. (1994). More than talk: A Bakhtinian perspective on drama in education and change in understanding. *National Association for Drama in Education Journal, 18* (2), 25-36.

Edmiston, B., & Wilhelm, J. (in press). Repositioning views/reviewing positions: Forming complex understandings in drama. In B. J. Wagner (Ed.), *What drama can do.* Portsmouth, NH: Heinemann.

Hardy, B. (1977). Towards a poetics of fiction. In M. Meek, G. Barton, & A. Warlow (Eds.), *The cool web: The pattern of children's reading,* pp. 12-23. London: The Bodley Head. 12-23.

Heathcote, D., & Bolton, G. (1995). *Drama for learning: Dorothy Heathcote's mantle of the expert approach for teaching.* Portsmouth, NH: Heinemann.

NASSP. (1996). *Breaking ranks.* Alexandria, VA: National Association of Secondary School Principals.

O'Neill, C. (1994). *Drama worlds.* Portsmouth, NH: Heinemann.

O'Neill, C., & Lambert, A. (1982). *Drama structures.* Portsmouth, NH: Heinemann.

O'Neill, C., Lambert, A., Linnell, R., Warr-Wood, J. (1976). *Drama guidelines.*

London: Heinemann Educational Books.

Perkins, D. N. (1988). Art as understanding. *Journal of Aesthetic Education, 22* (1), 111-131.

Postman, N. (1995). *The end of education.* New York: Basic Books.

Rethinking schools. Fall, 1992, 7 (1). Milwaukee, WI.

Schank, R. (1992). *Tell me A story: Narrative and artificial intelligence.* New York: Scribner's.

Social Issues Resource Services (SIRS), P.O. Box 2348, Boca Raton, FL 33427.

Wells, G., & Chang-Wells, G. L. (1992). *Constructing knowledge together: Classrooms as a center of inquiry and literacy.* Portsmouth, NH: Heinemann.

Wilhelm, J. (1997). *You gotta be the book: Teaching engaged and reflective reading with adolescents.* New York: Teachers College Press.

Wilhelm, J., & Edmiston, B. (1997). *Imagining to learn: Drama to support learning and valuing across the curriculum through drama.* Portsmouth, NH: Heinemann.

Part IV

Quality Nonfiction Literature: More About Authors and Their Books

In this final section of the book, we first offer readers eleven response guides to well-written nonfiction titles. The purpose of these guides is to offer teachers and librarians a model for helping children examine and appreciate the richness of well-crafted nonfiction literature. Included in each guide is a synopsis of the book, a section highlighting distinguishing features of the book, response suggestions that will help challenge readers to think more critically about nonfiction, and a list of connecting books.

We conclude our book with an annotated Bibliography of Orbis Pictus Award-Winning, Honor, and Notable nonfiction titles. Distinguished nonfiction literature has been chosen every year for the last six years by the Orbis Pictus Committee of the National Council of Teachers of English. This annotated bibliography will provide teachers and librarians with a source of some of the best nonfiction titles for children from kindergarten through grade 8.

Response Guides to Nonfiction Children's Literature

by Rosemary A. Bamford & Janice V. Kristo

What Do Response Guides Offer Teachers and Librarians?

Our intent in designing this set of 11 nonfiction response guides is to highlight the work of a sample of notable nonfiction writers. The guides offer readers ways to look more deeply into nonfiction and to explore and appreciate interesting aspects about the book and the writer. The format of the guide offers teachers and librarians ways to consider what a nonfiction title offers to stretch and challenge inquiring young minds.

What Is Found in Each Guide?

Each guide is comprised of the following:

- bibliographical information
- suggested interest levels
- specific distinguishing features
- a synopsis describing the content and features
- response suggestions for the classroom that expand upon the features
- a sample of connecting books
- excerpts from interviews with authors on their research and writing processes

The list of connecting books includes other titles by the author as well as books by additional writers who use similar features. In some response guides, we have identified connecting books on the same topic that also use those features. We envision that teachers and librarians will expand upon these ideas for any of the titles they wish to use and will also see the format of the guides as a useful model for selecting and sharing nonfiction titles with children.

How Did We Choose Books for the Response Guides?

We used the criteria, as discussed in Chapters 2-5, to guide our choices: accuracy, organizational structures, style, and format and access features. Questions such as the following helped identify distinguishing features for each book: How do we find out what the author knows? How do the organizational structures help the reader?; How does the style of language draw in and support the reader? How do the access features explain and expand the content of the book? and How does the format clarify and increase reader interest? Distinguishing features also include the author's research strategies (*e.g.*, using a variety of primary source materials, interviewing procedures, going on site to do research, etc.), interesting organizational structures, and engaging graphics and access features. We also chose titles representative of different curricular areas and grade levels and those with features that elementary and middle school students might emulate in the products of their own inquiries.

Response Guide Authors and Their Nonfiction Books

Jim Brandenburg—*To The Top of the World: Adventures with Arctic Wolves*

Joanna Cole—*The Magic School Bus Inside a Beehive*, Illustrated by Bruce Degen

Peter Dodson—*An Alphabet of Dinosaurs*, Paintings by Wayne D. Barlowe

Linda Granfield—*Cowboy: An Album*

Diane Hoyt-Goldsmith—*Pueblo Storyteller*, Photographs by Lawrence Migdale

Philip M. Isaacson—*A Short Walk Around the Pyramids & Through the World of Art*

Kathyrn Lasky—*The Librarian Who Measured the Earth*, Illustrated by Kevin Hawkes

Patricia Lauber—*Hurricanes: Earth's Mightiest Storms*

Jim Murphy—*The Great Fire*

Jerry Stanley—*Children of the Dust Bowl: The True Story of the School at Weedpatch Camp*

Diane Swanson—*Safari Beneath the Sea: The Wonder World of the North Pacific Coast*

To the Top of the World:
Adventures with Arctic Wolves

Jim Brandenburg. (1993). *To the Top of the World: Adventures with Arctic Wolves.* New York: Walker and Company. 44 pp. Orbis Pictus Honor Book.

Suggested Interest Levels—Ages 6 and up.

Distinguished Features—Photographic essay, observational writing, chronological organization, on-site research, and table of contents.

Synopsis—A spectacular white arctic wolf striding across the harsh snow-covered island of Ellesmere entices readers to explore the unique photographs of these wolves. Award-winning photographer Jim Brandenburg shares his awe-inspiring two-month experience of living on this island with the arctic wolves. Beginning with what Brandenburg felt at the time was his ultimate photograph, a wolf on an iceberg illuminated by a single shaft of light, he reveals not only his daily life with photographing the wolf pack but also his many thoughts and questions. As he does so, he creates a sense of immediacy, of being on the island with him, as he follows the wolves and their pups. Brandenburg's descriptive personal narrative, accompanied by his crisp and dramatic photographs, informs readers about the behaviors of this isolated wolf pack.

Response Suggestions—

- On-site research is used by many of today's nonfiction authors/photographers. These experiences and photographic shoots result in authentic descriptive photographic essays. Arrange for your students to visit a nearby site to gather information on a specific topic (*e.g.*, treatment of animals at the local zoo, information on a production line at a factory or mill, observation of animals at a wildlife sanctuary, etc.). Photograph the experience and using either a diary approach or notebooks, encourage the students not only to write what they observe but also to include their personal reflections of the experience. Help the students engage in interviewing workers, owners, etc. Children can write their own photographic essays using notes from observations and interviews, personal reflections, photographs, and information from other readings on the topic.

- Students can write captions describing or explaining the content of the photograph as a way to expand upon the text. Brandenburg uses a combination of caption structures: extended labels, phrases, and descriptive sentences.

Connecting Books—

- Other Books by Jim Brandenburg:
    An American Safari: Adventures on the North American Prairie
    Sand and Fog: Adventures in Southern Africa
    Scruffy: A Wolf Finds His Place in the Pack
- Look for Adult Nonfiction on This Topic Written by Brandenburg
- Other Books about the Arctic and Wolves:
    Arctic Memories by Normee Ekoomiak
    Wolves by R. D. Lawrence
    Wolves by Seymour Simon
- Other Photographic Essays Using On-Site Research of Wildlife:
(Also look for other books by the following authors.)
    The American Alligator by Dorothy Hinshaw Patent
    Arctic Foxes by Downs Matthews
    Polar Bear Cubs by Downs Matthews
    Raptor Rescue: An Eagle Flies Free by Sylvia Johnson
    Nights of the Pufflings by Bruce McMillan
    Summer Ice: Life Along the Antarctic Peninsula by Bruce McMillan

An Interview With Jim Brandenburg...

We asked Jim Brandenburg to discuss the experience of doing on-site research on Arctic wolves. Going on site to such a harsh climate was a challenge in writing this book. Seventy cases of equipment and food had to be carried from Minnesota. In addition, temperatures were as extreme as the hoards of mosquitoes. Because the wolves were tolerant and curious, Jim was able to take extensive pictures.

Jim told us that his books for young readers are "born of out his books for adults, but no adult book has ever given him the response or joy he has gotten from doing *To the Top of the World*." He has been interested in wolves since he was a young boy. Jim has tried to write a wolf book for years, but the wolves in Northern Minnesota are so allusive he could only get a few portraits. While on an expedition to cover a dog sled trip to the North Pole, he came across these arctic wolves that showed no fear of him—the pack of wolves out of curiosity came toward him "like ghosts in white." He knew he would go back to do a story about them and, subsequently, spent the next three years on Ellesmere Island photographing and studying the wolves.

Jim says it is not easy to write for young children, because they tend to believe everything they read. Therefore, he is careful not to anthromorphize the wolves to the point readers would think of them as human. Because of the way his mind works, Jim does not write many notes. Instead, he takes lots of photographs and examines them to recall the details of the experiences. One photograph is like taking pages and pages of notes. The photographs become little miniature sketches and scenes, similar to working from a storyboard. As he looks at his photographs, he gets a rough idea of how he will write the book and then tape records this. His editor works closely with him to keep the thread of the narrative. She helps him avoid tangents and monitors the style so it is appropriate for children.

We asked Jim why he writes in the first person. He told us the decision to use first person may come from talking into the tape recorder when working with his editor. He also said that his experience of being with the wolves was so powerful that using his own voice was a very natural way to write.

The Magic School Bus Inside a Beehive

Joanna Cole. (1996). *The Magic School Bus Inside a Beehive*. Illustrated by Bruce Degen. New York: Scholastic. 48 pp.

Suggested Interest—Levels- Ages 7-12.

Distinguished Features—Varied format offering multiple sources of information on each page (*e.g.*, definition of new words, report writing, labeled illustrations and diagrams, lists of facts, etc.), story-within-a-story format, fantasy and nonfiction elements, and a section that serves as an afterword.

Synopsis—Writer Joanna Cole and illustrator Bruce Degen team up once again to bring readers another Magic School Bus adventure. They set the stage for the journey to the beekeeper's hives by first providing readers with brief background information about insects. Ms. Frizzle and her class are transported to the inside of the beehive to examine how bees live and work together and to explore how honey is produced.

Readers who dare take The Magic School Bus adventure along with Ms. Frizzle and her class will learn a myriad of new insect-related terms and facts about bees. Each page is uniquely designed to inform readers about bees, their community, and the making of honey while at the same time entertaining readers with an imaginary jouney inside a beehive.

Response Suggestions—

• Each title in *The Magic School Bus* series combines a lively, fast-moving fantasy narrative with informational text on every page. This format can be challenging to share aloud. After introducing the book, invite students to browse through *The Magic School Bus Inside a Beehive*. Ask students to talk about the book. What did they find most interesting ? What did they learn about bees? What facts would they want to go back and check? What additional questions do they have about bees and the making of honey?

• Spend time focusing on particular pages of this book as a way to discuss the differences between factual information and the accompanying fantasy story of *The Magic School Bus*. Consider preparing a transparency of one page to facilitate a closer examination. Ask students to consider the many different ways factual information is displayed on each page (*e.g.*, list of facts, report writing, labeled diagrams, etc.).

• Invite students to browse through other books in *The Magic School Bus* series. Many of these are listed in the Connecting Books section below. What are the common elements they find in all the books? Although the information on a page is presented in a variety of formats, it is all inter connected as well as being carried from page to page. This format allows a writer and an illustrator to include important information that

doesn't necessarily fit within the flow of the text. As a class, students might enjoy designing their own Magic School Bus adventure incorporating a fantasy story along with the results of research on a topic of interest.

Connecting Books—

- A Sample of *The Magic School Bus* books by Joanna Cole and Bruce Degen:
    The Magic School Bus in the Time of the Dinosaurs
    The Magic School Bus on the Ocean Floor
    The Magic School Bus Lost in the Solar System
    The Magic School Bus Inside the Human Body
    The Magic School Bus Inside the Earth
    The Magic School Bus at the Waterworks

- Other Books Offering Varied Formats and Multiple Sources of Information:
    African Animal Giants by James M. Dietz
    Castle: Stephen Biesty's Cross Sections by Richard Platt
    Eyewitness Series Published by Dorling Kindersley/Knopf
    Inside Dinosaurs and Other Prehistoric Creatures by Steve Parker and
        Illustrated by Ted Dewan
    It's All in your Brain by Sylvia Funston & Jay Ingram
    Man-of-War: Stephen's Biesty's Cross Sections by Richard Platt
    National Geographic Action Book Series Published by National
        Geographic Society
    One Small Square series by Donald M. Silver and Illustrated by Patricia
        J. Wynne
    *Scholastic Voyager of Discovery Series on Natural History, Science and
        Technology, Visual Arts, and Music and Performing Arts* Published
        by Scholastic

- Other Books on Bees:
    A Beekeeper's Year by Sylvia A. Johnson
    The Honey Makers by Gail Gibbons
    Killer Bees by Bianca Lavies
    The Life and Times of the Honeybee by Charles Micucci

An Interview With Joanna Cole...

When asked about some of the challenges of writing *The Magic School Bus* books, Joanna Cole responded by quoting Einstein: "It should be as simple as possible, without being simpler." A big challenge of writing *The Magic School Bus* books is to simplify the material without distorting the facts; the information has to be understandable and interesting to children.

We also wanted to know how Joanna combines fact with fantasy in her books. Joanna stated that "The first order of business in writing for children is the science; the science determines the story." She talked further about the magic in the books not being antithetical to science. Instead, "It works as a literary device to get kids into a place to observe reality. It's important for children to be able to see things that they aren't able to see in everyday life, to see places that are impossible to go to."

We also asked Joanna to comment on the format of the book. There is so much for readers to look at on each page—conversation bubbles, labeled diagrams, report writing, plus the storyline incorporating factual information. Joanna and illustrator Bruce Degen orchestrate text and illustrations so that all the information is interrelated and has an internal organization. She said that it really doesn't matter what you read first, because the concept is mentioned elsewhere on the page. Each piece of information reinforces another piece.

Joanna discussed the nature of the collaboration she has with Bruce Degen. "His contribution is incalculable," says Joanna. "Bruce makes things funny, he helps with the layout, and he makes it all work; he's so inventive." We agree; *The Magic School Bus* books are ingenious and a fun "way" into the world of science. Joanna Cole says it best: "It's better for a child to read one good science trade book than a whole textbook that teaches you that science is boring."

An Alphabet of Dinosaurs

Peter Dodson. (1995). *An Alphabet of Dinosaurs*. Paintings by Wayne D. Barlowe. New York: Scholastic. Unpaged.

Suggested Interest Levels—Ages 7- 12.

Distinguished Features—Collaborative working relationship between author and illustrator, alphabetic organizational structure, summary guide of dinosaurs, and an appendix on "What Happened to the Dinosaurs?".

Synopsis—Dr. Peter Dodson, a professor of anatomy, and Wayne D. Barlowe, an illustrator, collaborated on *An Alphabet of Dinosaurs*. This book offers young dinosaur afficionados sensational illustrations and the newest facts about 26 of these creatures.

Each page of this alphabet book uses a consistent format including a brief description of the dinosaur, a pen and ink skeletal drawing of the entire dinosaur or a particularly distinctive feature, and a detailed caption of the painting on the next page. The paintings are dramatic and portray dinosaurs as active creatures in their environments.

"A Guide To The Dinosaurs In This Book" at the end provides the following information for each dinosaur: a pronunciation key, what its name means, what it ate, when it lived, where the fossils were found, and its length. There is also a two-page endnote speculating on "What Happened to the Dinosaurs?"

Response Suggestions—

- After an examination of this book, as well as other informational alpha bet books, discuss the organizational format of an alphabet book. For example, what does the author and illustrator choose to depict in words and pictures about their subject? What kind of written information is included? What is not included? What are the limitations of an alphabet book in terms of the extent of coverage of the topic? What are the advantages?

- Invite pairs of students to create their own alphabet book on a topic being studied in one of the content areas to generate one page of a class alphabet book.

- Using the format of a chart, students could summarize information in their reports as well as include additional material that did not fit well into the body of the report.

Connecting Books—

- Adult Nonfiction by Peter Dodson:
    The Dinosauria
    Evolution: Process and Product
    The Horned Dinosaurs: A Natural History

- Other Alphabet Books:
    The Butterfly Alphabet Book by Brian Cassie and Jerry Pallotta
    Geography A to Z by Jack Knowlton
    Navajo ABC: A Diné Alphabet Book by Luci Tapahonso and Eleanor Schick
    Under the Sea from A to Z by Anne Doubilet
    V for Vanishing: An Alphabet of Endangered Animals by Patricia Mullins
- Other Books about Dinosaurs:
    Dinosaur Worlds by Don Lessem (Peter Dobson-scientific consultant)
    Dinosaurs by Gail Gibbons
    Dinosaurs Bones by Aliki
    Dinosaurs: The Fastest, the Fiercest, the Most Amazing by Elizabeth MacLeod
    Dinosaurs! Strange and Wonderful by Laurence Pringle
    Dinosaurs Walked Here and Other Stories Fossils Tell by Patricia Lauber
    Dougall Dixon's Dinosaurs by Dougall Dixon (Peter Dobson-scientific consultant)
    Inside Dinosaurs and Other Prehistoric Creatures by Steve Parker
    Living with Dinosaurs by Patricia Lauber
    The Magic School Bus in the Time of the Dinosaurs by Joanna Cole
    The News about Dinosaurs by Patricia Lauber
    Raptor! The Nastiest Dinosars by Don Lessem

An Interview With Peter Dodson...

Knowing that Peter Dodson is a professor of anatomy, paleontology, and geology at the University of Pennsylvania, our first question was how he came to write an alphabet book on dinosaurs. It started out that Peter was to act as a consultant on the project, providing a list of dinosaurs from A to Z. About midway through the project, he was then asked to write the text that would accompany each letter. As Peter says he "came to writing this book through the back door."

Appreciating Peter's extensive knowledge about dinosaurs, we wondered how he decided on what to write about each dinosaur, given the limitations of an alphabet book. Peter's aim was to include information about each dinosaur that was "engaging, interesting, and unique."

Peter described his collaboration with natual history illustrator Wayne Barlowe as active and interesting. Although Wayne depicts the dinosaurs in color and as action oriented, we have no knowledge of their actual color, but we do have some understanding of skin texture. However, being related to birds and reptiles, dinosaurs probably had color vision. Peter related an interesting story of the dinosaur for the letter Q—Quaesitosaurus. Only the skull of this dinosaur has been found. So, interestingly, Wayne depicted only the large neck and head of this dinosaur feeding under water.

Peter finds it interesting to write for children and enjoys making science accessible for a wide audience.

Cowboy: An Album

Linda Granfield. (1994). *Cowboy: An Album.* New York: Ticknor & Fields.

Suggested Interest Levels—Ages 7 and up.

Distinguished Features—Organizational structure, album format, and author's use of primary sources and artifacts, table of contents, author-created letters, sidebars, acknowledgments, list of additional books to read, index, picture credits.

Synopsis—The tan rawhide-like stitched dust jacket, the title depicted in large wooden cut-out letters, and a cowboy on horseback with lasso in hand, beckons readers to open the cover and have a look inside. Organizational structure and format work together as an album. By its very nature, an album encourages browsing and sampling. Granfield presents readers with a variety of interesting and intriguing facts behind the legend and lore of cowboys. The information is presented chronologically in brief pieces of narrative, author-created letters, as well as in fascinating tidbits on charts, diagrams, boxes, and in captions describing historical photographs, photos of modern-day cowboys, and cartoons.

Don't miss the lengthy list of author acknowledgments after the title page. Granfield lists such sources as museums, the Western Folklife Center, galleries, and libraries. Also of merit in this book is a table of contents divided into 5 parts from "The Historical Cowboy" to "Cowboys Today" and an index.

Response Suggestions—

- Children are natural collectors, so invite them to bring in collections, albums, or scrapbooks from home. Encourage discussion about how they were assembled, the themes or topics represented, and how they are organized.

- Use several of the connecting books listed below to discuss how authors have presented information in album-like books through writing and other graphics. Explore how authors include additional information through the use of graphic features.

- Offer the album as a format for students to consider for their own research projects, as stories about their families, or as a way to write about their collections. Students will need to decide how they will organize the nonfiction album and what written information they want to include. If it is of a historical nature, discuss the reporting of events chronologically. Also, children will need to think about the variety of materials to include in their albums—photos, newspaper clippings, their own illustrations, magazine pictures, recipes, etc.

Connecting Books—

- Other Books by Linda Granfield:
  All About Niagara Falls
  Extra! Extra! The Who, What, Where, When and Why of Newspapers
  In Flanders Fields: The Story of the Poem of John McCrae
- Other Books Using Primary Sources and Artifacts to Create Album-Like Structures:
  Cowboys: A Library of Congress Book by Martin W. Sandler
  Cowboys, Indians, and Gunfighters: The Story of the Cattle Kingdom by Albert Marrin
  A Desert Scrapbook: Dawn to Dusk in the Sonoran Desert by Virginia Wright-Frierson
  For Home and Country: A Civil War Scrapbook by Norman Bolotin and Angela Herb
  Free to Dream: The Making of a Poet: Langston Hughes by Audrey Osofsky
  The Great American Gold Rush by Rhoda Blumberg
  Pioneers: A Library of Congress Book by Martin W. Sandler
  Ranch Dressing: The Story of Western Wear by M. Jean Greenlaw
  Rosie the Riveter: Women Working on the Home Front in World War II by Penny Colman
  Texas Traditions: The Culture of the Lone Star State by Robyn Montana Turner
  Where Will This Shoe Take You? A Walk through the History of Footwear by Laurie Lawlor

An Interview With Linda Granfield...

We asked Linda Granfield to discuss her unique album-like format and organization, how she finds her primary sources, and decisions about how she organizes her materials.

Linda told us that in searching for what was available for children on cowboys, she found that books were dated and contained inaccurate information. The challenge in her research is finding "the truth and new ways to present her findings." As she researched, she found a wide variety of visuals, probably due to the invention of the stereoscope and camera. Linda saw this as an opportunity to create a book that was an analogy for the family album, with the hope that this would help children to consider their family's own background as part of a bigger view of history.

Using the album structure, Linda devoted a double-page spread for each topic, giving readers an opportunity to "dip into" the book, browse, and sample the contents. This structure allowed her to include additional information through extended captions and sidebars. The letters Linda created to the character "Jenny" became another device for presenting information about life on the trail in a more creative way.

Linda said she was very involved with the design of the layout. Because she wanted materials and photographs that hadn't been used in other books, she searched antique shops for postcards, trade cards, and business advertising, etc. By using these materials (which often were no longer copyrighted), the cost of the book was reduced, because the publisher did not have to pay for expensive permissions to use photographs from museums.

When Linda does workshops for schools, she suggests to teachers and librarians that they help students to create a "research depot" in the library. The research depot would include inexpensive and free materials such as flyers, food wrappers, bags or boxes, handouts from trade shows, photographs, campaign buttons, and advertisements, etc. These materials could be used for research projects or short research papers. Contents of a home junk drawer can also result in some interesting research topics. This can be a great source for encouraging children to find out where an item comes from, how it is made, and writing to companies for further information. Linda believes that research definitely does not need to be boring!

Pueblo Storyteller

Diane Hoyt-Goldsmith. (1991). *Pueblo Storyteller*. Photographs by Lawrence Migdale. New York: Holiday House. 28 pp.

Suggested Interest Levels—Ages 6-12.

Distinguished Features—Photographic essay, first-person narrative told through the eyes of a child of the culture depicted in the book, detailed acknowledgments, addresses for further information, photographs with detailed captions, a Pueblo legend, glossary, and index.

Synopsis—Ten-year-old April introduces readers to the culture of the Cochiti Pueblo near Santa Fe, New Mexico. We learn about April's everyday life and areas of the culture that are important to Pueblo Indians—baking bread, designing and making pottery, making Cochiti drums, and the significance of the Buffalo Dance. Because the storyteller is such a very important person for Pueblo people, the storyteller is depicted in the form of clay figures. Readers will learn about the process of finding just the right clay, the preparation of the clay, and the sculpturing process. A Pueblo legend, "How the People Came to Earth," is included at the end of the book.

April's story grew out of the many hours Diane Hoyt-Goldsmith interviewed the family while Lawrence Migdale took photographs. This powerful combination of narrative and photographs gives readers an inside look at one family of the Pueblo culture. The family is presented as a part of contemporary culture without bias and stereotyping.

Response Suggestions—

- Share other books by Diane Hoyt-Goldsmith and Lawrence Migdale that are listed in the Connecting Books section. Ask students to consider the common elements of these books. What do they learn about each culture from a first-person narrative? To what extent is telling the story about a person's everyday life through the eyes of a child more successful than if the story was told from a third-person point of view? Notice how the books are divided into sections with each describing something special about the culture.

- Invite students to consider writing their own stories. Children could interview each other and then design books about their lives including many of the features they noticed in *Pueblo Storyteller*. For example, include family photographs depicting everyday events, as well as special happenings. Develop detailed captions for these. Interview members of the family for additional information to include in the book, along with a list of acknowledgements. Divide the written information into chapters or sections.

Connecting Books—

- Other Books by Diane Hoyt-Goldsmith and Lawrence Migdale:
    Apache Rodeo
    Arctic Hunter
    Celebrating Kawanzaa
    Cherokee Summer
    Day of the Dead: A Mexican-American Celebration
    Hoang Anh: A Vietnamese-American Boy
    Mardi Gras: A Cajun Country Celebration
    Totem Pole

- Other Photographic Essays Resulting from On-Site Visits and Interviews, Using a Child as Narrator, or Ones Focusing on the Children of the Culture: (Also look for other books by these authors.)
    Chi Hoon: A Korean Girl by Patricia McMahon
    The Children of Micronesia by Jules Hermes
    Eskimo Boy: Life in an Inupiaq Eskimo Village by Russ Kendall
    Kodomo: Children of Japan by Susan Kuklin
    Mongolia: Vanishing Cultures by Jan Reynolds
    Olbalbal: A Day in Maasailand by Barbara A. Margolies
    The Spirit of Maya: A Boy Explores his Poeple's Mysterious Past by Guy Garcia
    Yanomami: People of the Amazon by David M. Schwartz

- Other Books on the Pueblo Indians:
    Pueblo Boy: Growing up in Two Worlds by Marcia Keegan
    The Pueblo by Charlotte Yue and David Yue

An Interview With Diane Hoyt-Goldsmith...

We asked Diane Hoyt-Goldsmith to discuss the research she does to write about a child and family from another culture and how she goes about writing from a first-person perspective. Diane said that part of the adventure of writing books like *Pueblo Storyteller* is the search for the child and the family. She writes the book from the viewpoint of a child within the culture and not as an outsider making judgements about the culture.

Diane's interest in Native American art led to the writing of *Totem Pole* and then to a fascination with storyteller pottery. The writing of *Pueblo*

Storyteller began with visits to the Cochiti Pueblo in New Mexico. She learned that the pottery was first made there in the 1970s and that grandmothers pass down their skills to their daughters and granddaughters.

Diane's purpose in writing about children from another culture is to show readers how different people live. She wants to tell their story, so it's important that she and photographer Lawrence Migdale spend whole days with the family photographing them as they go about their daily activities. The photography gives the narrative direction and involves the subjects in the project because of their participation in the picture taking. Diane requests permission to tape record interviews with family members. The tape recordings offer clues that enable Diane to later recall the place where she did the research, allowing her to capture the voice and special qualities of the child and family. Next, she writes a draft of the book and returns it to the family for feedback. Because the writing is very much a collaboration between the photographer, the family, and herself, Diane commented that she wouldn't publish anything to which the family objected.

Diane sees herself as a kind of journalist. She said that she goes out into a world that's new to her and opens up her heart, her eyes, and her ears to absorb everything that's around her. Diane also suggested that children can learn more about people who live around them by writing from a reporter's point of view just as she does.

A Short Walk Around the Pyramids & Through the World of Art

Philip M. Isaacson. (1993). *A Short Walk Around the Pyramids & Through the World of Art*. New York: Alfred A. Knopf. 120 pp.

Suggested Interest Levels—Ages 10 and up.

Distinguished Features—Photographs of art, combination of observational writing and emotional responses to various art forms, information on the works of art presented in *text* with no captions, text refers to specific photographs of art using plate numbers, *endnotes* describe the works of art using the plate numbers as reference, and the *index* includes the illustrations.

Synopsis—Philip Isaacson's book is one in which both the extraordinary and ordinary are depicted in the majesty of the pyramids, in the beauty of famous paintings, in intricate and simple sculpture, exquisite photographs, and in the appeal of everyday objects. This introduction to the world of art challenges readers to think about such artistic aspects as the beauty, color, and harmony of the objects around them.

Response Suggestions—

* After sharing *A Short Walk Around the Pyramids & Through the World of Art*, take students on a field trip around the school. Invite them to observe, in new ways, objects they may have seen many times before. Ask students to sketch the object and describe it in terms of its shape, color, texture, etc. Perhaps the ordinary will become the extraordinary! After students have an opportunity to revise their work, gather all the drawings and descriptions and assemble them into a book.

* Take students on a field trip to an art museum. Share and discuss the contents of a museum catalog. Invite them to view different kinds of works of art using some of Isaacson's statements as ways to begin discussion. For example, he discusses how art stirs our emotions. Students could discuss how various art forms move their emotions.

* Have students create a class art gallery, which may include some of their own art work. Take photographs of the various works of art and write a short description of their observations of each work using Isaacson's writing as a model. Asssemble the photographs and writing into a class museum catalog using plate numbers.

Connecting Books—

* Other Books by Philip Isaacson:
  The American Eagle (adult book)
  Round Buildings, Square Buildings & Buildings That Wiggle Like a Fish

- Examples of Books Using Observational (Descriptive) Writing:
  The Amazing Paper Cuttings of Hans Christian Andersen by Beth
      Wagner Brust
  The American Eye: Eleven Artists of the Twentieth Century by Jan
      Greenberg and Sandra Jordan
  Bibles and Bestiaries: A Guide to Illuminated Manuscripts by
      Elizabeth B. Wilson
  The Clover & the Bee: A Book of Pollination by Anne Ophelia Dowden
  Creepy, Crawly Baby Bugs by Sandra Markle
  Extra Cheese, Please! Mozzarella's Journey from Cow to Pizza by Cris
      Peterson
  Jack-in-the-Pulpit by Jerome Wexler
  Roy Lichtenstein: The Artist at Work by Lou Ann Walker

An Interview With Philip Isaacson...

Since Philip Isaacson is a lawyer, we were curious about his second career as an art critic and as an author of children's books on art. He described himself as having a "good eye" like someone who has a "good ear." Philip found that he always analyzed things in terms of proportion, harmony, color, etc. He is a self-taught critic whose responses to art are appreciated by many who read his weekly column in the *Maine Sunday Telegram*.

We asked him to talk about how *A Short Walk* came about. He stated that it was a follow-up to his previous children's book, *Round Buildings, Square Buildings & Buildings That Wiggle Like a Fish*, in which he explored the personalities of buildings. In *A Short Walk*, he expands this notion of responding emotionally to other art forms. His objective was not to do a book on art history; he wanted to reach out to children to get them to think about art and the emotional qualities within art. He wanted to encourage readers to ask themselves how they respond to any given piece of art.

In organizing his book, Philip said that his goal was to weave it all together into a comprehensive whole. He began with the general term, harmony, and then expanded to consider other aspects of art such as the artist's skill and execution as well as the qualities of animation that exist in various pieces of art. He applies these ideas to all types of art. He wants readers to think about how color affects us and how images can be presented in various emotional ways. As Philip talks about each art form, he weaves connections to previous sections of the book helping readers see the problems and limitations faced by the artist of each form. He stated that all the arts are integrated and reflect the culture of a given time. There is unity and the various arts do influence each other. Philip hopes his books will help children understand what art is and will provide a model of responding emotionally to art.

The Librarian Who Measured the Earth

Kathryn Lasky. (1994). *The Librarian Who Measured the Earth.* Illustrated by Kevin Hawkes. Boston: Little, Brown and Company. 48 pp.

Suggested Interest Levels—Ages 9-12.

Distinguished Features—Author's note, afterword, speculative biographical writing, and a bibliography of sources used by Lasky and Hawkes.

Synopsis—In the author's note, Lasky shares how she became interested in the life and times of Eratosthenes, a Greek geographer and astronomer, who lived more than 2,000 years ago. Although we have some understanding about that time period, very little is known about Eratosthenes. He became the chief librarian in Alexandria, Egypt and determined a method for measuring the circumference of the earth within 200 miles of what technology found it to be in the last several years.

In her note, Lasky discusses the challenges of writing about someone of which little is known. She has written some of the text in this picture book in a speculative way because of limited information on Eratosthenes.

In the afterword, Lasky discusses the mathematical achievements made by the time of the third century B.C. She explains the inaccuracies of the maps used by Columbus, prepared by Greek geographers after the time of Eratosthenes, and concludes by reinforcing the notion that curiosity leads to challenging old ways of thinking in order to create new knowledge.

Response Suggestions—

- Before sharing aloud this picture book, talk about the times in which Eratosthenes lived. Investigating some of the books included in Lasky and Hawkes' bibliography will provide background information. Invite students to speculate on the differences between life in ancient times and today. This could take the form of a comparison chart or Venn diagram.

- Share both the author's note and the afterword with students. Discuss why an author would include this information. In *The Librarian Who Measured the Earth*, Lasky points out that not much is known about Eratosthenes. Ask students why they think this may be the case. In her writing about Eratosthenes, she had to take what is known about living in that time period in order to speculate on other areas of his life.

- Share additional books in which an author had to speculate about a person's life. Several titles are listed in the Connecting Books section of this response guide. Examine the books to find information about the author's research process—what is known and not known. Is this information in the author's notes, the afterword, and/or indicated by the language the author uses? For example, an author might use words, *e.g.*, could have happened, it is reasonable to consider, or we are unsure, etc.

- As you share *The Librarian Who Measured the Earth*, ask students to consider what Lasky may have found as fact and areas in which she had to extrapolate.

- Have students identify a person in history, mathematics, science, or the arts. After listing questions they want to investigate, encourage students to read several books about that person. What questions were they able to answer? Invite students to share their written and illustrated reports. Other classmates can ask the author which facts in the report can be substantiated and where the author speculated on information. What facts did the author find that allowed for reasonable speculations?

Connecting Books—

- Other Books by Kathryn Lasky:
    Days of the Dead
    Dinosaur Dig
    A Journey to the New World: The Diary of Remember Patience Whipple
    Pond Year
    Surtsey: The Newest Place on Earth
    Think Like an Eagle: At Work with a Wildlife Photographer

- Other Books in Which the Author Addresses the Problem of Incomplete Information:
    Bard of Avon: The Story of William Shakespeare by Diane Stanley and Peter Vennema
    Cleopatra by Diane Stanley and Peter Vennema
    Marco Polo: His Notebook by Susan L. Roth
    Theodoric's Rainbow by Stephen Kramer

- Examples of Books with Afterwords and Epilogues about the Research Process:
    Big Annie of Calumet: The True Story of the Industrial Revolution by Jerry Stanley
    Leonardo da Vinci by Diane Stanley
    A Long Hard Journey: The Story of Pullman Porter by Patricia McKissack and Fredrick McKissack
    North Star to Freedom: The Story of the Underground Railroad by Gena K. Gorrell

An Interview With Kathryn Lasky...

In the author's note at the beginning of *The Librarian Who Measured the Earth*, Kathryn Lasky discusses the challenges of writing biographical material when not much is known about the person. We asked her to talk further about these challenges. She reiterated that not much is known about Eratosthenes, but she said that even if much were known, writers must "extrapolate responsibly." For example, she begins by writing about Eratosthenes being a curious baby. As a young child he would follow a path of ants and also wondered why the stars stayed in the sky. Kathryn said that in all her research she did not read about these specific events in Eratosthenes' early life. However, she said that it is a responsible assumption that Eratosthenes was a curious young boy. Kathryn said she reads a lot of books about science topics and biographies of contemporary scien

tists. She found many commonalities in the early lives of these scientists— they were curious children, full of wonder. Therefore, she assumed that Eratosthenes was also a child who had a "capacity for playful observation." Later in the book, Lasky includes information pertaining to Eratosthenes keeping lists of the important dates in Greek history. She said that when she is that specific, there is evidence to support her writing such a statement. Kathryn feels that this book "is really about curiosity—a kind of celebration of thinking."

Kathryn mentioned that this is one of the most collaborative books she has done, having worked closely with a mathematician and the illustrator of the book, Kevin Hawkes. A grapefruit was suggested as a metaphor to explain how Eratosthenes measured the circumference of the earth. Kathryn commented on how valuable it is for her to use metaphors as a way to make sense of complicated issues in nonfiction.

We also learned that Kathryn is a "devotee of author's notes and afterwords." She would like to see these features in more picture books. They provide readers with the opportunity to learn more, without this information cluttering the main body of the text. For example, readers learn in Lasky's author's note about how she became fascinated about Eratosthenes. This provides readers with insight on how Kathryn's curiosity and questions led her to read and research this fascinating individual who lived over 2,000 years ago. She said that, "Authors are drawn to a topic—there's a slow kind of seduction" to investigate a subject and write about it. Children can become involved in a similar kind of inquiry—teachers need only help them pursue their questions and curiosities about the world.

Hurricanes: Earth's Mightiest Storms

Patricia Lauber. (1996). *Hurricanes: Earth's Mightiest Storms.* New York: Scholastic. 64 pp.

Suggested Interest Levels—Ages 8 and up.

Distinguished Features—Captioned photographs; maps; diagrams; and additonal information in sidebars, metaphors to explain concepts, selected information in blue-colored pages, further readings, picture credits, and index.

Synopsis—In newspaper-report style writing, Lauber begins by describing the "monster storm" of 1938. Her writing will capture readers with its mounting intensity as she describes this mighty and devastating storm. This first chapter builds the foundation for subsequent chapters that discuss how hurricances are made, how they are predicted, tracked, named, and the damage they cause. It also discusses hurricane frequency cycles, the dangers created by recent population shifts, and ecological effects. Lauber also discusses famous hurricanes, the names hurricanes are called in other parts of the world, and what people can do to help themselves.

Response Suggestions—

- Walk students through *Hurricanes*, helping them to notice and understand the special access features of this book. They may want to incorporate these in their own written investigations, *e.g.*, sidebars, maps, labeled diagrams, and the use of colored pages to include additional information.

- Discuss the use of similes and metaphors to explain complex concepts in nonfiction. Ask students to speculate on why many nonfiction authors use metaphors in their writing. Locate examples of metaphors in Hurricanes and in other books by Patricia Lauber. Find other good examples of nonfiction writing in which authors use metaphors to explain concepts. Brainstorm additional metaphors with students to describe concepts in the books shared and how these metaphors relate a new idea to one(s) readers have experienced. Invite students to create metaphors in their own writing. Discuss how metaphors can also limit understanding of a new concept.

- Have pairs of students research one of the famous hurricanes mentioned by Lauber, other storms, or natural disasters. The products of their investigations can include such features as sidebars, additional information on colored sheets, maps, diagrams, and the use of metaphor.

Connecting Books—

• Other Books by Patricia Lauber:
  Be a Friend to Trees
  Dinosaurs Walked Here and Other Stories Fossils Tell
  Fur, Feather, Flipper: How Animals Live Where They Do
  Journey to the Planets
  Living with Dinosaurs
  The News about Dinosaurs
  Seeing Earth from Space
  Summer of Fire: Yellowstone 1988
  Volcano: The Eruption and Healing of Mount St. Helens
  Who Discovered America? Mysteries and Puzzles of the New World

• Other Books That Use Access Features (Diagrams, Maps, etc.):
  Eagles by Aubrey Lang
  From the Beginning: The Story of Human Evolution by David Peters
  The Italian American Family Album by Dorothy and Thomas Hoobler
  My Costume Book by Cheryl Owen
  Postcards from Pluto: A Tour of the Solar System by Loreen Leedy

An Interview With Patricia Lauber...

Patricia Lauber begins *Hurricanes* in a compelling and dramatic way using rich and vivid descriptions to recount the horrific storm that hit Long Island and the New England coast in 1938. We were interested in the types of resources Patricia Lauber used to help her write this book. She said she made extensive use of contemporary accounts of this hurricane and also her own experiences in a lifetime spent on the New England coast.

Hurricanes is filled with archival photographs and interesting graphics and maps. Although Patricia doesn't illustrate her own books, she searched for illustrations, maps, and graphics for this book. Patricia says that she plays a major role in selecting access features, such as diagrams and graphics, because she is the "local expert" who has done all the background research. She also thinks about possible illustrations while writing because she feels that they both extend the text and enhance comprehension. A professor of meteorology reviewed the text and graphics for accuracy before publication.

Several other features make *Hurricanes* an interesting example of nonfiction. Throughout the book are blue-colored pages that include information that can stand alone; it is material that doesn't fit in with the main text of the book. The "blue pages" contain information Patricia "could get into" but "not out of" in order to continue the narrative. The information that ends one chapter ought to lead into the next chapter. Patricia does think of herself as creating a storyline but is careful to remain within the bounds of what is accurate.

Since scientists don't fully understand how hurricanes form, explaining clearly and explicitly was one of Patricia's biggest challenges in writing this book. She used metaphors to help describe the nature of hurricanes and their destructive powers. One of her goals is to use metaphors that children will understand based on their experiential level. Having written over 90 books for children, she said that she just naturally thinks in terms of analogies.

Patricia is a collector of book ideas, often gathering materials for years before she commits to actually writing a book. In her first draft she typically includes everything, and in the revising stage normally cuts the material by a third. She aims to make her books "page turners"—with writing that is exciting and interesting while creating a narrative thread that pulls the book together and leads readers from one concept to another.

She advises children to write about subjects that interest them and to allow their enthusiasm for the topic to shine through their writing. The best way to learn to write is to read a lot, absorbing a host of different ways to express ideas.

The Great Fire

Jim Murphy. (1995). *The Great Fire*. New York: Scholastic. 144 pp. Orbis Pictus Award Winner.

Suggested Interest Levels—Ages 9 and above.

Distinguished Features—Use of primary sources, integration of primary source material such as newspaper reports, eyewitness accounts, and personal histories into the narrative account, maps, newspaper headlines, acknowledgments, introduction, table of contents, archival photographs, bibliography and sources, and index.

Synopsis—decision to write an account of the disastrous Chicago fire of 1871 was prompted by finding an interesting book titled, *The Great Conflagration*, in an antiquarian bookstore. In *The Great Fire*, Murphy weaves the interesting personal histories of people who lived through this disaster into a gripping narrative. This riveting documentary includes numerous archival photographs with detailed captions and a map of the city that changes in each chapter illustrating the disastrous spread of the fire.

In the final chapters of the book, Murphy takes some of the lingering issues about the cause of the fire and reasons for its rapid spread and places them within a historical perspective. For example, in discussing the cause of the fire, he describes how rumors quickly spread caused by inaccuracies in news-reporting procedures of the day. Although the fire was started in the O'Leary barn, there is no firm evidence regarding the cause of the fire and who was actually to be blamed for this calamity. Murphy also discusses possible explanations for the seeming ineptitude of the fire department in quelling the spread of the fire. The last few pages of the book describe the rebuilding of Chicago.

Response Suggestions—

- Share this book by inviting students to peruse the old photographs and captions throughout the book as a way into Murphy's description of the great Chicago fire. Students can follow the spread of the fire by focusing on the map at the end of each chapter.

- Examine other books below that incorporate primary sources and discuss how each author has approached the use of these materials. Pay particular attention to the following: the storylike narrative, the use of quoted material to suggest dialog, how chapters are titled, sources used by the author, and the use of other facsimile archival material.

- Take students to the library to read about famous local events in old newspapers. Compare these accounts to diaries and other archival materials of the same time period. The historical society might be a good source for these materials, as well as speakers. As a next step, young writers could talk and write about the event by weaving the various pieces of historical data into a narrative account of the event. They might also try incorporating quoted material, as Murphy does in his book.

Connecting Books—

- Other Books by Jim Murphy:
    Across America on an Emigrant Train
    The Boys' War: Confederate and Union Soldiers Talk about Civil War
    Into the Deep Forest with Henry Thoreau
    The Last Dinosaur
    The Long Road to Gettysburg
    A Young Patriot: The American Revolution as Experienced by One Boy
- Other Books Using Primary Sources to Weave a Chronological Narrative: (Examine other books by these authors.)
    Gold: The True Story of Why People Search for it, Mine it, Trade it, Steal it, Mint it, Hoard it, Shape it, Wear it, Fight and Kill for it by Milton Meltzer
    The Gold Rush by Liza Ketchum
    The Oregon Trail by Leonard Everett Fisher
    Till Victory Is Won: Black Soldiers in the Civil War by Zak Mettger
    Unconditional Surrender: U. S. Grant and the Civil War by Albert Marrin
    Who Were the Founding Fathers? Two Hundred Years of Reinventing American History by Steven H. Jaffe
    The Wright Brothers: How They Invented the Airplane by Russell Freedman

An Interview With Jim Murphy...

We were curious about Jim Murphy's strategies for merging the four eyewitness voices that help to tell the story of the Great Chicago Fire. Jim said that finding each of these people in his research helped to bring a fresh new perspective or angle on understanding the fire. He also wanted to make sure that he presented a balanced view. A particular challenge was being able to orient readers to each new voice, and to make those transitions in the text as clear as possible.

As part of his research, Jim bought a

map of Chicago and began tracing the route of the fire. He realized that a map found near the end of each chapter would serve as a way to help readers keep track of the action and the spread of the fire. Without the maps, he said that it would have taken too much text to explain who was where and what was happening. The maps serve as a valuable access feature for readers. Jim feels that once a reader becomes disoriented while reading the text, the "spell of the scene" is lost. In order to see the text as a new reader would, he often did not read sections he had written for weeks in order to revisit them later to see if they all made sense.

We found chapter titles such as "'The Dogs of Hell Were Upon the Housetops'" and "'A Surging Ocean of Flame'" especially appealing. Jim said he wanted to tease readers, as some 19th century authors did, using titles that would not give away too much of what was going to happen next in the book. In many cases, the chapter titles are quotes he found while doing his research.

Writing captions is also another important component of the book. Jim stated that in writing his own, he does not want to provide readers with obvious information. He uses a magnifying glass to examine each photograph to note details to share with readers.

We also asked Jim to what extent writing *The Great Fire* stretched his research skills. In researching this very focused topic, he read each footnote in every book he read. This led him to further explore social issues such as conflicts between the rich and the poor and the formulation of building codes as a result of the fire. These issues, and others, became the focus of the last two chapters of the book. His editor helped Jim to consolidate information, as these chapters were becoming too lengthy. Jim commented on not wanting to overwhelm readers; he had given them a "roller coaster ride through the fire," and at the end he did not want to simply "feed" readers information.

As a former editor, he believes that the design and look of a book is crucial as to how well a book will be received. Books need to be both "friendly and accessible." His final remarks to us were that he does a lot of self-editing, but he's not a good speller!

Children of the Dust Bowl: The True Story of the School at Weedpatch Camp

Jerry Stanley. (1992). *Children of the Dust Bowl: The True Story of the School at Weedpatch Camp.* New York: Crown. 85 pp. Orbis Pictus Award Winner.

Suggested Interest Levels—Ages 9 and up.

Distinguished Features—Acknowledgments, table of contents, author's note, introduction, use of primary sources, interview data, maps, songs, archival photographs, afterword, bibliographic note and picture credits, and index.

Synopsis—Stanley's stunning historical narrative account describes the hardships of the Okies, their journey to California, and the eventual settlement in government built farm-labor camps in the San Joaquin Valley. He focuses his attention on Weedpatch Camp and Leo Hart, the newly elected superintendent of Kern County, who started Weedpatch School. Stanley's numerous interviews with Leo Hart, teachers, and former students provided him with an almost eyewitness account of the creation and building of the Weedpatch School.

Hart understood and empathized with the situation of the Okies and began the Weedpatch School as a project that would cost the county nothing. Hart's dedication to the children and families of Weedpatch was only matched by his perseverance to recruit the best new teachers and search for donations of building materials. He envisioned the curriculum to be broad, enriching, and one that would help students gain practical life skills. The school became so successful that residents outside of the camp wanted their children enrolled. Much of the school was rebuilt after a 1952 earthquake and is now known as Sunset School.

Response Suggestions—

- Discuss the Great Depression of the 1930s with students. Share the brief author's note in which Stanley comments on the term *Okie* and the way Okies use the term to mean "pride, courage, and a determination to accept hardship without showing weakness." Ask students to speculate on why Stanley included this in the author's note. Browse through *Children of the Dust Bowl* by examining the many photographs and captions in the book. This is a good way to acquaint students with the life and times of the Okies. Share sections of the narrative and ask students to think of the kinds of questions Stanley might have posed to Leo Hart, former teachers, and students in order to aquire the information he needed to write his account of Weedpatch School.

- See Donald Graves' book, *Investigating Nonfiction* (Heinemann, 1989), for a description of data gathering and interviewing techniques. Invite students to develop a list of questions to interview each other. After sharing *Children of the Dust Bowl*, encourage them to interview family members who lived during this time. Also engage students in a discussion about other people in the community they might like to interview and why. One strategy they can use to think about this is to consider the questions they have about the world around them. For example, if their school is named for a person, do they know why this person was chosen? Interview the principal and others to gain information and to write responses from this data.

Connecting Books—

- Other Books by Jerry Stanley:
    Big Annie of Calumet: A True Story of the Industrial Revolution
    Digger: The Tragic Fate of the California Indians from the Missions to the Gold Rush
    I Am an American: A True Story of Japanese Internment

- Other Books Using Primary Sources with Interview Data:
    The Bones Detectives: How Forensic Anthropologists Solve Crimes and Uncover Mysteries of the Dead by Donna M. Jackson
    Growing Up in Coal Country by Susan Campbell Bartoletti
    Red-Tail Angels: The Story of the Tuskegee Airmen of World War II by Patricia McKissack and Fredrick McKissack

- See Books by Diane Hoyt-Goldsmith in Response Guides

- See Other Books about the Depression:
    Growing Up in the Great Depression by Richard Wormser
    John Steinbeck by Catherine Reef
    Kids at Work: Lewis Hine and the Crusade Against Child Labor by Russell Freedman

An Interview With Jerry Stanley...

Because Jerry Stanley used interviews to explore his topic, we asked him to describe how the book came about. As a new assistant professor at California State University 21 years ago, his dean requested that he interview Leo Hart about the School at Weedpatch Camp, which Hart helped start at Bakersfield for the Okies during the Depression. What began reluctantly as assigned writing, eventually became a scholarly article, a magazine piece, a children's book, and shortly will be a Hollywood movie. In that

initial interview, Jerry became captivated with Hart's story, which if it had not been written, might never have become history. Jerry says that,"Unless history is written down, it vanishes."

As a historian, Jerry uses interviews to collect information about his topic. He believes that students need to be encouraged to go out and talk to people in order to capture and preserve the past through writing. In sharing his approach to the initial interview he conducted with Leo Hart, he started with about 30 questions. From Mr. Hart and the principal, Pete Bancroft, Jerry obtained the names and addresses of other teachers and students. Many of the local interviews took place over the phone. He stated that, "The more interviews you do, the better the questions you have to ask" about various events. From these interviews, he compiled a lengthy questionnaire, which he sent to other students and teachers. Jerry commented that the great challenge was to synthesize the different recollections into a composite.

We asked Jerry how he integrated all the notes from the interviews into a "story." He firmly advised, "Don't write up your notes—the writing will be stiff and unreadable." He uses the historian's methodology with his goal being to create a factual account, in a narrative style, promoting the reader to turn the page to find out what happens next. To achieve this natural retelling, he places notes on the same topic on 4 x 6 cards. By repeatedly sorting through the cards for the individual chapters, he absorbs the events. He then puts the notes away and writes the way he remembers it. Jerry assured us that the important events and people rise to the surface. Then he checks the manuscript against his notecards for any misinformation. Jerry said that his goal is to tell the story and that the worst thing you can do is to feel you have to write in a certain order, such as you might with an outline. To help him remain honest with the past during a writing project, he keeps one photograph from his research opposite his writing desk where he can see it, and it can see him and serve as a check on him.

Jerry's research and writing about the School at Weedpatch Camp began in 1975. He likened the experience to "a dog chasing a car for 21 years and finally catching it!" Jerry and those involved in the story of Weedpatch Camp are looking forward to viewing the premier of the movie based on *Children of the Dust Bowl*. It will be a particularly poignant moment to return to the theatre in Bakersfield that once posted a sign declaring: "Okies sit in the balcony!"

Safari Beneath the Sea: The Wonder World of the North Pacific Coast

Diane Swanson. (1994). *Safari Beneath the Sea: The Wonder World of the North Pacific Coast.* Photographs by the Royal British Columbia Museum. San Francisco: Sierra Club Books for Children. 58 pp. Orbis Pictus Award Winner.

Suggested Interest Levels—Ages 8-12.

Distinguished Features—Sierra Club note, table of contents, photographs with captions, major headings, sidebars, bulleted information, organizational structure (enumeration), and index.

Synopsis—A diver, cradling an octopus in some dark and mysterious underwater place, is the cover photograph of Diane Swanson's Orbis Pictus Award Winner. Diane invites readers into the world of the North Pacific with her highly imaginative lead: "Imagine fish that tie themselves in knots...."

Swanson offers readers a rich feast for the eyes using many photographs by the Royal British Columbia Museum to accompany the five chapters, whose content ranges from plants to mammals of the North Pacific. Each chapter title is creatively phrased, but descriptive of its content. For example, Chapter 3—"Spineless Superstars" begins with a statement about the giant Pacific octopus that makes the reader a little less fearsome about a creature that Swanson says can weigh up to 150 pounds and stretches 23 feet from arm to arm. Swanson's lead sentence is so fascinating that readers will be swept into the rest of the chapter and not be disappointed.

Response Suggestions—

- Share a chapter of *Safari Beneath the Sea* aloud with students. In addition to talking about the interesting information, ask students to focus on all of the different access features in each chapter and how these work together successfully: use of headings to discuss each subtopic; enumeration as the organizational structure (a listing of topics); use of sidebars to include additional information; bullets to highlight facts; captions and photographs that explain and expand textual information. Next, examine other chapters in the book to see the consistent use of these features. Note that chapters can be sampled and not necessarily read in order. Ask students why they think this is the case.

- Demonstrate how to take additional information about a topic and ways to include this "outside" of the text using access features. Examine other books in which authors organize the text in interesting ways and also use access features. Encourage students to use these features in their own report writing.

Connecting Books—

- Other Books by Diane Swanson:
    Buffalo Sunrise: The Story of a North American Giant
    *Coyotes in the Crosswalk: True Tales of Animal Life in the Wilds of
      the City!*
    The Day of the Twelve-Story Wave
    Sky Dancers: The Amazing World of North American Birds
    *Squirts and Snails and Skinny Green Tails: Seashore Nature Activities
      for Kids*
    A Toothy Tongue & One Long Foot: Nature Activities for Kids
- Other Books about Ocean Study:
    Coral Reefs: Earth's Undersea Treasures by Laurence Pringle
    Deep-Sea Vents: Living World without Sun by John F. Waters
- Other Books with Bullets, Sidebars, Captions, Interesting Chapter
  Headings and Titles:
    Careers in Baseball by Howard J. Blumenthal
    Hurricane: Earth's Mightest Storms by Patricia Lauber
    Nature All Year Long by Clare Walker Leslie
    Ticket to the Twenties: A Time Traveler's Guide by Mary Blocksma
    Vanilla, Chocolate, & Strawberry: The Story of Your Favorite Flavors by
      Bonnie Busenberg

An Interview With Diane Swanson...

We were very impressed with the
organization and format of *Safari Beneath
the Sea.* This book is amazing in terms of
the consistency in each chapter—the
number of topics covered, sidebars, and
bulleted remarks. Diane Swanson's
response to our observation is that consistency of format is not only helpful to her
as a writer, but that it is also helpful to
readers. Her work as a Literacy Volunteeer
has helped her to appreciate the reading
challenges that many people face. By vary-
ing the format with a variety of access features, she finds that readers do not have
to approach reading it necessarily from
cover to cover. Instead, they can browse through the book, enjoying parts
of it—the sidebars, bulleted points, etc.

Diane commented on the fact that the boxes and bulleted information
she includes gives her freedom as a writer. She can explore a point more in

depth, write about a related topic, as well as write from different points of view. Diane also writes her own captions for the photographs in the book. She believes that it is very important for her to do that. She likes to add new information in the captions, rather than reiterating material already in the text. The captions should be able to stand alone without referring back to the text.

Diane also discussed the role of the SAFARI team as part of the research process in writing this book. Using modern technology, the SAFARI team divers had the capabilities of interacting with an audience to discuss what fish and other marine life were around them. Diane was responsible for writing the study guide that was used with this program. The work of the SAFARI team and the photographs from the Royal British Columbia Museum were important aspects in the writing of this book and are identified in the acknowledgments.

Diane said it's fun to write and likes to consider format first. Her aim is to write highly interesting and captivating nonfiction books that readers not only find informative but also entertaining.

Orbis Pictus Award-Winners, Honor Books, and Notables: An Annotated Bibliography

by Rosemary A. Bamford & Janice V. Kristo

Each year the Orbis Pictus Committee of the National Council of Teachers of English recognizes well-written nonfiction for children—one winner and a selection of Honor and Notable books. Awards are based on the following criteria: accuracy, organization, design, style, and usefulness in K-8 classrooms. The following is an annotated bibliography of these books. The "DF" notation indicates distinguished features for each book such as specific organizational structures, access features, or unique aspects. Subject headings at the end of each entry suggest possible use for thematic studies.

Adler, David. (1989). *We Remember the Holocaust.* Holt. 147 pp. Ages 10 and up.
Describes the Holocaust and includes accounts from survivors. DF: Table of Contents (chapter titles are quotes); Map; Historic photographs with captions; Preface; Chronology; Glossary; Suggested Readings (includes nonfiction and fiction); Bibliography; Acknowledgments; Index. JEWISH HOLOCAUST; WORLD WAR II

Alexander, Sally Hobart. (1990). *Mom Can't See Me.* Photographs by George Ancona. Simon & Schuster. Unpaged. Ages 6-10.
Through photographs and text, this heart-warming story shows family life of a blind woman and her family from the perspective of her 9-year-old daughter. DF: First-person narrative; Black and white photographs that closely match the text. BLINDNESS

Aliki. (1989). *The King's Day: Louis XIV of France.* Crowell. Unpaged. Ages and up.
Describes a day in the life of King Louis XIV of France. DF: Detailed illus-

trations; Chronology of King Louis X1V; Definitions of French words. KINGS

Ancona, George. (1989). *The American Farm Family.* Text by Joan
    Anderson. Harcourt, Brace Jovanovich. Unpaged. Ages 6 and up.
Photographic essay of three farming families from Massachusetts, Georgia,
and Iowa. DF: Address for Farm Aid for further information; Introduction;
Interviews; Afterword. FARM LIFE

Apfel, Necia H. (1991). *Voyager to the Planets.* Clarion. 48 pp. Ages 8 and
    up.
Examines the findings of the Voyager I and II missions in space. DF:
Photographs; Index; Further Reading list; Pronunciation Guide. PLANETS;
SPACE EXPLORATION

Arnosky, Jim. (1996). *Nearer Nature.* Lothrop, Lee & Shepard. 160 pp. Ages
    10 and up.
Noted naturalist and artist presents a personal perspective and extensive
collection of sketches of his observations of wild animals on his Vermont
farm. DF: Table of Contents; Observational writing; Introduction; Drawings
with labels; Index. NATURE; VERMONT

Ashabranner, Brent. (1996). *A Strange and Distant Shore: Indians of the
    Great Plains in Exile.* Cobblehill. 54 pp. Ages 10-14.
Using reproductions of the original art work done by imprisoned Great
Plains Indian leaders, the author describes how Richard Henry Pratt
encouraged art and education as a means of emotionally surviving their
exile in St. Augustine. DF: Multiple perspectives; Quotes from the exiled
Indians and generals; Speculative writing; Reproductions of original art;
Archival photographs; Illustration credits; Bibliography; Index; Informal
afterword explores debate of Pratt's intentions. NATIVE AMERICANS; ART

Bartoletti, Susan Campbell. (1996). *Growing Up in Coal Country.* Houghton
    Mifflin. 127 pp. Ages 9-14.
Describes the life and work of coal miners, especially their children, during
the 19th and 20th centuries. DF: Acknowledgments; Table of Contents with
small photographs representative of content; Introduction presents personal involvement of author; Each chapter introduced with quotes from
interviews; Enumerative organization; Photographs; Captions; Bibliography.
COAL MINING

Bash, Barbara. (1993). *Shadows of Night: The Hidden World of the Little
    Brown Bat.* Sierra Club. Unpaged. Ages 6-10.
Describes the life cycle and characteristics of the Little Brown Bat, one of
the most common bats of North America. DF: Information is accessible to

young children; More About Bats page; Things to Remember. BATS

Bash, Barbara. (1994). *Ancient Ones: The World of the Old-Growth Douglas Fir.* Sierra Club. Unpaged. Ages 7 and up.
The author invites the reader for a walk into an old-growth forest to discover the flora and fauna and the process of the regrowth of a Douglas fir. DF: Endpages depict growth of a forest from 1 year to 1,000+ years; Verso of title page, Sierra Club note; Acknowledgments; Author note about research process. TREES; ECOLOGY

Bial, Raymond. (1995). *The Underground Railroad.* Houghton Mifflin. 48 pp. Ages 9 and up.
Although much is not known about the underground railroad, this book documents what we do know about the routes, lives and trying times of the "passengers" and "conductors." DF: Foreword describes on-site research; Historical photographs; Detailed captions; Chronology of antislavery movement; Further readings; Acknowledgments. SLAVERY

Bial, Raymond. (1996). *With Needle and Thread: A Book about Quilts.* Houghton Mifflin. 48 pp. Ages 10 and up.
Discusses the history of quilts and quiltmaking as an art form handed down through generations of women. DF: Acknowledgments; Author's Note equates writing to the process of quilting; Photographs; Captions; Further Reading; Address for Kentucky Quilt Project. QUILTING; CRAFTS; ART

Blumberg, Rhoda. (1989). *The Great American Gold Rush.* Bradbury. 135 pp. Ages 12 and up. (1990 HONOR BOOK).
Describes the forty-niners search for gold in the West by emigrants from the East Coast of the United States and Europe. DF: Acknowledgments; Table of Contents; Original photographs, artwork; cartoons and posters; Captions; Maps; Notes; Bibliography; Index; Author's Biography. THE GOLD RUSH; CALIFORNIA; WESTWARD MOVEMENT

Blumberg, Rhoda. (1991). *The Remarkable Voyages of Captain Cook.* Bradbury. 137 pp. Ages 10 and up.
The story of one of the world's most reknown navigators and explorers, British Captain James Cook, discoverer of Hawaii, Australia, and other Pacific Ocean areas. DF: Table of Contents; Historic illustrations; Maps; Subheadings within each chapter; Words defined in text; Contrasts conditions explorers found on the islands with those in England; Notes for each chapter; Bibliography including primary and secondary sources; About the Artists section; Index. EXPLORERS

Blumberg, Rhoda. (1996). *Full Steam Ahead: The Race to Build a Transcontinental Railroad.* National Geographic Society. 159 pp. Ages 12 and up. (HONOR BOOK)
An in-depth discussion of the vision and the drama of building the Transcontinental Railroad. DF: Acknowledgments; Archival photographs; Captions; Maps; Bibliography includes list of primary and secondary soures, as well as newspapers; Notes for each chapter and additional information; Index. RAILROAD; WESTERN MOVEMENT; CHINESE

Brandenburg, Jim. (1993). *To the Top of the World: Adventures with Arctic Wolves.* Walker. 44 pp. Ages 6 and up. (1994 HONOR BOOK)
Through photographs and text, Brandenburg chronicles the months he spent with a pack of Arctic wolves on Ellesmere Island in the Northwest Territories. DF: Table of Contents; Photographs, Descriptive observational writing. WOLVES

Brooks, Bruce. (1993). *Making Sense: Animal Perception and Communication.* Farrar Straus Giroux. 74 pp. Ages 10 and up. (1994 HONOR BOOK)
Explores the five senses (plus a sixth—feelings) of animals, insects, and birds as ways to communicate and perceive the world. DF: Title is one in the *Knowing Nature* series (Brooks wrote two others in this series—*Nature by Design* and *Predator!*); Table of Contents; Glossary; Index. SENSES; ANIMALS; ANIMAL PERCEPTIONS

Brown, Mary Barrett. (1992). *Wings Along the Waterway.* Orchard. 80 pp. Ages 7 and up.
Describes 21 different water birds including a discussion of their habitat, appearance, and aspects of their survival. DF: Author acknowledgments; Table of Contents; Introduction; Epilogue; Bibliography; Index; Watercolor illustrations of the water birds. WATER BIRDS

Burleigh, Robert. (1991). *Flight: The Jouney of Charles Lindbergh.* Illustrated by Mike Wimmer. Philomel. Unpaged. Ages 7 and up. (1992 ORBIS PICTUS AWARD-WINNER)
Documents the nonstop solo flight of Charles Lindbergh from New York to Paris in 1927. DF: Acknowledgments; Introduction by Jean Fritz; Full color paintings. FLIGHT; AVIATION

Busenberg, Bonnie. (1994). *Vanilla, Chocolate, & Strawberry: The Story of Your Favorite Flavors.* Lerner. 112 pp. Ages 10 and up.
Discusses the history, biology and chemistry, current farming and processing techniques, and use of three favorite flavors—vanilla, chocolate, and strawberry. DF: Table of Contents; Introduction; Sidebars; Detailed graph-

ics; Photographs; Engravings; Detailed captions; Maps; Inserted sections; Recipes; Metric Conversion Chart; Hints on Cooking; Glossary; Index; Acknowledgments. DESSERTS; FOOD

Calabro, Marian. (1989). *Operation Grizzly Bear.* Four Winds. 118 pp. Ages 10 and up.
Describes John and Frank Craighead's research on the grizzly bears of Yellowstone National Park, which included many new tracking devices such as the radio collar. DF: Acknowledgments; Table of Contents; Maps; Photographs; Quotes from researchers; Bibliography; Further Reading; Index. BEARS; HUMAN-ANIMAL RELATIONSHIPS; YELLOWSTONE NATIONAL PARK

Calmenson, Stephanie. (1994). *Rosie, A Visiting Dog's Story.* Photographs by Justin Sutcliffe. Clarion. 47 pp. Ages 6-10.
A photographic essay describing the training of a working dog who visits people in such places as hospitals and nursing homes. DF: Author note describes the dog breed and the visiting dog programs. HUMAN-ANIMAL RELATIONSHIPS; PETS

Carrick, Carol. (1993). *Whaling Day.* Woodcuts by David Frampton. Clarion. 40 pp. Ages 8 and up.
Weaving in information on the physical and behavioral aspects of the whale, Carrick describes the whaling industry from its early times to current efforts of regulation and conservation. DF: Acknowledgment; Woodcuts; Labeled diagrams; Whaling Terms; Selected Bibliography; Index. WHALES; WHALING

Cha, Dia. (1996). *Dia's Story Cloth: The Hmong People's Journey of Freedom.* Stitched by Chue and Nhia Thao Cha. Lee and Low/Denver Museum of Natural History. 24 pp. Ages 10-12.
Personal narrative of the story cloth, pan'dau, created by the author's Hmong relatives describing their journey to freedom. DF: Close-up photographs of sections of the cloth; Afterword from Curator of the Denver Museum of Natural History. HMONG; IMMIGRATION

Cole, Joanna. (1990). *The Magic School Bus Lost in the Solar System.* Illustrated by Bruce Degen. Scholastic. Unpaged. Ages 7-10.
Humorous, but informative, visit to the planets with Ms. Frizzle and The Magic School Bus. DF: Each page loaded with factual information; Narrative storyline; Conversation bubbles; Charts. SOLAR SYSTEM; ASTRONOMY

Colman, Penny. (1995). *Rosie the Riveter: Women Working on the Home Front in World War II.* Crown. 120 pp. 12 and up. (1996 HONOR BOOK)
Using more than 60 archival photographs documenting the role of women

in the workplace during WW II. DF: Archival photographs, posters and advertisements; Select list of women's wartime jobs; Facts and figures about women war workers; Chronology; Bibliography and notes (including articles, videos, books, and films); Picture credits; Acknowledgments; Index. World War II; WOMEN'S HISTORY

Cone, Molly. (1992). *Come Back, Salmon: How a Group of Dedicated kids Adopted Pigeon Creek and Brought it Back to Life.* Photographs by Sidnee Wheelwright. Sierra Club. 48 pp. Ages 8-12. (1993 HONOR BOOK)
Describes the efforts and success of the Jackson Elementary School in Everett, Washington to restore a stream where salmon would return to spawn. DF: Detailed acknowledgments; Dialog in the book was based on interviews; Table of Contents; Captioned photographs; Sidebars; Glossary; Index. FISH; ENVIRONMENTAL PROTECTION

Conrad, Pam. (1991). *Prairie Visions: The Life and Times of Solomon Butcher.* HarperCollins. 85 pp. Ages 10 and up. (1992 HONOR BOOK)
Describes the photographic work of Solomon Butcher and, through his photographs, the life of the people of Nebraska during the turn of the century. DF: Acknowledgments; Table of Contents; Introduction; Original Butcher photographs; Captions; Bibliography. BIOGRAPHY; PHOTOGRAPHER; PRAIRIE

Cooper, Floyd. (1996). *Mandela: From the Life of the South African Statesman.* Philomel. Unpaged; Ages 8-12.
Describes Mandela's youth, schooling, and work as a lawyer with particular emphasis on the development of his character. DF: Acknowledgments; Illustrations; Pronunciation key; Bibliography; Author's Note. BIOGRAPHY; APARTHEID; SOUTH AFRICA

Cummings, Pat (Editor). (1992). *Talking with Artists: Conversations with Victoria Chess, Pat Cummings, Leo and Diane Dillon, Richard Egielski, Lois Ehlert, Lisa Campbell Ernst, Tom Feelings, Steven Kellogg, Jerry Pinkney, Amy Schwartz, Lane Smith, Chris Van Allsburg, and David Wiesner.* Bradbury. 96 pp. All Ages. (1993 HONOR BOOK)
A combination of fourteen autobiographies of artists of children's books and interviews in which the artists respond to eight of the questions most often asked by children. DF: Table of Contents; Introduction; Photographs of the artists; Samples of the artist's artwork (both as child and adult); Glossary; Books by the Artists; Acknowledgments. BIOGRAPHY; ARTISTS; ART

Davidson, Rosemary. (1994). *Take a Look: An Introduction to the Experience of Art.* Viking. 128 pp. Ages 10 and up.
With activities and experiments, discusses the history, techniques, and functions of art. DF: Acknowledgments; Table of Contents; Black and white

photographs; Graphics; Experiments and activities for readers; Photographs in color of original art; Metaphors; Sidebars; Time line of the history of art; Glossary; Further readings; Illustration Credits; Index. ART

Dewey, Jennifer Owings. (1994). *Wildlife Rescue: The Work of Dr. Kathleen Ramsay.* Photographs by Don MacCarter. Boyds Mills. 64 pp. Ages 7 and up. (1995 HONOR BOOK)
Describes the rehabilitative work to help injured animals return to the wild through photographs and text. DF: Note acknowledgments; Table of Contents; Personal narrative lead. WILDLIFE RESCUE; VETERINARY SCIENCE

Dowden, Anne Ophelia. (1990). *The Clover & the Bee: A Book of Pollination.* HarperCollins. 90 pp. Ages 10 and up.
Describes the process of pollination and the relationship of insects, water, the wind, and animals in this process. DF: Acknowledgments of research; Detailed botanical drawings and labeled diagrams (Dowden is a world-renown botanical illustrator); Table of contents; Index of Plants and Pollinators; Subject Index. POLLINATION; FLOWERS

Ekoomiak, Normee. (1990). *Arctic Memories.* Holt. Unpaged. Ages 8 and up. (1991 HONOR BOOK)
In text written in both English and Inuktitut and drawings by the author, the vanishing lifestyle and customs of the Inuit are described. DF: Text in English and Inuktitut; Map on back cover; Editor's Notes describe the Inuit, their language, and art; Notes on author's life. INUITS

Fisher, Leonard Evertt. (1990). *The Oregon Trail. Holiday House.* 64 pp. Ages 10 and up.
Describes the arduous journey of 19th-century pioneers who traveled the Oregon Trail by wagon train until the advent of the cross-country railroad. DF: Numerous historic photographs; Acknowledgments; Maps; Index. OREGON TRAIL; JOURNEYS

Fleischman, Sid. (1996). *The Abracadabra Kid: A Writer's Life.* Greenwillow. 198 pp. Ages 10 and up.
An informative autobiography describing Sid Fleischman's life including his youth, interest in magic, and life as a writer, with sound advice to writers. DF: Table of Contents; Each chapter opens with quote from a reader; Photographs; Reproductions of pages from his manuscripts and personal memorabilia; Bibliography of his works. AUTOBIOGRAPHY; CHILDREN'S AUTHOR

Fradin, Dennis Brindell. (1996). *"We Have Conquered Pain": The Discovery of Anesthesia.* McElderry/Simon & Schuster. 148 pp. Ages 11 and up.

Story of the discovery of anesthesia in the mid-19th century and the ongoing debate over which of the four doctors should get the credit. DF: Table of Contents; Note from author introducing four doctors; Photographs; Prints; Captions; Bibliography; Photo Credits; Index. MEDICINE

Fraser, Mary Ann. (1995). *In Search of the Grand Canyon: Down the Colorado with John Wesley Powell.* Holt. 70 pp. Ages 9 and up.
Using the journals and reports of Powell and his crew, Fraser traces their exploration of the Grand Canyon River. DF: Original photographs; Labeled diagrams; Sidebars of status reports of boats, men, and supplies; Maps; Bibliography. WESTERN EXPLORATION

Freedman, Russell. (1990). *Franklin Delano Roosevelt.* Clarion. 200 pp. Ages 12 and up. (1991 ORBIS PICTUS AWARD-WINNER)
Photographs and text chronicle the life and times of Franklin D. Roosevelt from his birth in 1882 to his death in 1945. DF: Table of Contents; Photographs; Quote precedes each chapter; Political cartoons; Books about FDR; Acknowledgments; Picture Credits; Index. FRANKLIN D. ROOSEVELT; PRESIDENTS; BIOGRAPHY

Freedman, Russell. (1991). *The Wright Brothers: How They Invented the Airplane.* With Original Photographs by Wilbur and Orville Wright. Holiday House. 129 pp. Ages 10 and up.
Tells the story of Wilbur and Orville Wright's life and their invention of the airplane. DF: Includes 94 photographs by the Wright Brothers with captions; Table of Contents; About the Photographs; Places to Visit; For Further Reading; Index. AVIATION; AIRPLANES

Freedman, Russell. (1992). *An Indian Winter.* Paintings and Drawings by Karl Bodmer. Holiday House. 88 pp. Ages 10 and up.
Freedman chronicles the 1833 journey of German Prince Alexander Philipp Maximilian and artist Karl Bodmer during a winter spent exploring the Missouri River Valley and its inhabitants. DF: Table of Contents; Historic paintings of Karl Bodmer with captions; Map; Afterword; A list of Places to Visit depicting aspects of the journey; List of Illustrations; Bibliography and a note by Freedman indicating his adaptation of the original translation of the journey by H. Evans Lloyd; Acknowledgments; Index. NATIVE AMERICANS; EXPLORATION

Freedman, Russell. (1993). *Eleanor Roosevelt: A Life of Discovery.* Clarion. 198 pp. Ages 12 and up.
Thoughtfully describes Eleanor Roosevelt's life from childhood to her later years as a much respected advocate of others. DF: Table of Contents; Quotes from Eleanor's writings woven into the narrative; Family Photo-

graphs and Album; Quotes to introduce chapters; Captions; Description of Val-Kill Cottage; Books about and by Eleanor Roosevelt; Acknowledgments and Picture Credits; Index. BIOGRAPHY; FIRST LADIES

Freedman, Russell. (1994). *Kids at Work: Lewis Hine and the Crusade Against Child Labor.* Photographs by Lewis Hine. Clarion. 104 pp. Ages 10 and up. (1995 HONOR BOOK)
Decribes the life and pioneering work of Lewis Hine to combat child labor. DF: Original Hine photographs; Bibliography including a film title; Index; Acknowledgments. CHILD LABOR; SOCIAL REFORM

Freedman, Russell. (1996). *The Life and Death of Crazy Horse.* Drawings by Amos Bad Heart Bull. Holiday House. 166 pp. Ages 12 and up. (1997 HONOR BOOK)
An engaging narrative of the life of Crazy Horse from his youth until his death. DF: Narrative style; Chronological organization; Acknowledgments; Historical list of "Main Characters"; Table of Contents; Chapter 1 serves as introduction and identifies interviews done in the 1930s as major primary source; Quotes from interviews; Maps; Captions; Drawings; "About the Drawings" section presents the role of band historians who maintained pictorial records of the tribe's history; Chronology of Crazy Horse's life; Selected Bibliography; Index. BIOGRAPHY; NATIVE AMERICANS

Fritz, Jean. (1989). *The Great Little Madison.* Putnam. 159 pp. Ages 10 and up. (1990 ORBIS PICTUS AWARD-WINNER)
Chronicles the life and times of the fourth president of the United States James Madison. DF: Maps; Prints and engravings; Divided into chapters; Notes for specific pages throughout the book; Bibliography; Index; Illustration credits. BIOGRAPHY; PRESIDENTS

Fritz, Jean. (1991). *Bully for You, Teddy Roosevelt!* Illustrated by Mike Wimmer. Putnam. 127 pp. Ages 10 and up.
Documents the varied life of Theodore Roosevelt, the twenty-sixth president of the United States, who besides having an interest in politics, wrote books, went on an expedition to Brazil, and studied birds. DF: Divided into chapters; Afterword; Notes about individual pages throughout the text; Bibliography; Index. BIOGRAPHY; PRESIDENTS

Gelman, Rita Golden. (1991). *Dawn to Dusk in the Galapagos: Flightless Birds, Swimming Lizards, and Other Fascinating Creatures.* Photographs by Tui De Roy. Little, Brown. Unpaged. Ages 6 and up.
Describes an array of animal life in the unusual and relatively untouched Galapagos Islands. DF: Photographs; Narrative style includes many details. UNUSUAL ANIMALS, EVOLUTION

George, Jean Craighead. (1994). *Animals Who Have Won Our Hearts.*
    HarperCollins. 56 pp. Ages 7 and up.
Ten stories of famous animals who have made great accomplishments. DF:
Preface; Table of Contents; Bibliography of further reading about each ani-
mal. ANIMALS

George, Jean Craighead. (1995). *Everglades.* Paintings by Wendell Minor.
    HarperCollins. Unpaged. Ages 6-10.
A storyteller relates the beginning of the Everglades and the human impact
on this area. DF: Green tinted endpages; Author and illustrator dedications;
Chart of the Symbols of the Vanishing Everglades. WETLANDS; EVER-
GLADES; ECOLOGY

Gibbons, Gail. (1992). *The Great St. Lawrence Seaway.* Morrow. Unpaged.
    Ages 7-10.
Chronicles the early exploration of the St. Lawrence Seaway to modern
times. DF: Map on endpages; Acknowledgments; Illustrations define words
used in text; Labeled illustrations; List of facts and accompanying illustrations about the St. Lawrence Seaway. WATERWAYS; SAINT LAWRENCE SEA-
WAY

Giblin, James Cross. (1990). *The Riddle of the Rosetta Stone.* Harper. 85 pp.
    Ages 9 and up.
Examines the discovery and significance of the Rosetta Stone in deciphering Egyptian hieroglyphics. DF: Acknowledgments; Notes about illustrations; Table of Contents; Reproductions of original engravings;
Photographs of museum antiquities; Afterword; Bibliography with titles
asterisked indicating those appropriate for young readers; Author's note
about his research; Bibliography; Index. EGYPT; LANGUAGE

Giblin, James Cross. (1993). *Be Seated: A Book About Chairs.* HarperCollins.
    136 pp. Ages 10 and up.
Documents the history and significance of the chair in the United States,
Africa, Asia, and Europe. DF: Quote by Henry David Thoreau at the begin-
ning of the book; Acknowledgments; Table of Contents; Photographs;
Bibliography and Source Notes with books written for young people aster-
isked; Sources organized by chapter; Index. SOCIAL HISTORY; FURNITURE

Giblin, James Cross. (1995). *When Plague Strikes: The Black Death,*
    Smallpox, AIDS. Woodcuts by David Frampton. HarperCollins. 212 pp.
    Ages 12 and up.
Vivid description of three of the most killing plagues—black plague, smallpox and AIDS. DF: Woodcuts; Afterword on bacteria and antibodies; Source
notes; Annotated bibliography; Index. DISEASES; PLAGUES; MEDICINE

Greenberg, Jan, & Jordan, Sandra. (1991). *The Painter's Eye. Learning to Look at Contemporary American Art.* Delacorte. 96 pp. Ages 10 and up.
Introduction to the world of art through an exploration of contemporary American works. DF: Table of Contents; Preface; Brief biographies of artists organized according to the art movement with which they were identified; Glossary; List of Paintings; Bibliography; Further Reading; Index. ART APPRECIATION

Hamilton, Virginia. (1993). *Many Thousand Gone: African Americans from Slavery to Freedom.* Illustrated by Leo and Diane Dillon. Knopf. 151 pp. Ages 10 and up.
Chronicles the advent of slavery in the United States, profiles such figures as Harriet Tubman and Frederick Douglass, and depicts the harsh life of slaves and their escape to freedom using the underground railroad. DF: Divided into three parts with individual brief chapters in each; Afterword by Virginia Hamilton; Bibliography and Useful Sources; Index. SLAVERY; UNDERGROUND RAILROAD

Harrison, Barbara, & Terris, Daniel. (1992). *A Twilight Struggle: The Life of John Fitzgerald Kennedy.* Lothrop, Lee & Shepard. 159 pp. Ages 10 and up.
Biography of John F. Kennedy, including his childhood, family, and political career. Based upon research for the television documentary "JFK: In His Own Words." DF: Inaugural Address; Table of Contents; Frost's poem "Birches" and portions of it are used to introduce chapters; Original photographs; Afterword; Sources of Information; Chronology of Events; Source Notes; Index. BIOGRAPHY; PRESIDENT

Hoyt-Goldsmith, Diane. (1990). *Totem Pole.* Photographs by Lawrence Migdale. Holiday House. 32 pp. Ages 8-12.
Told in first-person narrative this is the story of David, a member of the Tsimshian tribe, working with his father, a master artisan, to carve a totem pole. DF: Photographs with detailed captions; Includes "The Legend of the Eagle and the Young Chief: A Tsimshian Tale" within the text; Glossary; Index. TOTEM POLES; NATIVE AMERICANS

Hoyt-Goldsmith, Diane. (1991). *Pueblo Storyteller.* Photographs by Lawrence Migdale. Holiday House. 26 pp. Ages 6-12.
Ten-year-old April, a Cochito Indian, describes the traditions and modern life of her family including bread and drum making, pottery, storytelling, and the ancient Buffalo Dance. DF: Photographs with detailed captions; Pueblo legend; Glossary; Index; Detailed acknowledgments include sources for further information. NATIVE AMERICANS; PUEBLO

Hunt, Jonathan. (1989). *Illuminations.* Bradbury. Unpaged. Ages 7 and up.
Using each letter of the alphabet, Hunt depicts words significant to medieval life. DF: Note From the Author; About the Art notes; Suggested Reading with a note to readers; Selected Bibliography. MEDIEVAL TIMES; ALPHABET BOOK

Jacobs, Francine. (1992). *The Tainos: The People Who Welcomed Columbus.*
   Illustrated by Patrick Collins. Putnam. 107 pp. Ages 12 and up.
Describes the history, culture, and the inhumane exploitation and extinction of the Tainos, the first Native Americans Columbus met in 1492. DF: Map; Table of Contents; Notes; Museum and Exhibits; Bibliography; Index. NATIVE AMERICANS; COLUMBUS, EXPLORATION

Jaffe, Steven H. (1996). *Who Were the Founding Fathers?* Holt. 227 pp.
   Ages 13 and up.
Explores many debates from earliest times to present about the intent of our Founding Fathers in their writing of the Declaration of Independence and the Constitution. DF: Introduction; Table of Contents; Chronological organization; Compares and contrasts political positions; Excerpts from primary sources used to expand debated issues; Photographs and prints of archival primary sources; Captions; Bibliography; Index. AMERICAN REVOLUTION; CONSTITUTION

Johnson, Sylvia A. (1995). *Raptor Rescue! An Eagle Flies Free.* Photographs
   by Ron Winch. Dutton. 32 pp. Ages 7 and up.
Photographs and text describe the care and treatment of an injured bald eagle, as well as providing additional information about other features of the rehabilitation center catering to raptors or birds of prey. DF: Note acknowledgments; Excellent photographs, many with detailed captions; Informational page at the end about what readers can do to help raptors; More About Raptors—list of points. BALD EAGLES; BIRDS OF PREY; WILDLIFE RESCUE

Jurmain, Suzanne. (1989). *Once upon a Horse: A History of Horses and
   How They Shaped History.* Lothrop, Lee & Shepard. 176 pp. Ages 10
   and up.
Combining folklore, literature, and history, Jurmain traces the history of horses and how their involvement with humans has helped to change the world. DF: Table of Contents; Introduction, Photographs; Original photographs, posters, and artwork; Detailed captions; Notes; Principal Sources; Illustration Credits; Index. HORSES; HISTORY; ANIMALS

Keegan, Marcia. (1991). *Pueblo Boy: Growing up in Two Worlds.* Cobblehill. Unpaged. Ages 9-14.
An account of Timmy Roybal, a 10-year-old Pueblo boy's daily life, and the

importance of maintaining traditions. DF: Photographs depicting traditional Pueblo practices. PUEBLOS; NATIVE AMERICANS; SOCIAL LIFE AND
CUSTOMS

Keeler, Patricia A., & McCall, Francis X., Jr. (1995). *Unraveling Fibers.*
Atheneum. 36 pp. Ages 8-12.
Description of the manufacturing of cloth fibers made from plants and ani-
mals and synthetic chemicals. DF: Table of Contents; Acknowledgments;
Photographs and diagrams including enlargements of fibers; Captions;
Index. TEXTILES; CLOTHING

Knight, Amelia Stewart. (1993). *The Way West: Journal of A Pioneer
Woman.* Illustrated by Michael McCurdy. Simon and Schuster.
Unpaged. Ages 8-12.
Excerpts from the journal of the Stewart family as they travel by wagon
from Iowa to the Oregon Territory in 1853. DF: Introduction provides a
brief description of Amelia Stewart Knight's family and the hardships of a
journey west. WESTWARD MOVEMENT; JOURNAL; WAGON TRAINS

Krull, Kathleen. (1994). *Lives of Writers: Comedies, Tragedies (And What
the Neighbors Thought).* Harcourt Brace. 96 pp. Ages 9 and up.
Unique interesting facts are in included in biographical sketches of 19 writ-
ers. DF: Acknowledgments; Table of Contents; Full-page portraits;
Bookmarks (additional information); Literary Terms; Index of Writers;
Further Readings.WRITERS; BIOGRAPHY

Lankford, Mary D. (1992). *Hopscotch around The World.* Illustrated by
Karen Milone. Morrow. 48 pp. Ages 6-10.
Nineteen ways to play hopscotch around the world. DF: Map; Table of
Contents; Introduction about playing hopscotch; For each version author
gives hopscotch name, directions, diagram, and brief information about the
country accompanied by an illustration; Bibliography; Index. GAMES; MUL-
TIETHNIC

Lasky, Kathryn. (1990). *Dinosaur Dig.* Photographs by Christopher G.
Knight. Morrow. Unpaged. Ages 7-12.
Chronicles the author and photographer's family trip to the Badlands to
search for dinosaurs. DF: Narrative style; Divided into chapters.
DINOSAURS

Lasky, Kathryn. (1992). *Surtsey: The Newest Place on Earth.* Photographs
by Christopher G. Knight. Hyperion. 64 pp. Ages 8- and up.
Examines the creation of an island from volcanic activity in 1963, south of
Iceland and how animal and plant life begin. DF: Table of Contents;
Opening quotes for each chapter adapted from the "The Prose Edda," an

Icelandic epic; Index. VOLCANOES; ISLANDS; GEOLOGY

Lauber, Patricia. (1989). *The News about Dinosaurs.* Bradbury. 48 pp. Ages 6 and up. (1990 HONOR BOOK)
Recent discoveries about dinosaurs are discussed by contrasting old information with new findings. DF: Pronunciation guide; Detailed captions; Writing pattern contrasts old information with recent discoveries by using "The News Is" for each new finding; Speculative language; Evidence of discoveries through text and illustrations; Index. DINOSAURS

Lauber, Patricia. (1990). *Seeing Earth from Space.* Orchard Books. 80 pp. Ages 10 and up. (1991 HONOR BOOK)
Explores the way Earth looks from space through photographs and text and the ways Earth is changing due to human behaviors, such as the thinning of the ozone layer. DF: Table of Contents; Glossary; Further Reading (asterisks indicating those books that are appropriate for young readers); Index. EARTH

Lauber, Patricia. (1991). *Summer of Fire: Yellowstone 1988.* Orchard. 64 pp. Ages 8 and up.
Lauber examines the devastation of the 1988 fires in Yellowstone Park and the growth and renewal of the forest after the aftermath of the fire. DF: Table of Contents; Acknowledgments; Photographs with detailed captions; Map; Glossary; Further Reading (asterisks indicate those books that are appropriate for young readers); Index. FIRES; ECOLOGY

Lauber, Patricia. (1994). *Fur, Feather, and Flippers: How Animals Live Where They Do.* Scholastic. 48 pp. Ages 7 and up.
Explores five habitats around the world and the animals inhabiting these places. DF: Table of Contents; Maps; Detailed captions; Index. ANIMALS; HABITATS

Lauber, Patricia. (1996). *Hurricanes: Earth's Mightiest Storms.* Scholastic. 64 pp. Ages 9 and up.
Describes how hurricanes develop, how we study them, and how they impact our lives and environment. DF: Acknowledgments; Chronological organization; Maps; Photographs; Graphics; Detailed captions; Metaphors to explain concepts; Selected information in blue-paneled pages; Further Readings; Picture Credits; Index. METEOROLOGY; HURRICANES

Lawrence, Jacob. (1993). *The Great Migration: An American Story.* HarperCollins, 1993. Unpaged. Ages 8 and up.
The story of the migration of African-Americans from the south to the north in the early 20th century told through text and 60 paintings. DF: "Migration" poem by Walter Dean

Myers at end of book; Information about the author, the poet, and the art. AFRICAN-AMERICANS

Lawrence, R. D. (1990). *Wolves.* Sierra Club/Little, Brown. 64 pp. Ages 7 and up.
Describes the life cycle of wolves from puppy to adulthood. DF: See note about the Sierra Club at the beginning of the book; Table of Contents; First chapter is written as a first-person narrative; Captivating lead; Photographs with captions; Pages colored in blue include additional information, such as wolf tracks, wolf faces, and leaders of the wolf pack; Maps; Index. WOLVES

Levinson, Nancy Smiler. (1990). *Christopher Columbus: Voyager to the Unknown.* Lodestar/Dutton. 118 pp. Ages 8 and up.
Chronicles the life story of Christopher Columbus and his explorations. DF: Table of Contents; Maps; Photographs, reproduction of paintings and engravings; Captions; Author's Note; Chronology of Events; Articles of Capitulation; Letter of Introduction; List of Crew on the First Voyage; Suggested Readings; Index; Sample of one of Columbus' letters. CHRISTO-PHER COLUMBUS; BIOGRAPHY; EXPLORATION

Luenn, Nancy. (1994). *Squish! A Wetland Walk.* Illustrated by Ronald Himler. Atheneum. Unpaged. Ages 5-8.
Explores the many aspects of nature in a wetland, such as a variety of birds, reptiles, and insects. DF: Simple, poetic language brings the wetland alive for young children. WETLANDS; ECOLOGY

Maestro, Betsy, & Maestro, Giulio. (1991). *The Discovery of the Americas.* Lothrop, Lee & Shepard. 48 pp. Ages 8 and up.
Chronicles both actual and speculative voyages to the Americas by the Vikings, Saint Brendan of Ireland, Columbus, and others. DF: Maps; Table of Dates; Some People of the Ancient and Early Americas; Description of important events happening during The Age of Discovery; How the Americas Got Their Name; and Other Interesting Voyages. EXPLORATION; DISCOVERY

Markle, Sandra. (1994). *Science to the Rescue.* Atheneum. 48 pp. Ages 10 and up.
Examines problems and ways science helps solve challenges such as pollution, the need for crops resistant to pests and disease, and ways to surgically improve the lives of amputees. DF: Table of Contents; Organized into eight problems including a "Tackle the Challenge" and "See for Yourself" sections for each problem; Index. SCIENCE PROJECTS

Marrin, Albert. (1994). *Unconditional Surrender: U. S. Grant and the Civil War.* Atheneum. 200 pp. Ages 12 and up.
Describes Grant's life and his reluctant role in the Civil War. DF: Table of Contents; Prologue; Original photographs; Quotes in sidebars to introduce each chapter; Detailed captions; Map; Notes for each chapter; Bibliography; Index. CIVIL WAR; PRESIDENTS

Matthews, Downs. (1989). *Polar Bear Cubs.* Photographs by Dan Guravich. Simon and Schuster. Unpaged. Ages 7-10.
Describes the life of a female polar bear and her two cubs through an Arctic summer from gestation to independence. DF: Enticing lead; Photographs. POLAR BEARS; ANIMALS

McKissack, Patricia C., & McKissack, Fredrick L. (1994). *Christmas In The Big House, Christmas In The Quarters.* Illustrated by John Thompson. Scholastic. 68 pp. Ages 9 and up. (1995 HONOR BOOK)
Descriptions of Christmas traditions prior to the Civil War in a southern plantation house contrasted with those in the slave quarters. DF: Table of Contents; Acknowledgments; Authors' Note at beginning of book; Detailed notes at end; Bibliography. SLAVERY

McMahon, Patricia. (1995). *Listen for the Bus: David's Story.* Photographs by John Godt. Boyds Mills. Unpaged; Ages 5-8.
Photographic essay of the life of a blind kindergarten boy. DF: Good photograph/text match. BLINDNESS; HANDICAPS

McMillan, Bruce. (1995). *Summer Ice: Life Along the Antarctic Peninsula.* Houghton Mifflin. 48 pp. All ages.
Photo-essay describes the life in the Antarctic during the summer months with detailed information on penguins, whales, and seals. DF: Headings; Comparisons; Photographs with inserted enlargements; Detailed captions; Latin names within text; Maps; Glossary; Bibliography; Author Note; Index. ANTARCTIC

Meltzer, Milton. (Ed.). (1989). *Voices from the Civil War: A Documentary History of the Great American Conflict.* Crowell. 203 pp. Ages 10 and up.
Chronicles the Civil War through illustrations, diaries, interviews, speeches, letters, and ballads. DF: Table of Contents; Forward; Introduction; Notes about Further Reading; Index. CIVIL WAR

Meltzer, Milton. (1990). *Columbus and the World around Him.* Franklin Watts. 192 pp. Ages 10 and up.
Drawing from Columbus' journal and other resources, Meltzer describes the culture that influenced Columbus and the devastating impact of his voyage to America on native populations, as well as how life was influ-

enced in the Old World. DF: Table of Contents; Photographs; Reproductions of paintings; Maps; A Note on Sources; Index. CHRISTOPHER COLUMBUS; EXPLORATION

Meltzer, Milton. (1992). *The Amazing Potato: A Story in which the Incas, Conquistadors, Marie Antoinette, Thomas Jefferson, Wars, Famines, Immigrants and French Fries All Play a Part.* HarperCollins. 116 pp. Ages 8 and up.
Chronicles the fascinating history of the potato and its important role in history. DF: Table of Contents; Foreword by Milton Meltzer; Introduction; Boxed information throughout the text; Labeled diagrams; Illustrations; Old photographs; Lithographs; Bibliography; A Note on Sources; Index; About the Author page. FOOD; POTATOES

Meltzer, Milton. (1993). *Lincoln: In His Own Words.* Illustrated by Stephen Alcorn. Harcourt Brace. 226 pp. Ages 12 and up.
Excerpts from Lincoln's speeches and writings with commentary. DF: Table of Contents; Author's Note; Brief Profiles of Lincoln's Contemporaries; Lincoln and the World Around Him: A Chronology; A Note on Sources; Illustrator's Note; Index. ABRAHAM LINCOLN; CIVIL WAR

Meltzer, Milton. (1994). *Cheap Raw Material: How Our Youngest Workers Are Exploited and Abused.* Viking. 167 pp. Ages 12 and up.
A historical exploration of child labor from earliest civilization to today's sweatshops, farms, and the fast food industries. DF: Table of Contents; Plates and photographs; Summary of recent proposed legislation; Questions to consider regarding teenage employment; Bibliography; Source Notes; Index. LABOR; CHILD LABOR; SOCIAL REFORM

Micucci, Charles. (1995). *The Life and Times of the Honeybee.* Tinknor & Fields. 32 pp. All ages.
A witty, but detailed description of the life cycle of bees, the organization of hives, and the production of honey. DF: Labeled diagrams; Table of Contents; Historical notes. INSECTS

Monceaux, Morgan. (1994). *Jazz: My Music, My People.* Knopf. 64 pp. Ages 10 and up.
Biographical sketches of major jazz musicians and singers organized according to three eras of jazz. DF: Introduction; Foreword by Wynton Marsalis; Table of Contents; Glossary; Index. MUSIC

Morimoto, Junko. (1990). *My Hiroshima.* Viking. Unpaged. Ages 10 and up.
The story of the bombing of Hiroshima told through the author's childhood memories. DF: Endpages contain photographs and a letter from the author to parents and teachers; The Facts About Hiroshima. WORLD WAR II

Moser, Barry. (1993). *Fly: A Brief History of Flight Illustrated.* HarperCollins. Unpaged. Ages 8 and up.
Depicts the history of aviation through 16 scenarios from the hot-air balloon to space shuttles. DF: Introduction by Barry Moser; Sixteen one-page episodes about flight with an accompanying watercolor illustration by Moser; Time line of important events at bottom of each page; Detailed Historical Notes. HISTORY OF FLIGHT

Murphy, Jim. (1992). *The Long Road to Gettysburg.* Clarion. 116 pp. Ages 12 and up.
Building on the first-hand accounts from the diaries of two young soldiers, Murphy presents the Battle of Gettysburg from the perspective of both the Union and Confederate armies. DF: Acknowledgments; Table of Contents; Introduction; Original photographs; Maps of the battles; Line drawings; Engravings; Conclusion; Second draft of Gettysburg Address in Lincoln's handwriting; Bibliography; Index. CIVIL WAR

Murphy, Jim. (1993). *Across America on an Emigrant Train.* Clarion. 150 pp. Ages 10 and up. (1994 ORBIS PICTUS AWARD-WINNER)
Combines Robert Louis Stevenson's trip from Scotland to the West Coast and the history of the American railroad. DF: Acknowledgments; Maps; Table of Contents; Introduction; Original photographs and drawings; Detailed captions; Quotes from Stevenson's writings about the trip; A Final Word; Bibliography; Index. BIOGRAPHY; WRITER

Murphy, Jim. (1995). *The Great Fire.* Scholastic. 144 pp. Ages 9 and up. (1996 ORBIS PICTUS AWARD-WINNER)
Weaving personal accounts with the historical events, Murphy reconstructs the Chicago Fire of 1871 and the aftermath. DF: Acknowledgments; Table of Contents; Introduction; Original photographs; Reprints from magazines; Street maps; Headlines from newspapers; Bibliography and Sources; Index. CHICAGO FIRE; AMERICAN HISTORY

Myers, Walter Dean. (1991). *Now is Your Time! The African-American Struggle for Freedom.* HarperCollins. 292 pp. Ages 12 and up. (1992 HONOR BOOK)
Beginning with the capture of Africans in the early 1600s, Myers traces 400 years of history of the African-Americans' struggle for freedom and equality. DF: Acknowledgments; Table of Contents; Introduction; Historical maps; Original photographs; Reprints of slavery-related documents; Reprints of plantation records; Posters; Letters; Afterword; Author's Note; Select Bibliography; Index. SLAVERY; AFRICAN-AMERICAN HISTORY

Osborne, Mary Pope. (1990). *The Many Lives of Benjamin Franklin.* Dial.
  127 pp. Ages 9 and up.
Biography of Benjamin Franklin from his younger years in Boston to his
death in Philadelphia in 1790. Describes his role in American history and
his many achievements: writer, printer, inventor, and politician among
many others. DF: Chronological organization; Last chapter contains list of
accomplishments; Time line; Bibliography; Reproductions of black and
white illustrations from newspapers and other sources; Index. AMERICAN
HISTORY; BIOGRAPHY; REVOLUTIONARY WAR

Osborne, Mary Pope. (1996). *One World, Many Religions.* Knopf. 86 pp.
  Ages 9 and up. (1997 HONOR BOOK)
Illustrated comparison and coherent discussion of seven major religions:
Christianity, Judaism, Confucianism, Taoism, Islam, Hinduism, and
Buddhism. DF: Acknowledgments; Comparative time line of major events
associated with each religion; Photographs; Demographic map; Glossary;
Bibliography; Index. RELIGIONS

Osofsky, Audrey. (1996). *Free to Dream: The Making of a Poet: Langston
  Hughes.* Lothrop, Lee & Shepard. 112 pp. Ages 10 and up.
Chronicles his growth as a poet, writer, lecturer, and traveler with a focus
on his early years. DF: Album quality; Table of Contents with sections called
Variations; Excerpts from Hughes' writings; Photographs; Ends with poem
set to music; Notes for each Variation; Bibliography categorized by types;
Suggested Readings; Index. BIOGRAPHY; AUTHOR

Pandell, Karen. (1995). *Learning from the Dalai Lama: Secrets of the Wheel
  of Time.* With Barry Byrant. Photographs by John B. Taylor. Concept
  by Manuel C. Menendez. Dutton. 40 pp. Ages 10 and up.
Photo-essay highlights the intricate details of the creation of the
Kalachakra, the Wheel of Time mandala, during the International Year of
Tibet celebration with the Dalai Lama at Madison Square Garden in 1991.
DF: Table of Contents; Acknowledgments; Foreword by Richard Gere;
Photographs; Captions; Instructions on creating a mandala; Glossary;
Index. RELIGIONS

Patent, Dorothy Hinshaw. (1989). *Wild Turkey, Tame Turkey.* Photographs
  by William Muñoz. Clarion. 57 pp. Ages 8 and up.
A photographic essay of the wild turkey, a native of North America, and
how it compares to the domesticated turkey. DF: Acknowledgments and
Dedication; Table of Contents; Photographs with captions; Index. WILD
TURKEYS

Paulsen, Gary. (1990). *Wood-Song.* Bradbury. 132 pp. Ages 10 and up.

Autobiographical sketches from the popular writer Gary Paulsen, which-captures his love for nature and his first dogsled race across Alaska. DF: Map of the Iditarod; Powerful lead. AUTHOR BIOGRAPHY; OUTDOOR LIFE

Peet, Bill. (1989). *Bill Peet: An Autobiography.* Houghton Mifflin. 190 pp. All ages.
Bill Peet tells his own story of his life and his work through illustrations and text. DF: List of books by Bill Peet; Illustrations including original artwork. AUTOBIOGRAPHY; CHILDREN'S AUTHOR AND ILLUSTRATOR

Pinkney, Andrea Davis. (1993). *Seven Candles for Kwanzaa.* Illustrated by Brian Pinkney. Dial. Unpaged. Ages 5 and up.
Describes the 7-day celebration of Kwanzaa, as well as the origins and traditional practices of this African-American festival. DF: Note to Readers at the beginning of the book; Pronunciation of words given within the context of the text; Bibliography. CELEBRATIONS; KWANZAA; AFRICAN-AMERICANS

Pringle, Laurence. (1991). *Batman: Exploring the World of Bats.* Photographs by Merlin Tuttle. Charles Scribner's Sons. 42 pp. Ages 10 and up.
Describes the work and contributions of the scientist and bat expert Merlin Tuttle; in his efforts to increase appreciation of bats through Bat Conservation International. DF: Table of Contents; Photographs; Detailed captions; Further Readings; Index. BATS; ECOLOGY

Pringle, Laurence. (1992). *Antarctica: The Last Unspoiled Continent.* Simon & Schuster. 56 pp. Ages 10 and up.
Describes Antarctica, 10 percent of the earth's surface and the fifth largest continent, as a land of contrasts. DF: Table of Contents; Photographs; Maps; Glossary; Index. ANTARCTICA

Pringle, Laurence. (1995). *Dolphin Man: Exploring the World of Dolphins.* Photographs by Randall S. Wells and Dolphin Biology Research Institute. Atheneum. 42 pp. Ages 9 and up. (1996 HONOR BOOK)
Account of Randall Wells' (photographer of this book) early interest in dolphins leading to a career studying this mammal. DF: Table of Contents; Captions; Further Reading list; Index. DOLPHINS; SEA MAMMALS

Pringle, Laurence. (1995). *Fire in the Forest: A Cycle of Growth and Renewal.* Paintings by Bob Marstall. Atheneum. 32 pp. Ages 8-13.
This photo-essay describes and shows how a forest fire is part of the natural cycle of forest growth using paintings of a forested landscape before, during, and after a forest fire. DF: Acknowledgments; Detailed captions include approximate sizes of animals and plants; Full-spread paintings; Headings; Further Reading and Sources. FOREST FIRES

Reef, Catherine. (1996). *John Steinbeck.* Clarion. 163 pp. Ages 10 and up. Introduction to life, writing career, and significant works of John Steinbeck with a detailed description of the writing of *Grapes of Wrath.* DF: Acknowledgments; Table of Contents; Photographs; Bibliography; List of works by Steinbeck; Index. BIOGRAPHY; AUTHOR

Robbins, Ken. (1995). *Air.* Holt. Unpaged. All ages. Photo-essay of the role and importance of air in the environment and our lives, devoting a full-page spread to each subtopic such as sky, oxygen, etc. DF: Title is third book in *The Elements* series (Robbins also wrote *Earth, Water,* and *Fire*); Hand-tinted photographs; Poetic text; Acknowledgments. AIR; PHYSICAL SCIENCES

Rylant, Cynthia. (1991). *Appalachia: The Voices of Sleeping Birds.* Illustrated by Barry Moser. Harcourt Brace Jovanovich. 24 pp. Ages 7 and up.
Chronicles life in Appalachia. DF: Narrative style describes social customs; Transparent watercolor illustrations. APPALACHIA; SOCIAL LIFE AND CUS-TOMS

St. George, Judith. (1989). *Panama Canal: Gateway to the World.* Putnam. 159 pp. Ages 10 and up.
A history of the Panama Canal from Columbus through the U.S.-Panama treaties of 1977. DF: Cross Section of the Panama Canal; Acknowledgments; Historic photographs and illustrations with captions; Maps; Labeled diagrams; Quotations from letters, records, newspapers, and official government documentation; Bibliography; Statistics—Panama Canal—1914; Index. PANAMA CANAL

San Souci, Robert. (1991). *N. C. Wyeth's Pilgrims.* Chronicle Books. Unpaged. Ages 7-10.
Chronicles the settling of Plymouth Colony and dispels some common myths about the story of the Pilgrims. DF: Endpages are copies of the list of those who sailed on the Mayflower; Author's Note describes sources consulted; Information about the artist, N. C. Wyeth, and the history of the paintings. PILGRIMS; PLYMOUTH COLONY

Sattler, Helen Roney. (1989). *Giraffes, the Sentinels of the Savannas.* Illustrated by Christopher Santoro. Lothrop, Lee & Shepard. 80 pp. Ages 8 and up.
Describes the giraffe from its evolution to modern times. Includes information on its habitat, habits, physical characteristics, and relationship with humans. DF: Acknowledgments; Table of Contents; A Glossary of Giraffes with illustrations; A Geological Timetable for Giraffes; Classification of

Giraffes; For Further Reading; Index. GIRAFFES

Sattler, Helen Roney. (1995). *The Book of North American Owls.* Illustrated by Jean Day Zallinger. Clarion. 64 pp. Ages 9 and up.
Detailed description of the life and behaviors of owls of North America ending with a handbook section devoting one page to each species. DF: Table of Contents; Definitions and technical terms woven into text; Personal accounts; Metaphors; Detailed drawings of owls and body parts depicting comparative sizes; Detailed captions; Glossary of Owls with range maps and detailed descriptions of each species; List of North American Owls by family, genus, and species; Bibliography; Index. ANIMALS; BIRDS; OWLS

Sills. Leslie. (1989). *Inspirations: Stories about Women Artists.* Albert Whitman. 56 pp. Ages 8 and up.
Through text and color reproductions, Sills describes the work and art of four women artists: Georgia O'Keeffe, Frida Kahlo, Alice Neel, and Faith Ringgold. DF: Table of Contents; Photographs; Art reproductions; Picture Credits; Bibliography of each artist. BIOGRAPHY; WOMEN ARTISTS

Simon, Seymour. (1989). *Whales.* Crowell. Unpaged. Ages 5 and up.
Describes the characteristics, habits, and habitat of a variety of species of whales. DF: Photographs; Metaphors used to explain concepts. WHALES

Simon, Seymour. (1990). *Oceans.* Morrow. Unpaged. Ages 8 and up.
Explores aspects of oceans such as tides, waves, sealife, and how the oceans influence our weather patterns. DF: Map on the endpages; Diagrams; Maps; Color. OCEANS

Simon, Seymour. (1991). *Earthquakes.* Morrow Junior. Unpaged. Ages 7 and up.
Examines why and how earthquakes occur, as well as the damage they cause. DF: Excellent photos; New terms defined in context. EARTHQUAKES

Sís, Peter. (1996). *Starry Messenger: A Book Depicting the Life of a Famous Scientist, Mathematician, Astronomer, Philosopher, Physicist.* Farrar, Straus Giroux. Unpaged. All Ages.
Life and times of Galileo with primary focus on him as an original thinker. DF: Illustrations; Numerous quotes from Galileo in cursive off to side of illustrations. BIOGRAPHY; SCIENTIST

Stanley, Diane. (1996). *Leonardo da Vinci.* Morrow. Unpaged. Ages 11 and up. (1997 ORBIS PICTUS AWARD-WINNER)
This biography of Italian Renaissance artist and inventor Leonardo da Vinci describes his life, art, exploration into the unknown, inventions, and com-

mentary on life. DF: Acknowledgments; Reproductions of da Vinci's art and drawings from his notebooks; Illustrations; Introduction describes Period; Quotes of da Vinci woven into narrative; Pronunciation Key; Recommended Readings; Bibliography. BIOGRAPHY; RENAISSANCE PERIOD; ARTIST

Stanley, Diane, & Vennema, Peter. (1990). *Good Queen Bess: The Story of Elizabeth I of England.* Illustrated by Diane Stanley. Four Winds. Unpaged. Ages 10 and up.
Tells the story of the much-admired Queen Elizabeth I of England. DF: Acknowledgments; Authors' Note at the beginning of the book; Bibliography. BIOGRAPHY; GREAT BRITAIN; QUEENS

Stanley, Diane, & Vennema, Peter. (1992). *Bard of Avon: The Story of William Shakespeare.* Illustrated by Diane Stanley. Morrow. Unpaged. Ages 10 and up.
Tells the story of the world's most famous playwright, William Shakespeare. DF: Authors' note at beginning of book; Postscript; Bibliography with asterisked texts indicated for children. BIOGRAPHY; SHAKESPEARE

Stanley, Diane, & Vennema, Peter. (1994). *Cleopatra.* Illustrated by Diane Stanley. Morrow. Unpaged. Ages 10 and up.
Tells the story of the famed Queen of Egypt, Cleopatra. DF: Note authors' acknowledgments; Preface; Note on Ancient Sources at beginning of book; Maps; Mosaic-framed pages; Epilogue; Pronunciation Guide; Bibliography. BIOGRAPHY; EGYPT; QUEENS

Stanley, Jerry. (1992). *Children of the Dustbowl: The True Story of the School at Weedpatch Camp.* Crown. 85 pp. Ages 9 and up. (1993 ORBIS PICTUS AWARD-WINNER)
Describes the hardships of the migrant workers who left Oklahoma and the Dust Bowl to work in California only to be restricted to federal labor camps where, with the help of Superintendent Leo Hart, the adults and children built their own school. DF: Table of Contents; Author's Note; Introduction; Original photographs; Maps; Quotes from interviews; Afterword; Bibliographic Note and Picture Credits; Acknowledgment; Index. MIGRANT WORKERS; CHEAP LABOR; SOCIAL REFORM

Stanley, Jerry. (1994). *I Am an American: A True Story of Japanese Internment.* Crown. 102 pp. Ages 10 and up.
Using interviews and original photographs, the author describes the Japanese internment at Manzanar. DF: Family photographs; Table of Contents; Introduction. WORLD WAR II; JAPANESE; INTERNMENT

Swanson, Diane. (1994). *Safari Beneath the Sea: The Wonder World of the North Pacific Coast.* Photographs by the Royal British Columbia Museum. Sierra Club. 58 pp. Ages 8 -12. (1995 ORBIS PICTUS AWARD-WINNER)
Describes a myriad of marine life beneath and above the waters of the North Pacific. DF: Note information about the Sierra Club at the beginning of the book; Table of Contents; Photographs with captions; Major headings in bold print within each chapter; Additional information in boxes on pages; Bulleted information; Index. MARINE LIFE

Switzer, Ellen. (1995). *The Magic of Mozart: Mozart, The Magic Flute, and the Salzburg Marionettes.* Photographs by Costas. Atheneum. 90 pp. Ages 8 and up.
Told in three sections, Switzer briefly tells the life and struggles of Mozart, presents in colored photographs the "The Magic Flute" as performed by the Salzburg Marionettes, and provides a brief history and background information about the Salzburg Marionette Theater. DF: Acknowledgments; Table of Contents; Introduction; Opera of "The Magic Flute" with photographs of the marionettes; Bibliography. BIOGRAPHY; MUSIC; COMPOSER; PUPPETS

Toll, Nelly S. (1993). *Behind the Secret Window: A Memoir of a Hidden Childhood during World War II.* Dial. 161 pp. Ages 12 and up.
In this autobiography, using artwork from her childhood, Toll recounts her 13-month experience of hiding from the Nazis in a small cubicle behind a false window. DF: Acknowledgments; Preface; Historical Note; Original artwork; Epilogue. AUTOBIOGRAPHY; WORLD WAR II

Verhoeven, Rian, & van der Rol, Ruud. (1993). *Anne Frank: Beyond the Diary.* Viking. 113 pp. Ages 10 and up.
Photographic biography of Anne Frank including diary excerpts, maps, and interviews. DF: Acknowledgments; Table of Contents; Introduction; Photos from the Anne Frank House archives in Amsterdam and from other collections; Excerpts from original diaries; Detailed maps; Information about the Anne Frank House; Chronology of the Frank Family and the Families of the Secret Annex; Notes on the Different Versions of the Diary of Anne Frank; Sources of Quotations and Photographs; Index of People and Places. BIOGRAPHY; JEWISH HOLOCAUST; WORLD WAR II

Waldman, Neil. (1995). *The Golden City: Jerusalem's 3,000 Years.* Atheneum. Unpaged. Ages 10 and up.
Briefly traces the history of the city of Jerusalem from the times of King David's empire to 1967 and the 6-Day War. DF: Pastel illustrations; Introduction; Chronological summary of Jerusalem's history. MIDDLE EAST; RELIGION; CITIES

Wright-Frierson, Virginia. (1996). *A Desert Scrapbook: Dawn to Dusk in the Sonoran Desert.* Simon & Schuster. Unpaged. Ages 7 and up.
Descriptions and sketches of the animals, plants, and surrounding Sonoran Desert presented as a 1-day trip. DF: Acknowledgments; Address of the Arizonian-Sonoran Desert Museum; Excerpted diary pages; Photographs of original sketches with handwritten captions; Scientific drawings; Valuable as a writing model for children condensing many experiences into 1 day. DESERT; NATURE

Zhensun, Zheng, & Low, Alice. (1991). *A Young Painter: The Life and Paintings Of Wang Yani—China's Extraordinary Young Artist.* Photographs by Zheng Zhensun. Scholastic. 80 pp. Ages 8 and up.
Describes the life and work of the young Chinese artist Wang Yani who started painting at the age of 3 and exhibited at the Smithsonian as a teenager. DF: Introduction by Jan Stuart; Preface; Maps; Photographs; Original artwork; Detailed captions; Foldout pages; Quotes from the artist; Description of Traditional Chinese Painting; Glossary; Index. BIOGRAPHY; ARTIST; ART

Bibliography of Children's Books Cited

Adler, David. (1989). *We remember the Holocaust.* Henry Holt.

Adler, David. (1992). *A picture book of Harriet Tubman.* Illustrated by Samuel Byrd. Holiday House.

Aikman, Troy, & Brown, Greg. (1995). *Things change.* Illustrated by Doug Keith. Taylor Publishing.

Albert, Burton. (1991). *Where does the trail lead?* Illustrated by Brian Pinkney. Simon & Schuster.

Alexander, Sally Hobart. (1990). *Mom can't see me.* Photographs by George Ancona. Simon & Schuster.

Aliki. (1988). *Dinosaur bones.* Crowell.

Aliki. (1989). *The king's day: Louie XIV of France.* Crowell.

Aliki. (1993). *My visit to the aquarium.* HarperCollins.

Allison, Linda. (1976). *Blood and guts.* Little, Brown.

Ancona, George. (1989). *The American farm family.* Text by Joan Anderson. Harcourt Brace Jovanovich.

Ancona, George. (1994). *The piñata maker/El piñatero.* Harcourt Brace.

Andersen, Honey. (1996). *Breathing.* Illustrated by Jane Tanner. Greenvale, NY: Mondo Publishing.

Andersen, Honey. (1996). *Floating and sinking.* Illustrated by Meredith Thomas. Greenvale, NY: Mondo Publishing.

Anderson, Joan. (1993). *Twins on toes: A ballet debut.* Photographs by George Ancona. Lodestar.

Anno, Masaichiro, & Anno, Mitsumasa. (1983). *Anno's mysterious multiplying jar.* Illustrated by Mitsumasa Anno. Philomel.

Anno, Mitsumasa. (1980). *Anno's medieval world.* Philomel.

Anno, Mitsumasa. (1982). *Anno's counting house.* Crowell.

Anno, Mitsumasa. (1987). *Anno's math games.* Philomel.

Anno, Mitsumasa. (1989). *Anno's faces.* Philomel.

Anno, Mitsumasa. (1989). *Anno's math games II.* Philomel.

Anno, Mitsumasa. (1991). *Anno's math games III.* Philomel.

Apfel, Necia. (1991). *Voyager to the planets.* Clarion.

Archer, Jules. (1991). *Breaking barriers: The feminist revolution.* Puffin.

Ardley, Neil. (1995). *A young person's guide to music.* Music by Poul Ruders. Dorling Kindersley.

Arenas, J. F. (1990). *The key to renaissance art.* Minneapolis, MN: Lerner.

Arnold, Caroline. (1994). *Killer whale.* Photographs by Richard Hewett. Morrow.

Arnosky, Jim. (1990). *A kettle of hawks and other wildlife groups.* Lothrop, Lee & Shepard.

Arnosky, Jim. (1995). *I see animals hiding.* Scholastic.

Arnosky, Jim. (1996). *Crinkleroot's guide to knowing butterflies & moths.* Simon & Schuster.

Arnosky, Jim. (1996). *Nearer nature.* Lothrop, Lee & Shepard.

Asch, Frank. (1997). *One man show.* Photographs by Jan Asch. Richard C. Owen.

Ash, Russell. (1996). *The top 10 of everything of 1996.* Dorling Kindersley.

Ashabranner, Brent. (1996). *A strange and distant shore: Indians of the Great Plains in exile.* Cobblehill.

Asimov, Isaac. (1992). *Why are the rain forests vanishing?* Milwaukee, WI: Gareth Stevens.

Axelrod, Alan. (1991). *Songs of the wild west.* Simon & Schuster.

Baker, Lucy. (1990). *Life in the rain forest.* Scholastic.

Barrow, Lloyd. (1991). *Adventures with rocks and minerals: Geology experiments for young people.* Springfield, NJ: Enslow.

Barrow, Lloyd. (1995). *Adventures with rocks and minerals: Book II geology experiments for young people.* Springfield, NJ: Enslow.

Bartoletti, Susan Campbell. (1996). *Growing up in coal country.* Houghton Mifflin.

Barton, Byron. (1995). *Big machines.* Greenwillow.

Bash, Barbara. (1993). *Shadows of night: The hidden world of the little brown bat.* Sierra Club.

Bash, Barbara. (1994). *Ancient ones: The world of the old-growth Douglas fir.* Sierra Club.

Beattie, Owen, & Geiger, John. (1992). *Buried in ice: The mystery of a lost Arctic expedition.* (With Shelley Tanaka). Scholastic.

Berger, Melvin. (1994). *Oil spill!* Illustrated by Paul Mirocha. HarperCollins.

Bernhard, Emery. (1994). *Eagles: Lions of the sky.* Illustrated by Durga Bernhard. Holiday House.

Bial, Raymond. (1995). *The underground railroad.* Houghton Mifflin.

Bial, Raymond. (1996). *With needle and thread: A book about quilts.*

Houghton Mifflin.

Birch, David. (1988). *The king's chessboard.* Illustrated by Davis Grebu. Penguin.

Bird, Bettina, & Short, Joan. (1996). *Some machines are enormous.* Illustrated by Amanda Barrett. Greenvale, NY: Mondo Publishing.

Björk, Christina. (1985). *Linnea in Monet's garden.* Illustrated by Lena Anderson. New York: R & S Books.

Björk, Christina, & Anderson, Lena. (1988). *Linnea's windowsill garden.* New York: R & S Books.

Blocksma, Mary. (1993). *Ticket to the twenties: A time traveler's guide.* Illustrated by Susan Dennen. Little, Brown.

Blos, Joan. W. (1996). *Nellie Bly's monkey: His remarkable story in his own words.* Illustrated by Catherine Stock. Morrow.

Blum, Raymond. (1991). *Mathemagic.* New York: Sterling.

Blumberg, Rhoda. (1989). *The great American gold rush.* Bradbury.

Blumberg, Rhoda. (1991). *The remarkable voyages of Captain Cook.* Bradbury.

Blumberg, Rhoda. (1996). *Full steam ahead: The race to build a Transcontinental Railroad.* National Geographic Society.

Blumenthal, Howard. (1993). *Careers in baseball.* Little, Brown.

Bolton, Faye. (1995). *Melting.* Illustrated by Meredith Thomas. Greenvale, NY: Mondo Publishing.

Bolotin, Norman, & Herb, Angela. (1995). *For home and country: A Civil War scrapbook.* Lodestar.

Bonafoux, Pascal. (1992). *A weekend with Rembrandt.* New York: Rizzoli.

Bowen, Betsy. (1995). *Gathering: A northwoods counting book.* Little, Brown.

Bowen, Gary. (1994). *Stranded at Plimoth Plantation 1626.* Introduction by David Freeman. HarperCollins.

Brandenburg, Jim. (1993). *To the top of the world: Adventures with arctic wolves.* Walker.

Brandenburg, Jim. (1994). *Sand and fog: Adventures in southern Africa.* Walker.

Brandenburg, Jim. (1995). *An American safari: Adventures on the North American Prairie.* Edited by JoAnn Bren Guernsey. Walker.

Brandenburg, Jim. (1996). *Scruffy: A wolf finds his place in the pack.* Edited by JoAnn Bren Guernsey. Walker.

Branley, Franklyn M. (1993). *Keeping time.* Illustrated by Iris Van Rynbach. Houghton Mifflin.

Branley, Franklyn M. (1994). *Venus: Magellan explores our twin planet.* HarperCollins.

Brenner, Barbara. (1997). *Thinking about ants.* Illustrated by Carol Schwartz. Greenvale, NY: Mondo Publishing.

Brooks, Bruce. (1993). *Making sense: Animal perception and communication.* Farrar Straus Giroux.

Brown, Mary Barrett. (1992). *Wings along the waterway.* Orchard.

Brust, Beth Wagner. (1994). *The amazing paper cuttings of Hans Christian Andersen.* Ticknor & Fields.

Burleigh, Robert. (1991). *Flight: The journey of Charles Lindbergh.* Illustrated by Mike Wimmer. Philomel.

Burnie, David. (1988). *Bird.* Dorling Kindersley/Knopf.

Burns, Diane L. (1993). *Rocky mountain seasons: From valley to mountain top.* Photographs by Kent & Donna Dannen. Macmillan.

Burns, Marilyn. (1982). *Math for smarty pants.* Illustrated by Martha Weston. Little, Brown.

Busch, Phyllis. (1995). *Backyard safaris: 52 year-round science adventures.* Illustrated by Wayne J. Trimm. Simon & Schuster.

Busenberg, Bonnie. (1994). *Vanilla, chocolate, & strawberry: The story of your favorite flavors.* Minneapolis, MN: Lerner.

Calabro, Marian. (1989). *Operation grizzly bear.* Four Winds Press.

Calmenson, Stephanie. (1994). *Rosie, a visiting dog's story.* Photographs by Justin Sutcliffe. Clarion.

Carlson, Nancy. (1988). *I like me!* Puffin.

Carlstrom, Nancy W. (1993). *How does the wind walk?* Macmillan.

Carlstrom, Nancy W. (1994). *What would you do if you lived at the zoo?* Illustrated by Lizi Boyd. Little, Brown.

Carrick, Carol. (1993). *Whaling days.* Woodcuts by David Frampton. Clarion.

Cassie, Brian, & Pallotta, Jerry. (1995). *The butterfly alphabet book.* Illustrated by Mark Astrella. Watertown, MA: Charlesbridge.

Cerullo, Mary M. (1994). *Lobsters: Gangsters of the sea.* Photographs by Jeffrey L. Rotman. Cobblehill.

Cha, Dia. (1996). *Dia's story cloth: The Hmong people's journey to freedom.* Stitched by Chue and Nhia Thao Cha. Lee & Low/Denver Museum of Natural History.

Chermayeff, Ivan. (1995). *Scaley facts.* Harcourt Brace.

Cherry, Lynne. (1990). *The great kapok tree: A tale of the Amazon rain forest.* Harcourt.

Cherry, Lynne. (1992). *A river ran wild.* Harcourt Brace Jovanovich.

Chinery, Michael. (1992). *Rainforest animals.* Random House.

Clarke, Barry. (1990). *Amazing frogs and toads.* Knopf.

Clement, Rod. (1991). *Counting on Frank.* Milwaukee: Gareth Stevens.

Cobb, Vicki. (1990). *Natural wonders.* Lothrop.

Cole, Alison. (1992). *Perspective.* Dorling Kindersley.

Cole, Alison. (1993). *Color.* Dorling Kindersley.

Cole, Joanna. (1985a). *Large as life: Daytime animals, life size.* Illustrated by Kenneth Lilly. Knopf.

Cole, Joanna. (1985b). *Large as life: Nighttime animals, life size.* Illustrated by Kenneth Lilly. Knopf.

Cole, Joanna. (1986). *The magic school bus at the waterworks.* Illustrated by Bruce Degen. Scholastic.

Cole, Joanna. (1987). *The magic school bus inside the earth.* Illustrated by Bruce Degen. Scholastic.

Cole, Joanna. (1989). *The magic school bus inside the human body.* Illustrated by Bruce Degen. Scholastic.

Cole, Joanna. (1990). *Large as life animals series: In beautiful life-size paintings.* Illustrated by Kenneth Lilly. Knopf.

Cole, Joanna. (1990). *The magic school bus lost in the solar system.* Illustrated by Bruce Degen. Scholastic.

Cole, Joanna. (1992). *The magic school bus on the ocean floor.* Illustrated by Bruce Degen. Scholastic.

Cole, Joanna. (1994). *The magic school bus in the time of the dinosaurs.* Illustrated by Bruce Degen. Scholastic.

Cole, Joanna. (1995). *The magic school bus inside a hurricane.* Illustrated by Bruce Degen. Scholastic.

Cole, Joanna. (1995). *My new kitten.* Photographs by Margaret Miller. Morrow.

Cole, Joanna. (1996). *The magic school bus inside a beehive.* Illustrated by Bruce Degen. Scholastic.

Cole, Joanna. (1996). *On the bus with Joanna Cole: A creative autobiography* (with Wendy Saul). Portsmouth, NH: Heinemann.

Coles, Robert. (1995). *The story of Ruby Bridges.* Illustrated by George Ford. Scholastic.

Collins, Michael. (1995). *Dinosaurs.* Illustrated by Margaret Dannatt. Greenvale, NY: Mondo Publishing.

Colman, Penny. (1995). *Rosie the riveter: Women working on the home front in World War II.* Crown.

Cone, Molly. (1992). *Come back, salmon: How a group of dedicated kids adopted Pigeon Creek and brought it back to life.* Photographs by Sidnee Wheelwright. Sierra Club.

Cone, Molly. (1996). *Squishy, misty, damp & muddy: The in-between world of wetlands.* Sierra Club.

Conrad, Pam. (1991). *Prairie visions: The life and times of Solomon Butcher.* HarperCollins.

Cooper, Floyd. (1996). *Mandela: From the life of the South African Statesman.* Philomel.

Corrain, Lucia. (1995). *Giotto and medieval painting: The lives and works of medieval artists.* New York: Peter Bedrick.

Cowly, Joy. (1987). *Little car.* Illustrated by Martin Bailey. Bothell, WA: The Wright Group.

Craighead, Charles. (1994). *The eagle and the river.* Photographs by Tom Mangelsen. Macmillan.

Creasy, Rosalind. (1994). *Blue potatoes, orange tomatoes.* Illustrated by Ruth Heller. Sierra Club.

Cummings, Pat. (Ed.). (1992). *Talking with artists.* Bradbury.

Cummings, Pat. (Ed.). (1995). *Talking with artists, volume two.* Simon & Schuster.

Cutting, Brian, & Cutting, Jillian. (1988). *Underwater journey.* Illustrated by Jeff Fowler. Bothell, WA: The Wright Group.

Darling, Kathy. (1996). *Amazon ABC.* Photographs by Tara Darling. Lothrop.

Darling, Tara, & Darling, Kathy. (1996). *How to babysit an orangutan.* Walker.

Davidson, Rosemary. (1994). *Take a look: An introduction to the experience of art.* Viking.

Davies, Kay, & Oldfield, Wendy. (1990). *My Balloon.* Photographs by Fiona Pragoff. Doubleday.

Demi. (1997). *One grain of rice: A mathematical folktale.* Scholastic.

dePaola, Tomie. (1977). *The quicksand book.* Holiday House.

dePaola, Tomie. (1978). *The popcorn book.* Holiday House.

Dethier, Vincent. (1981). *Newberry: The life and times of a Maine clam.* Illustrated by Marie Litterer. Camden, ME: Down East Books.

Dewey, Jennifer Owings. (1993). *Spiders near and far.* Dutton.

Dewey, Jennifer Owings. (1994). *Wildlife rescue: The work of Dr. Kathleen Ramsay.* Photographs by Don MacCarter. Boyds Mills Press.

Dietz, James M. (1994). *African animal giants.* Illustrated by Robert Cremins. National Geographic Society.

Dijs, Carla. (1993). *What do I do at eight o'clock?* Simon & Schuster.

Dixon, Dougall. (1993). *Dougall Dixon's dinosaurs.* Boyds Mills Press.

Dodson, Peter. (1995). *An alphabet of dinosaurs.* Paintings by Wayne D. Barlowe and Drawings by Michael Meaker. Bryon Preiss Visual Publications/Scholastic.

Dooley, Norah. (1991). *Everybody cooks rice.* Illustrated by Peter J. Thornton. Minneapolis, MN: Carolrhoda.

Dorris, Michael. (1992). *Morning girl.* Hyperion.

Dorros, Arthur. (1990). *Rain forest secrets.* Scholastic.

Dorros, Arthur. (1994). *Elephant families.* HarperCollins.

Dorros, Arthur. (1997). *A tree is growing.* Illustrated by S. D. Schindler. Scholastic.

Doubilet, Anne. (1991). *Under the sea from A to Z.* Crown.

Dowden, Anne Ophelia. (1990). *The clover and the bee: A book of pollination.* HarperCollins.

Dowden, Anne Ophelia. (1994). *Poisons in our path: Plants that harm and heal.* HarperCollins.

Dunphy, Madeleine. (1994). *Here is the tropical rain forest.* Illustrated by Michael Rothman. Hyperion.

Durston, G. (1968). "The Wolf" In *Time for poetry*. Edited by M. Arbuthnot. Scott Foresman.

Earth Works Group. (1994). *Fifty simple things kids can do to recycle.* Illustrated by Michele Montez. Berkeley, CA: Earth Works Press.

Edelman, Bernard. (Ed.). (1985). *Dear America: Letters home from Vietnam.* Norton.

Edmonds, William. (1994). *Big book of time.* Illustrated by Helen Marsden. New York: Readers Digest Kids.

Ehlert, Lois (1990). *Feathers for lunch.* Harcourt Brace Jovanovich.

Ehlert, Lois. (1991). *Red leaf, yellow leaf.* Harcourt Brace Jovanovich.

Ehlert, Lois. (1995). *Snowballs.* Harcourt Brace.

Ehlert, Lois. (1996). *Under my nose.* Richard C. Owen.

Ekoomiak, Normee. (1990). *Arctic memories.* Holt.

Esbensen, Barbara Juster. (1990). *Great northern diver: The loon.* Illustrated by Mary Barrett Brown. Little, Brown.

Eyewitness series. Dorling Kindersley/Knopf.

Facklam, Margery, & Thomas, Margaret. (1992). *The kids' world almanac of amazing facts about numbers, math and money.* Illustrated by Paul Facklam. New York: World Almanac.

Felder, Deborah G. (1996). *The kids' world almanac of animals and pets.* Illustrated by John Lowe. Pharos Books.

Filipovic, Zlata. (1994). *Zlata's diary: A child's life in Sarajevo.* Viking.

Fisher, Leonard Everett. (1989). *The White House.* Holiday House.

Fisher, Leonard Everett. (1990). *The Oregon trail.* Holiday House.

Fisher, Leonard Everett. (1992). *Galileo.* Macmillan.

Fisher, Leonard Everett. (1994). *Marie Curie.* Macmillan.

Fix, Philippe. (1994). *Not so very long ago: Life in a small country village.* Dutton.

Fleischman, Paul. (1993). *Bull run.* HarperCollins.

Fleischman, Sid. (1996). *The abracadabra kid: A writer's life.* Greenwillow.

Fradin, Dennis Brindell. (1996). *"We have conquered the pain": The discovery of Anesthesia.* Simon & Schuster.

Fraser, Mary Ann. (1993). *One giant leap.* Henry Holt.

Fraser, Mary Ann. (1993). *Ten mile day and the building of the Transcontinental Railroad.* Henry Holt.

Fraser, Mary Ann. (1995). *In search of the Grand Canyon: Down the Colorado with John Wesley Powell.* Holt.

Fredericks, Anthony. D. (1996). *Exploring the rainforest.* Golden, CO: Fulcrum Publishing.

Fredericks, Anthony D. (1996). *Surprising swimmers.* Minocqua, WI: NorthWord Press.

Fredericks, Anthony D. (1996). *Weird walkers.* Minocqua, WI: NorthWord Press.

Fredericks, Anthony D. (1997). *Clever camouflagers.* Minocqua,WI: NorthWord Press.

Freedman, Russell. (1983). *Children of the wild west.* Clarion.

Freedman, Russell. (1985). *Cowboys of the wild west.* Clarion.

Freedman, Russell. (1988). *Buffalo hunt.* Holiday House.

Freedman, Russell. (1989). *Lincoln: A photobiography.* Clarion.

Freedman, Russell. (1990). *Franklin Delano Roosevelt.* Clarion.

Freedman, Russell. (1991). *The Wright brothers: How they invented the air plane.* Original photographs by Wilbur and Orville Wright. Holiday House.

Freedman, Russell. (1992). *An Indian winter.* Paintings and drawings by Karl Bodmer. Holiday House.

Freedman, Russell. (1993). *Eleanor Roosevelt: A life of discovery.* Clarion.

Freedman, Russell. (1994). *Kids at work: Lewis Hine and the crusade against child labor.* Photographs by Lewis Hine. Clarion.

Freedman, Russell. (1996). *The life and death of Crazy Horse.* Drawings by Amos Bad Heart Bull. Holiday House.

French, Vivian. (1994). *Spider watching.* Illustrated by Alison Wisenfeld. Candlewick.

Fritz, Jean. (1969). *George Washington's breakfast.* Illustrated by Paul Galdone. Coward, McCann & Geoghegan.

Fritz, Jean. (1974). *Why don't you get a horse, Sam Adams?* Illustrated by Trina Schart Hyman. Coward-McCann.

Fritz, Jean. (1987). *Shh! We're writing the Constitution.* Illustrated by Tomie dePaola. Putnam.

Fritz, Jean. (1989). *The great little Madison.* Putnam.

Fritz, Jean. (1991). *Bully for you, Teddy Roosevelt!* Illustrated by Mike Wimmer. Putnam.

Fritz, Jean. (1992). *Surprising myself.* Photographs by Andrea F. Pfleger. Richard C. Owen.

Funston, Sylvia, & Ingram, Jay. (1994). *It's all in your brain.* Illustrated by Gary Clement. Grosset & Dunlap.

Garcia, Guy. (1995). *The spirit of the Maya: A boy explores his people's mysterious past.* Photographs by Ted Wood. Walker.

Gardner, Jane Mylum. (1993). *Henry Moore: From bones and stones to sketches and sculptures.* Four Winds.

Garelick, May. (1988). *What makes a bird a bird?* Illustrated by Trish Hill. Greenvale, NY: Mondo Publishing.

Gelman, Rita Golden. (1991). *Dawn to dusk in the Galápagos: Flightless birds, swimming lizards, and other fascinating creatures.* Photographs by Tui De Roy. Little, Brown.

George, Jean Craighead. (1996). *Vulpes the red fox.* HarperCollins.

George, Jean Craighead. (1972). *Julie of the wolves.* Pictures by John

Schoenherr. Harper and Row.

George, Jean Craighead. (1994). *Animals who have won our hearts.* HarperCollins.

George, Jean Craighead. (1995). *Everglades.* Paintings by Wendell Minor. HarperCollins.

Gersting, Judith L., & Kuczkowski, Joseph E. (1977). *Yes-no, stop-go: Some patterns in mathematical logic.* Illustrated by Don Madden. Crowell.

Gherman, Beverly. (1990). *Agnes DeMille, dancing off the Earth.* Atheneum.

Gherman, Beverly. (1992). *E. B. White: Some writer!* Atheneum.

Gibbons, Gail. (1987). *Dinosaurs.* Holiday House.

Gibbons, Gail. (1990). *Beacons of light: Lighthouses.* Morrow.

Gibbons, Gail. (1990). *Weather words and what they mean.* Holiday House.

Gibbons, Gail. (1991). *Whales.* Holiday House.

Gibbons, Gail. (1992). *Sharks.* Holiday House.

Gibbons, Gail. (1992). *The great St. Lawrence Seaway.* Morrow.

Gibbons, Gail. (1993). *Spiders.* Holiday House.

Gibbons, Gail. (1993). *The planets.* Holiday House.

Gibbons, Gail. (1994). *Nature's green umbrella: Tropical rain forests.* Morrow.

Gibbons, Gail. (1995). *The reasons for seasons.* Holiday House.

Gibbons, Gail. (1995). *Bicycle book.* Holiday House.

Gibbons, Gail. (1997). *The honey makers.* Morrow.

Giblin, James Cross. (1987). *From hand to mouth: Or, how we invented knives, forks, spoons, and chopsticks & the table manners to go with them.* Crowell.

Giblin, James Cross. (1988). *Let there be light: A book about windows.* Crowell.

Giblin, James Cross. (1990). *The riddle of the Rosetta stone.* HarperCollins.

Giblin, James Cross. (1993). *Be seated: A book about chairs.* HarperCollins.

Giblin, James Cross. (1994). *Thomas Jefferson: A picture book biography.* Illustrated by Michael Dooling. Scholastic.

Giblin, James Cross. (1995). *When plague strikes: The Black Death, small pox, AIDS.* Woodcuts by David Frampton. HarperCollins.

Giganti, Paul, Jr. (1992). *Each orange had eight slices: A counting book.* Illustrated by Donald Crews. Greenwillow.

Ginns, Russell. (1994). *Puzzlooney! Really ridiculous math puzzles.* New York: W. H. Freeman.

Gioglio, Gerald. (1989). *Days of decision: An oral history of conscientious objectors in the military during the Vietnam War.* Trenton, NJ: The Broken Rifle Press.

Giovanni, Nikki. (1996). *The genie in the jar.* Illustrated by Chris Raschka. Holt.

Gomi, Taro. (1993). *Everyone poops.* Translated by Amanda Mayer

Stinchecum. Brooklyn, NY: Kane/Miller.

Goodman, Susan E. (1995). *Unseen rainbows, silent songs: The world beyond the human senses.* Atheneum.

Gorrell, Gena K. (1996). *North star to freedom: The story of the under ground railroad.* Foreword by Rosemary Brown. Delacorte.

Granfield, Linda. (1989). *All about Niagara Falls: Fascinating facts, dramatic discoveries.* Morrow.

Granfield, Linda. (1993). *Extra! Extra! The who, what, where, when and why of newspapers.* Illustrated by Bill Slavin. Orchard.

Granfield, Linda. (1994). *Cowboy: An album.* Ticknor and Fields.

Granfield, Linda. (1996). *In Flander's Fields: The story of the poem by John McCree.* Illustrated by Janet Wilson. Doubleday.

Gray, Libba Moore. (1995). *My mama had a dancing heart.* Illustrated by Raúl Colón. Orchard.

Green, Robyn. (1986). *Caterpillars.* Illustrated by Sadie Pascoe. Greenvale, NY: Mondo Publishing.

Green, Robyn. (1996). *Slugs and snails.* Photographs by Kathie Atkinson and Densey Clyne. Greenvale, NY: Mondo Publishing.

Greenberg, Jan, & Jordan, Sandra. (1991). *The painter's eye: Learning to look at contemporary American art.* Delacorte.

Greenberg, Jan, & Jordan, Sandra. (1993). *The sculptor's eye: Looking at contemporary American art.* Delacorte.

Greenberg, Jan, & Jordan, Sandra. (1995). *The American eye: Eleven artists of the twentieth century.* Delacorte.

Greene, Bob. (1989). *Homecoming: When the soldiers returned from Vietnam.* Putnam.

Greenlaw, M. Jean. (1993). *Ranch dressing: The story of western wear.* Lodestar.

Greenspun, Adele Aron. (1991). *Daddies.* Philomel Books.

Guiberson, Brenda. (1991). *Cactus hotel.* Illustrated by Megan Lloyd. Henry Holt.

Guiberson, Brenda. (1994). *Spotted owl: Bird of the ancient forest.* Holt.

Hakim, Joy. (1993). *From colonies to country.* Oxford University Press.

Hakim, Joy. (1994). *Liberty for all?* Oxford University Press.

Hamanaka, Sheila. (1990). *The journey: Japanese Americans, racism and renewal.* Orchard Books.

Hamilton, Virginia. (1993). *Many thousand gone: African Americans from slavery to freedom.* Illustrated by Leo and Diane Dillon. Knopf.

Harness, Cheryl. (1995). *The amazing impossible Erie Canal.* Macmillan.

Harrison, Barbara, & Terris, Daniel. (1992). *A twilight struggle: The life of John Fitzgerald Kennedy.* Lothrop, Lee & Shepard.

Hart, George. (1990). *Ancient Egypt.* Knopf.

Harvey, Paul. (1977). *Paul Harvey's the rest of the story.* Doubleday.

Haskins, Jim. (1989). *Count your way through Mexico.* Minneapolis, MN: Carolrhoda Books.

Haskins, Jim. (1995). *The day Fort Sumpter was fired upon: A photo history of the Civil War.* Scholastic.

Hausman, Gerald. (1994). *Turtle Island ABC: A gathering of Native American symbols.* Illustrated by Cara and Barry Moser. HarperCollins.

Heinst, Marie. (1992). *My first number book.* Dorling Kindersley.

Hermes, Jules. (1994). *The children of Micronesia.* Carolrhoda.

Hertzberg, Hendrik. (1993). *One million.* Random House.

Heslewood, Julie. (1993). *Introducing Picasso.* Little, Brown.

Highwater, Jamake. (1995). *Songs for the seasons.* Illustrated by Sandra Speidel. Lothrop, Lee & Shepard.

Hirschi, Ron. (1990). *Winter.* Photographs by Thomas D. Mangelsen. Cobblehill Books.

Hirschi, Ron. (1994). *Save our prairies and grasslands.* Photographs by Erwin and Peggy Bauer. Delacorte.

Hoban, Tana. (1985). *Is it larger? Is it smaller?* Greenwillow.

Hoban, Tana. (1989). *Of colors and things.* Greenwillow.

Hoban, Tana. (1992). *Spirals, curls, fanshapes, and lines.* Greenwillow.

Hoff, Syd. (1958). *Danny and the dinosaur.* Harper & Row.

Hollander, Phyllis, & Hollander, Zander. (1986). *Amazing but true sports stories.* Scholastic.

Hoobler, Dorothy, & Hoobler, Thomas. (1994). *The Italian American family album.* Introduction by Governor Mario M. Cuomo. Oxford University Press.

Hoyt-Goldsmith, Diane. (1990). *Totem pole.* Photographs by Lawrence Migdale. Holiday House.

Hoyt-Goldsmith, Diane. (1991). *Pueblo storyteller.* Photographs by Lawrence Migdale. Holiday House.

Hoyt-Goldsmith, Diane. (1992). *Arctic hunter.* Photographs by Lawrence Migdale. Holiday House.

Hoyt-Goldsmith, Diane. (1992). *Hoang Anh: A Vietnamese American boy.* Photographs by Lawrence Migdale. Holiday House.

Hoyt-Goldsmith, Diane. (1993). *Celebrating Kwanzaa.* Photographs by Lawrence Migdale. Holiday House.

Hoyt-Goldsmith, Diane. (1993). *Cherokee summer: Cwy ay.* Photographs by Lawrence Migdale. Holiday House.

Hoyt-Goldsmith, Diane. (1994). *Day of the dead: A Mexican-American celebration.* Photographology by Lawrence Migdale. Holiday House.

Hoyt-Goldsmith, Diane. (1995). *Apache rodeo.* Photographs by Lawrence Migdale. Holiday House.

Hoyt-Goldsmith, Diane. (1995). *Mardi Gras: A Cajun country celebration.* Photographs by Lawrence Migdale. Holiday House.

Hudson, Wade, & Wesley, Valerie W. (1988). *Afro-Bets book of Black heroes from A to Z: An introduction to important Black archives.* East Orange, NJ: Just Us Books.

Hunt, Jonathan. (1989). *Illuminations.* Bradbury.

Hunt, Irene. (1964). *Across five Aprils.* Follett.

Hunt, Joni Phelps. (1995). *A chorus of frogs.* Silver Burdett Press.

Hutchins, Pat. (1986). *The doorbell rang.* Scholastic.

Hyde, Margaret O., & Forsyth, Elizabeth H. (1996). *AIDS: What does it mean to you?* Walker.

Isaacson, Philip M. (1975). *The American eagle.* Boston: New York Graphic Society.

Isaacson, Phillip. (1988). *Round buildings, square buildings and buildings that wiggle like a fish.* Knopf.

Isaacson, Phillip. (1993). *A short walk around the pyramids & through the world of art.* Knopf.

Irvine, Joan. (1993). *Build it with boxes.* Illustrated by Linda Hendry. Morrow.

Jackson, Donna M. (1995). *The bone detectives: How forensic anthropologists solve crimes and uncover mysteries of the dead.* Photographs by Charlie Fellenbaum. Little, Brown.

Jacobs, Francine. (1992). *The Tainos: The people who welcomed Columbus.* Illustrated by Patrick Collins. Putnam.

Jaffe, Steven. (1996). *Who were the Founding Fathers? Two hundred years of reinventing American history.* Holt.

James, Sylvia. (1996). *Meet the octopus.* Illustrated by Cynthia A. Belcher. Greenvale, NY: Mondo Publishing.

Jenness, Aylette. (1990). *Families: A celebration of diversity, commitment, and love.* Houghton Mifflin.

Johnson, Stephan. (1995). *Alphabet city.* Viking.

Johnson, Sylvia A. (1994). *A beekeeper's year.* Photographs by Nick Von Ohlen. Little, Brown.

Johnson, Sylvia. (1995). *Raptor rescue! An eagle flies free.* Photographs by Ron Winch. Dutton.

Johnston, Norma. (1994). *Harriet: The life and world of Harriet Beecher Stowe.* Four Winds.

Jonas, Ann. (1989). *Aardvarks disembark!* Greenwillow.

Jones, Charlotte F. (1991). *Mistakes that worked.* Illustrated by John O'Brien. Doubleday.

Jurmain, Suzanne. (1989). *Once upon a horse: A history of horses and how they shaped history.* Lothrop, Lee & Shepard.

Keegan, Marcia. (1991). *Pueblo boy: Growing up in two worlds.* Cobblehill.

Keeler, Patricia, & McCall, Francis, Jr. (1995). *Unraveling fibers.* Atheneum.

Kendall, Russ. (1992). *Eskimo boy: Life in an Inupiaq Eskimo village.*

Scholastic.

Ketchum, Liza. (1996). *The gold rush.* With an Introduction by Stephen Ives and Ken Burns. Little, Brown.

Kierein, Tom. (1994). *Weather: A National Geographic action book.* National Geographic Society.

Kindersley, Barnabas, & Kindersley, Anabel. (1995). *Children just like me: A unique celebration of children around the world.* Photo-illustrated by Barnabas Kindersley. Dorling Kindersley.

King-Smith, Dick. (1994). *I love guinea pigs.* Illustrated by Anita Jeram. Candlewick.

Kinney, Rowena. (1995). *Fall.* Orono, ME: University of Maine.

Knight, Amelia Stewart. (1993). *The way west: Journal of a pioneer woman.* Illustrated by Michael McCurdy. Simon & Schuster.

Knight, Margy Burns. (1992). *Talking walls.* Illustrated by Anne Sibley O'Brien. Gardner, ME: Tilbury House.

Knight, Margy Burns. (1996). *Talking walls: The stories continue.* Illustrated by Anne Sibley O'Brien. Gardner, ME: Tilbury House.

Knowlton, Jack. (1988). *Geography from A to Z: A picture glossary.* Illustrated by Harriett Barton. Crowell.

Kovacs, Deborah, & Madin, Kate. (1996). *Beneath blue waters: Meetings with remarkable deep-sea creatures.* Photographs by Larry Madin. Viking.

Kovic, Ron. (1976). *Born on the Fourth of July.* Pocket Books.

Kraft, Betsy Harvey. (1995). *Mother Jones: One woman's fight for labor.* Clarion.

Kramer, Stephen. (1995). *Theodoric's rainbow.* Illustrated by Daniel Mark Duffy. W. H. Freeman.

Kroll, Steven. (1996). *Pony express!* Illustrated by Dan Andreasen. Scholastic.

Krull, Kathleen. (1993). *Lives of the musicians: Good times, bad times (and what the neighbors thought).* Illustrated by Kathryn Hewitt. Harcourt Brace Jovanovich.

Krull, Kathleen. (1994). *Lives of the writers: Comedies, tragedies (and what the neighbors thought).* Harcourt Brace.

Krull, Kathleen. (1995). *Lives of the artists: Masterpieces, messes (and what the neighbors thought).* Illustrated by Kathleen Hewitt. Harcourt Brace.

Krupp, Robin Rector. (1996). *Let's go traveling in Mexico.* Morrow.

Kuklin, Susan. (1989). *Going to my ballet class.* Bradbury.

Kuklin, Susan. (1995). *Kodomo: Children of Japan.* Putnam.

Lake, Mary Dixon. (1995). *I love bugs.* Illustrated by Deborah Drew-Brook and Allan Cormack. Greenvale, NY: Mondo Publishing.

Landau, Elaine. (1991). *Tropical rain forests around the world.* Franklin Watts.

Lang, Aubrey. (1990). *Eagles.* Photographs by Wayne Lynch. Sierra Club/ Little, Brown.

Langley, Andrew, & DeSouza, Philip. (1996). *The Roman news.* (Edited by A. Powell & P. Steele) Candlewick.

Lankford, Mary. (1992). *Hopscotch around the world.* Illustrated by Karen Milone. Morrow.

Lankford, Mary D. (1996). *Jacks around the world.* Illustrated by Karen Dugan. Morrow.

Lasky, Kathryn. (1990). *Dinosaur dig.* Morrow.

Lasky, Kathryn. (1992). *Surtsey: The newest place on earth.* Photographs by Christopher G. Knight. Hyperion.

Lasky, Kathryn. (1992). *Think like an eagle: At work with a wildlife photographer.* Photographs by Christopher G. Knight and Jack Swedberg. Little, Brown.

Lasky, Kathryn. (1994). *Days of the dead.* Photographs by Christopher G. Knight. Hyperion.

Lasky, Kathryn. (1994). *The librarian who measured the earth.* Illustrated by Kevin Hawkes. Little, Brown.

Lasky, Kathryn. (1995). *Pond year.* Illustration by Mike Bostock. Candlewick.

Lasky, Kathryn. (1996). *A journey to the new world: The diary of Remember Patience Whipple.* Scholastic.

Lauber, Patricia. (1982). *Journey to the planets.* Crown.

Lauber, Patricia. (1986). *Volcano: The eruption and healing of Mount St. Helens.* Bradbury.

Lauber, Patricia. (1987). *Dinosaurs walked here, and other stories fossils tell.* Bradbury.

Lauber, Patricia. (1989). *The news about dinosaurs.* Bradbury.

Lauber, Patricia. (1990). *An octopus is amazing.* Illustrated by Holly Keller. Collins.

Lauber, Patricia. (1990). *Seeing earth from space.* Orchard.

Lauber, Patricia. (1991). *Living with dinosaurs.* Illustrated by Doug Henderson. Bradbury.

Lauber, Patricia. (1991). *Summer of fire: Yellowstone 1988.* Orchard.

Lauber, Patricia. (1992). *Who discovered America? Mysteries and puzzles of the new world.* (New Edition). Illustrated by Mike Eagle. HarperCollins.

Lauber, Patricia. (1994). *Be a friend to trees.* Illustrated by Holly Keller. HarperCollins.

Lauber, Patricia. (1994). *Fur, feather, and flippers: How animals live where they do.* Scholastic.

Lauber, Patricia. (1996). *How dinosaurs came to be.* Illustrated by Douglas Henderson. Simon & Schuster.

Lauber, Patricia. (1996). *Hurricanes: Earth's mightiest storms.* Scholastic.

Lavies, Bianca. (1994). *Killer bees.* Dutton.

Lawlor, Laurie. (1996). *Where will this shoe take you? A walk through the history of footwear.* Walker.

Lawrence, Jacob. (1993). *The great migration: An American story.* HarperCollins.

Lawrence, R. D. (1990). *Wolves.* Sierra Club/Little, Brown.

Lawson, Don. (1986). *An album of the Vietnam War.* Franklin Watts.

Leedy, Loreen. (1992). *The monster money book.* Holiday House.

Leedy, Loreen. (1993). *Postcards from Pluto: A tour of the solar system.* Holiday House.

Leedy, Loreen. (1994). *Fraction action.* Holiday House.

Leedy, Loreen. (1995). *2 x 2 = boo!: A set of spooky multiplication stories.* Holiday House.

Lerner, Carol. (1994). *Backyard birds of winter.* Morrow.

Leslie, Clare Walker. (1991). *Nature all year long.* Greenwillow.

Lessem, Don. (1994). *The Iceman.* Crown.

Lessem, Don. (1996). *Dinosaur worlds.* Boyds Mills Press.

Lessem, Don. (1996). *Raptors! The nastiest dinosaurs.* Illustrated by David Peters. Little, Brown.

Lester, Julius. (1968). *To be a slave.* Illustrated by Tom Feelings. Scholastic.

Levinson, Nancy Smiler. (1990). *Christopher Columbus: Voyager to the unknown.* Lodestar/Dutton.

Lewin, Ted. (1996). *Market!* Lothrop.

Lewis, Barbara A. (1991). *The kid's guide to social action: How to solve the social problems you choose—and turn creative thinking into positive action.* Minneapolis: Free Spirit.

Lindbergh, Reeve. (1994). *What is the sun?* Illustrated by Stephen Lambert. Candlewick.

Little, Douglas. (1994). *Ten little-known facts about hippopotamuses: And more little-known facts and a few fibs about other animals.* Houghton Mifflin.

Littlefield, Bill. (1993). *Champions: Stories of ten remarkable athletes.* Illustrated by Bernie Fuchs. Little, Brown.

Livingston, Myra Cohn. (1994). *Animal, vegetable, mineral: Poems about small things.* Viking.

Llewellyn, Claire. (1992). *My first book of time.* Dorling Kindersley.

Locker, Thomas. (1995). *Sky tree: Seeing science through art.* (With Christiansen, Candace). HarperCollins.

London, Jonathan. (1993). *Voices of the wild.* Illustrated by Wayne McLoughlin. Crown.

Lovell, Scarlett, & Snowball, Diane. (1995). *Is this a monster?* Greenvale, NY: Mondo Publishing.

Lovett, Sara. (1992). *Extremely weird frogs.* Santa Fe, NM: John Muir Publications.

Lucero, Jaime. (1996). *How to make salsa.* Illustrated by Francisco X. Mora. Greenvale, NY: Mondo Publishing.

Luenn, Nancy. (1994). *Squish! A wetland walk.* Illustrated by Ronald Himler. Atheneum.

Lyons, Mary E. (1992). *Letters from a slave girl: The story of Harriet Powers.* Scribner's.

Lyons, Mary E. (1993). Starting home: The story of Horace Pippin, painter. Scribner's.

Lyons, Mary E. (1993). *Stitching stars: The story quilts of Harriet Jacobs.* Scribner's.

Lyons, Mary E. (1994). *Deep blues: Bill Traylor, self-taught artist.* Scribner's.

Lyons, Mary E. (1994). *Master of mahogany: Tom Day, free black cabinet-maker.* Scribner's.

Lyons, Mary E. (1995). *Keeping secrets: The girlhood diaries of seven women writers.* Henry Holt.

Lyons, Mary E. (1996). *Painting dreams: Minnie Evans, visionary artist.* Houghton Mifflin.

Mabie, Margot C. (1985). *Vietnam: There and here.* Holt, Rinehart & Winston.

Machotka, Hana. (1992). *Breathtaking noses.* Morrow.

MacLeod, Elizabeth. (1994). *Dinosaurs: The fastest, the fiercest, the most amazing.* Illustrated by Gordon Sauvé. Viking.

Maestro, Betsy, & Maestro, Giulio. (1991). *The discovery of the Americas.* Lothrop, Lee & Shepard.

Maestro, Betsy. (1994). *Bats: Night flyers.* Illustrated by Giulio Maestro. Scholastic.

Maestro, Betsy. (1996). *Coming to America: The story of immigration.* Illustrated by Susannah Ryan. Scholastic.

Malnig, Anita. (1985). *Where the waves break: Life at the edge of the sea.* Photographs by Jeff Rotman, Alex Kerstitch, and Franklin H. Barnwell. Minneapolis, MN: Carolrhoda.

Books. Marchon-Arnaud, Catherine. (1994). *A gallery of games.* Illustrated by Marc Schwartz. Ticknor & Fields.

Margolies, Barbara A. (1994). *Olbalbal: A day in Maasailand.* Four Winds.

Markle, Sandra. (1994). *Science to the rescue.* Atheneum.

Markle, Sandra. (1995). *Pioneering ocean depths.* Atheneum.

Markle, Sandra. (1996). *Creepy, crawly baby bugs.* Walker.

Marrin, Albert. (1993). *Cowboys, Indians, and gunfighters: The story of the cattle kingdom.* Atheneum.

Marrin, Albert. (1994). *Unconditional surrender: U. S. Grant and the Civil War.* Atheneum.

Marsalis, Wynton. (1995). *Marsalis on music.* Norton.

Matthews, Downs. (1989). *Polar bear cubs.* Photographs by Dan Guravich.

Simon & Schuster.

Matthews, Downs. (1995). *Arctic foxes*. Photographs by Dan Guravich and Nikita Ovsyanikov. Simon & Schuster.

McDonald, Megan. (1990). *Is this a house for a hermit crab?* Illustrated by S. D. Schindler. Orchard.

McFarlan, Donald, & McWhirter, Norris. (1996). *The Guinness book of world records*. Sterling Publishing.

McKissack, Patricia, & McKissack, Fredrick. (1989). *A long hard journey: The story of the Pullman porter*. Walker.

McKissack, Patricia. (1992). *A million fish...more or less*. Knopf.

McKissack, Patricia, & McKissack, Fredrick. (1992). *Sojourner truth: Ain't I a woman?* Scholastic.

McKissack, Patricia, & McKissack, Fredrick. (1994). *Christmas in the big house, Christmas in the quarters*. Illustrated by John Thompson. Scholastic.

McKissack, Patricia, & McKissack, Fredrick. (1995). *Red-tail angels: The story of the Tuskegee airmen of World War II*. Walker.

McKissack, Patricia. (1997). *Can you imagine?* Photographs by Myles Pickney. Richard C. Owens.

McMahon, Patricia. (1993). *Chi-Hoon: A Korean girl*. Photographs by Michael F. O'Brien. Boyds Mills.

McMahon, Patricia. (1995). *Listen for the bus: David's story*. Photographs by John Godt. Boyds Mills.

McMillan, Bruce. (1986). *Counting wildflowers*. Lothrop, Lee & Shepard.

McMillan, Bruce. (1991). *Eating fractions*. Scholastic.

McMillan, Bruce. (1992). *Going on a whale watch*. Scholastic.

McMillan, Bruce. (1995). *Puffins climb, penguins rhyme*. Gulliver/Harcourt Brace.

McMillan, Bruce. (1995). *Nights of the Pufflings*. Houghton Mifflin.

McMillan, Bruce. (1995). *Summer ice: Life along the Antarctic Peninsula*. Houghton Mifflin.

McMillan, Bruce. (1996). *Jelly beans for sale*. Scholastic.

Meltzer, Milton. (1980). *All times, all peoples: A world history of slavery*. Illustrated by Leonard E. Fisher. HarperCollins.

Meltzer, Milton. (Ed.). (1989). *Voices from the Civil War: A documentary history of the great American conflict*. Crowell.

Meltzer, Milton. (1990). *Columbus and the world around him*. Franklin Watts.

Meltzer, Milton. (1992). *The amazing potato: A story in which the Incas, Conquistadors, Marie Antoinette, Thomas Jefferson, wars, famines, immigrants, and french fries all play a part*. HarperCollins.

Meltzer, Milton. (1993). *Gold: The true story of why people search for it, mine it, trade it, steal it, mint it, hoard it, shape it, wear it, fight and kill for it.* HarperCollins.

Meltzer, Milton. (1993). *Lincoln in his own words.* Illustrated by Stephen Alcorn. Harcourt Brace.

Meltzer, Milton. (1994). *Cheap raw material: How our youngest workers are exploited and abused.* Viking.

Mettger, Zak. (1994). *Till victory is won: Black soldiers in the Civil War.* Lodestar.

Meyer, Susan E. (1990). *Mary Cassatt.* Abrams.

Micklethwait, Lucy. (1993). *A child's book of art: Great pictures, first words.* Dorling Kindersley.

Micklethwait, Lucy. (1992). *I spy: An alphabet book in art.* Greenwillow.

Micklethwait, Lucy. (1993). *I spy two eyes: Numbers in art.* Greenwillow.

Micklethwait, Lucy. (1994). *I spy a lion, animals in art.* Greenwillow.

Micklethwait, Lucy. (1996). *A child's book of play in art:* Dorling Kindersley.

Micklethwait, Lucy. (1996). *I spy a freight train: Transportation in art.* Greenwillow.

Micucci, Charles. (1995). *The life and times of the honeybee.* Ticknor & Fields.

Miller, Margaret. (1990). *Who uses this?* Greenwillow.

Miller, Margaret. (1991). *Whose shoe?* Greenwillow.

Miller, Margaret. (1994). *Guess who?* Greenwillow.

Monceaux, Morgan. (1994). *Jazz: My music, my people.* Knopf.

Moody, Anne. (1968). *Coming of age in Mississippi.* Dell.

Moore, Helen H. (1996). *Beavers.* Illustrated by Terri Talas. Greenvale, NY: Mondo Publishing.

Mooser, Stephen. (1991). *The man who ate a car and tons of other weird true stories.* Illustrated by George Ulrich. Dell.

Mori, Tuyosi. (1986). *Socrates and the three little pigs.* Illustrated by Mitsumasa Anno. Philomel.

Morimoto, Junko. (1990). *My Hiroshima.* Viking.

Morris, Ann. (1989). *Bread, bread, bread.* Photographs by Ken Heyman. Lothrop.

Morris, Ann. (1990). *Loving.* Photo-illustrated by Ken Heyman. Lothrop, Lee & Shepard.

Morris, Ann. (1990). *On the go.* Photo-illustrated by Ken Heyman. Lothrop, Lee & Shepard.

Morris, Ann. (1992). *Houses and homes.* Photographs by Ken Heyman. Lothrop, Lee and Shepard.

Morris, Ann. (1993). *Tools.* Photo-illustrated by Ken Heyman. Lothrop, Lee & Shepard.

Morris, Ann. (1994). *700 kids on grandpa's farm.* Photographs by Ken Heyman. Dutton.

Morris, Ann. (1996). *Weddings.* Photographs by Ken Heyman. Lothrop.

Moser, Barry. (1993). *Fly! A brief history of flight illustrated.* HarperCollins.

Moss, Lloyd. (1995). *Zin! Zin! A violin.* Illustrated by Marjorie Priceman. Simon & Schuster.

Mühlberger, Richard. (1993). *What makes a Bruegel a Bruegel?* Viking/ Metropolitan Museum of Art.

Mullins, Patricia. (1994). *V for vanishing: An alphabet of endangered animals.* Illustrated by Marjorie Priceman. HarperCollins.

Murphy, Jim. (1988). *The last dinosaur.* Illustrated by Mark Alan Weatherby. Scholastic.

Murphy, Jim. (1990). *The boys' war: Confederate and Union soldiers talk about the Civil War.* Clarion.

Murphy, Jim. (1992). *The long road to Gettysburg.* Clarion.

Murphy, Jim. (1993). *Across America on an emigrant train.* Clarion.

Murphy, Jim. (1995). *Into the deep forest with Henry David Thoreau.* Illustrated by Kate Kiesler. Clarion.

Murphy, Jim. (1995). *The great fire.* Scholastic.

Murphy, Jim. (1996). *A young patriot: The American Revolution as experienced by one boy.* Clarion.

Myers, Walter Dean. (1991). *Now is your time! The African-American struggle for freedom.* HarperCollins.

Myller, Rolf. (1986). *How big is a foot?* Dell.

National Geographic Action Book Series. National Geographic Society.

N. E. Thing Enterprises. (1993). *Magic eye: A new way of looking at the world.* Kansas City, MO: Andrew and McMeel.

N. E. Thing Enterprises. (1994). *Magic eye II: Now you see it ....* Kansas City, MO: Andrew and McMeel.

N. E. Thing Enterprises. (1994). *Magic eye III: Now you see it....* Kansas City, MO: Andrew and McMeel.

Nelson, Joanne. (1990). *Half and half.* Cleveland: Curriculum Press.

Nichol, Barbara. (1993). *Beethoven lives upstairs.* Illustrated by Scott Cameron. Orchard.

Nickens, Bessie. (1994). *Walking the log: Memories of a southern childhood.* Rizzoli.

Norden, Beth B., & Ruschak, Lynette. (1993). *Magnification.* Lodestar.

Nozaki, Akihiro. (1985). *Anno's hat tricks.* Illustrated by Mitsumasa Anno. Philomel.

Ockenga, Starr. (1990). *A book of days: Then and now.* Houghton Mifflin.

Olivastro, Dominic. (1993). *Ancient puzzles: Classic brainteasers and other timeless mathematical games of the last ten centuries.* Bantam.

Onyefulu, Ifeoma. (1993). *A is for Africa.* Cobblehill.

Onyefulu, Ifeoma. (1995). *Emeka's gift: An African counting story.* Cobblehill.

Onyefulu, Ifeoma. (1996). *Ogbo: Sharing life in an African village.* Harcourt.

Osborne, Mary Pope. (1990). *The many lives of Benjamin Franklin.* Dial.

Osborne, Mary Pope. (1996). *One world, many religions: The way we worship.* Knopf.

Osofsky, Audrey. (1996). *Free to dream: The making of a poet: Langston Hughes.* Lothrop, Lee & Shepard.

Owen, Cheryl. (1993). *My costume book.* Little, Brown.

Owens, Mary Beth. (1988). *A caribou alphabet.* Illustrated by Mark McCollough. Gardner, ME: Tilbury House.

Owens, Mary Beth. (1993). *Counting cranes.* Little, Brown.

Pallotta, Jerry. (1986). *The ocean alphabet book.* Photographs by Frank Mazzola, Jr. Watertown, MA: Charlesbridge Publishing.

Pallotta, Jerry. (1991). *The icky bug counting book.* Illustrated by Frank Mazzola, Jr. Watertown, MA: Charlesbridge Publishing.

Pandell, Karen. (1993). *Land of dark, land of light: The Arctic national wildlife refuge.* Dutton.

Pandell, Karen, & Bryant, Barry. (1995). *Learning from the Dalai Lama: Secrets of the wheel of time.* Photographs by John B. Taylor. Dutton.

Parker, Nancy Winslow, & Wright, Joan R. (1990). *Frogs, toads, lizards and salamanders.* Illustrated by Nancy Winslow Parker. Greenwillow.

Parker, Steve. (1994). *Inside dinosaurs and other prehistoric creatures.* Illustrated by Ted Dewan. Delacorte.

Parker, Steve. (1994). *Frogs and toads.* San Francisco: Sierra Club.

Patent, Dorothy Hinshaw. (1989). *Wild turkey, tame turkey.* Photographs by William Muñoz. Clarion.

Patent, Dorothy Hinshaw. (1990). *Yellowstone fires: Flames and rebirth.* Photographs by William Muñoz and others. Holiday House.

Patent. Dorothy Hinshaw. (1994). *The American alligator.* Photographs by William Muñoz. Clarion.

Patent, Dorothy Hinshaw. (1995). *Eagles of America.* Photographs by William Muñoz. Holiday House.

Patent, Dorothy Hinshaw. (1995). *Why mammals have fur.* Photographs by William Muñoz. Cobblehill/Dutton.

Patterson, Francine. (1985). *Koko's kitten.* Photographs by Ronald Cohn. Scholastic.

Paulsen, Gary. (1990). *Wood-song.* Bradbury.

Paulsen, Gary. (1993). *Nightjohn.* Delacorte.

Peet, Bill. (1989). *Bill Peet: An autobiography.* Houghton Mifflin.

Pelta, Kathy. (1991). *Discovering Christopher Columbus: How history is invented.* Lerner.

Peppin, Anthea. (1991). *Nature in art.* Brookfield, CT: Millbrook.

Peppin, Anthea. (1991). *People in art.* Brookfield, CT: Millbrook.

Peppin, Anthea. (1991). *Places in art.* Brookfield, CT: Millbrook.

Perl, Lila. (1993). *It happened in America: True stories from the fifty states.*

Illustrated by Ib Ohlsson. Holt.

Peters, David. (1991). *From the beginning: The story of human evolution.* Morrow.

Peterson, Cris. (1994). *Extra cheese, please!: Mozzarella's journey from cow to pizza.* Photographs by Alvis Upitis. Boyds Mills.

Pfeffer, Wendy. (1994). *From tadpole to frog.* Illustrated by Holly Keller. HarperCollins.

Philip, Neil. (1995). *Singing America: Poems that define a nation.* Illustrated by Michael McCurdy. Viking.

Pillar, Marjorie. (1992). *Join the band.* HarperCollins.

Pinczes, Elinor J. (1993). *One hundred hungry ants.* Illustrated by Bonnie MacKain. Houghton Mifflin.

Pinczes, Elinor J. (1995). *A remainder of one.* Illustrated by Bonnie MacKain. Houghton Mifflin.

Pinkney, Andrea Davis. (1993). *Seven candles for Kwanzaa.* Illustrated by Brian Pinkney. Dial.

Pinkney, Andrea Davis. (1994). *Dear Benjamin Banneker.* Illustrated by Brian Pinkney. Harcourt.

Platnick, Norman I. (1995). *Tarantulas are spiders.* Greenvale, NY: Mondo Publishing.

Platt, Richard. (1992). *Incredible cross-sections.* Illustrations by Steven Biesty. Knopf.

Platt, Richard. (1993). *Man-of-war: Stephen's Biesty's cross-sections.* Illustrated by Stephen Biesty. Dorling Kindersley.

Platt, Richard. (1994). *Castle: Stephen Biesty's cross-sectons.* Illustrated by Stephen Biesty. Dorling Kindersley.

Plazy, Giles. (1993). *A weekend with Rousseau.* New York: Rizzoli.

Pratt, Kristin J. (1992). *A walk in the rain forest.* Nevada City, CA: Dawn Publications.

Pratt, Kristin J. (1994). *A swim through the sea.* Nevada City, CA: Dawn Publications.

Pringle, Laurence. (1991). *Batman: Exploring the world of bats.* Photographs by Merlin Tuttle. Scribner's.

Pringle, Laurence. (1992). *Antarctica: The last unspoiled continent.* Simon & Schuster.

Pringle, Laurence. (1995). *Coral reefs: Earth's undersea treasures.* Simon & Schuster.

Pringle, Laurence. (1995). *Dinosaurs! Strange and wonderful.* Illustrated by Carol Heyer. Boyds Mills.

Pringle, Laurence. (1995). *Dolphin man: Exploring the world of dolphins.* Photographs by Randall S. Wells and Dolphin Biology Research Institute. Atheneum.

Pringle, Laurence. (1995). *Fire in the forest: A cycle of growth and renewal.*

Paintings by Bob Marstall. Atheneum.

Pringle, Laurence. (1995). *Vanishing ozone: Protecting earth from ultravio let radiation.* Morrow.

Pringle, Laurence. (1997). *Nature! Wild and wonderful.* Photographs by Tim Holmstrom. Richard C. Owen.

Provensen, Alice, & Provensen, Martin. (1983). *The glorious flight: Across the channel with Louis Blériot, July 25, 1909.* Viking.

Provensen, Alice, & Provensen, Martin. (1984). *Leonardo da Vinci: The artist, inventor, scientist in three-dimensional movable pictures.* Viking.

Quinlan, Susan E. (1995). *The case of the mummified pigs and other mysteries in nature.* Illustrated by Jennifer Owings Dewey. Boyds Mills.

Raimondo, Lois. (1994). *The little Lama of Tibet.* Scholastic.

Raschka, Chris. (1992). *Charle Parker played be-bop.* Orchard.

Ray, Mary L. (1992). *Pumpkins.* Harcourt Brace Jovanovich.

Reef, Catherine. (1996). *John Steinbeck.* Clarion.

Reynolds, Jan. (1993). *Amazon Basin.* Harcourt Brace.

Reynolds, Jan. (1994). *Mongolia: Vanishing cultures.* Harcourt Brace.

Richardson, Wendy, & Richardson, Jack. (1992). *Cities: Through the eyes of artists.* Children's Press.

Ride, Sally, & Okie, Susan. (1986). *To space and back.* Lothrop, Lee, & Shepard.

Roalf, Peggy. (1992). *Dancers.* Hyperion.

Roalf, Peggy. (1992). *Families.* Hyperion.

Roalf, Peggy. (1993). *Children.* Hyperion.

Robbins, Ken. (1992). *Make me a peanut butter sandwich and a glass of milk.* Scholastic.

Robbins, Ken. (1994). *Water: The elements.* Holt.

Robbins, Ken. (1995). *Air: The elements.* Holt.

Robbins, Ken. (1995). *Earth: The elements.* Holt.

Robbins, Ken. (1996). *Fire: The elements.* Holt.

Rogow, Zack. (1988). *Oranges.* Illustrated by Mary Szilagyi. Orchard.

Rosenberg, Maxine B. (1994). *Hiding to survive: Stories of Jewish children rescued from the Holocaust.* Clarion.

Ross, Catherine S. (1992). *Circles: Fun ideas for getting a-round math.* Illustrated by Bill Slavin. Toronto: Kids Can Press.

Ross, Michael. (1996). *Cricketology.* Minneapolis, MN: Carolrhoda.

Roth, Susan. (1990). *Marco Polo: His notebook.* Doubleday.

Roth, Susan, L. (1994). *Buddha.* Doubleday.

Ryan, Pam Munoz. (1994). *One hundred is a family.* Illustrated by Benrei Huang. Hyperion.

Ryden, Hope. (1995). *Out of the wild: The story of domesticated animals.* Lodestar.

Ryden, Hope. (1991). *Your cat's wild cousins*. Lodestar/Dutton.

Ryder, Joanne. (1993). *Sea elf*. Illustrated by Michael Rothman. Morrow.

Rylant, Cynthia. (1991). *Appalachia: The voices of sleeping birds*. Illustrated by Barry Moser. Harcourt Brace Jovanovich.

St. George, Judith. (1989). *Panama Canal: Gateway to the world*. Putnam.

San Souci, Robert. (1991). *N. C. Wyeth's Pilgrims*. Chronicle.

Sandler, Martin. (1994). *Cowboys: A Library of Congress book*. Introduction by James H. Billington. HarperCollins.

Sandler, Martin. (1994). *Pioneers: A Library of Congress book*. Introduction by James H. Billington. HarperCollins.

Sarrett, Lew. (1968). "Wolf cry." In *Time for poetry*. Edited by M. Arbuthnot. Scott Foresman.

Sattler, Helen Roney. (1989). *Giraffes, the sentinels of the Savannas*. Illustrated by Christopher Santoro. Lothrop, Lee & Shepard.

Sattler, Helen Roney. (1995). *The book of North American owls*. Illustrated by Jean Day. Zallinger. Clarion.

Sayre, April Pulley. (1995). *If you should hear a honey guide*. Illustrated by S. D. Schindler. Houghton Mifflin.

Schaefer, Carole Lexa. (1996). *The squiggle*. Illustrated by Pierr Morgan. Crown.

Scheid, Margaret. (1988). *Discovering Acadia: A guide for young naturalists*. Bar Harbor, ME: Acadia Publishing Company.

Scholastic Voyager of Discovery series on natural history, visual arts, science and technology, and music and performing arts. Scholastic.

Schwartz, David. M. (1985). *How much is a million?* Illustrated by Steven Kellogg. Lothrop, Lee & Shepard.

Schwartz, David M. (1989). *If you made a million*. Illustrated by Steven Kellogg. Lothrop, Lee & Shepard.

Schwartz, David. (1995). *Yanomami: People of the Amazon*. Photographs by Victor Englebert. Lothrop, Lee & Shepard.

Scholastic. (1995). *Water, the source of life: Glaciers, springs, oceans, tide pools, lakes, swamps, rivers, and oases (Scholastic Voyages of Discovery Series)*. Scholastic.

Scieszka, Jon, & Smith, Lane. (1995). *Math curse*. Viking.

Seddon, Tom. (1995). *Atom bomb*. New York: W. H. Freeman.

Seifert, Patti. (1994). *Exploring tree habitats*. Illustrated by Peg Doherty. Greenvale, NY: Mondo Publishing.

Sewell, Marcia. (1995). *Thunder from the clear sky*. Atheneum.

Showers, Paul. (1994). *Where does garbage go?* Illustrated by Randy Chewning. HarperCollins.

Sills, Leslie. (1989). *Inspirations: Stories about women artists*. Morton Grove, IL: Albert Whitman.

Sills, Leslie. (1993). *Visions: Stories about women artists*. Morton Grove, IL:

Albert Whitman.

Silver, Donald M. (1995). *Extinction is forever*. Illustrated by Patricia J. Wynne. Silver Burdett.

Silver, Donald M. (1995). *One small square: Cactus desert*. Illustrated by Patricia J. Wynne. New York: W.H. Freeman.

Silverstein, Alvin, & Silverstein, Virginia. (1990). *Life in a tidal pool*. Illustrated by Pamela Carroll and Walter Carroll. Little, Brown.

Simon, Seymour. (1976). *The optical illusion book*. Illustrated by Constance Ftera. Morrow.

Simon, Seymour. (1981). *Strange creatures*. Illustrated by Pamela Carroll. Four Winds Press.

Simon, Seymour. (1984). *Earth: Our planet in space*. Four Winds.

Simon, Seymour. (1986). *The sun*. William Morrow.

Simon, Seymour. (1989). *Whales*. Crowell.

Simon, Seymour. (1990). *Oceans*. Morrow.

Simon, Seymour. (1991). *Big cats*. HarperCollins.

Simon, Seymour. (1991). *Earthquakes*. Morrow.

Simon, Seymour. (1991). *Mirror magic*. Boyds Mills.

Simon, Seymour. (1993). *Autumn across America*. Hyperion.

Simon, Seymour. (1993). *Wolves*. HarperCollins.

Simon, Seymour. (1994). *Winter across America*. Hyperion.

Simon, Seymour. (1995). *Earth words: A dictionary of the environment*. Illustrated by Mark Kaplan. HarperCollins.

Simon, Seymour. (1995). *Sharks*. HarperCollins.

Singer, Marilyn. (1995). *A wasp is not a bee*. Illustrated by Patricia O'Brien. Holt.

Sís, Peter. (1996). *Starry messenger: A book depicting the life of a famous scientist, mathematician, astronomer, philosopher, physicist*. Farrar, Straus & Giroux.

Skira-Venturi, Rosabianca. (1991). *A Weekend with Leonardo da Vinci*. Rizzoli.

Skira-Venturi, Rosabianca. (1991). *A Weekend with Renoir*. Rizzoli.

Skira-Venturi, Rosabianca. (1991). *A Weekend with Van Gogh*. Rizzoli.

Skira-Venturi, Rosabianca. (1992). *A Weekend with Degas*. Rizzoli.

Skurzynski, Gloria. (1994). *Zero gravity*. Bradbury.

Sloan, Peter, & Sloan, Sheryl. (1995). *Animal homes*. Littleton, MA: Sundance Publishing.

Smith, Ray. (1993). *An introduction to watercolor*. Dorling Kindersley.

Snedden, Robert. (1994). *What is a reptile?* Photographs by Oxford Scientific Films and Illustrated by Adrian Lascom. Sierra Club.

Snow, Alan. (1995). *The truth about cats*. Little, Brown.

Snowball, Diane. (1995). *Chickens*. Illustrated by Mary Werther. Greenvale, NY: Mondo Publishing.

Spatt, Leslie E. (1995). *Behind the scenes ballet: Rehearsing and performing the Sleeping Beauty.* Viking.

Spruyt, E. Lee. (1986). *Behind the golden curtain: Hansel and Gretel at the Great Opera House.* Four Winds.

Spurr, Elizabeth. (1991). *The biggest birthday cake in the world.* Harcourt Brace Jovanovich.

Squire, Ann. (1996). *101 questions and answers about backyard wildlife.* Illustrated by Jennifer DiRubbio. Walker.

Stanley, Diane, & Vennema, Peter. (1990). *Good Queen Bess: The story of Elizabeth I of England.* Illustrated by Diane Stanley. Four Winds.

Stanley, Diane, & Vennema, Peter. (1992). *Bard of Avon: The story of William Shakespeare.* Illustrated by Diane Stanley. Morrow.

Stanley, Diane, & Vennema, Peter. (1994). *Cleopatra.* Illustrated by Diane Stanley. Morrow.

Stanley, Diane. (1996). *Leonardo da Vinci.* Morrow.

Stanley, Fay, & Stanley, Diane. (1991). *The last princess: The story of Princess Kaíulani of Hawaii.* Illustrated by Diane Stanley. Four Winds.

Stanley, Jerry. (1992). *Children of the Dust Bowl: The true story of the school at Weedpatch Camp.* Crown.

Stanley, Jerry. (1994). *I am an American: A true story of Japanese internment.* Crown.

Stanley, Jerry. (1996). *Big Annie of Calumet: A true story of the industrial revolution.* Crown.

Stanley, Jerry. (1997). *Digger: The tragic fate of the California Indians from the Missions to the Gold Rush.* Crown.

Stevens, Janet. (1995). *From pictures to words: A book about making a book.* Holiday House.

Sullivan, Charles. (1989). *Imaginary gardens: American poetry and art for young people.* Abrams.

Sullivan, Charles. (1992). *Children of promise: African-American literature and art for young people.* Abrams.

Sullivan, Charles. (1994). *Here is my kingdom: Hispanic-American literature and art for young people.* Abrams.

Sullivan, George. (1994). *Mathew Brady: His life and photographs.* Cobblehill.

Swanson, Diane. (1994). *Safari beneath the sea: The wonder world of the North Pacific coast.* Photographs by the Royal British Columbia Museum. Sierra Club.

Swanson, Diane. (1994). *Squirts & snails & skinny green tails: Seashore nature activities for kids.* Rainier, WA: Adams Pub.

Swanson, Diane. (1994). *Toothy tongue & one long foot: Nature activities for kids.* Rainier, WA: Adams Pub.

Swanson, Diane. (1995). *Coyotes in the crosswalk: True tales of animal life in the wilds—of the city!* Illustrated by Douglas Penhale. Stillwater, MN. Voyageur.

Swanson, Diane. (1995). *Sky dancers: The amazing world of North American birds.* Voyageur.

Swanson, Diane, & Cook, Laura. (1995). *The day of the twelve-story wave.* Marietta, GA: Longstreet Pr. Inc.

Swanson, Diane. (1996). *Buffalo sunrise: The story of a North American giant.* Sierra Club.

Swanson-Natsues, Lyn. (1995). *What comes first?* Illustrated by Lynn Krause. Greenvale, NY: Mondo Publishing.

Switzer, Ellen. (1995). *Magic of Mozart: The Magic Flute, and the Salzburg marionettes.* Photographs by Costas. Atheneum.

Tapahonso, Luci, & Schick, Eleanor. (1995). *Navajo ABC: A Diné alphabet book.* Illustrated by Eleanor Schick. Simon & Schuster.

Taylor, Barbara. (1992). *Rain forest.* Dorling Kindersley.

Taylor, Mildred. (1976). *Roll of thunder, hear my cry.* Dial.

Thaler, Mike. (1989). *The teacher from the black lagoon.* Scholastic.

Thompson, Wendy. (1991). *Wolfgang Amadeus Mozart.* Little, Brown.

Thompson, Wendy. (1993). *Claude Debussy.* Little, Brown.

Thornhill, Jan. (1995). *Wild in the city.* Sierra Club.

Toll, Nelly. (1993). *Behind the secret window: A memoir of a hidden childhood during World War Two.* Dial.

Tomblin, Gill. (1992). *Small and furry animals: A watercolor sketchbook of mammals in the wild.* Putnam & Grosset.

Tunnell, Michael, & Chilcoat, George. W. (1996). *The children of Topaz: The story of a Japanese-American internment camp based on a classroom diary.* Holiday House.

Turner, Ann. (1987). *Nettie's trip south.* Illustrated by Ronald Himler. Macmillan.

Turner, Robyn M. (1991). *Georgia O'Keeffe.* Little, Brown.

Turner, Robyn M. (1991). *Rosa Bonheur.* Little, Brown.

Turner, Robyn M. (1992). *Mary Cassatt.* Little, Brown.

Turner, Robyn M. (1993). *Frida Kahlo.* Little, Brown.

Turner, Robyn M. (1994). *Dorothea Lange.* Little Brown.

Turner, Robyn M. (1996). *Texas traditions: The culture of the Lone Star State.* Little, Brown.

van der Rol, Ruud, & Verhoeven, Rian. (1993). *Anne Frank: Beyond the diary.* Viking.

Van Loon, Hendrik. (1985). *The story of mankind.* New York: Liveright.

van Noorden, Djinn. (Ed.). (1994). *The lifesize animal counting book.* Dorling Kindersley.

Vandine, JoAnn. (1995). *I eat leaves.* Illustrated by Cynthia A. Belcher. Greenvale, NY: Mondo Publishing.

Vaughan, Marcia. (1996). *The dancing dragon.* Illustrated by Stanley Wong Hoo Foon. Greenvale, NY: Mondo Publishing.

Ventura, Piero. (1995). *Darwin: Nature reinterpreted.* Houghton Mifflin.

Verhoven, Rian, & van der Rol, Ruud. (1993). *Anne Frank, beyond the diary: A photographic remembrance.* Viking.

Vieira, Linda. (1994). *The ever-living tree: The life and times of a coast redwood.* Illustrated by Christopher Canyon. Walker.

Vogel, Carole G. (1995). *The great midwest flood of 1993.* Little, Brown.

Vogel, Carole G. (1996). *Shock waves through Los Angeles: The Northridge earthquake.* Little, Brown.

Voyages of Discovery. (1996). *Boats and ships.* Scholastic.

Waldman, Neil. (1995). *The golden city: Jerusalem's 3000 years.* Atheneum.

Walker, Lou Ann. (1994). *Roy Lichtenstein: The artist at work.* Photographs by Michael Abramson. Lodestar/Dutton.

Wallace, Karen. (1993). *Think of an eel.* Illustrated by Mike Bostock. Candlewick Press.

Wallace, Marianne. (1996). *America's deserts: Guide to plants and animals.* Golden, CO: Fulcrum Publishing.

Ward, Geoffrey C., & Burns, Ken with O'Connor, Jim. (1994). *Shadow ball: The history.* Knopf.

Waters, John F. (1994). *Deep-sea vents: Living worlds without sun.* Cobblehill.

Waters, Kate. (1989). *Sarah Morton's day: A day in the life of a Pilgrim girl.* Photographs by Russ Kendall. Scholastic.

Waters, Kate. (1993). *Samuel Eaton's day: A day in the life of a Pilgrim boy.* Photographs by Russ Kendall. Scholastic.

Waters, Kate. (1996). *On the Mayflower: Voyage of the ship's apprentice and a passenger girl.* Photographs by Russell Kendall. Scholastic.

Watts, Barrie (photographer). (1992). *See how they grow: Rabbit.* Dorling Kindersley/Dutton/Lodestar.

Wechsler, Doug. (1995). *Bizarre bugs.* Cobblehill.

Wells, Robert E. (1993). *Is a blue whale the biggest thing there is?* Morton Grove, IL: Albert Whitman.

Wells, Robert E. (1995). *What's smaller than a pygmy shrew?* Morton Grove, IL: Albert Whitman.

Westray, Kathleen. (1994). *Picture puzzler.* Ticknor & Fields.

Westray, Ruth. (1993). *Color sampler.* Ticknor & Fields.

Westridge Young Writers' Workshop. (1994). *Kids explore the gifts of children with special needs.* Santa Fe, NM: John Muir.

Wexler, Jerome. (1993). *Jack-in-the pulpit.* Dutton.

White, Laurence B., Jr., & Broekel, Ray. (1990). *Math-a-magic: Number tricks for magicians.* Whitman.

Wick, Walter. (1997). *A Drop of water: A book of science and wonder.*

Scholastic.

Wilcox, Charlotte. (1993). *Mummies and their mysteries.* Minneapolis, MN: Carolrhoda.

Wilkes, Angela. (1989). *My first cookbook.* Photographs by David Johnson. Knopf.

Williams, Helen. (1991). *Stories in art.* Brookfield, CT: Millbrook Press.

Wilson, April. (1990). *Look!.* Penguin.

Wilson, Clive. (Ed.). (1996). *The Kingfisher young people's book of music.* Kingfisher.

Wilson, Elizabeth B. (1994). *Bibles and bestiaries: A guide to illuminated manuscripts.* Illustrations by Pierpoint Morgan Library. Farrar, Straus and Giroux.

Wilson, Janet. (1996). *The ingenious Mr. Peale: Painter, patriot and man of science.* Simon.

Wilson, Laura. (1994). *Daily life in a Victorian house.* Grinnell, IA: Preservation.

Winkleman, Katherine. K. (1996). *Police patrol.* Illustrated by John S. Winkleman. Walker.

Winner, Cherie. (1995). *Coyotes.* Minneapolis, MN: Carolrhoda.

Wittstock, Laura Waterman. (1993). *Ininatig's gift of sugar: Traditional sugarmaking.* Photo-illustrated by Dale Kakkak. Minneapolis, MN: Lerner Publishing.

Wolf, Sylvia. (1994). *Focus: Five women photographers.* Morton Grove, IL: Albert Whitman.

Wood, Don, & Wood, Audrey. (1984). *The little mouse, the red ripe strawberry, and the big hungry bear.* New York: Child's Play.

Woolf, Felicity. (1990). *Picture This: A First Introduction to Paintings.* Doubleday.

Woolf, Felicity. (1993). *Picture This: An Introduction to Twentieth Century Art.* Doubleday.

Wormser, Richard. (1994). *Growing up in the Great Depression.* Atheneum.

Wright, Courtni. (1994). *Journey to freedom: A story of the underground railroad.* Illustrated by Gershom Griffith. Holiday House.

Wright-Frierson, Virginia. (1996). *A desert scrapbook: Dawn to dusk in the Sonoran Desert.* Simon & Schuster.

Wyler, Rose, & Elting, Mary. (1992). *Math fun with money puzzlers.* Julian Messner.

Yenawine, Phillip. (1991). *Colors.* Delacorte.

Yenawine, Phillip. (1991). *Lines.* Delacorte.

Yenawine, Phillip. (1991). *Shapes.* Delacorte.

Yenawine, Phillip. (1993). *People.* Delacorte.

Yenawine, Phillip. (1993). *Places.* Delacorte.

Yenawine, Phillip. (1993). *Stories.* Delacorte.

Yolen, Jane. (1992). *Letting Swift River go.* Illustrated by Barbara Cooney. Little, Brown.

Yolen, Jane. (1993). *Welcome to the green house.* Illustrated by Laura Regan. Putnam.

Yue, Charlotte, & Yue, David. (1986). *The Pueblo.* Houghton Mifflin.

Zhensun, Zheng, & Low, Alice. (1991). *A young painter: The life and paintings of Wang Yani—China's extraordinary young artist.* Photographs by Zheng Zhensun. Scholastic.

Zubrowski, Bernie. (1991). *Blinkers and buzzers: Building and experimenting with electricity and magnetism.* Illustrated by Ray Doty. Morrow.

Zubrowski, Bernie. (1992). *Mirrors: Finding out about the properties of light.* Morrow.

Zubrowski, Bernie. (1994). *Making waves: Finding out about rhythmic motion.* Illustrated by Roy Doty. (A Boston Children's Museum Activity Book). Morrow.

Zubrowski, Bernie. (1995). *Shadow play: Making pictures with light and lenses.* Illustrated by Roy Doty. (A Boston Children's Museum Activity Book). Morrow.

INDEX

Author & Illustrator Index

Title Index

Subject Index

EDITORS

Rosemary A. Bamford is a Professor of Education at the University of Maine where she specializes in children's literature, writing process, and literacy. She is also Site Coordinator for the Center of Early Literacy who oversees Maine's Reading Recovery training program. She received her M.L.S. from the University of Maine and her Ed. D. from the University of Georgia in English Education and Children's Literature. She was Associate Dean of the University of Maine Graduate School (1982-1986). In 1991, she was the recipient of the New England Reading Association's Special Recognition Award and was President of the New England Reading Association (1988-1990). A member of the Orbis Pictus Award Committee from its inception (1989), she served on the selection committee from 1991- 1996. She was the co-founder of International Reading Association's Special Interest Group in Children's Literature and Reading. Dr. Bamford (formerly Rosemary A. Salesi) has published numerous articles and chapters. She has been a member of the Editorial Board for *Language Arts* of the National

Council of Teachers of English (1989-1993); and on the Board of Editors of the University of Maine Press (1994-1997). Her current area of research interest is nonfiction literature and its use in the classroom.

Janice V. Kristo is a Professor of Education at the University of Maine. She is a member of the literacy faculty and a member of the University of Maine Center for Early Literacy Research Advisory Board which provides guidance on issues with early literacy, teacher talk in literacy instruction, and classroom based research. She received her Master's Degree from Teachers College, Columbia University and her Ph.D. from the University of Connecticut. Her areas of specialization are children's literature, reading, and integrated literacy learning, with extensive instructional experience in these areas at the preservice and graduate levels. She currently serves on the Children's Literature Assembly Advisory Board of the National Council

of Teachers of English and as President of the Children's Literature and Reading Special Interest Group of the International Reading Association. She also served as chair of the Notable Children's Books in the Language Arts Committee of the Children's Literature Assembly. Dr. Kristo is co-author of several texts and numerous articles and chapters on literacy learning. She is currently on the Editorial Review Board of the *Journal of Children's Literature.* Her current area of research interest is nonfiction literature and its use in the classroom.

CONTRIBUTORS

Carol Avery has been an elementary librarian, a high school English teacher and an elementary classroom teacher. She is the author of *And With a Light Touch: Learning About Reading, Writing and Teaching with First Graders* and numerous educational articles and book chapters. In 1997 she served as President of the National Council of Teachers of English.

Anthony D. Fredericks is an Associate Professor of Education at York College in York, Pennsylvania where he teaches methods courses in language arts and science. He is the author/co-author of three college textbooks, more than thirty teacher resource books, and five highly acclaimed children's books. In addition, he is well known for his energetic, fast-paced, and highly practical presentations for strengthening science instruction through children's literature.

Susan Hepler is a children's literature specialist and consultant based in Alexandria, Virginia. She currently works with school systems and organizations to develop literature based curricula. She received her Ph.D. from Ohio State University in 1982 and has taught there as well as at Central Connecticut State University, and American University. She is a co-author with Charlotte S. Huck, Janet Hickman, and Barbara Kiefer, of *Children's Literature in the Elementary School* 6th

edition published by McGraw-Hill (1997), and an editor of *Children's Literature in the Classroom: Extending Charlotte's Web*, published by

Christopher-Gordon Publishers, Inc. (1994). Dr. Hepler is a long-time reviewer for School Library Journal and has published numerous articles and book chapters about children's literature, reading, and language arts. She is an active member of The Children's Book Guild of Washington, DC

Richard Kerper is an Assistant Professor at the Millersville University of Pennsylvania. He received his Ph.D. from The Ohio State University in Children's Literature and Language. He is interested in nonfiction literature for children and adolescents, and their response to literature. He is involved with The National Council of Teachers of English's Children's Literature Assembly, as well as the International Reading Association.

Barbara Kiefer is an Associate Professor in the Department of Curriculum and Teaching at Teachers College, Columbia University where she teaches courses in Reading and Children's Literature. She has served as chair of the Elementary Section Committee of the National Council of Teachers of English, as a member of the NCTE Executive Board, and was a member of the 1988 Caldecott Award Committee of the American Library Association. She has published articles and

book chapters about reading and children's literature. She is author of *The Potential of Picturebooks: From Visual Literacy to Aesthetic Understanding*, and the co-author of the books *An Integrated Language Perspective in the Elementary School: Theory Into Action*, with Christine Pappas and Linda Levstik, and *Children's Literature in the Elementary School with*, Charlotte Huck, Susan Hepler, and Janet Hickman.

Linda Levstik is Professor of Social Studies Education in the College of Education at the University of Kentucky. She received her Ph.D. from The Ohio State University. Her research interests focus on the development of historical understanding in children and adolescents and the development of classroom communities of inquiry. She is co-author with Keith C. Barton of *Doing History: Investigating with Children in Elementary and Middle School Classrooms* (Erlbaum), and with

Christine Pappas and Barbara Kiefer of *An Integrated Language Perspective in the Elementary School* (Longman).

Donna Maxim teaches third- and fourth-grade at
The Center for Teaching and Learning, a demonstra-
tion school in Edgecomb, Maine. The school accepts
seven teams of intern teachers, for a week at a time,
each year to observe and make plans for ways to
change their teaching practices in their own school
systems. Donna has taught at this level for the past
seven years and previously taught third and fourth
grade for 17 years. She has taught inservice courses
and conducted workshops about writing, literature,
and integrating curriculum throughout the Northeast. She has presented
sessions at numerous conferences about using literature and writing in science and social studies. Donna has served as President of the New England
Reading Association and is currently serving a four year commitment on
the Elementary Section Committee of NCTE where she is co-editor of their
publication *School Talk.*

Amy McClure taught in public schools for ten years
as a classroom teacher, reading specialist and coor-
dinator of gifted children programs. She is currently a Professor of Education and Director of
Elementary Education at Ohio Wesleyan University
where she teaches courses in reading and children's
literature, supervises student teachers and directs
the university's honors program. A long-time
International Reading Association member, she has
served the organization in various capacities,
including member of the Intellectual Freedom Committee, Editorial Boards
of *Reading Teacher* and *Ohio Reading Teacher*, and President of the Ohio
affiliate. She is active in the National Council of Teachers of English, serving on various committees and as President of the Children's Literature
Assembly. She has spoken at many state and national conventions. Dr.
McClure was named NCTE's Promising Young Researcher in 1985.

Paula Moore has worked in public schools as a pri-
mary teacher, literacy specialist, and school admin-
istrator for twenty years before moving to
University work. As part of her Doctoral program
she worked for a year in New Zealand schools an
studied at the Auckland College of Education.
Currently, she is Assistant Professor for early literacy at the University of Maine and Director of the
Center for Early Literacy where she teaches and

coordinates graduate programs for early primary teachers. In addition, Dr. Moore is working with childcare programs to enhance early literacy learning opportunities for pre-school children.

Yvonne Siu-Runyan is an Associate Professor of Literacy at the University of Northern Colorado-Greeley, where she teaches undergraduate and graduate courses in literacy development. Dr. Siu-Runyan has spoken widely and written book chapters and articles about whole language instruction, integrative learning, writing and reading instruction, children's literature, and supervision. In addition to chairing committees for IRA, NCTE, and CCIRA, she is a founding executive board member for the Whole Language Umbrella, an International Confederation of Teachers.

Sylvia Mergeler Vardell is currently associate professor at the University of Texas at Arlington, where she teaches graduate and undergraduate courses in literature-based teaching of reading, multicultural children's literature, teaching the writing process, and other literature/ literacy courses. Her research and publications have focused on techniques for teaching literature and writing, on nonfiction children's literature, on the development of reading and writing abilities in young people, on sexism in language, as well as articles profiling children's authors. Vardell has published in *Language Arts*, *English Journal*, *The Reading Teacher*, *The New Advocate*, *Young Children*, and *Horn Book*, as well as several chapters in books on language and literature. She has presented at many state, regional, national, and international conferences, and has received numerous grants from various institutions

Sandra Wilde teaches and conducts research at Portland State University in Oregon. She has taught elementary school and junior high school, and has worked with teachers in universities and other settings since 1977. Her two areas of special expertise are spelling from a holistic perspective and the role of children's literature in teaching mathematics. She speaks frequently at the annual conferences of IRA, NCTE, and the Whole Language Umbrella.

Sandra is a lively presenter who communicates her appreciation of both children and teachers as creative learners. Her unique approach is both theoretically sound and rewarding for teachers to carry out. Children, their writing, and their invented spelling are always at the center of Sandra's presentations and workshops.

Jeffrey Wilhelm was a teacher of reading and the language arts at the middle and secondary school level for thirteen years. Currently, he is an assistant professor at the University of Maine where he teaches courses in middle and secondary level literacy. His interests include team teaching, co-constructing inquiry driven curriculum with students, and pursuing teacher research. In Maine, he co-ordinates the fledgling Adolescent Literacy Project and summer institutes in literacy and technology. He is the author of Standards in Practice: Grades 6-8, an addendum to the NCTE and IRA's national standards for Reading and the Language Arts. *You Gotta Be the Book: Teaching Engaged and Reflective Reading with Adolescents* (Teachers College Press and NCTE), and *Imagining to Learn: Extending Reading, Learning and Valuing Across the Curriculum through Drama* (Heinemann) are his two most recent books.

Myra Zarnowski teaches courses in reading and children's literature at Queens College of the City University of New York. She is the author of *Learning About Biographies: A Reading -and-Writing Approach for Children* (NCTE, 1990) and co-editor of *Children's Literature and Social Studies: Selecting and Using Notable Books in the Classroom* (NCSS, 1993). She is the current chair of the Orbis Pictus Award Committee of the National Council of Teachers of English, a committee which recognizes and promotes the use of outstanding nonfiction literature for children.

1748

YORK COLLEGE OF PENNSYLVANIA 17403

0 2003 0109309 8

LB1575.5.U5 M45 1998

Making faces come alive
: choosing quality
c1998

DISCARDED

GAYLORD FG